ss&Administration
STANDARDS

# Student Handbook
## Level3

cfa
business skills
at work

**Vic Ashley & Sheila Ashley**

Published by Council for Administration
6 Graphite Square, Vauxhall Walk, London, SE11 5EE
Registered charity number 1095 809

Cover design, typeset, graphics and
additional photography by Richard Jane

Cover photography by Craig Jones

Printed and bound by Adare Halcyon Ltd.

The authors have made reasonable efforts to ensure that all information
provided throughout this book is accurate at the time of going to print.
However, there may be inadvertent and occasional errors for which the
authors apologise.

Whilst care is taken to ensure the accuracy of the information contained
within this book, it is provided on the understanding that no responsibility
attaches to the authors or the publishers and we shall not be liable under
the contract or otherwise for any consequential loss or damages.

Microsoft product screen shots reprinted with permission
from Microsoft Corporation.

Adobe product screen shots reprinted with permission from
Adobe Systems Incorporated.

www.cfa.uk.com
020 7091 9620

This book is dedicated to our son Graham and his wife Rachel, who presented us with our first grandchild, Matthew, during the writing of it.

# CONTENTS

# INTRODUCTION

Welcome to the Level 3 Business & Administration Student Handbook. This book can be used as a student resource for anyone working towards a vocational qualification based on the 2005 Business & Administration National Occupational Standards.

Business & Administration is a varied and important area of work. The opportunities to develop your career are endless.

Almost five million people are directly employed in Business & Administration job roles throughout the UK. Another ten million people need some Business & Administration skills to carry out a part of their job.

As technology improves the job roles in Business & Administration will change so it is important that people in business support roles continue to update their skills.

This book provides guidance to anyone working in, or studying for, a Level 3 role in Business & Administration.

The 31 chapters of this book cover the content of Business & Administration qualifications at Level 3 including:

- National Vocational Qualification (NVQ)
- Scottish Vocational Qualification (SVQ)
- Technical Certificate (TC)
- Apprenticeship programmes

The book will also help you achieve:

- Other Business & Administration Vocational Qualifications (VRQs)
- Key Skill Qualifications
- Core Skill Qualifications

We hope that you enjoy using this book as much as we have enjoyed writing it. A career in Business & Administration can be an exciting, interesting and challenging one. We hope that this book helps you on your way towards a long and rewarding career

**Good Luck!!**

Throughout the book you will come across the following symbols. These are there to remind you of the key points, skills needed and the types of evidence you can gather for each unit.

The likely skills needed to complete each unit of learning are listed at the beginning of each chapter. All of these skills are explained for you within the four sections of chapter 1.

Your understanding is tested in the 'What you need to know' sections in each chapter.

Each chapter also contains activities in the 'Are you ready for assessment' section that will give you valuable practice and generate evidence towards your qualification.

All of the evidence that you generate during your course can be stored on-line using *forward* ePortfolio PLUS.

For more information, please visit www.cfa.uk.com/*forward*

# CHAPTER 1
# SKILLS AT WORK

Working in Business & Administration requires a wide range of skills.  Each chapter of this book refers to the set of skills you will need to meet the requirements of the chapter.

You may find it useful to read this chapter through before starting on any of the other chapters you have chosen to study.  You can then return to the individual skills identified in each chapter as you work your way through the book.

 The skills have been organised into four groups

## Part 1 - Personal Skills

Empathising, following, interpersonal skills, listening, networking, obtaining feedback, personal presentation, providing feedback, questioning, stress management, valuing and supporting others.

## Part 2 - Information Skills

Analysing, checking, communicating, designing, evaluating, managing information, noting, presenting information, recording, researching and using technology.

## Part 3 - Organisational Skills

Managing time, negotiating, organising, planning, prioritising, problem solving, reading, team working, using number, working safely and writing.

## Part 4 – Supervisory Skills

Decision making, consulting with and involving others, developing others, leading by example, managing conflict, managing resources, monitoring, motivating, setting objectives and team building.

# PART 1 – PERSONAL SKILLS

## Empathising

It is easy to confuse empathising with sympathising. The difference is that while sympathising is about feeling sorry for someone, empathising is about understanding how that person feels. Empathy allows you to understand other people and what is important to them. It will help you to deal with people who otherwise might appear difficult. If you can empathise with them you may be able to see beyond the differences and understand their interests and perspective.

We all see everything and everybody through our own experiences and if you have formed a very specific view of what is right it is very difficult to understand that other people may have an equally specific but totally different view. When you come across people whose views are totally opposed to your own you consider them to be either mad or bad. The more you are able to understand where your own beliefs have come from, the more open you will be to accepting that other people have different beliefs that are equally valid.

## Following

Following may seem an odd description of a skill. You may feel that it is something that everybody can do without any need for learning or training. If following were just a matter of doing as you are told then you would be right, but the skill of following involves giving active support to the person that is giving the lead.

The skilful leader will communicate the reasons for their decisions and seek feedback on them. The skilful follower will encourage their leader to develop the skills of communication and delegation so that the outcome is achieved to the benefit of all concerned.

Following is not about blindly tagging along behind but actively participating in the process of taking the issue forward. A good follower will support their leader, taking as much as possible of the pressure off them by anticipating opportunities to help.

## Interpersonal skills

### Self awareness

You can't interact successfully with others until you are aware of your own strengths and weaknesses. It is more likely that other people will recognise your strengths once you have identified them for yourself. Understanding your own weaknesses will help you to work towards overcoming them.

You can become more self-aware by:

- Asking other people how they see you
- Looking at references or appraisals
- Identifying the tasks you enjoy and those you don't
- Identifying areas where you need further training

### Self motivation

The next interpersonal skill is self-motivation. You will need to motivate yourself if you are not getting sufficient motivation from outside. Work is more enjoyable if you are motivated. There is nothing more boring than not having enough to do. Show you are motivated by keeping yourself busy; there is always something that needs doing. Does somebody else need a hand with their work? Are there tasks due tomorrow that you could do today? Be adaptable; offer to help other people if they are busy and you aren't. This will make you more popular as well as widening your skills and experience. If there really is nothing that you can do, use your time to master new tasks and learn new skills. That way you can gain more knowledge to help in the future.

## Tact and diplomacy

Care must be taken to display tact and diplomacy when dealing with other people.  Don't give the impression that you are offering to help because you feel that your colleague is incapable of completing the task on their own.  If you are responsible for allocating tasks consider the feelings of people.  Try not to always give the difficult or interesting tasks to the same people.  Also be considerate of people's personal feelings.  Don't make remarks about their appearance or demeanour; they may not be looking their best because of personal problems that they don't wish to discuss.  Try to let them see that you are available if they have something they want to talk about without being intrusive.

## Assertiveness

There will be times when it will be necessary to be assertive. Don't confuse assertiveness with aggressiveness.  You are entitled to expect co-operation from your colleagues when you ask for assistance.  If you don't receive it you will need to assert your right to ask:

- Explain why you need help
- Ask for what you really want
- Don't be tempted to use bribery
- Don't apologise for asking

This differs from aggressiveness, which is telling rather than asking.  It avoids bullying and emotional blackmail and enables you to assert your authority.

Be realistic about what you are able to achieve.  If asked to complete a task in an unrealistic timescale it is not helpful to agree and then fail to achieve it.  It is much better to explain that the target is not achievable, give the reasons and negotiate an extended deadline or further resources.  Also don't over-estimate your own abilities.  If asked to carry out a task you have not been trained for, it is better to say so at the time than to attempt the task and complete it unsatisfactorily.

Try this exercise.

Complete a SWOT analysis of your interpersonal skills. This involves identifying:

- **Strengths** - What are you particularly good at when it comes to dealing with other people?
- **Weaknesses** - Where could your skills benefit from some improvement?
- **Opportunities** - What situations offer you the chance to practise your skills?
- **Threats** - Are there any internal or external influences that make it difficult to use or improve your skills?

| STRENGTHS | WEAKNESSES |
|---|---|
| | |
| OPPORTUNITIES | THREATS |
| | |

Now discuss your development needs with your manager or tutor.

## Listening

It is often said that communication is a two-way process. If you don't listen to what someone is saying they are wasting their time talking to you. There is more to listening than simply being within hearing distance of the message. It is possible to tell whether somebody is actively listening, i.e. making an effort to hear and understand, or simply passively listening, i.e. hearing without taking in what is being said. Passive listening involves:

- Listening but not hearing
- Switching off
- Slouching
- Not making eye contact
- Impassive expression
- Moving about restlessly
- Appearing disinterested
- Making no response

Active listening involves:

- Appearing involved
- Leaning towards the speaker
- Making eye contact
- Mirroring the speaker's facial expression and body posture
- Nodding or shaking your head
- Paying attention
- Responding with 'mm', 'yes', 'I' 'see', 'really'
- Asking for clarification

## Networking

You will have heard the expression 'it's not what you know but who you know'. While this is a little cynical it contains at least a germ of truth. A dictionary definition of a network is 'a large and widely distributed group of people or things such as shops, colleges, or churches that communicate with one another and work together as a unit or system'. From a skills point of view the important parts of the definition to concentrate on are:

- Large and widely distributed group
- Communicate with one another
- Work together as a unit

You will benefit from building up and maintaining informal relationships, especially with people whose friendship could bring advantages such as job or business opportunities. The bigger your network, the more varied your contacts.
Everyone that you meet in a work context, or have dealings with, is a potential member of your network. Each of them has the possibility of being helpful to you at some point in the future. If you feel that this is 'using people' console yourself with the idea that you will also be a member of each of their networks with the possibility of being helpful to them.

Communication is the key to successful networking.  If the first time a contact hears from you in years is when you are looking for a huge favour, you are much less likely to be successful than if you have kept in regular contact and have been able to provide small favours to each other along the way.

Working together as a unit should not be interpreted as creating any form of cartel or operating a 'closed shop' to the exclusion of non-members of the network.  Having a beneficial network of contacts helps everyone.  It enables you all to keep in touch with trends and know what's going on outside your immediate sphere of responsibility at work. Contacts can be used to provide advice or introductions. They can also be used to help resolve your difficulties. Remember they may also be looking for the services that you are able to offer.

The business will not be placed with your organisation because you are known, but the opportunity to make potential customers aware of what you can offer will be brought about by your networking.  Networking can be seen, therefore, as a form of free advertising.  Your potential customer base is expanded by word of mouth recommendation, and you reciprocate this for other members of the network.

Try this exercise.

Draw a diagram of the people in your network.  Include business contacts, friends and family.  Indicate on the diagram what they can offer that you may need.

On the same diagram indicate what you can do or provide that could help anybody else.  You may be surprised to find out just how large and varied your network is.

## Obtaining feedback

It is difficult to know what your staff or your line manager think about you unless they tell you.  Your line manager will probably tell you during your regular appraisal or they may be particularly good at giving feedback on an ongoing basis.  Unless you have a 360° appraisal system in operation in your organisation you will probably have to ask your staff for feedback.

You will need to ask specific questions in order to encourage the sort of feedback you are looking for.  You may not be too pleased with the response if your relationship with your staff is such that they feel able to be brutally honest with you.  Despite this it is a worthwhile exercise to carry out.  Feedback from your staff will help you to be more aware of their perception of your performance.  It is important to understand what people think you meant when you gave them an instruction, or passed on some information.

Negative feedback, provided it is constructive, will enable you to spot areas where your skills can be improved.  Positive feedback will reassure you that you are doing well.  Try to avoid falling into the trap of complacency.  You will need to seek continuous feedback if you are to be sure that your performance levels are not slipping.

## Personal Presentation

Although it may be unfair, people do judge us on our appearance.  Take the time to think about the way you look and the impression that you give to your clients, customers and colleagues.  Your personal presentation will send out messages about your attitude and your efficiency.

The most important aspect of personal presentation is to dress appropriately for the position that you hold.  While a business suit is appropriate for working in an office, it would be totally inappropriate for a swimming pool attendant.  The way you dress, the type and amount of jewellery you wear and your hair style should reflect the values of the organisation rather than your own personal taste.

There are a number of reasons for dressing appropriately:

- To identify you as a member of staff
- To avoid making colleagues feel uncomfortable
- Practicality, long hair and dangling jewellery may become entangled in equipment
- Self esteem, if you look good you feel good
- Comfort, appropriate clothing will be more comfortable to wear through the day

As well as dressing appropriately you need to think about:

- **Shoes** - Your shoes should be comfortable enough to wear all day, and always clean and polished
- **Personal hygiene** - Absolute cleanliness and the use of deodorants will show consideration to your colleagues
- **Hair** - Make sure it is clean and tidy, if your hair is long it may need to be tied back when you are using equipment such as shredders or photocopiers

Equally important is the way you behave at work.  You are only at work for a few hours a day so concentrate on why you are there.  Treat other people the way that you want to be treated yourself.  Always be polite to others as this will make it difficult for them not to be polite in turn.  When you make a mistake admit it as soon as possible and accept the criticism for it.  The important thing is to learn from the mistake.

## Providing feedback

In the same way that you should be encouraging feedback on your performance in order to improve, you should be offering feedback on the performance of others.  When giving feedback remember that it should be based on fact rather than opinion and you must always be prepared to back up your feedback with examples. Positive feedback should reinforce what the receiver has done well and identify opportunities to continue to perform well. Corrective action may be necessary where performance has not been satisfactory but the individual should be encouraged to recognise this for themselves. Take time to encourage individuals to identify their own poor performance. By doing this, you will find they take responsibility for the mistake and will be more willing to work towards improvement. It is important to be positive and objective when giving feedback and remember people will only be able to deal with a reasonable level of information at any one time. One of the most effective ways of giving feedback is to deliver a 'praise sandwich' – highlight the things that have been done well at the beginning and end of your feedback and point out the areas for improvement in the middle. Feedback should:

- Relate to observed behaviour
- Describe actual events
- Seek the individual's opinion as to the cause of events
- Allow the individual to decide what happened and why
- Encourage corrective action rather than reprimanding

## Appraisals

When giving formal feedback or carrying out an appraisal, effective planning is essential. At an appraisal meeting most of the talking should be done by the person being appraised and the listening by the person giving the appraisal. Remember that good listeners concentrate on what the speaker is saying and don't interrupt unnecessarily. Good listeners will also ask questions to clarify issues and demonstrate understanding without interrupting the flow of the speaker.

The appraisee should be given the opportunity to self-assess prior to the meeting to consider:

- Their achievements against previously set objectives
- Reasons for non-achievement of objectives
- Their training needs
- Their own aspirations
- Where they feel support is needed

You should prepare by:

- Reviewing the individual's performance
- Reviewing progress against the last development plan
- Collating evidence to support your intended feedback
- Considering training opportunities
- Considering the individual's potential to progress
- Considering where support can be offered

During the meeting ask open questions which allow the individual to expand on their answers and probing questions which seek more specific information on what happened and why. The appraisal should look at performance over the whole period under review, recognise the individual's achievement and produce a development plan which the individual is able to agree with.

## Questioning

Questions are used to elicit information. All questions can be categorised as either 'open' questions or 'closed' questions. Closed questions are those which can be answered 'yes' or 'no'. You would use a closed question if you wanted a definite answer. For instance, 'Do you want it copied?'

Open questions are used if more information is needed. For instance, 'Do you want it copied in colour or black and white?' Open questions can also be used to get an opinion. For instance, 'How do you think I should lay it out?' Open questions usually begin with 'who', 'what' 'when', 'where', 'how' 'which' and 'why'.

Try this exercise.

Which of the following are open questions?

1. How many copies shall I make?
2. Do you take sugar in your tea?
3. How many sugars do you take in your tea?
4. When is the new copier being delivered?
5. Are we having a day off on Monday?
6. Can I take this down to despatch?
7. Why didn't you finish the accounts yesterday?
8. Where is the paper for the printer kept?

# Stress management

Stress can cause physical illness such as raised blood pressure and depression.  It is caused by a number of things:

- The feeling that there is never enough time to do all the things that need to be done
- The demands placed upon us by others
- Any kind of change in our circumstances, especially life changing events such as bereavement, divorce or moving house
- Conflict with colleagues
- Conflict with friends and family

You should not however, be aiming for a completely stress-free existence.  The amount of stress each of us can tolerate differs and it is the excess of stress, above our usual tolerance level, which makes us complain about being stressed.

Stress management is about identifying the cause of your stress and deciding whether there is anything that can be done about it.  Some things can be dealt with, for instance the demands made on you by others may be negotiable.  Some things can't be dealt with so easily, for instance bereavement.  Tackle the things that you can do something about.  Think positively about them and take steps to change them.  This alone will reduce your stress.

Handle the things that you can't do anything about by accepting the fact that nothing can be done.  Try to remain as positive as possible and remember that there will come a time when the things that seem unbearable now will become a distant memory.

A technique you might find useful at work is to rest your brain for five or so minutes every hour.  During these five minutes clear your mind of everything to do with work and either think about nothing in particular or think about something personal that has nothing to do with work.  Plan a treat for yourself such as a holiday or a trip to the theatre.  Whether you actually get the treat or not is unimportant, it is thinking about it that will reduce your stress.

# Valuing and supporting others

Your most valuable resource is the ability of the people who work with you. It is important that you make them aware of this fact regularly. Simple things such as always saying 'good morning' and 'good night' will go a long way. A manager who values people allows them the opportunity to develop. Always remember to thank colleagues when they have completed a task satisfactorily or gone out of their way to achieve a deadline. Always give credit where it is due and make people feel needed and useful. Treat people as equals and delegate responsibility to them. Utilise their abilities and offer them the opportunity to learn new skills whenever possible. Try to concentrate on their strengths rather than any weaknesses they may have, and when it is necessary to give feedback on their weaknesses make it constructive.

People will sometimes need emotional support. This can be as important as actual support with their work. Recognise that personal circumstances can affect performance at work and try to be understanding in these circumstances. Sometimes it is necessary to allow colleagues some leeway. Encourage them to put forward their views and listen to them when they do. If they have constructive suggestions to make, support them in putting their ideas forward. If you identify that they have development needs ensure that opportunities to meet them are provided. If problems occur avoid the temptation to blame or penalise others unreasonably.

Treat your most valuable resource with the care and consideration that you would treat any other resource.

# PART 2 – INFORMATION SKILLS

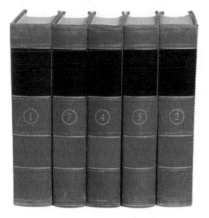

## Analysing

Analysis is the examination of facts in sufficient detail to understand them or discover more about them. In an office environment it is used to examine information that has been gathered by research in order to draw conclusions.

A frequently used method of analysis is SWOT analysis, in which the strengths, weaknesses, opportunities and threats of a situation are compared. The strengths and weaknesses focus on the internal environment and the opportunities and threats focus on the external environment.

Analysis reduces an unmanageable volume of information to an amount that can be handled more easily. This is not necessarily done by discarding information but by combining two or more pieces of information to produce a third, allowing the original information to be discarded.

## Checking

The purpose of checking is to confirm the accuracy of text, data or figures. Before sending out any form of information or irrevocably entering it into the system, it is important that you check its accuracy. Sending out inaccurate information will, at the very least, give a poor impression. At worst it could lead to serious consequences if decisions are made based on the inaccurate information. Inputting inaccurate information into a spreadsheet or database can lead to effects far more serious than the original error. For instance, if you input incorrect dosage information onto a patient's records the effects could be catastrophic.

Probably the best way to check the accuracy of text is to first use the spell check facility and the grammar check facility on your computer to pick up any blatant errors. Then print a draft copy as it is usually easier to proof read on paper than on screen. At this point you will be looking for errors that can't be picked up electronically such as the substitution of one word for another. At the same time you will be looking for more subtle changes that may be required such as the order in which facts are presented or repetition.

When inputting data to a database it is essential that you check the accuracy before you complete a record as the database will automatically be updated on completion of each record. There is only one way to do this, and that is to input the data then check against the source document before completing the record.

Figures are probably the most difficult when it comes to checking because every single digit must be checked against the source document. Whereas words with transposed letters will stand out as incorrect, transposed figures will appear to be as accurate as correct figures. When inputting rows of figures it is a good idea to use a ruler to prevent your eye from straying from the line of figures. It may also be possible to check the accuracy of figures by estimating the outcome. For instance if the total number of hours worked in a week by an employee comes to 375 there is a strong chance that you have input the decimal point in the wrong place!

| | A | B | C | D | E | F | G | H |
|---|---|---|---|---|---|---|---|---|
| 1 | **Income** | | | | | | | |
| 2 | Sales | £1,000.00 | | | | | | |
| 3 | Publications | £500.00 | | | | | | |
| 4 | Subtotal | | | | | | | |
| 5 | **Outgoings** | | | | | | | |
| 6 | Accomodation | £200.00 | | | | | | |
| 7 | **Balance** | £1,300.00 | | | | | | |
| 8 | | | | | | | | |
| 9 | | | | | | | | |

If you are using a printing calculator to total a column of figures, check the print-out against the source document, ticking each entry in case you get interrupted in the middle. If you are using a non-printing calculator input the figures twice to check that the same result is achieved.

## Designing

Designing is the planning or making of something in a skilful or artistic way.  Its most common use in an administrative setting will be in creating documents and presentations or preparing for projects.

Visual design is very important when producing documents, especially important documents like reports and presentations.  Good designs are usually based on good design elements and principles.

The elements of good visual design are:

- Line
- Shape
- Direction
- Size
- Texture
- Colour
- Value

The principles of good visual design are:

- **Balance** - A large shape close to the centre of the slide can be balanced by a small shape close to the edge.  A large light shape will be balanced by a small dark shape
- **Gradation** - Gradation of size and direction produce linear perspective.  Gradation of colour from warm to cool and tone from dark to light produce aerial perspective.  Gradation from dark to light causes the eye to move along the shape
- **Repetition** - Repetition with variation is interesting, without variation repetition becomes monotonous
- **Contrast** - The major contrast should be located at the centre of interest
- **Harmony** - Harmony is achieved by combining similar, related elements such as adjacent colours on the colour wheel, similar shapes etc

- **Dominance** - Dominance can be applied to one or more of the elements to give emphasis
- **Unity** - Unity refers to the visual linking of various elements

A well designed slide show will consider all of the elements and principles of design in order to add interest and make the presentation more effective.  For instance red is the most exciting colour, green the most restful and blue the most cheerful so thoughtful use of colour will help you get the message across.  Be careful not to over use colours as different colours have different physical effects on the audience.

You will be involved in more intellectual processes when you design projects.  Try to remember the five 'Ps' – planning and preparation prevent poor performance.  When you design a project you need to consider:

- **Aim** - identify the aim
- **Objectives** - state what the objectives will be
- **Plan** - design a plan that will deliver the aim and objectives
- **Resources** - identify the resources you need.  This could include people, space, time, equipment and materials
- **Budget** - agree a budget with your line manger

## Evaluating

Evaluating is a systematic and objective examination of the way that things are done.  There are two types of evaluation:

- **Formative evaluation** - Looks at the way things are being done at present to judge whether you are doing the right things in the right way
- **Summative evaluation** - Looks at a project after completion or processes after amendments have been put in place to judge their efficiency, effectiveness, impact and sustainability

You will be using formative evaluation regularly to assess all the things that you do on a day-to-day basis to see if there are any improvements that can be made.  Self-evaluation involves reviewing your regular tasks to confirm that you are using the most efficient methods to complete them.  External evaluation involves asking the people you do the tasks for and those you work with for feedback. They will be able to tell you if you are satisfying their requirements and give you any suggestions for how completing the task may be made easier.

Summative evaluation is a more formal process in that you are evaluating a specific project or change of process. This can be done by seeking structured feedback from everybody involved, possibly by the use of a questionnaire or feedback form, in order that the feedback is received in a manner that allows it to be analysed. This provides an evaluation that includes credible and useful information on the level of achievement and the effective use of resources.

Many organisations are involved in continuous evaluatory cycles as part of a continuous improvement model at work:

Gather Information

Analyse Performance

Change Business Practices

Improve Performance

Try this exercise.

Look at a process that you carry out regularly, for instance organising a meeting or managing the reprographic process. Carry out an evaluation of the process, seeking feedback from all those involved. Write an evaluation report stating what you have discovered, what changes you recommend and why.

## Communication

Communication is a two-way process. It is the process of giving and receiving information. It is important that you exercise skill in communication so that you:

- Pass the information effectively
- Comprehend the information you are receiving
- Create the right impression
- Encourage others to communicate with you

There are a number of methods of communication including verbal, non-verbal and written. The skills required in each are different.

Verbal communication, or face-to-face communication, requires you to consider not only what you are saying but also your tone of voice, volume, clarity and speed. Your tone of voice will convey the way you feel about what you are saying; excited, angry, distressed, tired, happy, positive for example. The volume will need to be moderated according to the audience; if you are speaking to an audience in a large room you will need to speak louder than if you are speaking to one person who is close by. Clarity is important in ensuring the message is received accurately, especially if you are speaking in a language or accent that is unfamiliar to the listener. Similarly the speed at which you speak needs to be regulated according to the level of understanding of the listener.

The wording of the message will affect how well it is received and understood. Using sensory words will help communicate more effectively by creating a picture, a sound or a feeling that the listener can associate with. This is particularly useful if you are trying to persuade the listener to agree with the message. There are three main types of sensory words:

- **Seeing** - 'I see what you mean'
- **Hearing** - 'I hear what you say'
- **Feeling** - 'I feel good about what I hear'

Choose words that will put the message across in the way that you want it to be received; if you are unsure, use a mixture.

Non-verbal communication is also known as body language. This is the messages you send out whether you are speaking or not, by the way you sit, stand, fold your arms, and use facial expressions. Body language can either reinforce or take away from what you are saying. When speaking, positive body language involves:

- Good posture.  Stand or sit straight
- Not fidgeting
- Not tapping your feet
- Not drumming your fingers
- Not folding your arms
- Looking at your audience
- Relaxing your facial muscles
- Not giving the impression of being bored, nervous or disinterested

Telephone communication is similar to face-to-face communication except that you are unable to see the person you are speaking to.  Remember that tone of voice, volume, clarity and speed are equally as important when speaking on the telephone, because you can't gauge the listener's reaction from their facial expression.

The way in which telephone calls are made and answered is very important.  Your organisation will probably have a standard format for answering calls.  Use it, it may not be your personal style but it is the company style.  External callers will base their impression of the organisation on what they hear; the impression you're aiming for is friendly and efficient.

Remember to smile when you answer the phone as this will project a positive image of yourself and the organisation.  Experienced communicators will always tell you they can 'hear' the smile in your voice.  Don't answer the phone while eating, chewing gum or yawning.

Before making a call consider whether the telephone is the best way of communicating.  Although most people nowadays carry a mobile phone, giving you access to them when they are away from their workplace, they may be in the car or on a train and variable reception or background noise may make communication difficult.

In conclusion all telephone calls whether internal or external must be given importance.  Callers will receive an impression of the organisation from the way you answer the phone.  Make sure you are polite, receptive and let the caller know you are listening.  If you are giving information keep it relevant and accurate, if you are receiving information have a pen and paper handy.  Don't 'lose' callers when transferring them or leave them to repeat themselves.  Use message systems efficiently, both your own and other people's.

Try this exercise.

Here are some examples of sensory words.  Which are 'seeing', 'hearing' and 'feeling' words?

| | | |
|---|---|---|
| sound | grasp | imagine |
| picture | fight | accent |
| voice | harmonise | colour |
| appearance | blunt | touch |
| search | image | tune in to |
| celebrate | hate | move |
| tone | speak | show |

## Managing information

It is said that 'Knowledge is power'.  Information is a valuable commodity, so the way it is managed is important to the efficient operation of the business.  Most organisations are aiming for a 'paper-free' office, but there always seems to be papers waiting to be filed.  These will require a variety of filing systems and equipment.  Our computers also contain more and more files of information, and a system to enable us to find this information quickly saves a great deal of time.  Much of this information, whether on paper or on computer, will need to be kept long after it ceases to be current.  It is just as important that archived information is managed in a way that enables easy retrieval.

There are a surprising number of Acts of Parliament which refer to records retention and disposal:

- Occupiers Liability Act 1957
- Employers' Liability (Compulsory Insurance) Act 1969
- Equal Pay Act 1970
- Taxes Management Act 1970
- Prescription and Limitations (Scotland) Act 1973
- Health and Safety at Work Act 1974
- Sex Discrimination Act 1975
- Race Relations Act 1976
- Limitation Act 1980
- Social Security Contributions and Benefits Act 1992
- Education Act 1994
- Value Added Tax Act 1994

- Disability Discrimination Act 1995
- Data Protection Act 1998

As well as a large number of Statutory Instruments. Each of these tells you how long you have to keep documents. Among those you are most likely to come across in your working day are:

- Employment records
- Contracts and agreements
- Accounts records
- Transport records

If the information you are responsible for is not listed above, check the relevant Act.

Managing an information system may not seem to be the most important job in the organisation but in many ways it is. There are a lot of decisions to be made and the success of the whole organisation may depend on access to reliable and up-to-date information. Only if the storage system is efficient will it be possible to find information quickly. This applies equally to archived information as there is legislation to be complied with, and failure to do so could have serious consequences.

## Noting

A note is something that is written down, often in abbreviated form, as a record or a reminder. You may make notes during a meeting, on the bus or train on the way to work, when you are being given instructions or when taking a message.

Nobody can remember everything that is said during a meeting, or exactly what instructions they have been given, or all the details of a complex message. Rather than try, it is best to jot down notes which will enable you to recall the main points and fill in the gaps later.

If you have a difficult task to complete when you get to work you may choose to make notes during your journey to work. It is best not to try to write out whole sentences but just to write headings or keywords to remind you of the ideas you had.

Most people have developed their own individual method of note taking. Some write just the keywords and omit all of the connecting language, some write as much as they can, often abbreviating the words; for example, two people attending a meeting and making notes of a decision to increase the fees for conveyancing from £180 per hour to £200 per hour with effect from the following Monday might make the following notes:

- conveyance fees £200 Monday
- inc. fees conv. 180-200 w.e.f. Mon

Don't try to write down every word as, although you may be able to do so, the meeting will have moved on and you will have missed the next point. Even if you are able to write shorthand you can't concentrate on taking part in the meeting and write verbatim notes at the same time.

Whatever method you adopt, it is unlikely that anybody else will be able to make sense of the notes you take. Even you may find it difficult to remember exactly what they meant after a time, so it is important that you make use of them as quickly as possible. Either take action straight away or write up your notes later so that you have a fuller record.

Try this exercise.

Find a busy spot and make notes on what you see. This may be:

- A busy road junction. Note the make, model and colour of the first 20 cars that pass

- A busy bus stop or train station.  Note as much as you can about the first 20 people that get off a bus or train

These are only suggestions, you can choose any situation where you can take notes on what is happening but you don't have time to write full details.  Don't forget to note anything unusual that may happen while you are there.

Now imagine that an incident has occurred during your note taking and you are asked to supply the fullest possible details of every car that passed or person that was in the area. Write up a witness statement from your notes.

## Presenting information

Whether you are going to present information in writing or verbally, you will need to organise your material so that your presentation has a clear beginning, middle and end.  There are a number of techniques which will help you to get started:

- **List the ideas you want to cover** - For instance an announcement of a meeting may include the time and place, people involved, reason for the meeting, any preparation required and any follow-up action needed
- **Use index cards** - Write each idea on a card, lay out all the cards on a flat surface and move the cards around until you get the ideas into a coherent order
- **Use Post-it notes** - Similar to index cards except that you can stick your Post-it notes with the ideas written on onto the wall and move them about

If you struggle to start, give yourself a limited amount of time to think and at the end of that time, write whatever you have thought of.  This is always better than sitting around endlessly waiting for inspiration.

There are a number of different ways that you can organise the ideas.  Probably the most often used is to state your ideas in the order of their importance.  Using this method means that:

- The recipient will understand the purpose of the communication immediately

- If not all the information is read, the most important will be
- People can make their minds up whether to read the information or not more quickly

An alternative is to organise your ideas in chronological order. This simply means putting it in date order either by listing past events starting with the earliest, or listing future events starting with the soonest.

A third option, similar to chronological, is sequential. This involves listing the events in the order in which they will occur without allocating times or dates to them.

Another method is to organise the information into two sets that can be compared with each other. For instance, if recommending the purchase of a laser printer over an inkjet printer you might state the features of the laser printer followed by the comparable features of the inkjet printer.

**Remember** to be precise. If you have gathered all the information, you will need to make a series of judgements about what will be included in the final presentation. This is your decision. You may work in an organisation that expects a huge amount of detail or maybe in an environment where summaries are expected, with fuller information provided upon request.

Plan your presentation so that it has:

- An introduction to what you are going to present
- An interesting and compelling content
- A conclusion, that confirms what you have said

Try this exercise:

You have been asked to write a report on the feasibility of launching a new insurance product. Below are the ideas that you have produced on your index cards, sort them into the final order that they will appear in the report.

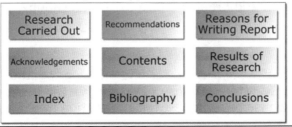

# Recording

Recording is keeping an account of something, preserved in a lasting form, e.g. in writing or electronically. The decisions that have to be made in an administrative environment are:

- **What to record** - Basically you should record anything that you may need to refer to at a later date. You will need to bear in mind the principle of the Data Protection Act 2000 which states 'personal data shall be obtained only for one or more specified and lawful purposes' when recording any personal information. The temptation is to record everything 'because it might be useful one day' so a degree of selectivity is required
- **How to record it** - Essentially there are two choices, hard copy or electronic record. Legal documents and those requiring original signatures need to be retained in hard copy. Most other records can be recorded electronically as hard copies can be produced should they be required. It is important to carry out computer back up operations every day, so none of your computer records get lost or damaged
- **How to reference records for ease of retrieval** - Whether your records are in hard copy or electronic it is important that you are able to find them quickly. Hard copy records can be filed alphabetically, numerically, alpha-numerically or chronologically; electronic records can be filed in folders or directories
- **How long to record it for** - There are three criteria to consider; some records such as payroll records and VAT records for instance, must be retained for specific periods; the Data Protection Act 2000 states that personal records 'shall not be kept for longer than is necessary'; records should be kept only as long as they are useful

The overriding issue in recording anything is that the recording must be accurate. Inaccurate records can cause all manner of confusion and problems for your organisation.

# Researching

Effective research is the searching for and bringing together of information relevant to a purpose. Usually this will be carried out in response to a request for information from your line manager or supervisor, or for an internal or external customer. This request for information may be from inside or outside the organisation. If you are asked to research a subject it is important to be thorough and find all of the available information. The obscure fact that you are tempted to overlook could be the decisive factor in future decisions made as a result of the research. At the same time you must be careful not to be sidetracked into including information that is not directly relevant to your search.

When asked to research information make sure you get clear 'terms of reference' so you know exactly what it is you have been asked for. The terms of reference should cover how much or how little information is required, by when, in what format and how the information should be reported. If in any doubt seek clarification from the person asking for the information before you waste time producing irrelevant or unnecessary information.

Once you are sure what it is you are going to research, you need to decide where you are going to research. There are four main sources of information available:

- Previous research you may have carried out
- Paper-based reference material
- The Internet
- The experience of other people

Each of these has short-cuts which will reduce the time taken to research the information. You will be able to find information in previous research you may have carried out if you have kept accurate and comprehensive records of the research and properly referenced them so that the information in them can be readily accessed.

Paper-based reference material includes reference books, publications, company documents, catalogues, price lists and directories. There are short-cuts to looking up information in reference books:

- **Look in the preface** - This will help you decide whether there is likely to be useful information in the book
- **Look at the publication date** - This will tell you how up-to-date the information is

- **Look in the index** - Using the key word that will lead you to the pages where the subject you are looking for may be found
- **Look in the contents** - This may lead you to the relevant chapter
- **Look in the bibliography** - This will guide you to other books that might be useful

The Internet holds information on almost everything; the drawback is that there is so much information it can be difficult to find exactly what you are looking for. The shortcut on the Internet is to use a good 'search engine'. Having chosen your search engine there are some tips for narrowing the search:

- Think of keywords you would expect to find in the article you are searching for
- Avoid using lengthy combinations of keywords
- Start with seven words
- Spell the keywords correctly
- Use a thesaurus to choose keywords
- Use lower case letters

To use the experience of other people, start with those in your own network and ask them if they have any information on the subject you are researching. Then ask if they know anybody who has any information and ask them, if necessary, to introduce you to them.

At this stage gather together all the relevant information you can find, discarding none until you have compiled all of it.

Try this exercise.

Research all the appropriate qualifications available to you in Business & Administration.

## Using technology

The modern workplace is teeming with technology. It is everywhere you look. Many offices now have all of the following:

- Computers
- Printers
- Telephones

- Photocopiers
- Fax machines
- Franking machines
- Shredders
- Calculators
- Laminators
- Scanners
- Conference facilities – tele or video conferencing

In fact it is impossible to make a cup of coffee in many workplaces as the ubiquitous coffee machine has taken over. When you put your 20p in for a cup of coffee you are using technology. This doesn't require much training (if any) and if the machine goes wrong the solution is to put an 'out of order' notice on it and go and use another one. However, this is not a satisfactory solution to using other forms of technology.

Before operating any form of technology that you haven't had any previous experience of it is important that you receive training and that you read the manufacturer's manual. The manual will contain vital safety and operating information as well as a number of functions or time-saving features which you may otherwise be unaware of. Keep the manual close to the equipment for easy reference.

Remember that the equipment costs a great deal of money to replace, so treat it with respect. Where necessary, clean it after use and leave it ready for the next user.

# PART 3 – ORGANISATIONAL SKILLS

## Managing time

Time is the one resource that can't be replaced. Although time is infinite we never have enough of it. You need to make the best use of every minute of your time at work, but this doesn't mean you need to be 'doing' something all the time. Time spent planning, reviewing and reflecting is time well spent.

Do you know how you spend your time at work now? You probably think you spend most of your time on the important tasks that you have to complete each day, but you might be surprised to find how much time you actually spend on the trivia. You might think that a few minutes spent on an unnecessary task don't matter too much, but if you work out how much your time is worth you might be surprised. Try the following calculation:

- Multiply your monthly salary by 1.5 to allow for overheads
- Divide by four
- Divide by the number of hours you work in a week
- Divide by 60

This will give you the cost to the organisation of every minute of your time. Next time you spend five minutes staring out of the window, think about how much it has cost.

If you have kept a log of your time and analysed it you will probably find that you are spending 60% of your time on routine tasks, 25% on urgent tasks and 15% on important tasks; you should be spending exactly the opposite proportions, 60% on important tasks, 25% on urgent tasks and only 15% on routine tasks.

The chart below may help.

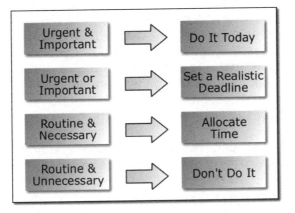

Be realistic when planning. Don't plan more than you know you can achieve, it will de-motivate both you and others involved if you consistently fail to achieve everything you have planned for the day.

Be flexible, remember 'the best laid plans of mice and men often go awry'. Demands will change and your plans will need to change to reflect the new priorities. The important thing is to re-adjust to accommodate the new demands, not just to push everything back.

## Negotiating

Negotiation is not about getting your own way, it is about reaching a situation where everybody gains. This is known as a win:win situation. The skill involves persuading people to agree rather than in persuading them to change their mind.

It is important to remember that in order for both parties to win, both parties will probably have to agree to lose something. The aim is a compromise that both parties feel comfortable with and if you have to lose a minor battle in order to win the war, this is a small price to pay. Decide before you begin negotiating what you are prepared to lose and what you are absolutely determined not to give up. Try to find out what the other person's 'must haves' are and what they might be prepared to sacrifice. A successful outcome is one in which both keep what they were determined to keep and give up as little as possible of what they were prepared to lose.

At the beginning of negotiation you will need to identify the issue that you are negotiating on and not confuse the problem with the people concerned. It may be that you think you can't work successfully with someone, but if you identify the reasons you think that and negotiate on the reasons, there is a chance that you will find an acceptable compromise. Too often people base their negotiation on their emotions about the issue rather than the facts.

Try to find common ground, that is areas where you both agree, rather than focussing on areas of disagreement. You will often be surprised to find that there is much more common ground than you expected. Try to keep an open-mind and listen actively to what the other person is saying; they may not take the position you are expecting and if you don't listen you may miss an opportunity.

Know when to stop. Recognise when you have achieved your main objective and that you are unlikely to gain any more by continuing and summarise the agreement before the moment passes. Sometimes there is only one moment when everybody is prepared to agree, miss it and the negotiations can go on endlessly.

The stages of negotiation are:

- State your case
- Listen to their case
- Identify common ground
- Give sensible reasons for your views
- Explain the reasons
- Overcome their objections without dismissing them or becoming aggressive

- Confirm agreement

There are people who are naturally good at negotiating, but don't worry if you come up against them; if they are really good they will want you to come out with a win situation too.

## Organising

Organising work involves allocating tasks between the available people, deciding who is going to do what, by when, as well as organising your own work and your workspace.

The extent to which you will be involved in allocating tasks to other people will depend on your job role. You may think if you have no staff reporting directly to you, you won't be able to delegate tasks, but delegation is a skill which can be practised in any direction, upwards and sidewards as well as downwards. The critical thing to remember is that abdication is not the same thing as delegation. If it is your responsibility to complete a task but you delegate it to a colleague, the responsibility remains yours. You need to be sure the colleague has the necessary skills and experience to complete the task successfully and you must monitor their progress so that you don't lose control of the project.

Organising your work requires discipline. It is difficult to avoid the danger of tasks being neglected because you have forgotten about them if you don't have any system of arranging the flow of work across your desk. Most people do this either electronically or manually. They use a system based on 'in' and 'pending' trays. This means that new work will be placed in the 'in-tray'.

At the start of each day go through the contents of your in-tray and make a decision about each item:

- If it requires no action, either delete it (if the original is in electronic format), throw it away or file it
- If it requires action, but not by you, pass it on
- If it requires action but you aren't in a position to take the action today, diarise the action so that it is not forgotten and keep the paper in your pending tray
- If it requires action today, put it on your to-do list

Don't allow the pending tray to become a hiding place for tasks that you don't want to do. A task that can be put off indefinitely doesn't need doing at all.

You will work much more efficiently if your workspace is well organised. Think about which files, books or reference material you use most often and place these where they are most accessible. For instance, if you keep them in a bookcase place the most often needed in the centre shelves with the things you use only occasionally at the top and the bottom.

You will spend most of your time at your desk so it is important that this is as organised as possible. If you have an L-shaped working area split the two areas so that one is free working space. Put the computer monitor in the corner of the 'L' where it will take up least space. Make sure the telephone is easily accessible and keep a message pad and pen nearby. Organise your drawers so that you know where to lay your hands on:

- Stationery
- Pens and pencils
- Telephone numbers
- Diary
- Dictionary
- Thesaurus
- Calculator
- Address book
- Regularly used documentation

Keep your desk top clear of things you are not using at the time. Always put everything away before you go home at night. You will find it much easier to get started the next day if you have a clear desk when you arrive.

Try this exercise.

Look at your workspace. Are the things you use regularly in the most accessible places and the things you rarely use in the least accessible? If you work in an office with lots of desks, is yours the tidiest at the end of the day?

## Planning

There are a number of methods of planning your work, people who use each method will tell you it is infallible and the only method to use. Research all the methods, settle on the one that suits you best and, most importantly, use it. Remember to include every task however trivial, or those that are not included will be forgotten.

The simplest method is to make a list at the beginning of each day of all the tasks that need to be completed or worked on that day. Add to the list any new tasks that you are given during the day, cross off any tasks that you complete and carry forward any tasks that remain incomplete. This may not mean carrying them forward to the following day. There may be a task that you are working on periodically. This will need to be carried forward to the list for the next day that you are planning to work on that task.

You will need to prioritise the tasks on your list as the chances are that you will not complete them all within the day. Categorise the tasks as important, urgent, routine or trivial. Some tasks will appear in more than one category as some routine tasks are important while some urgent tasks are trivial. Deal with the important first, then the urgent, but don't ignore the routine as they will become urgent if they are not dealt with.

Carrying forward the uncompleted tasks will enable you to identify those that simply never get done. This may be because you don't like doing them or because they are too trivial to ever become urgent. If the reason is that you don't like doing them, try dealing with one of them as your first job of the day and rewarding yourself with a cup of coffee when you have completed it. Look closely at each of the tasks that aren't done because they are trivial. Decide if you can delegate them to somebody else or simply stop putting them on the list as it is clearly of no importance whether they ever get done.

A supplementary method to list-making is keeping a diary, either electronically or manually. Some people use the diary to record events or appointments that are to take place at a specific time on a specific day, and keep a separate daily list of tasks; others combine the two by keeping their list in their diary. The benefit of keeping your list in your diary is that it shows in advance where there is likely to be some 'slack' in your workload so that if you are asked to agree a deadline for a task you will be able to look forward and project a completion date.

However, lists can have limitations. When several people need to be involved with work tasks over a period of time, you will need a separate action plan. The action plan will need to analyse the overall task and show which actions have to be taken and when. Each action must have a starting date and a completion date. There should be milestones for key events and specified outcomes.

Choose the method that best meets your requirements, but don't use a mixture of all the methods as this will lead inevitably to confusion and tasks being missed completely. Keep your schedule of tasks to be done constantly to hand and refer to it regularly throughout the day.

# Prioritising

The thesaurus gives the following synonyms for priority; first concern, greater importance, precedence, pre-eminence, preference, prerogative, rank, right of way, seniority, superiority, supremacy, the lead. The art of prioritising involves the ability to recognise which task of the many that need your attention deserves to be given priority. Every task will have its claim to be the first. It may be simple, so you could do it and get it off the list. It may be that the person you are doing the task for is constantly on the phone asking when it will be done. It may just be it's a task you actually enjoy doing. Accepting any of these as a good reason for giving a task priority will only lead to greater problems in the future when the task that you should have done first passes its deadline without being achieved.

Tasks should be sorted into:

- **Must do tasks** - Jobs which are important and have a deadline which requires them to be started on today
- **Should do tasks** - Jobs which are not so important but will need to be done soon
- **Could do tasks** - Jobs which it would be nice to get done if you only had the time

Must do tasks must then be given the priority followed by should do tasks and finally could do tasks. If you are responsible for allocating tasks to others, the question of priority is given another dimension. Considerations such as comparative competence, development needs and staff morale have to be taken into account. Must do tasks should be allocated to colleagues who you are confident will be able to complete them satisfactorily by the deadline. Should do tasks can be allocated to colleagues who require some training or assistance and this should be used to develop them so that they can move on to the must do tasks in the future. Avoid giving the could do tasks to the same people every time as this will both de-motivate them and not help to develop their skills so that you have a larger pool of people that you can delegate must do tasks to.

# Problem solving

Problem solving is a very important activity at work. Unexpected situations are always arising. You or your colleagues can experience all sorts of problems in just one day. Employers value people who can resolve problems calmly. There are six stages to problem solving:

1. **Identify the problem** - This will often be done for you as a customer or colleague will point out that you or your department is not providing the service required. If you are monitoring your own performance you may have recognised the fact that there is a problem before you are told

2. **Define the effects of the problem** - If the problem has been pointed out to you by somebody else they will probably have told you what the effects are. For instance, if you have failed to meet a deadline, you will probably have been told in no uncertain terms why it was important. If, on the other hand, you have identified the problem yourself, you need to find out what, if any, the effects have been. You may have a task on your list as a priority and be surprised to find, if you fail to carry it out, that nobody actually notices. Defining the effects of the problem allow you to decide the importance that needs to be given to solving the problem

3. **Find the cause of the problem** - This stage is not about apportioning blame but about finding out why a problem has arisen. This may require some tact and diplomacy in asking other people what their contribution has been to the problem, or may need some honesty on your own part to admit that the fault lies with you. It may be that you have failed to give the task sufficient priority or that other tasks have been added to your list and caused a backlog

4. **Identify possible solutions** - If it is a one-off problem then a short-term solution will need to be found; either the task will have to be re-assigned or you may have to stop what you are doing and deal with the problem. Repetitive problems need a longer-term solution. When you have identified the causes you will be able to look at alternative ways of dealing with them. If in the example above additional tasks have caused a backlog, you should have advised the people involved that a deadline will be missed or that

you are unable to take on additional tasks as you already have priority tasks to complete

5. **Choose between the solutions** - As in any matter of choice you need to look at the advantages and disadvantages of each solution and identify the one that has the most advantages and the least disadvantages.  In this situation you should weigh up the advantages and disadvantages to the whole organisation rather than to yourself or your department

6. **Plan the way forward** - If other people are involved in the chosen solution, make sure you involve them in planning the way forward to prevent the problem re-occurring.  Get the agreement of everyone involved that the chosen solution is the best way forward; involving them in choosing the solution will ensure their commitment to its success

## Team working

A team is a group of people working collectively to achieve a common aim.  You will find yourself working in a number of teams during your career.  If you work in a large or complex organisation you will probably find yourself working in more than one team at a time.  For instance, you may be part of the accounts team at the same time as being part of a project team.  You will also be part of a team that stretches outside of the organisation to include your contacts in suppliers, customers and contractors.  As the various teams are likely to overlap it is essential that there is effective communication both within the team and between the teams.

Each member of a team has their own strengths and weaknesses and you will need to integrate those with your own if you are to work effectively.

Successful teams have the following characteristics:

- **Honesty** - Members of the team must be prepared to express their opinions openly with the rest of the team
- **Willingness** - to take on any task.  There are bound to be jobs that you would not choose to do, but in a team each must be prepared to do what is needed

- **Clear objectives** - Every member of the team must understand their purpose and be committed to its achievement
- **Results oriented** - The focus in a team must be on achieving its goals rather than on the process required
- **Mutual trust** - You must be able to rely on every other member of the team to achieve their part of the whole
- **Support** - Each member of the team needs to know that if they are having difficulty completing their part they can expect help from others

Each member of a team will have their own role, utilising their individual skills to the best advantage of the team. For instance, to produce a magazine the features editor will choose the subjects to be included; writers will write the articles; sales staff will sell the advertising; graphics designers will organise the layout; sub-editors will edit the content; printers will print the magazine and the distribution manager will see that copies reach the news stands. Each will be taking their particular role because it best matches their skills.

Each team needs people to undertake one or more of the following roles:

- **Initiator** - The person who starts the whole process
- **Clarifier** - The person who turns generalisations into specifics
- **Information provider** - The person who either has the knowledge the team needs or knows where to get it
- **Questioner** - The person who raises doubts in the team and challenges assumptions
- **Summariser** - The person who doesn't add anything new but ensures the team knows how far it has got
- **Supporter** - The person who supports members of the team as necessary
- **Joker** - The person who helps the team to keep their perspective
- **Process observer** - The person who overcomes difficulties by referring to a known method

There may or may not be an appointed team leader, but the leadership role will be assumed by one or other of the team depending on the situation. Leadership is derived from power, and power comes from a variety of sources, the importance of which will vary from situation to situation.

Whatever their roles in the team it is vital that everyone knows what the goals of the team are and is kept informed of the team's progress towards achieving those goals. There are various ways of motivating team members; some organisations have set incentives while others leave this to the team leader.

In any team there will always be people you get on with better than others. There will always be some people that you just don't understand, but that doesn't mean you can't work with them. Everybody has some positive attributes, if you concentrate on those you will be able to find a way of working together.

## Reading

You can obviously read already, otherwise you wouldn't be able to read this book. There is more to reading, however, than being able to make out the words on a page. Reading for business purposes requires you to be able to:

- Obtain relevant information from various types of documents
- Gain a general idea of the content of documents by skim-reading them
- Identify the required information from documents
- Understand the writer's meaning
- Identify the main points, ideas and lines of reasoning from text and images

Working in the field of Business & Administration you will be required to read a wide range of material from simple memos to complex reports. Some of your work will require careful reading, while some will require you only to skim through the material and pick out the points that you need. Skim-reading, however, requires the ability to understand the meaning of what you are reading. For instance, if you read 'I saw the man with the binoculars', who has the binoculars: you or the man? Misunderstanding an instruction can have serious repercussions. It would be dangerous to follow the instruction often seen on the roadside 'use both lanes' when what is meant is 'use either lane'.

There is only one way to improve your reading skills and that is to practise. This doesn't have to be hard work; try carrying a book with you and reading it on the bus or during your coffee break. If you prefer, magazines and newspapers may be an acceptable alternative. Not only will this improve your reading skills, it will increase your knowledge base.

Try to read things that contain words you won't immediately understand and make the effort to find out what they mean, as this will widen your vocabulary.

Highlight the words that you aren't sure you fully understand. Make a list of these words and when you get home or to the office, look them up in a good dictionary. Words in a dictionary are arranged in alphabetical order, so it is easy to find the word you want. The dictionary will then give the definition of the word. Sometimes this won't fully explain the meaning of the word in the context that you have read it. Another really useful source of information is a thesaurus. A thesaurus lists words alphabetically, exactly the same as a dictionary, but instead of giving definitions it gives synonyms, words which mean the same as or similar to the word you look up. This can sometimes be more helpful when searching for an alternative word or to gain a fuller meaning of the original word. The dictionary definition of 'intelligent' for example is 'having, showing good intellect'. The thesaurus gives 'acute, alert, apt, brainy, bright, clever, discerning, enlightened, instructed, knowing, penetrating, perspicacious, quick, quick-witted, rational, sharp, smart, thinking, well-informed'. If you didn't know the meaning of intelligent, which would you find more useful?

Try the following exercises as examples of understanding what you read.

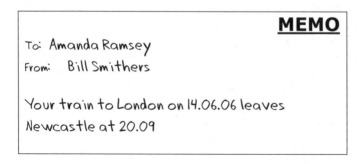

**MEMO**

To: Amanda Ramsey
From: Bill Smithers

Your train to London on 14.06.06 leaves Newcastle at 20.09

Does this mean:

- The train leaves at 9 minutes past 8 in the morning
- The train leaves at 9 minutes past 8 in the evening
- The train leaves at 20 minutes past 9 in the morning
- The train leaves at 20 minutes past 9 in the evening?

> For more information on forthcoming attractions at this theatre ring 0854 659 369 and leave your telephone number. Somebody will get back to you.

What will happen if you ring 0854 659 369?

- You can ask about forthcoming attractions
- You can ask for times of the shows
- You can leave a message and someone will call back
- You can request brochures be sent to you

**INTERNATIONAL TELEPHONE CALLS**

15 PENCE PER MINUTE
BETWEEN 9AM AND 6PM

**FIRST THREE
MONTHS
SUBSCRIPTION FREE***

CALL 016659 365418
TODAY TO REGISTER

*then £14.99 per month

What does this information tell you?

- You can register now or in three months' time
- You can only make international calls between 9am and 6pm
- You have to pay £14.99 after three months
- You have to call today to take advantage of the offer

You will find four book reviews overleaf, read them and answer the questions that follow.

### The Scottish Story by William Waterfield

The main character, Simon Bretherton, is down-to-earth, maybe at times a little too down-to-earth. The descriptions of the countryside are very realistic and the characters almost seem like old friends. The story leads you down dead-ends with the occasional light to be seen; it will keep you spell-bound to the very end when the twist that you never saw coming hits you in the face. It all becomes very clear and you will wonder why you never saw it coming. This is one of the best books I have ever read. I sat and read it from end-to-end, it was so difficult to put down.

### The Numerical Mystery by Christopher Agate

This is an outstanding example of Agate's work. His ubiquitous private detective is lead on a wild goose chase across the country on the trail of a fiendishly inventive murderer using numerical connections to taunt the, as usual, dull-witted police as they try desperately to bring his reign of terror to an end. The murders of a milkman in Manchester, a driver in Derby and a publican in Perth appear unconnected and only the lateral thinking of Achilles Crowe can unravel the mystery. The 1930's setting adds to the charm of this excellent whodunnit.

### The Man in the White Coat by Phillipa Barker

If you like your romantic novels, you will love this one. It is set in the early 17th century. The romantic hero is a well-to-do man who lives in the big house on the hill, he notices Amanda when she comes to the house to become the understairs maid. How long can she resist his charms? Does she really want to? What will the family make of it all? These questions will all be answered, but not necessarily in the way that you think. The twists and turns of their romantic encounters will keep you on the edge of your seat right up to the very, unusual and unexpected, end.

### Blue Horizons by Demitri Kassakov

This book, like the others in the series, is set on an imaginary planet somewhere in the far reaches of space. The characters are drawn from a wide spectrum of alien races, yet all have clearly human characteristics and their failings and concerns will be instantly recognisable to all of us. The story follows the attempt by the United Planetary Corporation to extract valuable minerals from the planet Syrius 0 with disastrous consequences for all the inhabitants. A renegade space trader proves to be a thorn in the side of the inter-galactic corporation as he rallies the inhabitants of the endangered planet to thwart their plans.

1. Which book is set on Syrius 0?
2. Which book describes the countryside in which it is set?
3. Amanda is mentioned in which book?
4. What is Amanda's occupation?
5. Where does the murder of the milkman take place?
6. Who solves The Numerical Mystery?

7. How is Simon Bretherton described?
8. Which book has an unusual and unexpected end?
9. Why couldn't the police in the Numerical Mystery use DNA to track down the killer?
10. Which book is one of a series?

# Using number

Using number involves understanding and using mathematical information given by numbers, symbols, diagrams and charts for a range of different purposes.

The degree to which you will use number in your working experience will depend on the job roles you undertake. In this section we will try to cover all of the common mathematical applications that you might come across in your day-to-day work. You will find you are using mathematics all the time without realising it, so try and relate the examples given below to your everyday work.

### Accuracy

In most applications absolute accuracy will be essential. For instance if you are ordering a carpet for a room 9.15m x 8.67m a carpet measuring 9m x 8.5m would not be enough. But there are times when an approximation is good enough. For instance if you are asked your annual turnover, £6million is close enough if the actual answer is £6,027,136.55. This form of approximation is called 'rounding up' or 'rounding down' and the general rule is if the number after the number you are going to give as the answer is five or over round the answer up, four or less round it down.

Try these exercises.

Round the following numbers to three decimal places:

1. 2563.5568
2. 56.36894521
3. 96.969696
4. 6369.65459
5. 9.36549

Round the following times to the nearest quarter hour:

1. 09.42
2. 21.24
3. 10.56
4. 03.05
5. 08.12

Calculate the following weekly wage to the nearest pound:

1. 35hrs @ £6.37per hour
2. 16hrs @ £5.20per hour
3. 46hrs @ £14.56per hour
4. 2 days @ £126 per day
5. 20hrs @ £6.20per hour

**Tolerances**

Connected to the concept of accuracy is the question of tolerance. Tolerance is the amount of inaccuracy you are prepared to accept. For example printers often work to a tolerance of 10% on volume work, so if you order 10,000 copies of a brochure they will deliver 10,000 copies plus or minus 10%. It is important that an acceptable tolerance is agreed in any situation where inaccuracy may be acceptable. In the exercises above the tolerance is set by the instruction, so the tolerance in the exercise 'calculate the following weekly wage to the nearest pound' is 50p, since that is the furthest from an exact answer that is acceptable.

## Probability

Probability is a mathematical way of describing the chance that something will happen. For instance, if a member of staff is off sick one week in every ten, the probability of them being off sick is one in ten. Probability theory is used in occupations such as insurance and medicine.

Try these exercises:

1. If you pick one card from a standard pack of 52 playing cards what is the probability of picking an ace?
2. If there are 25million cars on the road and 5million break-downs a year, what is the probability that an individual car will break down?
3. If there are 47million households and 13million claims for accidental damage a year, what is the probability of any one household having a claim for accidental damage?

## Area and perimeter

The perimeter of a space is the distance around the outside (the black line in the drawing below). The area is the space contained within the perimeter (the grey space in the drawing).

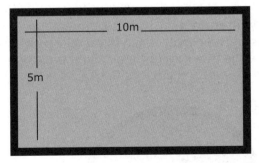

To find the perimeter of the space you must add together the lengths of all the sides. In the example above this is 10m + 5m + 10m + 5m, a total of 30m.

To find the area of the space you must multiply the length of one side by the length of the other. In the example above this is 10m x 5m, a total of 50 metres square (50m²). This formula is only effective in a square or rectangular space.

In an irregularly shaped space you will have to divide the space into rectangles, calculate the area of each and add them together.

In the diagram below there are a total of three rectangles, one 10m x 8m and two 2m x 4m. The total area is, therefore, 80m² + 8m² + 8m² = 96m².

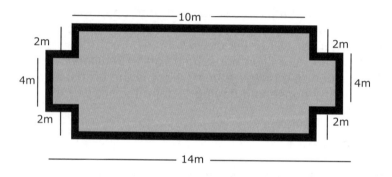

The total perimeter is 10m + 2m + 2m + 4m +2m + 2m + 10m +2m + 2m + 4m + 2m + 2m = 44m.

The area of a circle is calculated by using the formula Pi r squared which is written as $\pi r^2$. In this formula Pi = 3.14 and r = the radius of the circle, which is the distance from the centre to the edge in a straight line. So if a circle has a radius of 10m the area of the circle is 3.14 x 10 x 10 = 314m².

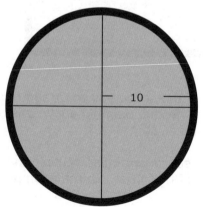

The perimeter of a circle is called the circumference. To calculate the circumference of a circle use the formula $2\pi r$, so a circle with a radius of 10m has a circumference of 2 x 3.14 x 10 = 62.8m.

## Averages

To find the average of a set of numbers add together all the numbers and divide by the number of numbers. For instance, from the table below, to find the average sales per day add the six sales figures together and divide by six. (269,610 ÷ 6 = 44,935).

| Day | Sales |
|-----------|--------|
| Monday | 56,998 |
| Tuesday | 26,569 |
| Wednesday | 36,256 |
| Thursday | 75,556 |
| Friday | 14,984 |
| Saturday | 59,247 |

44,935 is the average sales per day. This is known as the mean average. There are three other expressions that are used in relation to sets of numbers such as these: mode, median and range.

| Day | Number of staff |
|-----------|-----------------|
| Monday | 8 |
| Tuesday | 5 |
| Wednesday | 5 |
| Thursday | 8 |
| Friday | 4 |
| Saturday | 8 |

The mean average of the table above is the total number of staff (38) divided by the number of days (6) = 6.33.

The mode is the number which appears most often in the set, in the table above the mode is 8.

The range is the difference between the highest and lowest numbers, so in the table above the highest number is 8 and the lowest number 4 so the range is 8 − 4 = 4.

The median is the middle number of the set, so in the table above the numbers are 4, 5 and 8, so the median is 5.

Try these exercises.

| Day | Number of staff | Sales |
|-----|-----------------|-------|
| Monday | 8 | 56,998 |
| Tuesday | 5 | 26,569 |
| Wednesday | 5 | 36,256 |
| Thursday | 8 | 75,556 |
| Friday | 4 | 14,984 |
| Saturday | 8 | 59,247 |

1. Calculate the mean average sales per head each day
2. Calculate the range of sales per day
3. Calculate the median sales per day
4. Calculate the median sales per head of staff per day

## Ratios

A ratio is the proportion between one number and another, most often expressed as 'per' as in miles per hour (mph) or pounds per square inch (psi). So if your rate of pay is £6 per hour the ratio between your pay and your time is 6:1, if there are five people working in an area measuring 400sq ft. the ratio between space and people is 400:5, or 80:1.

Try these exercises.

1. Using the area of the circle shown in the area and perimeter section, work out the ratio of space to people if six people work in the area.
2. If you had an office space of 50m$^2$ and the minimum ratio of space to people is 4:1, what is the maximum number of people that can be employed in the space?

## Fractions

A fraction is literally a part of a whole, for instance a half ($^1/_2$) or a quarter ($^1/_4$). They are mainly used in measuring and weighing. The number above the line is known as the numerator and the number below the line is known as the denominator.

To add fractions together they must have the same denominator. For instance to add $1/2$ to $1/4$ you must change the $1/2$ to $2/4$ then add the numerators together to give the answer ($2/4 + 1/4 = 3/4$). Remember not to add the denominators together.

To take away one fraction from another they must have the same denominator. For instance to take away $1/4$ from $1/2$ you change the $1/2$ to $2/4$ and take away the 1 from the 2 to give the answer ($2/4 - 1/4 = 1/4$). Remember not to take the denominators away.

To multiply fractions you simply multiply both the numerators and the denominators. For instance, to multiply $1/2$ by $1/4$, 1 x 1 = 1, 2 x 4 = 8. To give the answer ($1/2 \times 1/4 = 1/8$).

To divide fractions you simply invert the second fraction and multiply the fractions. For instance, to divide $1/4$ by $1/2$ invert the $1/2$ and multiply $1/4$ by $2/1$ 1 x 2 = 2, 4 x 1 = 4, to give the answer ($1/4 \times 2/1 = 2/4$ which = $1/2$).

## Interquartile range

Statistics can be distorted by freak results either at the top or the bottom of the range. For instance calculating average monthly sales can be distorted by Christmas when sales are disproportionately high or by freak weather conditions preventing customers from reaching you, making them disproportionately low. To avoid this distortion only the interquartile range is used.

The interquartile range is found within a set of figures. In order to find the interquartile range place the figures in order from lowest to highest then divide the number of numbers into four quarters. Disregard the top and bottom quarters and work out the range of the middle two quarters. Take away the lowest figure from the highest figure to get the interquartile range.

| January | 14,000 |
| February | 6,000 |
| March | 15,000 |
| April | 13,000 |
| May | 17,000 |
| June | 19,000 |
| July | 18,000 |
| August | 21,000 |

| | |
|---|---|
| September | 16,000 |
| October | 12,000 |
| November | 10,000 |
| December | 35,000 |

If the above table shows monthly sales you would need to re-arrange the table into descending order by sales.

| | |
|---|---|
| December | 35,000 |
| August | 21,000 |
| June | 19,000 |
| **July** | **18,000** |
| **May** | **17,000** |
| **September** | **16,000** |
| **March** | **15,000** |
| **January** | **14,000** |
| **April** | **13,000** |
| October | 12,000 |
| November | 10,000 |
| February | 6,000 |

To find the interquartile range you ignore the top three and the bottom three and concentrate on the six in the middle, highlighted in bold. The grey shading shows the highest and lowest figures in this range, 18,000 and 13,000. Take the lower from the higher and the interquartile range is 5,000.

## Negative numbers

A negative number is any number less than nought. They are usually written with a 'minus' sign in front of them or in brackets. An example would be this year's stationery budget is £2,500, last year's was £3,000 so this year's is -£500 compared with last year's.

To add negative numbers together you simply add the numbers together and put a minus in front so to add -101 to -879, add 101 + 879 = 980, put the minus in front to give the answer -980 or show the answer as (980).

To subtract negative numbers you change the sign of the second negative number to a positive so, to take away -3 from -6 write -6 minus –3. Change the sign on the second number to a positive and add the numbers together, so -6 + 3 = -3.

## Percentages

A percentage (%) is the rate per hundred so if 20 people in every 100 who work in an organisation are on holiday, 20%

of staff are on holiday.  In effect a percentage is a fraction where the denominator is always 100.  Therefore to add, subtract, multiply or divide percentages use the same rules as with fractions.

For instance:
- $20\% + 30\% = {}^{20}/_{100} + {}^{30}/_{100} = {}^{50}/_{100}$ or 50%
- $30\% - 20\% = {}^{30}/_{100} - {}^{20}/_{100} = {}^{10}/_{100}$ or 10%

However:
- $20\% \times 30\% = {}^{20}/_{100} \times {}^{30}/_{100} = {}^{600}/_{10000} = {}^{6}/_{100}$ or 6%

To divide:
- $20\%$ by $30\% = {}^{20}/100 \times {}^{100}/30 = {}^{2000}/3000 = 66.66\%$

## Working safely

It is the responsibility of everybody to work in such a way that they reduce the risk of harm to themselves and everybody else.  This responsibility is covered in legislation which requires that you:

- Take care of your own health and safety
- Take care not to put others at risk
- Wear any protective clothing that is provided
- Take care of any fire extinguishers

You should try to work safely at all times, including when you are away from your workplace, maybe visiting another site or clients' or customers' premises.  Accidents are costly, not only in terms of monetary loss to the organisation and the employee, but also in terms of the interruption of your career while recovering.

The most effective way to ensure that you work safely is to maintain good housekeeping standards.  Simply putting away things when you have finished with them, closing drawers and doors behind you, not leaving boxes and cartons in gangways and making sure there are no trailing wires when you use electrical equipment will all reduce the risk to yourself and others.

If you notice any hazards in the workplace don't ignore them. If possible take action yourself to correct them, if not report them to a supervisor or the Health and Safety representative. One of the major risks is fire, so be aware of the location of fire exits and fire fighting equipment.  Know what to do if there is a fire.  Your main priority is to save the lives of yourself, your colleagues and visitors.  Saving the property comes second.  The main causes of fire in buildings are electrical faults and smoking.

If any form of accident happens it must be entered in the accident book.  There should be qualified first-aiders in most workplaces.  Find out who they are and how you can contact them quickly in an emergency.  If you are not trained in first aid avoid moving anybody who is injured, call for a first-aider or an ambulance.

If your work involves lifting anything at all, learn the correct techniques for manual handling and make sure you carry them out every time.  This will reduce the risk of damaging your back or pulling muscles.  Similarly if you handle any hazardous substances make sure you know what they are and the risks they pose, and how to deal with any accidents involving them.

Try this exercise.

Look around your workplace and spot any risks to health and safety.  Correct those that you can immediately and report any that you cannot correct.

## Writing

Writing for business purposes means being able to:

- Write letters, e-mails, memos and reports
- Use different formats to present information
- Use spelling, punctuation and grammar accurately
- Alter your style of writing to suit the purpose and the reader
- Proof read your writing and correct or amend as necessary

The amount of writing that you do will vary enormously depending on your job role.  You may be heavily involved in producing written documents or you may only be required to make brief notes of conversations.  Writing letters, e-mails, memos and reports is covered in depth in later chapters in this book, as is proof reading.  In this chapter we will cover the basic skills of spelling, punctuation and grammar as these are needed by everybody.

The ability to spell is closely linked to the ability to read. The English language is more complex, irregular and eccentric than almost any other written language. It is the hardest European language to learn because of its inconsistent spelling. For this reason it is extremely difficult to learn to spell by learning rules such as 'i before e except after c'.

There are so many exceptions to every rule that you are almost as likely to make mistakes by following the rules as by guesswork. The only reliable way to learn to spell is by reading enough material that you recognise when words are misspelled because they 'look wrong'. This will also help you to pick the right spelling from two or more words that sound alike. For instance if you hear 'Threw the Looking Glass' by Lewis Carroll it will sound correct, but if you see it written down it should be immediately obvious that 'Threw' has been spelled incorrectly.

Try the following exercises.

Which spelling is correct?

| | | |
|---|---|---|
| administration | administrashun | adminnistration |
| paperwate | paperweight | paperwaite |
| committee | comittee | commitee |
| minimmum | minnimum | minimum |
| calandar | callandar | calendar |
| dictionery | dictionary | dixtionary |
| seprate | separate | seperate |
| telephonic | telefonic | tellephonic |
| goverment | guvernment | government |
| invironmental | environmental | enviromental |

Which word is correct?

- Read _threw/through_ the document very carefully.
- I was asked to _right/write_ to you _right/write_ away.
- It was time to have a new _tire/tyre_ fitted to the car.
- On my way to work I walked _past/passed_ the cinema and I _past/passed_ two people that I knew.
- The bride's mother was _complemented/complimented_ on her outfit at the wedding.

- She had been invited to be a *guessed/guest* at the ceremony.
- The administrator was asked to *hire/higher* a replacement car for the salesman.
- I have been asked to *write/right* an article on *gorilla/guerrilla* warfare in the jungle.
- He had spilt paint on his new *over all/overall*.
- She booked her holiday for the last *weak/week* in September.

In much the same way as using incorrect spelling will lead to confusion in the mind of the reader, so will the use of incorrect punctuation. Accurate punctuation is essential in business writing as the meaning of sentences can be completely distorted. For instance, 'Am I looking at your work or the typists'?' means something different from 'Am I looking at your work or the typist's?' Try saying these out loud, you will find that you automatically punctuate them differently when you speak.

There are a number of rules that can be learnt to help you punctuate accurately. If you remember the following, you will not go far wrong.

Capital (or upper case) letters are used to:

- Begin sentences
- Indicate proper names (Ahmed, Francesca, Belgrade, Africa)
- Begin titles (Mr., Mrs., Lord, Sir, Dr.)
- Begin days of the week

- Begin months of the year
- Indicate acronyms (RAF, CIA, FBI, MI5, RAC)

Commas are used:

- To separate words in a list (paper, pens, pencils and rubbers).  Note a comma is not used before the 'and'
- Before speech (Bill said, 'I would like the letter typed today.')
- In pairs to indicate part of a sentence that can be removed without changing the meaning of the sentence (Mrs. Patel, removing her earring, answered the telephone.)
- To indicate pauses in sentences ('I must finish photocopying my friend.' means something different from 'I must finish photocopying, my friend.')

Semi-colons are used to:

- Separate items in a list (The new office has the following features; central heating in the winter; air conditioning in the summer; reflective glass in the windows; wall-to-wall carpet and self-closing doors.)
- Emphasise contrasts (Byron liked to write poems; his manager preferred structured reports.)
- Link statements together (She wanted to pass her examination this year; promotion would be unlikely if she failed.)
- Add emphasis (Patrick answered the telephone; it was the Human Resources Director; he knew he was in trouble.)

Colons are used to:

- Introduce lists (Her manager asked for reports on: wages, hours worked, holidays booked, absenteeism and sickness.)
- Separate two parts of a sentence where the second part explains the first (Sales of coal had improved during November: it was the coldest month of the year.)

Hyphens are used:

- To avoid ambiguity (words such as co-respondent, re-formed, re-mark)

- When linking two nouns (Manchester-Birmingham coach) or two adjectives (Anglo-Italian heritage)
- When a noun phrase is used to qualify another noun (A self-closing door is self closing, a three-drawer filing cabinet has three drawers)
- For certain prefixes (Un-British, anti-hunting, pro-life or quasi-autonomous)
- To indicate words are to be spelled out (S-O-U-T-H-P-O-R-T)
- To avoid difficult looking compound words (coattail, belllike, deice look better and are easier to read, as coat-tail, bell-like and de-ice)

Brackets are used:

- For parenthesis.  Similar to a pair of commas, brackets separate a phrase within a sentence that could be removed without altering the sense.  (Mr. Muldoon (the new Managing Director) will visit the office next Wednesday.)

Full stops are used:

- To indicate the end of a sentence
- After initials or abbreviations (W. H. Smith, etc.)

Exclamation marks are used:

- In place of a full stop to indicate an exclamation (The machine went bang!)

Question marks are used:

- In place of a full stop to indicate a query (What time should I start work in the morning?)

Quotation marks are used:

- To indicate speech (Michael said, "I want you to work late tonight to finish the accounts.")
- To indicate a quote from another source (The letter from the supplier states ' that there is an outstanding balance of £48.80.')

Apostrophes are used:

- In place of missing letters (don't – do not; 'til – until; 'phone – telephone; B'ham – Birmingham.)
- To indicate possession

Possessive apostrophes follow certain rules:

- Where the noun is singular the apostrophe comes between the noun and the 's' (Carol's desk – the desk belonging to Carol)
- Where the noun is singular but ends in 's' the apostrophe still comes between the noun and the additional 's' (St. James's Square – the square of St. James)
- Where the noun is plural and ends in 's' the apostrophe comes after the 's' and there is no additional 's' (ladies' cloakroom– the cloakroom provided for ladies)
- Where the noun is plural and doesn't end in 's' the apostrophe comes between the noun and the 's' (children's books – the books belonging to children)

There is one exception to these rules and it's 'its'.  This is one of the most common mistakes to make.  If you mean 'it is' or 'it has' then the correct usage is 'it's' because you are replacing the missing letters with an apostrophe; if you mean 'belonging to it' then the correct usage is 'its', without the apostrophe.

Try these exercises.

Punctuate the following:

1. what time will the train be arriving in the morning I need to get there to collect someone
2. james letter to the publisher said I want you to proof read my manuscript carefully
3. the order for the stationer will need to include paperclips rubber bands sticky tape staples etc and photocopy paper for delivery on Wednesday
4. mr williams wife will be unable to attend the surgery on thursday as he will be in hospital
5. they were due to be in the office at 2pm as were going to have a meeting in the board room at 4pm

6. its going to be very difficult to finish the report on time as its going to be typed by its author who is not computer literate
7. today of all days the computer crashes have been unusually regular
8. the solicitors unable to see you today his wife has just delivered a note from his doctor saying hes unwell
9. I think the photocopier may well be broken it went off with a big bang
10. parents are not permitted to use the childrens door
11. information can be obtained from the citizens advice bureau between 9 and 5

Correct the following:

1. We need paper's, pencil's, rubbers', and staples.
2. Every one of the staff are invited to the meeting.
3. We want to get the 10am train?
4. In case of fire use neither the lift or the escalator.
5. When will the stationery order be delivered!
6. After the reports are finished should, we all meet in the pub for a drink.
7. Its been a long time since it's been this warm should, we open the windows.
8. Phillip has mastered the new printer hes worked out its idiosyncrasies.
9. The memo from accounts say will you forward all cheques as soon as they arrive.
10. If the diary is not kept up to date nobody will know were their supposed to be at any time.

The purpose of good grammar is to ensure that your meaning is clearly understood.  There are a few simple conventions to follow.  Divide up what you want to say into sentences and paragraphs.  A sentence is a set of words which make a complete statement.  As we have seen, sentences must start with a capital letter and end with a full stop, exclamation mark or question mark.  Sentences can be of almost any length, but for clarity it is as well if they are as short as possible.  As a minimum they must contain a subject and a verb.

A paragraph is a collection of sentences about a single subject.  Each paragraph must contain one sentence which describes the subject of the paragraph.  Paragraphs must contain at least two sentences and may be as long as is necessary to complete the subject. When a new subject is introduced, a new paragraph is begun.

Sentences are broken down into parts of speech. There are many different parts of speech in the English language but the main ones are:

- **Nouns** - A noun is the name of a thing (pencil, desk, computer, filing cabinet, clerk, supervisor)
- **Proper nouns** - A proper noun is the name of a person, a place, a day of the week or the month of the year (Joan, Islamabad, Tuesday, October)
- **Pronouns** - A pronoun is a word used in place of a noun (he, she, it, they)
- **Verbs** - A verb is a word that shows action (running, walking, speaks, reads, sits, jumped, followed)
- **Adverbs** - An adverb is a word that adds to a verb (slowly, quickly, efficiently, thoughtfully)
- **Adjectives** - An adjective is a word that describes a noun (blue, new, modern, antique, fast, pedantic)
- **Prepositions** - A preposition is a word that shows how one noun relates to another (towards, between, beside, behind)
- **Conjunctions** - A conjunction is a word that joins two other words (and, but, so, then, therefore)

Try this exercise:

Take a chapter from a book and analyse the grammar, checking that sentences and paragraphs are correctly formed. Try going through a few sentences and finding the different parts of speech that make them up.

## Decision making

We have touched on decision making in stage five of problem solving. A decision is a choice between two or more possibilities; it is impossible to choose correctly every time so don't despair if you find yourself making the wrong choice. It is only necessary to make a decision when there is more than one possibility. If there is only one option you may decide to delay making a decision. The skill lies in evaluating the choices, making the decision for the right reasons so that even if it turns out to have been an unwise decision you will be able to justify your reasons for making it.

You will be making decisions from the moment you wake up; what shall I wear today, shall I take the car or the bus to work, what shall I have for breakfast? You may feel you make these decisions without giving them a great deal of thought, but the process you go through is the same as the process you use for making major decisions; find the advantages and disadvantages of each option and select the option with the most advantages and least disadvantages.

When making a decision between a number of choices it may be possible to eliminate some as clearly impractical. This may be because the possible solution is far too expensive, will take far too long to implement or involves too great a risk should it fail.  This will leave you with a smaller list to choose from.  One technique for choosing between several options is to list them and then compare each with the one above and below it, moving them up and down the list.  For example, if you were asked to rank the following laptops in order of their suitability for your use:

1. Toshiba Satellite M30X-129
2. Toshiba Satellite M40-149
3. Toshiba Satellite L10-151
4. Toshiba Qosmio F10
5. Toshiba Qosmio G20
6. Toshiba Qosmio G10
7. Goodmans P50
8. Goodmans M40
9. Goodmans M20

First compare No.1 with No.2 looking at the features which matched your needs in each and if No.2 were preferable to No.1 move it to the No.1 position.  Compare No.3 with No.2 and again move them to the correct relative position. Continue this process with each pair in turn until you have an agreed ranking.  This is known as 'bubble up, bubble down' as each solution can finish anywhere in the list; No.9 could finish at No.1 but will have had to be favourably compared with all the other eight in order to do so.

If the decision is between a number of solutions to a problem it may be that two of the solutions are not mutually exclusive but would complement each other and work better than any single solution.  Test your decision by asking a number of questions.  If the answer to all the questions is 'yes' you may have found the best solution.

| QUESTION | YES | NO |
|---|---|---|
| Does it solve the problem? | | |
| Does it solve the cause of the problem? | | |
| Has everybody involved agreed to it? | | |
| Is it practical in terms of cost? | | |
| Is it practical in terms of time? | | |
| Is it practical in terms of people? | | |
| Is it practical in terms of resources? | | |
| Will it prevent the problem re-occurring? | | |
| Have you considered all the disadvantages? | | |
| Have you considered all the consequences? | | |

Remember that decisions are never final. Circumstances will change and today's best solution may not be tomorrow's. Be open to suggestions to reconsider decisions in the light of new circumstances.

## Consulting with and involving others

When you have to take important decisions that will affect other people you will often need to consult with them in order to get their commitment. People will usually be much more positive towards an idea that they feel they have been involved in. The advantages of consultation include:

- The decision will be seen as a group one rather than an individual choice which will reflect on you if it proves to be a poor decision
- Two (or more) heads are better than one. Others will have knowledge and experience that you don't have
- 'Experts' will be aggrieved if they perceive that decisions about their specialism are being taken without their involvement
- Others will have a different perspective and may suggest solutions you wouldn't have thought of

The disadvantages include:

- Consultation takes time
- Elements may be introduced into the decision making that impede the process

Consultation can take place in a number of different directions:

- You can consult with your subordinates. This needs to be carefully handled to avoid the possibility that it will be seen as a lack of leadership or, conversely, disappointment will be caused when not all of the suggestions can be included in the final decision. It is good management to ask for advice but not necessarily good management to act on it
- You can consult with your peers. They may have experience of the situation which you can use. They will also have an understanding of the parameters that apply to your level of responsibility and the knock-on effects of decisions at this level

- You can consult with your line manager. Present your idea to your line manager early on rather than when it is a fully fledged plan. You may find that there is a good reason not to go on with the idea and a great deal of time will be saved if you find this out as soon as possible. Find out why your line manager is not in favour. It may be that other decisions are in the pipe-line which will affect your plan or it may be simply that your manager has strong views on the subject

Remember there will be situations in which you will not be able to consult. If you are given a direct instruction or legislation does not allow any deviation from laid down procedures there is no point in discussing options, you just have to tell people the way it is. You will still be able to involve people in the implementation of the decision, even if you have been unable to consult with them in the making of the decision. Seek their opinions on the best way to carry out the decision and they will still feel ownership. If possible, set up a group to pilot the new procedure and report back on any amendments that they can suggest within the overall framework.

## Developing others

Developing others is a process which has advantages for everybody. Those being developed will find more job satisfaction and improved career prospects while those carrying out the development will have better trained staff that they can delegate tasks to. The vehicle for developing others is their appraisal.

Appraisals should lead to a development plan which will identify what needs to be done to achieve an acceptable level of performance and what opportunities there are for staff to fulfil their potential. The development plan will track progress towards the situation to be achieved in the next 12 months. Milestones will need to be set along the way so that you can review and amend targets. A well-written development plan will encourage staff to concentrate on the right parts of their job, improve their self-confidence, increase their motivation and focus on relevant tasks.

# Leading by example

For an organisation to succeed all levels of management need to be involved. While it is important to empower and involve others, don't underestimate what you can contribute when leading by example. Set an example by being open to change and being ready with advice if either line managers or colleagues ask for it. Lead by example, showing your own commitment to the organisation. Be ready to practise what you preach and take an active part in discussion and implementation.

Your wholehearted personal involvement as a leader together with that of your colleagues provides the best possible example and inspiration to subordinate staff. Make sure that your words and actions reinforce people's awareness of the benefits of commitment to the organisation and its values. Never refuse to contribute or respond to a question as if it is unimportant. Leading by example will give your colleagues an opportunity to grow as they progress from producing ideas to actually implementing change. You should be their mentor, informant, questioner and facilitator.

Never ask anybody to do something you wouldn't be prepared to do yourself. If you are prepared to turn your hand to any task that needs doing you will gain the respect of your team and find that they are much more willing to do the same.

# Managing conflict

Even in the best managed organisation there will occasionally be conflict between people. Each of us is different and we all have to learn to adapt our actions to suit the situation. What works one day with one person may be completely unsuitable on another day with someone else.

We all bring our own experiences, attitudes and needs to any situation; two or more people trying to work in harmony will find that their approaches may clash because of this. This may lead to conflict, which is not necessarily a bad thing as conflict can lead to innovation. It is the way that the conflict is managed that decides whether the experience is positive or negative.

When you find there is conflict between colleagues:

- Acknowledge the disagreement. Don't expect them to pretend to agree just for a quiet life or the conflict will simply grow
- Allow both to state the reasons for their opinion. You may find they will agree with each other's opinion once they have heard them
- If neither of them can agree completely with the other, look for the middle ground that they can both agree a compromise on
- If they can't compromise, see if it is possible to 'agree to disagree' and carry on working
- If compromise isn't possible and a solution is essential, attempt to mediate

This isn't an easy situation to be put in and you will have to:

- Be careful not to take sides. Let each have their say and try to let them find a solution
- Make sure the discussion is about the issues and not the personalities. However, it is not always possible to keep emotions out of things so allow for them
- Summarise regularly to make sure that both the protagonists understand what is being said
- Remember the object is to achieve agreement so focus everybody's efforts on this
- Be prepared to make the decision for them if after every opportunity they are unable to reach a compromise

The major problem with conflict is that the combatants take positions from which they can't retreat without loss of face. The only way to manage this situation is to get them both to recognise that, while they don't agree with the other person, they accept that the other person has a right to their point of view. Saying, 'I can understand why you may think that, but….' is much less likely to cause conflict than saying, 'I have never heard such a stupid idea in my life'.

## Managing resources

Excluding human resources and time, the majority of resources in an office environment are equipment and stationery. The management of equipment will consist of ensuring that it is kept in good order by arranging regular maintenance, avoiding careless acts that could cause damage and carrying out necessary cleaning.

Stationery resources can be divided into items that you would expect to last for some time and consumables which are used up and thrown away. Items you would expect to last include hole-punches, staplers, calculators, staple removers, scissors, box files and filing trays for example; consumables include paper, note pads, pens, sticky tape, correcting fluid, envelopes, stamps, plastic wallets and disks.

The management of stationery resources includes ordering, receiving, storage and handling. Efficient ordering requires some form of stock control so that you can place orders when stock is needed. Most organisations will operate a maximum and minimum stock level so that, for instance, if the maximum stock level of white C5 envelopes is five boxes of 500 and the minimum is three boxes, whenever the stock level reaches three, two boxes would be ordered to restore the stock to the maximum.

When the goods arrive, check that you have received the quantity and quality that you ordered. If there are any discrepancies report them to the supplier and arrange for the necessary corrective action to be taken.

Plan where items are to be stored taking into account such variables as their weight and the frequency with which they are used. Generally put heavier goods on lower shelves than lighter ones. Rotate stock so that new deliveries are placed behind or underneath existing stock so that the old stock gets used first. You may think this is unimportant with stationery but many items have a limited shelf-life; pens will dry out, the gum on envelopes will lose its stickiness, printer cartridges will dry out. In some cases poor storage conditions will render stationery unusable:

- Envelopes that get damp will seal themselves
- Disks stored near heat or magnets will be useless
- Unwrapped paper will discolour
- Damp paper will jam the printer
- Paper not stored flat will curl
- Sticky tape if stored near heat will lose its stick
- Rubber bands kept too long will perish

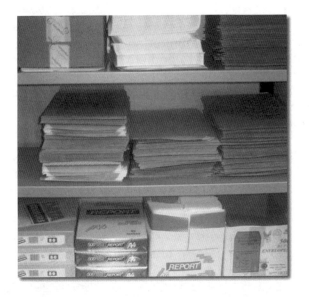

When handling stationery remember that paper is a very dense material and boxes of paper may be heavier than you expect.  Use correct handling methods when lifting heavy objects.  Don't leave boxes in gangways where people might trip over them and don't stack boxes too high as they pose a risk of falling on passers-by as well as possibly injuring someone trying to reach the top box.  Handling stationery also involves being careful in its use; if you are photocopying a large number of copies, make one copy first and check that it is correct before finding you have a large number of incorrect copies which have to be thrown away.  Don't leave the tops off marker pens, correcting fluid, felt tipped pens, so that when you come to use them again they have dried out. Store paper at the correct temperature and in a dry place to prevent deterioration.

You will also need to consider security of resources; should the stationery cupboard be kept locked and items issued only in exchange for requisitions so that a check on usage can be maintained?  Most people these days will have a use for stationery consumables at home and while you may think the taking of one biro or a couple of disks is not important, if every member of staff helped themselves regularly the cost of stationery would soon get out of hand.

# Monitoring

The dictionary definition of monitoring is 'to check something at regular intervals in order to find out how it is progressing or developing'. It won't be possible for you to monitor every task carried out by every member of staff so you will need to instigate some form of sampling system. There are a number of methods of sampling:

- **Random sample** - You pick tasks and members of staff to check completely at random. The advantage is that nobody can predict what will be sampled and make a special effort to ensure that particular task is carried out correctly
- **Structured sample** - A grid of tasks and time is drawn up and a pattern of sampling established

| | Monday | Tuesday | Wednesday | Thursday | Friday |
|---|---|---|---|---|---|
| Petty cash | X | | | | |
| Outstanding queries | | X | | | |
| Sales figures input | | | X | | |
| Filing | | | | X | |
| Security search | | | | | X |
| Housekeeping | X | | | | |
| Purchase orders | | X | | | |
| Invoices raised | | | X | | |
| Stationery supplies | | | | X | |
| Promotional material | | | | | X |

- The advantage is that everything is checked over a period of time. The disadvantage is that people can predict when checks will be carried out
- Informed structured sample. Starting from a grid as in the structured sample the level of sampling is adjusted over time to reflect the results of the sampling. Tasks which regularly indicate problems are sampled more often than those which are always up-to-date. The advantage is that your resource is directed towards areas that require attention. The disadvantage is that tasks that have historically been no problem may develop problems unnoticed

More in depth monitoring may take the form of an Internal Audit. These may look at processes such as:

- Purchase ledger
- Sales ledger
- Nominal ledger

- Sales ordering
- Purchase ordering
- Despatch
- Training
- Payroll
- Petty cash
- Bank reconciliation

An Internal Audit will look at the whole process in depth over a longer period of time. It will identify breaches of procedure but also failures of management and control.

## Motivating

Research into people's needs shows that some are more fundamental than others and, until the basic needs are met, there is no motivation to strive to meet the more advanced needs. For instance someone who has a well paid job which enables them to feed and clothe themselves and their family and provide a home will be more motivated by the offer of a course in management than someone who is unsure where their next meal is coming from.

The purpose of motivation is to improve performance. The key is encouraging people to improve willingly. This can be by offering rewards or incentives such as increased pay, bonuses, additional holiday or prizes but these tend to be short lived motivators as the improved conditions are soon seen as the norm. Better motivators are:

- Keeping staff informed
- Involving staff in decision making
- Support and advice when problems arise
- Challenging and interesting work
- SMART targets
- Praise for outstanding performance
- Delegation without abdication
- Opportunities for advancement

To effectively motivate a team requires you to understand the different individuals that make up the team and that they will not all be motivated by the same incentive. If someone carries out routine and boring work every day, simply the opportunity to do something different occasionally will be a major motivator.

## Setting objectives

Setting objectives is part of performance planning. You set the objectives and the standards that you expect from each member of the team and together plan how they are going to achieve them. Action plans state the specific ways that objectives will be achieved. They also define the actions needed by the employee to achieve the objectives.

Objectives need to be set for each individual based on their level of competence and their commitment to extend their current skills in order to progress within the organisation. They should be achievable over a 6–12 month period, and must be clearly defined, relevant to the person's job role and able to be measured. At the end of the period they must be reviewed against the measurement that was agreed and new objectives set for the next period.

If you have set realistic objectives your staff will reach their targets and will have a tremendous sense of achievement. This will motivate them to agreeing more challenging objectives for the next action plan, and your whole team will move forward. This will enable you to achieve your objectives and everybody will benefit.

# CHAPTER 2
## UNIT 110 – Ensure your own actions reduce risks to health and safety

It is important that the workplace is safe and conducive to the health of everybody who works there and any visitors or customers.  Any organisation with more than five employees must publish a Health and Safety Policy which should include:

- An outline of the policy
- Steps to be taken to fulfil the policy
- The legal responsibilities of employer and employees
- Information on training opportunities
- Information on how the policy will be displayed
- Plans to review and revise the policy
- Details of any relevant Codes of Practice
- Procedures for reporting accidents
- Names of those responsible for health and safety
- Reference to the organisation's rules on health and safety

No one wants to work somewhere that is unsafe, and visitors certainly don't want to feel in danger, or uncomfortable, when they enter the premises.  It is your responsibility as much as anybody else's to look out for potential hazards and to observe safe working practices.

Electrical equipment in particular is a source of hazards. You should not attempt any repairs or maintenance of electrical equipment unless you are properly qualified. The hazards to be aware of include:

- Insufficient insulation
- Lack of earth connection
- Incorrectly wired plugs or sockets
- Faulty wiring
- Worn insulation
- Poorly routed cables
- Incorrect fuse rating

Any of the above can lead to fire. A single spark can start a major fire. Sometimes the danger is not immediately apparent but there are warning signs that you should be aware of:

- Plugs or cables giving off excess heat
- Flickering lights or unreliable electrical supply
- Sparking noises
- Fuses blowing frequently
- A smell of burning

Other common causes of fire include:

- Overloaded electrical sockets
- Electrical equipment not switched off and disconnected overnight
- Smoking
- Heaters

Accidents can be very costly, and in the event of serious accidents they must be reported to the Health and Safety Executive. Compensation claims have become much more common in recent years. The law recognises that people and organisations are accountable for their actions, but claims are paid for out of the organisation's profits, which in turn impact on the job security of its employees. Dangerous occurrences, which are events that didn't actually cause any injury but could have done, also have to be reported. An example of this would be a fire caused by an electrical fault leading to the building being closed for more than 24 hours.

An important part of reducing risks to health and safety is good housekeeping. This involves ensuring the offices are kept clean, light bulbs are replaced as soon as they blow, broken furniture is repaired or replaced promptly, equipment is maintained properly, worn carpets are replaced and particular attention is paid to the condition of stairs and landings. Other areas that require attention include:

- Separate toilets should be provided for men and women. These should be well ventilated, clean, in working order and easily accessible
- A ventilated space must be provided between toilets and working areas
- Provision of wash basins with hot and cold running water
- Provision of soap and towels or a hand drier
- Regular emptying of waste bins
- Provision of clean drinking water
- Somewhere to heat up and eat food and drink

It is also important to consider the customer's perception of the organisation. If a customer is involved in an accident on the premises, they are not likely to hold the organisation in high regard and may not wish to deal with them again. They may even seek compensation from your employer through legal action.

 When ensuring your own actions reduce risks to health and safety you will need the following skills:

- Reading
- Analysing
- Decision making
- Communicating
- Working safely
- Personal presentation

These skills are covered in chapter 1.

# Health and Safety Legislation

Legislation makes health and safety at work everybody's responsibility, including yours. There are a number of relevant Acts of Parliament including:

Health and Safety at Work Act 1974. This makes it the employer's duty to provide:

- Safe entry and exit routes in and out of the workplace
- A safe working environment and adequate welfare facilities
- Safe equipment and systems of work
- Arrangements for ensuring the safe use, handling, storage and transport of articles and substances
- Information on health and safety, instruction, training and supervision
- The thorough investigation of any accidents

It also makes it the employee's duty to:

- Take reasonable care for their own health and safety
- Take reasonable care for the health and safety of other people who may be affected by their actions
- Co-operate with his or her employer or any other person carrying out duties under the Act

Reporting of Injuries, Diseases and Dangerous Occurrences Regulations (RIDDOR). This compels organisations to:

- Notify the Health and Safety Executive if any accidents occur resulting in serious or fatal injuries or have resulted in a lengthy period off work by an employee or employees
- Keep records of all notifiable injuries, dangerous occurrences and diseases

Control of Substances Hazardous to Health (COSHH). This requires organisations to:

- Identify any hazardous substances in use
- Eliminate the use of the substance if possible
- Substitute a safe substance where possible
- Enclose the substance so as few people as possible come into contact with it

Noise at Work Regulations. These require employers to:

- Assess noise hazards in the workplace
- Reduce noise hazards where possible
- Keep employees informed of noise hazards
- Provide ear protectors

The Management of Health and Safety at Work Regulations. These require employers to:

- Carry out risk assessments which assess significant risks both to employees and others affected by the organisation
- Keep a record of the assessment and the measures which have been identified to control the risk if there are more than five employees
- Appoint competent people to implement and monitor the health and safety arrangements
- Make arrangements to plan, organise, control, maintain and review health and safety arrangements
- Set up emergency procedures to deal with situations of serious or imminent danger
- Provide full information and training to all employees plus details of any risks involved in their work

Workplace (Health, Safety and Welfare) Regulations. These state minimum legal standards for:

- **Health** – lighting, ventilation and temperature; space and room dimensions; workstations and seating; cleanliness
- **Safety** – maintenance of the workplace and equipment, floors, windows and skylights; doors, gates and escalators; traffic routes, falls and falling objects
- **Welfare** – toilets and washing facilities; drinking water; changing rooms, rest rooms and eating facilities

Display Screen Equipment (DSE) Regulations. These apply to all who regularly use VDUs in their work, and relate to workstations as well as the equipment. They require employers to:

- Assess all workstations for health and safety risks and lower the risks as much as possible

- Plan work activities to incorporate rest breaks at regular intervals
- Arrange and pay for eye tests and pay for spectacles or lenses if these are prescribed specifically for VDU work
- Provide health and safety training for DSE users and re-train if the workstation is changed or modified
- Provide DSE users with information on all aspects of health and safety which apply to them and measures being taken to reduce risks to their health

Provision and Use of Work Equipment Regulations. Work equipment means any type of machine, appliance, apparatus or tools used at work. They require the employer to:

- Ensure that all equipment is suitable for the task and kept well maintained
- Take into account working conditions and potential hazards when selecting new equipment
- Issue appropriate information, instructions and training on its use
- Restrict access when necessary

Personal Protective Equipment at Work Regulations. These require employers to:

- Provide suitable personal protective equipment (PPE) without charge
- Ensure the PPE is suitable and fits properly
- Ensure the PPE is maintained in good condition
- Store the PPE safely
- Provide information on its use

Manual Handling Operations Regulations.  These require employers to:

- Avoid any manual handling operations in which employees could be injured
- Assess and reduce the risk of injury as much as possible
- Provide employees with information on specific loads which will help them avoid risk

Every organisation that employs more than ten people must keep an accident book.  This must record:

- Details of the injured person (name, address, age)
- Details of any injury sustained
- Details of the accident (what happened, when, where)
- First aid or medical treatment given
- Names of any witnesses

When the accident book is full it must be kept for three years after the date of the last entry.

**16** Report Number

**16** Report Number

# ACCIDENT RECORD

**1 About the person who had the accident**

Name    Abigail Inskip

Address  10 Rosedale Ave, Norwood, London

Postcode  SE-19 3PN

Occupation  PA to CEO

**2 About you, the person filling in this record**

▼ If you did not have the accident write your address and occupation.

Name    Heather Bellis

Address  6 Graphite Square, Vauxhall Walk, London

Postcode  SE-11 5EE

Occupation  Office Manager

**3 About the accident**  Continue on the back of this form if you need to

▼ Say when it happened.    Date  21 / 07 / 2005   Time  1025

▼ Say where it happened. State which room or place.

CEO's office, CfA offices

▼ Say how the accident happened. Give the cause if you can.

...ang on the... ...cho...

---

## ? What you need to know

How the legislation applies to your job role

Whose responsibility is it to provide safe equipment and systems of work?

Where escape routes are and why they must be kept un-blocked

What hazardous substances are in use in your workplace?

How your workplace complies with the Display Screen Equipment Regulations

What is the minimum legal temperature in your workplace?

Whether Personal Protective Equipment is in use in your workplace

What is the correct method of lifting heavy objects?

---

# Identifying hazards and evaluating risks

A hazard is a situation or an object that has the potential to cause injury, harm or ill health.  A risk is the likelihood of something causing harm because the hazard, or potential hazard, exists.  All organisations are required to carry out Risk Assessments which will identify where hazards exist and evaluate what the risks are.  There are five steps to carrying out an efficient Risk Assessment:

## STEP 1: LOOK FOR THE HAZARDS

Walk around your workplace and look at what could reasonably be expected to cause harm.  Only look at significant hazards which could result in serious harm or affect several people.  Ask your colleagues if they have noticed anything that might be a potential hazard, as they may have noticed something that is not immediately obvious. Look at accident records for trends or patterns to see if these can shed some light on dangers in your workplace.

## STEP 2: DECIDE WHO MIGHT BE HARMED AND HOW

As well as full-time members of staff consider people who are not in the workplace full-time such as cleaners, visitors, contractors, maintenance people and, of course, customers.

## STEP 3: WHAT ARE THE RISKS, WHAT IS BEING DONE?

There are probably precautions and systems in place already to reduce the risks created by the hazards that you have identified.  What you have to decide for each significant hazard is whether the remaining risk is high, medium or low.

- Ask yourself whether everything has been done that the law says must be done
- If so, ask yourself whether everything has been done that you would normally expect
- Then ask yourself whether there is still something practical that could be done to reduce the risk

If you find something needs to be done consider whether the hazard can be removed completely or, if not, how the risk can be controlled so that it can be significantly reduced.

## STEP 4: RECORD YOUR FINDINGS

If your workplace has five or more employees the Risk Assessment must be recorded.  This must show:

- The significant hazards
- Your conclusions
- That a proper check was made
- That employees who might be affected were asked
- That all obvious significant hazards were dealt with
- Precautions are reasonable
- The remaining risk is low

The written document should be kept for future reference.  It will help to show that the organisation has done what the law requires.

## STEP 5: REVIEW YOUR ASSESSMENT

It is not sufficient to carry out a Risk Assessment once, file it, and then forget about it until you are asked to produce it.

Things will inevitably change in the workplace; new equipment, new employees, new work practices. Anything that produces new hazards will mean a new Risk Assessment will need to be carried out.

You may feel that Health and Safety is the responsibility of someone else in the organisation, and, in fact, if you work in a reasonably large organisation there will be named people responsible for it. Remember, however, under The Health and Safety at Work Act everybody is responsible for taking reasonable care for the health and safety of themselves and others who may be affected by their actions.

If you come across a hazard that you can deal with immediately, for instance, a fire extinguisher propping open a fire-door or a carton left in a corridor, it is your responsibility to deal with it there and then. If you come across a hazard that you cannot deal with immediately for instance the fire door is padlocked, it is your responsibility to report it immediately to somebody who can deal with it.

If your organisation has appointed Health and Safety representatives and First Aiders, make sure you know who they are and how they can be contacted.

 **What you need to know**

Who your First Aiders are

What should you do if you find a hole in the stair carpet?

Who your Health and Safety representatives are

How should you deal with an unknown liquid spill on the floor in the corridor?

The five steps to Risk Assessment

How can you contact your First Aiders and Health and Safety Representatives?

How to recognise a hazard in the workplace

Why is it important to deal with risks immediately?

## Reducing risks to health and safety

You may think that an office is among the safest of places to work, but there are many hazards in even the most modern, up-to-date, paper-free environment. Everyone must be involved in noticing and either dealing with or reporting any risks.

It is probable that more working days are lost through illness caused by the actual office environment than there are through injury caused by accidents at work. You may not have considered that even the colour of the walls can have a significant effect. Paint or wallpaper should be a restful shade as patterns and bright colours can cause headaches. Nylon carpets can increase the risk of static electric shocks, while windows need curtains or blinds if there is a possibility of bright sunshine on computer screens.

Lighting and furniture are important. Background lighting should be restrained, complemented with directional light over work areas to reduce eye-strain. Desks should be large enough to take all the equipment and paperwork needed and high enough to get your legs under. Chairs should have a five-star base, adjustable seats and backs that give support. Filing cabinets need to be fitted with a device that prevents more than one drawer being opened at a time.

Computers can be a major source of problems. Using a monitor, or VDU, can cause headaches, eye-strain, neck problems, repetitive strain injury and stress. Of course, it is not the computer that causes the problems, it is the use of the computer. To avoid some of these there are steps that you can take:

- Sit on an adjustable chair with your back supported. Your arms should be horizontal when on the keyboard and the monitor should be immediately in front of your eyes
- Make sure the screen is the right distance from your eyes to enable you to focus easily. If necessary change the zoom facility

- Consider using a wrist rest to prevent repetitive strain injury and a foot rest to improve your posture to reduce the risk of back, shoulder and neck strain
- Adjust the screen brightness to reduce glare
- Clean the screen regularly to prevent the need to squint
- Take regular short breaks

If you have to lift and carry things in your work such as files, stationery, etc., use correct lifting techniques. If the load is too heavy to carry, use a trolley. When lifting from a low level:

- Bend your knees but do not kneel or over-flex the knees
- Keep your back straight (tucking in your chin)
- Lean forward a little over the load if necessary to get a good grip
- Keep your shoulders level and facing in the same direction as your hips
- Try to keep your arms within the boundary formed by your legs
- The best position and type of grip depends on the circumstances and individual preference: but it must be secure. A hook grip is less tiring than keeping your fingers straight
- Keep the load close to your body for as long as possible
- Keep the heaviest side of the load next to your body
- Lift smoothly, keeping control of the load
- Don't twist your body when turning to the side

To prevent accidents with equipment there are a few simple rules to follow:

- Don't overload filing cabinets
- Don't open more than one drawer at a time
- Don't place liquids on or near any electrical equipment
- Don't remove any safety guards
- Be careful not to get clothing, hair or jewellery caught in equipment
- If anything gets jammed in equipment don't try to free it without switching it off
- Make sure you know where and how to disconnect equipment in an emergency

- Don't attempt to repair equipment unless you are sure you know how and are authorised to
- Inform your supervisor immediately if equipment breaks down or fails to work, switch it off and put an out-of-order notice on it

Common causes of injury in offices are slips, trips and falls. Make sure any spillages are mopped up immediately they occur. Always close drawers after you have used them to avoid the risk of people falling over them or walking into them. Don't leave items such as boxes and handbags where people can trip over them. Be careful that cables are not left trailing, particularly when furniture and equipment are moved. This is not only a trip hazard but can also cause damage to the cables which could lead to risk of fire or electrocution. Portable equipment can be dangerous if not properly maintained. Look out for damaged plugs, sockets and leads. Don't use chairs or boxes to stand on to reach objects on high shelves or off the top of cabinets. Always use steps and make sure they are well-maintained.

Potentially the most devastating risk is fire. The priority must be to prevent fire, and to minimise the effect should one start. To prevent fire:

- Report any faulty equipment or wiring
- Switch off any faulty equipment until it has been repaired
- If smoking is allowed ensure cigarettes are properly extinguished and ashtrays are emptied into metal bins
- Don't put papers, clothing or other materials near heaters or equipment that gets hot
- Switch off all equipment at the end of the day

To minimise the effect of fire:

- Take fire drills seriously
- Don't block fire doors or fire exits
- Don't prop fire doors open
- Know where the fire exits are
- Know where your assembly point is
- Know where fire fighting equipment is and its uses
- Know how to raise the alarm

If you discover a fire raise the alarm and follow your organisation's procedures. This may require you to evacuate the building in all circumstances or may allow for attempts to extinguish the fire if it is small. In this case you will need to know what fire fighting equipment there is and how to use it. Equipment may include fire blankets which can be used to smother the flames, buckets of sand and fire extinguishers. Fire extinguishers come in a number of types which can be identified by colour coding.

| Colour | Contents | Use |
|--------|----------|-----|
| Red | Water | Most fires except liquids or electrical appliances |
| Blue | Dry powder | Flammable liquids or electrical appliances |
| Green | Halon | Flammable liquids or electrical appliances but not in confined spaces |
| Black | Carbon Dioxide | Flammable liquids or electrical appliances but not in confined spaces |
| Cream | Foam | Flammable liquids |

If you are the first on the scene of an accident it is important that you know how to react. If you are not a first aider it is vital that you know who the first aiders are and how to contact them quickly. There are a number of basic rules to follow:

- Is it safe for you to approach the casualty?
- Do not move the injured person
- Is the casualty conscious?
- Check to see if their airway is blocked
- Check whether they are breathing
- Check the casualty's circulation by taking their pulse at the wrist or neck
- Give any first aid that you are trained to give or find your company's trained first aider
- Place the patient in the recovery position and keep them warm
- Loosen any tight clothing
- Don't offer food, drink or cigarettes
- Dial 999 for an ambulance and stay on the line so that the operator can take all of your details

You also need to know how to deal with different types of medical emergency.

- In the case of someone who is bleeding badly, elevate the wound and apply pressure with a sterile dressing
- Where someone has been burnt or scalded, run cool water over the burn.  Do not pull clothing off the wound
- If someone has had an electric shock, turn off the electricity before you touch them or you are likely to get a shock as well
- If someone is choking, encourage them to cough at first.  If this does not work then deliver short sharp slaps between their shoulder blades to dislodge the item

Make sure you know the limits of your ability to deal with emergencies and don't attempt anything you have not been trained or feel confident to do.  In all of the cases mentioned above the casualty should go to the local Emergency Department.

# What you need to know

The steps that can be taken to avoid
health problems connected with the use
of computer equipment

What can you do to reduce the risk of
fire?

Correct lifting techniques

What type of fire extinguisher should
be used on an electrical equipment
fire?

Actions that can be taken to minimise the
effects of fire

What type of fire extinguisher should
be used on a paper fire?

Your organisation's health and safety
policy

Who should you report electrical
hazards to?

The benefits of good housekeeping

What indications might there be that an
electrical fire is imminent?

## The time to decide what to do in the case of an emergency is BEFORE the emergency happens

# Are you ready for assessment?

To achieve this unit of a Level 3 Business & Administration qualification you will need to demonstrate that you are competent in the following:

- Correctly name and locate the people responsible for health and safety in your workplace
- Identify which workplace policies are relevant to your working practices
- Identify those working practices in any part of your job role which could harm yourself or others
- Identify those aspects of the workplace which could harm yourself or others
- Evaluate which of the potentially harmful aspects of the workplace are those with the highest risks to you or to others
- Report those hazards with a high risk to the person responsible for health and safety in the workplace
- Deal with those hazards with low risks following workplace policies and legal requirements
- Carry out your working practices in accordance with legal requirements
- Follow the most recent workplace policies for your job role
- Put right those health and safety risks that you are able to within the scope of your job responsibilities
- Pass on any suggestions for reducing risks to health and safety within your job role to the responsible persons
- Make sure your personal conduct in the workplace does not endanger the health and safety of yourself or others
- Follow the workplace policies and suppliers' or manufacturers' instructions for the safe use of equipment, materials and products
- Report any differences between workplace policies and suppliers' or manufacturers' instructions as appropriate
- Make sure your personal presentation at work ensures the health and safety of yourself and others; meets

any legal duties and is in accordance with workplace policies

(Remember that you will need the skills listed at the beginning of this chapter. These are covered in chapter 1.)

You will need to produce evidence from a variety of sources. Carrying out the following activities will help you acquire competence at work.

**Activity 1**
Draw a floor plan of your workplace indicating:

- Fire exits
- Position and category of fire equipment
- Location of first aid boxes
- Location of first aiders
- Assembly points

Make a list of first aiders and health and safety representatives in your workplace, together with their location and telephone extensions.

**Activity 2**
Keep a work diary over the period of a month recording any incidents, fire drills, accidents or emergencies.

**Activity 3**
Carry out a Risk Assessment of your workplace.

**Activity 4**
You are sitting at your desk working on a report. You hear a cry and a crash from the next office. You go through to investigate and find a colleague on the floor apparently unconscious. It appears that they have fallen from a chair that they were standing on and may have struck their head on the edge of a desk. What steps do you take immediately? And what further action must you take once the initial emergency has been dealt with?

**Activity 5**
Imagine you have been given the responsibility of supervising a new member of staff. Prepare a help-sheet that would tell them:

- Who to report hazards to
- Who the safety representatives are
- What to do in the event of a fire
- Where the fire-fighting equipment is
- How to operate the fire-fighting equipment
- Who and where the first aiders are
- Where the first aid box is kept

- The contents of the first aid box
- Where the accident book is kept
- How to use correct lifting techniques

**Activity 6**

Which legislation covers each of the following:

- Identification of hazardous substances
- Legal standards for toilets and washing facilities
- Provision of Personal Protective Equipment without charge
- Provision of eye-tests
- Safe entry and exit routes
- Notification of accidents to the Health and Safety Executive
- The need to co-operate with employers
- Provision of training to employees on risks
- Provision of ear-protectors
- Carrying out of Risk Assessments
- The requirement to avoid any manual handling operations in which employees could be injured
- Investigation of accidents

The need to take into account working conditions when selecting new equipment

Remember:  Evidence will be generated for this unit while gathering evidence for all of the other units.

# CHAPTER 3
# UNIT 301 – Carry out your responsibilities at work

Whatever size or type of organisation you work in, you will have responsibilities that need to be carried out. These responsibilities will include the actual function of the job that you do. It will also include your responsibilities to the person or people you report to, the people who report to you, the team or teams in which you work and, perhaps most importantly, to yourself.

While you will hopefully enjoy your time at work, there will be frustrations, times when demands seem unreasonable, times when you feel you are being unfairly treated. It is the way you deal with these situations that will determine how much you enjoy your time at work. Working as part of a team will provide you with greater demands, but offer greater scope for development than working as an individual. Responding to the demands will improve your performance as you learn from other members of the team. Similarly your colleagues will benefit from working with you as they learn from your skills and experience. You will have the opportunity to lead a team and utilise the appropriate skills of leadership and delegation as well as developing the skills of other members of the team.

Modern organisations tend to give individuals more responsibility for their own work than was once the case. It is no longer enough not to make mistakes (or not to get caught making mistakes); everybody is now expected to be accountable for planning and organising their own work. The successful employee is no longer the one who keeps their head down and just does what is asked of them – initiative is now expected. Decisions are now delegated to everybody, problems are dealt with at a lower level than previously, all members of staff are expected to get involved in meetings, training colleagues and bringing forward suggestions to improve efficiency.

The key to working in this environment is effective communication. Information needs to be exchanged continually; not only information about the work being carried out but also information on your own situation and feelings. Effective communication will also enable you to progress your career, increase your skills base, expand your personal networks, improve your relationships with colleagues and your decision-making ability.

Giving and accepting feedback oils the wheels of communication. When you give feedback it can be positive or negative but must always be constructive. When you are given feedback you must take on board what is said. If it is positive, take it as confirmation that what you are currently doing is effective. If the feedback is negative, take steps to use the information to improve your performance.

 When carrying out your responsibilities at work you will need the following skills:

- Communicating
- Researching
- Negotiating
- Planning
- Managing time
- Solving problems
- Evaluating
- Team working

These skills are covered in chapter 1.

## Communicate information

The most important thing about communication is that it is two-way.  It is said that 'if the learner hasn't learnt, the teacher hasn't taught'.  It is equally true that if the receiver hasn't understood, the communicator hasn't communicated.  The fault, however, lies equally with the receiver if they haven't asked the necessary questions.  There are, of course, various methods of communicating; non-verbal, verbal and written.

There is a form of communication which is taking place all the time, although we may not be aware of it.  This is non-verbal communication, or 'body language'.  The messages you send out when you are not speaking.  The way you sit, stand, fold your arms, your facial expression, all of these communicate your attitude to others.  The messages may be deliberate, such as a nod or a shrug, or involuntary, such as a yawn.  Reading a person's body language will often tell you more than listening to what they are saying.  Look for:

- **The way people sit -** If they have their legs stretched out or their arms away from their body, they will be communicating confidence.  If their arms and legs are drawn in close to the body they will be communicating insecurity.  If a person's feet point out when sitting they are an extrovert, if they point in, an introvert
- **The way people stand** - Standing will always make people look more authoritative compared to those sitting down.  Moving around will accentuate this

effect. Posture shows how people will approach a situation. If their head is up, arms out and fists closed, they are ready to face any situation; shoulders down, arms folded, leaning to one side they either aren't interested or aren't ready face the problem

- **People's expressions** - A smile gives the message that all is well, a frown indicates either aggression or uncertainty. If they maintain eye contact they will give an impression of confidence and honesty; making little eye contact can indicate they are nervous, don't like you or believe they are superior to you. It may also indicate that they are not telling the truth. On the other hand, continuous eye contact is seen as aggression or even as a sign of instability. Another indicator of a person's confidence is the frequency of blinking, the less often a person blinks the more confident they feel.

- **Gestures** - Moving the head is an indication that a person is seeking approval. Keeping head movements to a minimum gives the impression of authority. Covering the front of the body with folded arms, raised hands or crossed legs is a defensive gesture which shows a lack of interest. As people become more interested and accepting of the conversation their arms will unfold, their legs uncross and they will turn towards you. A gesture that can be used deliberately to defuse a difficult situation is 'mirroring'. Sitting or standing in a similar posture to the person you are having a conversation with will make them feel at ease. People will make grooming gestures, straightening their hair or checking their clothes, to make themselves feel more confident when with strangers; this may be exaggerated into biting their nails or grinding their teeth to remove physical tension. Hand gestures emphasise what is being said, for instance hands pointing towards you with the palms up indicate agreement or acceptance. Hand to face gestures, such as scratching the chin, indicate a concern

You can use body language to give an impression of trustworthiness or confidence as the situation demands, if your audience understands how to read body language they will get the message. Try to read other people's body language, you may be able to adapt yours to overcome their concerns. Be careful of relying too heavily on it, however, as it is easy to misread the signs.

Another method is verbal communication. In the workplace verbal communication takes place all the time in:

- Meetings
- Presentations
- Discussions
- Telephone conversations
- Informally across the office or around the water cooler

It is a fact of life that you will attend numerous meetings in the course of your work. You should only be invited to meetings that you can actively contribute to. If you find yourself regularly attending meetings that don't seem to affect your work, you need to inquire, politely, why you are attending them. It may be that you have a particular knowledge that may be needed at the meeting, or possibly it is seen as a developmental activity. Pay close attention to everything that is being said during the meeting and you will be able to make a contribution at some point. Speak clearly and confidently but remember that others may not agree with your views. This does not mean you are necessarily incorrect, simply that there are differing views on the subject. Your opinions have more chance of being accepted if you remain calm and polite. You are unlikely to persuade anybody by being aggressive.

You will also instigate meetings in your role as a team leader. Bear in mind your experiences of attending meetings and ensure that your meetings are well organised, attended only by those who need to be there and give opportunities to everybody to participate. If it is your meeting make sure you remain in control and that it is you who decides when to put a stop to discussion and agree the way forward.

Discussions are basically spontaneous meetings. They are held to resolve immediate problems or to canvas opinion before decisions are taken. The thing to remember about discussions is that they are not a means of one person simply giving information to another, they are an exchange of information. Neither party necessarily has the answer before the beginning of the discussion but all that can change by the end of the discussion.

Even more than meetings, you will almost certainly spend a great deal of your working life on the telephone. There are specific techniques in using the telephone; learn what these are and you will communicate much more effectively. When making a call:

- Be clear why you are making the call
- Begin the call with a professional or friendly greeting. Remember to smile when you speak
- Say who you are and where you're from
- Make sure you state the purpose of your call
- Speak clearly and slowly in as simple terms as possible without being patronising
- If you have to use technical terms or pass on names and addresses repeat any words that may be difficult
- Try not to be side tracked
- Close the conversation when the purpose of your call has been achieved
- If necessary summarise your conversation
- Confirm any agreements or outstanding issues with the caller before you ring off

Remember why you made the call and make sure you get your point across. It will waste your time and theirs if you hold a meandering conversation without getting to the point. While keeping in mind that time is money remember you should be focused without being abrupt.

Informal chats may or may not be about work, but they still need to be carried out politely without being aggressive or patronising. Don't think you can speak inappropriately to people when you are chatting in a way that you wouldn't dream of in a more formal setting. Take notice of what others are saying during informal chats as you may pick up on something that they feel strongly about but are unwilling to raise in a more formal atmosphere.

Probably the most daunting form of verbal communication for most of us is giving a talk or presentation in front of a group of people. As with many things in life, careful preparation will make it seem a lot easier. If you have never given a presentation before, think about the kind of talk you may be asked to give. It might be a team talk to tell your colleagues about a new system or product, for instance.

You will want to know:

- Where the talk is to be given
- How long you are expected to speak
- How many people will be in the audience
- How much they are likely to know about the subject beforehand

Once you have this information you will be able to prepare the talk. To ensure that your own level of knowledge is superior to the audience's, research the subject carefully. If you anticipate any questions that you might be asked you probably won't be asked a question you don't know the answer to. Make notes of the main points you are going to cover but don't attempt to write a script and read it out. If you need handouts prepare sufficient copies well in advance; organise any equipment such as projectors, flip charts or whiteboards. Practice your presentation and ask someone to listen to it and give you feedback. This will also give you the opportunity to check your timing. If you have 30 minutes to give your talk you won't want it to last 15 or 45 minutes. When the time approaches to give your presentation, you will be nervous. People whose career depends on talking to groups will tell you they are always nervous before they start. If you have prepared adequately you can re-assure yourself that 'it will be all right on the night'.

- Think about presentations you have attended. What was the common feature of ones you enjoyed? It will probably be that they got off to a good start. The first few minutes will set the tone. Your audience will either get on your side or switch off
- Try to speak confidently, remember you know what you are talking about. The audience will be there to hear what you have to say
- Vary the tone and pitch of your voice as this will add interest. Speak as clearly as possible, remember the people at the back need to hear as much as those at the front
- Don't speak any more quickly than you would in normal conversation. You will find your nervousness will disappear after the first few minutes
- Talk to the whole audience; don't concentrate on one person or one group. If you do the rest will lose interest. Make eye contact with as many people as possible
- Avoid making jokes unless they really do add to what you are saying. If a joke falls flat your confidence will ebb away
- Some speakers prefer to stand still while they speak, others move about. Find your own style but avoid excessive movement, and particularly try not to wave your arms about too much or sway on your legs
- The classic format for a talk is tell them what you are going to tell them, tell them, and tell them what you have told them. In other words, an introduction, the body of the talk and then a summary
- Invite questions. If you know the answer, give it as briefly as possible. If you don't know the answer, admit it and offer to find out
- End by thanking your audience for listening. Ask someone that you trust to give you feedback on how it went. You may be surprised by the answer as it is

extremely difficult to judge while you are actually giving the presentation

There comes a point at which verbal communication is not reliable enough, either because the message is complicated or because a permanent record is needed.  The advantages of written communication are:

- A permanent record is produced
- Complex subjects can be covered
- Information can be amended during the preparation
- Care can be taken over the precise wording

There are a number of ways in which information is exchanged in writing within an organisation.  Relatively simple information will be communicated by e-mail or memo, while more complex information may be circulated in the form of a report.

A memo is a formal method of conveying information from one person to another, or to a group of people.  The important components are:

- Who the memo is from
- Who the memo is to
- The date
- The information

Take care to check the accuracy and completeness of the information as it is frustrating to receive a memo which requires you to telephone the sender to ask for clarification. For instance, if you are advising people that a meeting will be held on Thursday the 4th, if Thursday is actually the 5th people will need to ring to ask if you meant Wednesday the 4th or Thursday the 5th.

With the advent of electronic communication many memos are now sent by e-mail, which has the advantages of instant delivery and no cost of printing or despatch.  Documents, photographs or reports can be attached and distributed to large or small numbers of recipients simultaneously and a reply generated equally quickly.

Monday's Meeting - Message (Plain Text)

File  Edit  View  Insert  Format  Tools  Actions  Help

File...
Item...
Signature

To...    bluet
Cc...    simo
Bcc...
Subject:  Mon

Dear Laura

Monday's meeting has been re-scheduled and will now be held in Simon Thorpe's office at 9am on Tuesday the 25th.

Many thanks

Katie

Katie Jane
Personnel Director
Woodrow & Young
katiejane@woodrowyoung.com

Meeting
Record No...

If you are preparing a report some research and analysis will almost certainly be necessary.  The most appropriate source will depend on the type of information that you are researching.  In general terms, however, you will be guided by your own experience of similar research and the expertise of others that you can seek advice from.

Having identified relevant information from a number of sources, you will need to bring it all together into one format.

Try to sort all of the information into categories.  Once you have organised your information you will be able to look at it and select the facts which will be useful in producing a report.  When selecting the facts, care must be taken not to ignore those that do not seem to fit with the desired result.  There is always a temptation to include facts that support a preconceived idea and ignore those that contradict it.

The process of compiling a report is:

- Confirm the purpose of the report
- Research the information
- Analyse the information
- Sort the information into an introduction, a main body, a conclusion and recommendations
- Write a first draft
- Read and amend
- Write a final copy

More detailed information on researching and writing reports is covered in chapter 19.

# What you need to know

Why effective communication is important

> Why is it important to pay careful attention to what others are saying?

How to present clear and accurate information in a report

> Why is it important to consider the audience when communicating?

How to take part in discussions effectively

> What do you understand by the term 'body language'?

How to research information

> What can you learn from the way people stand?

Why it is important to take account of other people's ideas and opinions

> Why should you address the whole audience when giving a presentation?

How to analyse information

> What preparations should you make before making a telephone call?

## Plan and be accountable for your work

The key to planning your work is time management. Time is always limited and there are techniques which you can learn to help you make the most of it:

- **Prioritise your tasks** - Make a list of things you need to do and identify each as 'must do', 'should do' or 'could do'. Deal with the important, then the urgent, then the routine and finally the trivial if you have time. Consider how frequently you need to prioritise again, will it be later today, tomorrow or next week?

- **Plan your time** - Days, weeks, months and years can all be planned for. Set aside enough time to do the important and the urgent by their deadlines, but allow time for the routine and even the trivial
- **Delegate** - If you cannot do everything in the time available, ask someone else to do some of it
- **Plan meetings** - You may not be able to avoid attending them but you can try to make sure they are as brief as possible
- **Record the time you use** - This will help you identify where you have lost time
- **Deal with disruption** - If you have something important to do let it be known that you don't wish to be disturbed
- **Handle each piece of paper only once** - Don't keep thinking about dealing with something and putting it back on the pending pile
- **Control the telephone** - List the calls you need to make and make them all in a period of time set aside for telephone calls

You may feel that you are not in charge of your own time. If your boss brings you a task and requests that you do it immediately, you have no choice. This may be true, but you are able to discuss whether the timescale is realistic and to point out that completing the new task will affect other tasks that were planned. Beware of the temptation to agree to all requests. You may think it will make you indispensable, but if it means you never complete any task on time it will simply make you unreliable.

Monitoring progress towards the completion of tasks will avoid the need for last minute panic. Encourage your team to ask for help rather than discover that there is a backlog of work that they have been unable to complete and are unwilling to admit to. If problems occur which may affect your ability to meet an agreed deadline, let the person the work is being carried out for know as soon as possible. It may be possible to extend the deadline, or put more resources into completing the task.

If potential problems are reported sooner rather than later, action can be taken. If you simply carry on in hope, by the time it is obvious that the deadline will not be met it may be too late to do anything about it.

The same is true of mistakes. Mistakes are much more easily remedied immediately than they are further down the line. Acknowledging that you have made a mistake is the first step towards learning from mistakes. Encourage your team to own up to a mistake as soon as they discover it, and be willing to help them sort it out. Let them know that if they try to cover up the mistake, when the truth is uncovered there will be very little sympathy. Make sure you follow this policy yourself when you discover that you have made a mistake.

Don't change established ways of doing things without consultation. It is quite possible things are done the way they are 'because we've always done it that way' and that you have come up with an ingenious improvement. On the other hand it's quite possible things are done that way for very good reasons, possibly legal, and changes may have consequences that you cannot foresee. If you have come up with an idea to improve the way things are done, discuss whether the change is feasible with the people that may be affected. Similarly listen to suggestions for change and consider all the implications before deciding whether to implement the change. If you decide against making the change it is important that you explain your decision in order not to discourage your colleagues from bringing forward further suggestions.

# What you need to know

Why it is important to plan your work and
the work of others

Why is it important to negotiate and
agree realistic targets and timescales?

How mistakes can be seen as positive and
developmental

What do you understand by the term
'time management'?

Why you should pilot major changes
before implementing them

How would you monitor the progress of
your team's tasks?

Guidelines and procedures relevant to
your work

What tasks can you delegate?

Codes of practice relevant to your work

Why do other people need notice of
changes to plans?

## Improve your own performance

If you were playing music or sport, you know you would only
get better over time. You'd need to practise hard and gain
experience. The same is true of the tasks you perform at
work. Sports stars and musicians have coaches and
managers who analyse their performance and give them tips
on how to improve. Exactly the same process happens at
work. Some people have formal coaching sessions but
everyone receives feedback about their performance. The
most effective system is one of 360 degree feedback. This is
where you give and receive feedback both up the line with
the people who you report to and down the line with those
who report to you.

You should welcome and encourage feedback from others at
work. While it is very nice to hear that you have done
something particularly well, it is probably more useful to be

told when you have not done as well as you might have. The important thing about feedback is that it should be constructive. If someone is to tell you that your performance is not all it might be, they need to explain what you should have done, not just tell you what you should not have done. There will be occasions when feedback is given in a more formal way. There are a number of reasons for appraisals to be carried out:

- To identify your current level of performance
- To identify your strengths and weaknesses
- To reward your contribution towards achievement of goals
- To motivate
- To identify training and development needs
- To identify potential

Appraisals are an important opportunity for supervisors and staff to discuss performance. They should be seen as a joint review exercise in which opportunities and needs will be identified. The outcome of most appraisals is a development plan which will identify what you need to do in order to achieve an acceptable level of performance and what opportunities there are for you to fulfil your potential.

Appraisals are usually held annually, so the development plan will aim to track your progress from where you are now to where you hope to be in 12 months time. Milestones need to be set along the way so that you can review and amend targets. When you review your progress, if you are achieving your goals you will be encouraged. If you are not, you will need to identify the reasons preventing this before it is too late to take any corrective action. A well-written development plan will encourage you to:

- Improve performance of yourself and others
- Increase your area of responsibility
- Develop administration skills
- Develop management skills
- Address development needs

Use the activities identified in the development plan to improve the way you carry out your work. Check regularly that you are following the plan and evaluate the effectiveness of the actions that you have taken. You may find it necessary to review the plan with your manager between appraisals. You can then jointly amend the steps you need to take to achieve your objectives.

There are a number of points to remember when looking at your own development:

- Always confirm important information for yourself
- Working with successful people will reflect positively on you
- Keep in touch with people; they may be useful in the future
- Don't put off making unpopular decisions
- If you don't know, say so, and offer to find out
- Manage your stress, don't let it manage you
- When negotiating always have something in reserve

You are the only one who knows whether you really like the job you are doing now and whether you really want the responsibility that progress inevitably brings. While you will obviously benefit from the stimulation and motivation provided by your employer, don't forget how important self-motivation is.

## Improve the performance of others

In the same way that you should be encouraging feedback on your performance in order to improve, you should be offering feedback on the performance of others. When giving feedback remember that it should be based on fact rather than opinion and you must always be prepared to back up your feedback with examples. Positive feedback should reinforce what the receiver has done well and identify opportunities to continue to perform. Corrective action may be necessary where performance has not been satisfactory but the individual should be encouraged to recognise this for themselves. Be positive and objective and deliver a 'praise sandwich' – highlight the things that have been done well at the beginning and end of your feedback and point out the areas for improvement in the middle. Feedback should:

- Relate to observed behaviour
- Describe actual events
- Seek the individual's opinion as to the cause of events
- Allow the individual to decide what happened and why
- Encourage corrective action rather than reprimanding

When giving formal feedback or carrying out an appraisal, effective planning is essential. At an appraisal meeting most of the talking should be done by the person being appraised and the listening by the person giving the appraisal. Remember that good listeners concentrate on what the speaker is saying, don't interrupt, ask questions to clarify issues and demonstrate understanding without interrupting the flow of the speaker.

The appraisee should be given the opportunity to self-assess prior to the meeting to consider:

- Their achievements against previously set objectives
- Reasons for non-achievement of objectives
- Their training needs
- Their own aspirations
- Where they feel support is needed

You should prepare by:

- Reviewing the individual's performance
- Reviewing progress against the last development plan
- Collating evidence to support your intended feedback
- Considering training opportunities
- Considering the individual's potential to progress
- Considering where support can be offered

During the meeting ask open questions which allow the individual to expand on their answers and probing questions which seek more specific information on what happened and why. The appraisal should look at performance over the whole period under review, recognise the individual's achievement and produce a development plan which the individual is able to agree with.

 **What you need to know**

How to evaluate and continuously improve your overall performance

Why should you encourage and offer feedback?

The opportunities for career progression available to you and others

What are the benefits of continuous learning and development?

The opportunities for learning and development available to you and others

How do you develop a learning plan for yourself and others?

How to set high standards for your work and that of others

What preparations should you make prior to an appraisal?

# Behave in a way that supports effective working

One of the things that may be identified during an appraisal is whether you show sufficient drive and commitment. There is a lot of difference between doing all that is asked of you to a satisfactory standard and going out of your way to do as much as possible to the highest possible standard. If you set yourself targets well in excess of those that are required of you, you will find achieving the required standards easy.

From time to time there will inevitably be changes in what is expected of you. It may be that there is new software introduced, there may be new products to get to grips with, or a long serving colleague may leave and be replaced by somebody with different skills. Any of these changes will provide new challenges for you and your team. It is important that you view these challenges as opportunities rather than as problems. Your enthusiasm to embrace change will motivate others and raise morale at what might be a difficult time. Avoid the temptation to take on all the additional pressure yourself as this will inevitably lead to deterioration in your own performance as well as denying the members of your team the opportunity to develop.

If your team are struggling to cope with the new situation offer to help in any way that you can. Remember it is important to be honest about how much help you can give. You will still have your own work to complete and it will not be helpful in the long run if you either jeopardise your own deadlines or put yourself under undue stress in order to help your team through. The most honest approach may be to get the team together and explain that the change has produced unexpected difficulties. Ask them to suggest solutions as it will be much easier to get their commitment to ideas that have been brought forward by the team.

If there is a new member of staff try to remember how you felt on your first few days. Make allowances for the fact that they are probably feeling nervous and uncomfortable and don't jump to conclusions about either their abilities or their attitude. Until you get to know them give them the benefit of the doubt. Their attitude to you will be very much influenced by your attitude to them. Treat them with respect and consideration and you will get the same in return. At the same time there will come a point at which you can expect them to be competent at the tasks that they are set.

All of your colleagues should be treated with the respect and consideration that they deserve by being honest in your dealings with them. If they are doing their job well, tell them, if they are not, agree with them what improvements they need to make. There will be times when you will have to assert your authority. At these times it is important to be assertive not aggressive. Assertiveness is:

- Stating what you want
- Standing up for what you want
- Expressing opposition
- Aiming for a win:win situation

Aggressiveness is:

- Demanding what you want
- Taking what you want
- Suppressing opposition
- Aiming for a win:lose situation

It is better to learn techniques to increase your assertiveness rather than trying to become generally more assertive, as this often leads to aggression. Techniques for improving assertiveness include:

- Being ready to meet assertiveness from others
- Having your responses ready
- Gathering your facts before entering the discussion
- Having open questions ready

It should not be necessary to raise your voice in order to get your point across.

Honesty and respect should also be shown to your employers. This does not only mean not stealing from them, but also promoting the organisation internally and externally, recognising trends that will affect the performance of the business, encouraging the development of the business and doing your job to the best of your ability. Respect should be shown by always being positive about the organisation when talking to people from outside.

# What you need to know

The importance of behaving responsibly

> Why should you treat colleagues with honesty, respect and consideration?

How to cope with pressure

> How should you react to a setback?

Why it is important to embrace change

> What behaviour indicates a lack of honesty?

The importance of adapting readily to change

> Why should you always help and support others to the best of your ability?

The difference between assertiveness and aggressiveness

> Why is it important to show drive and commitment?

In carrying out your responsibilities at work you will need to manage yourself by taking responsibility for your own development, learning from mistakes, both your own and others', actively seeking feedback to identify strengths and weaknesses in your performance and using that feedback to change your behaviour. A major part of your job will involve thinking and taking decisions. To take effective decisions you will have to analyse systems into tasks, foresee the implications and consequences of decisions and identify different solutions to a problem before taking a realistic decision. You will need to be an excellent communicator, actively seeking questions to identify information needed and adapting your style of communication to meet the requirements of your audience.

Your responsibilities will require you to concentrate on the objectives that you have been set, taking personal responsibility for ensuring they are met and politely declining unreasonable requests. You will need to be ready to take advantage of opportunities as they arise, prioritise, make best use of time and resources by effective work scheduling and tackle problems in a positive way.

**The best kind of development is self-development. You are the only person who knows what you want to achieve and how much effort you are prepared to make to achieve it**

# Are you ready for assessment?

To achieve this unit of a Level 3 Business & Administration qualification you will need to demonstrate that you are competent in the following:

- Actively focussing on information that other people are communicating, questioning any points you are unsure about
- Providing accurate, clear and structured information confidently to other people and in a way that meets their needs
- Making useful contributions to discussions, developing points and ideas
- Giving others the opportunity to contribute their ideas and opinions and taking these into account
- Selecting and reading written material that contains information that you need
- Identifying and extracting the main points you need from written material
- Providing written information to other people accurately and clearly
- Negotiating and agreeing realistic targets for your work
- Prioritising targets and agreeing achievable timescales
- Planning how you will make best use of your time and the other resources you need and choose effective working methods
- Identifying and solving problems when they arise, using the support of other people when necessary
- Keeping other people informed of your progress
- Meeting your deadlines or re-negotiating targets, timescales and plans in good time
- Taking responsibility for your own work and accepting responsibility for any mistakes you make
- Following agreed guidelines, procedures and, where appropriate, codes of practice
- Encouraging and accepting feedback from other people
- Evaluating your own work and using feedback from other people to identify where you should improve

- Identifying ways to improving your work, consistently put them into practice and test how effective they are
- Identifying where further learning and development could improve your performance
- Developing and following through a learning plan that meets your own needs
- Reviewing your progress and updating your plans for improvement and learning
- Setting high standards for your work and showing drive and commitment in achieving these standards
- Coping with pressure and overcoming difficulties and setbacks
- Asserting your own needs and rights when necessary
- Showing a willingness to take on new challenges
- Adapting readily to change
- Treating other people with honesty, respect and consideration
- Helping and supporting other people

(Remember that you will need the skills listed at the beginning of this chapter. These are covered in chapter 1.)

You will need to produce evidence from a variety of sources. Carrying out the following activities will help you acquire competence at work.

**Activity 1**
Your department is being completely restructured and you have been asked to:

- Suggest options for re-organising the office layout, designing and presenting three alternatives with advantages and disadvantages of each, including relative costs and amount of disruption
- Re-allocate the tasks between yourself and the existing staff, identifying any training needs and/or duplication of resource

Prepare either a written report or a talk that you will present to your executive team.

**Activity 2**
A new member of staff is to start work in your department next week. You have asked a member of your team to carry out their induction to the whole organisation. Prepare a check-list of all the things that they will need to cover.

## Activity 3

Get your team to keep a precise log over a two month period, recording everything they do and exactly how long it takes. Review the log and look for time that could have been saved if you had planned and delegated more effectively. Use the information to plan the next period of time, communicate the changes and the reasons for them to the team and at the end, write a short account of how the planning has improved your team's efficiency.

## Activity 4

Complete the following self-appraisal by ticking the most appropriate box against each skill. For each tick in the 'training needs' column identify any action that needs to be taken.

|  | Can do | Training needs | Actions to be taken |
|---|---|---|---|
| Lead meetings |  |  |  |
| Encourage discussion |  |  |  |
| Motivate yourself |  |  |  |
| Motivate others |  |  |  |
| Give a presentation |  |  |  |
| Write a report |  |  |  |
| Write a memo |  |  |  |
| Research information |  |  |  |
| Prioritise tasks |  |  |  |
| Delegate |  |  |  |
| Deal with disruption |  |  |  |
| Say 'no' if necessary |  |  |  |
| Admit mistakes |  |  |  |
| Put forward ideas |  |  |  |
| Accept criticism |  |  |  |
| Cope with pressure |  |  |  |
| Set high standards |  |  |  |
| Accept new challenges |  |  |  |
| Embrace change |  |  |  |

Show the completed self-appraisal to your line manager to check that they agree with your findings. Negotiate with your line manager to ensure that the actions identified are addressed.

## Activity 5

Your department is to recruit a new office junior. The Human Resource department has asked for a job description, personnel specification and a written statement of terms and conditions. You have been asked to supply these.

## Activity 6

Make a list of all the decisions that you have to make at work over the next week. Identify which are the main issues and which are sub-tasks of the main issues. For each main issue decide whether it is important, urgent, both or neither. Re-list the issues in order of priority.

**Activity 7**

The week after carrying out Activity 6 reflect on your decision making the previous week.

- Did you deal with the issues in the order of priority that you decided?
- Were any of the decisions made by circumstances because you had delayed taking the decision?
- Identify the strengths you displayed in the way you made decisions
- Identify the weaknesses you displayed in the way you made decisions
- How can you build on the strengths and overcome the weaknesses?

Remember: Evidence will be generated for this unit while gathering evidence for optional units at Level 3. Assessment should be planned alongside the appropriate optional units.

# CHAPTER 4
# UNIT 302 – Work within your business environment

The economy of the United Kingdom is a mixed economy. This means there are organisations owned by individuals as well as organisations controlled by the state. Those owned by the state are known as the 'Public Sector' and include:

- Public Corporations such as the BBC
- Hospital Trusts
- Local Authorities such as local councils and local education authorities (LEAs)

Those owned by individuals are known as the 'Private Sector' and include:

- **Sole traders** - These are individuals who are self-employed
- **Partnerships** - This is a group of two or more self-employed people who have formed an organisation together in which each is a partner
- **Private Limited Companies (Ltd.)** - Two or more people form an organisation which is registered under the Companies Act 1985. Shares in the company can be sold privately
- **Public Limited Companies (plc.)** - A company whose shares can be bought and sold on the Stock Exchange

There is a third group of organisations which differ from the Public Sector. They are not owned by the state, and differ from the Private Sector, because they are not set up for the purpose of making a profit: they are often owned by their members. These organisations form the 'Mutuality Sector' and include:

- Those Building Societies which have not yet become Public Limited Companies
- Registered charities such as the RSPCA
- Co-operative Societies which operate in much the same way as Public Limited Companies except that any profit is returned to the customers

Organisations can also be divided into the following:

- **Service Providers** - These include Public Services, financial services such as banks and insurance companies, hotels and catering, call centres etc
- **Retailers** - These include High Street shops, on-line stores such as Amazon and mail-order catalogues such as Kays. They sell products direct to the public
- **Wholesalers** - These buy products direct from the manufacturer and sell them to retailers
- **Manufacturers** - These take raw materials and make them into a product which they sell to wholesalers

- **Extractive industries** - These include farming, mining, quarrying and fishing - they extract the product from natural resources

Wherever you work you will be working in one of the three sectors and one of the five types of organisation above. If you are unclear which it is, ask. Everyone employed has responsibilities to their employer and rights which they can expect their employer to respect. These are set out in your Contract of Employment and protected by legislation including the:

- National Minimum Wage Act 1998
- Disability Discrimination Act 1995
- Race Relations Act 1976
- Sex Discrimination Acts 1975 & 1986
- Equal Pay Act 1970
- Working Time Regulations Act 1998
- Data Protection Act 1998 (Employment)
- Employment Relations Act 1999
- Employment Rights Act 1996
- Human Rights Act 1998

Your responsibilities will involve you in:

- Acting in your organisation's best interests while you are at work
- Assessing risks to the business
- Taking any necessary action to maintain its security
- Supporting your employer's policy on diversity
- Respecting the confidentiality of information belonging to both your employer and clients or customers

Respecting confidentiality extends beyond the time spent at work to include your spare time and even after you have left the organisation. The information that you have had access to during your time at work must not be disclosed when you are out socially or when you start work at another organisation.

You will hear a lot about diversity in the workplace. Diversity means the qualities that make people unique including their race, religious beliefs, physical abilities, age, gender, sexual orientation, where they live, family status and background. There is legislation to protect the rights of employees against discrimination on grounds of:

- Ethnic origin
- Gender
- Marital status
- Sexual orientation
- Race
- Colour
- Pregnancy
- Physical impairment
- Mental impairment

Other diversity regulations and legislation is being planned including protection from ageism. You can play your part in supporting equal opportunities in the workplace by treating everybody fairly, learning from other people, not ignoring others who don't treat everybody fairly and by supporting equal opportunity programmes. Treat your colleagues fairly, just as you would want to be treated.

 When working within your business environment you will need the following skills:

- Planning
- Reading
- Communicating
- Monitoring
- Interpersonal skills
- Problem solving
- Team working

These skills are covered in chapter 1.

## Your organisation's purpose and values

Every organisation was set up with a purpose. It may be a commercial enterprise set up for the purpose of making money, a charitable organisation set up to relieve a need, or a public service. Each organisation will also have values, the principles by which it operates. These may be to raise as much money as possible for the cause, to operate in an ethical and environmentally friendly manner, or simply be the best in their field. In order to achieve their purpose and uphold those values, the people in charge will have set aims and objectives which will need to be amended in the light of changing circumstances.

This may be enshrined in a 'mission statement' which attempts to explain the organisation's purpose and values in a few words. For instance a training organisation may have a mission statement 'Helping to expand your horizons'.

Your role is to carry out your work in a way that helps your organisation to achieve its aims. For this reason you need to understand how your job fits in to the organisation as a whole. You may not feel your part is important but everybody has a part to play and it's the little cogs that make the big wheels turn. Remember that a complex organisation requires each member to carry out their part in the way that has been designated; while doing all you can to uphold the organisation's values.

Consider ways in which policies, systems and procedures can be improved in your work placement. Procedures are basically a standard way of doing things, making it easier for new staff to pick up a task or for somebody to stand in for the person who normally carries out the procedure when they are on holiday or off sick. If you are considering designing a new procedure it is wise to investigate first whether there is already a procedure in place, perhaps one that is not being followed. If this is the case, it may be the best idea simply to try to enforce the existing procedure. Procedures should:

- Make tasks easier to carry out
- Make work more cost-effective
- Deliver better service to your customers either external or internal

A procedure that does not achieve any of the above is pointless, and will probably not be carried out even if put in place.

Your ability to make changes to procedures will depend on your job role and level of authority. It is more likely that you will be able to make changes if they:

- Only affect your own department
- Have no legal or financial implications
- Do not impact on other procedures

Don't change the way you carry out your responsibilities without discussing them with your line manager, even if they fall within your authority to change, because you may inadvertently produce a major change in the way the whole organisation functions.

Before developing a new procedure or amending an existing procedure consider:

- The purpose of the procedure
- Ways of measuring its effectiveness
- The effects of implementing the procedure both positive and negative
- Who will use the procedure
- Whether to consult users or inform them when the procedure is ready to be implemented

The advantages of consulting users are:

- It may be unwise to implement a procedure 'behind the back' of your line manager
- You can draw on their expertise
- Two (or more) heads are better than one
- Others may foresee consequences of the procedure that you have overlooked
- Others, particularly in different departments, may have a different perspective on the procedure
- If they have first-hand knowledge of the task and you do not they may resent what they see as interference
- It's more likely users will follow a new procedure if they feel they have contributed to it

The disadvantages of consulting users are:

- They may make unhelpful, negative suggestions
- Consultation could be time consuming if the procedure needs to be implemented quickly
- You will probably receive conflicting suggestions
- People will be alienated from the procedure if they feel their suggestions have been ignored

If you decide to consult:

- Make it clear that you welcome suggestions
- Don't have a final solution in mind from the beginning
- Set a clear time limit for the consultation
- Involve those with expertise in the subject, those who will have to follow the procedure and those who will be affected by it
- Try to make at least one change from your original idea to incorporate others' suggestions
- Always explain your reasons for rejecting others' suggestions
- Consider operating the procedure for a trial period

If the procedure under consideration doesn't fall within your authority to implement, you will need approval from your line management to carry out changes. If you work in a small organisation getting approval may be a fairly simple process, if you work in a large or complex organisation there may be quite intricate procedures to follow. Many large organisations have a department responsible for monitoring and implementing procedures and any changes will have to be approved by them.

Approval may well depend on a consideration of the costs and benefits of the change. Costs will usually be:

- Financial
- Related to increased use of:
  - materials
  - equipment
  - labour
  - capital
- Quantifiable

Benefits will usually be:

- Financial

- Related to more effective use of:
    - materials
    - equipment
    - labour
    - capital
- Less quantifiable

It will be necessary to demonstrate that the benefits are likely to outweigh the costs.

There will be times when it is necessary to inform users of a change in procedure, rather than consulting with them, for instance when:

- There is no alternative to the procedure
- The procedure is imposed by government or senior management
- There are too many to consult with
- Legal requirements must be met
- Specialist advice is being followed
- The procedure is routine
- The timescale for implementation is extremely short

If you decide to inform without consultation:

- Tell the users why you have decided not to consult them
- Send out the procedure in writing, clearly and unambiguously
- Make sure they understand the consequences of not following the procedures
- Ensure any necessary training is organised
- Be prepared to answer questions

It is also important to understand that everything that you do in your job should reflect the organisation's values. Many organisations operate in an environmentally friendly way and everybody employed within that organisation is involved in that. This means reducing energy wastage, recycling, using low emission vehicles as company cars and using public transport on company business wherever possible. It can also mean considering which products are purchased for use within the organisation. If you work for an organic farmer then it would not be appropriate to order chemical fertilisers. If your job is in the public service sector, all of your actions should be aimed at serving the public.

Remember that to the public and people from outside your organisation, you represent the organisation. Their perception of your employer will be based on their impression of you. Every time you communicate with anyone you will give them an impression of the organisation you work for, whether you attend external meetings representing the organisation or simply communicate by telephone or letter. Think about situations when you have spoken to someone from another organisation. Have you ever been left with the feeling that they are not interested or couldn't care less? What was your impression of the organisation they worked for?

If you are to give the correct impression you need to know and understand your organisation's purpose and values. If you are not absolutely sure what these are ask for guidance.

 **What you need to know**

Your organisation's purpose

What three sectors make up the UK economy?

Your organisation's values

What sector does your organisation operate in?

How your organisation compares to other similar organisations

What are your main responsibilities?

How you contribute to the success of the organisation

How are the values of your organisation relevant to your role?

How to apply values in your day-to-day work

Who can you get guidance from on policies and values?

The process involved in improving procedures

How can you improve the organisation's objectives and values?

# Employment responsibilities and rights

Your responsibilities as an employee will be laid down in your job description, your staff handbook, your letter of appointment and contract of employment. Your workplace may also display some of your responsibilities in notices on notice boards, newsletters and policy documents. Your contract of employment will also state many of your rights as an employee, but there will be others not included in your contract.

When you first started your current job, your responsibilities will have been explained to you and you will have been issued with a job description. It is extremely unlikely, however, that you will be able to perform satisfactorily if you simply carry out the list of duties to the letter. All of us find, in practice, that there are many responsibilities attached to our jobs that are not listed on the job description (although sometimes the last item on the job description will be 'such duties as may from time to time be necessary' which is pretty much a 'catch-all'). It is much better for everybody if you are prepared to take on anything that needs doing, providing you have been trained to do it.

There are also responsibilities involved in your job that go beyond the duties required. These may be summed up as showing a positive attitude to work and involve such things as:

- Always looking your best and projecting the correct company image
- Being enthusiastic even when you're feeling a bit low
- Being flexible
- Welcoming change
- Accepting constructive criticism
- Dealing with pressure
- Using your initiative, especially to solve problems
- Having sound judgment
- Working well with other people even if you don't particularly like them
- Being punctual
- Not taking time off unnecessarily

All employers are required by the Employment Rights Act 1996 to give an employee a written statement of the terms and conditions of their employment within two months of their starting work. This is often in the form of a Contract of Employment, although legally speaking a contract exists whether it is in writing or not. The statement of employment particulars must contain:

- The names of the employer and employee
- The date employment started
- The date continuous employment started
- The rate and intervals of pay
- The hours of work
- Holidays and holiday pay
- Sickness and sick pay
- Pensions and pension schemes
- Length of notice required
- If non-permanent, the period for which employment is expected to continue or the date at which it is to end
- The job title or brief description
- The place of work
- Any collective agreements
- Disciplinary rules
- Grievance procedures

Your employment rights are also protected under the following legislation:

## National Minimum Wage Act 1998

All workers are entitled to be paid at least the National Minimum Wage. The minimum hourly rate is reviewed each year by the Low Pay Commission who set rates for those aged 22 or over and those aged 18–21. Excluded from this Act are company directors, those aged under 18 and the genuinely self employed.

## Equal Pay Act 1970

It is unlawful to offer different pay and conditions to men and women who perform the same type of work. This is defined as work of equal value in terms of effort and skills.

## Working Time Regulations 1998

In general these impose an obligation on employers to ensure that employees:

- Work an average week of no more than 48 hours calculated over a 17 week period including working lunches, job related travel and time spent on business abroad
- Have an 11 hour continuous rest period between working days
- Have a continuous 24 hour period off work each week
- Have a break of at least 20 minutes during the day if the day is more than six hours long

Workers above school leaving age but under 18 cannot work more than eight hours a day or 40 hours a week as part of their ordinary working pattern.

## Employment Relations Act 1999

Regardless of what may be written in the Contract of Employment, employees have a right to receive the following minimum periods of notice when employment is terminated:

- One week's notice for employees who have been employed for more than one month but less than two years
- Two weeks' notice for employees who have been continuously employed for more than two years, and one additional week's notice for each complete year of

continuous employment up to 12 weeks for a period of up to 12 years
- At least 12 weeks notice for employees who have been continuously employed for more than 12 years

Employees must give employers one week's notice if they have been employed continuously for one month or more.

## Human Rights Act 1998

This came into force in October 2000 and includes provisions on:

- Prohibition of discrimination
- Forced labour
- The right to privacy
- The right to join a Trade Union

There is other legislation which refers to employment rights. Information will be available from your Human Resources Department, your local Citizen's Advice Bureau, the internet or your public library.

Employers keep records on their employees which detail their attendance, time keeping, disciplinary records, appraisals and training. Employers also keep personal details such as address, National Insurance Number, next of kin, date of birth, current rate of pay and hours worked. If any of your details change you should inform your employer immediately. The employer is obliged to keep records regarding PAYE and other deductions from your pay.

 **What you need to know**

Where to find your terms and conditions of employment

Are there any regulations that apply specifically to the industry you work in?

The employment legislation that affects your role

How does legislation protect the rights of both employees and employers?

Where to obtain information on
employment legislation

Who would you contact if you had a
grievance?

What to do if you are ill or need time off
work

What information do employers keep
on employees?

## Supporting diversity

The dictionary definition of diversity is 'the state of being
different'.  You should deal with diversity by remembering that
everybody should be shown the same respect.  People with
disabilities or the elderly may require help with access to the
building.  Visitors, of both genders, with young children may
require baby-changing facilities.

Hearing impaired colleagues may need more visual aids.
Visually impaired colleagues may need documents in large print
or in audio format.  Also be aware that English may not be
someone's first language.

These are some examples of dealing with diversity.  Don't make
up your mind about somebody based on appearance, accent etc.
People have different requirements, help with access, help with
reading, help with understanding, but the important thing to
remember is they are all colleagues and should be shown the
same respect.

Many workplaces today are far more diverse than in the past.
You may well find yourself working with colleagues from a wide
range of cultures and abilities.  It's in the best interests of
everybody that you understand what is meant by Equal
Opportunities.  For employers Equal Opportunities is about good
business practice and can:

- Reduce costs
- Improve efficiency
- Lower staff turnover
- Improve customer relations

For employees it means they are judged on merit, ability and
past performance and covers:

- Recruitment
- Promotion
- Training
- Benefits
- Dismissal

Your organisation will probably have an Equal Opportunities programme which will be designed to:

- Improve team success through respect and dignity for all
- Reduce stress levels and therefore absenteeism
- Improve safety performance
- Reduce recruitment costs
- Increase sales through staff commitment
- Widen the customer base

Employers can make these programmes more successful by:

- Outlawing discrimination and harassment
- Treating everybody equally
- Providing advice and training
- Offering flexible working time
- Handling complaints promptly

Discrimination may be direct or indirect. Direct discrimination means treating people less favourably because of their gender, ethnicity or sexual orientation etc. For instance selecting a male for the supervisor's position ahead of a better qualified female because the majority of the staff are male and traditionally the role has been male.

Indirect discrimination occurs when a rule or practice discriminates against a particular group unintentionally, for instance stating that everyone applying for a job must have been to public school when there is no good reason for this.

Harassment is an unwelcome or offensive remark, request or other act that discriminates against a person by harming his or her job performance or satisfaction. Sexual harassment is a criminal offence. Other types of harassment may be criminal, for instance:

- Offensive jokes, remarks or insults based on ethnicity, nationality or other characteristics
- Bullying
- Threats, verbal or physical abuse

- Threatening or discriminating against someone for reporting a breach of the law

**Disability Discrimination Act 1995 (c. 50)**
© Crown Copyright 1995

**Race Relations Act 1976**
© Crown Copyright 1976

**Sex Discrimination Act 1975**
© Crown Copyright 1975

If you feel you are being discriminated against or harassed you are advised to tell the person involved that you find their behaviour offensive and want it to stop. If you feel you have been unfairly treated in terms of pay or promotion, ask for the decision to be reconsidered. If you feel unable to talk to the other person involved directly speak to their line manager. Make sure you have kept a record of what has happened and when.

The following legislation addresses Equal Opportunities at work:

## The Sex Discrimination Acts 1975 & 1986

These Acts prohibit discrimination against people based on their gender or marital status. It covers two main areas:

- **Recruitment** - This includes the job description, the person specification, the application form, the short-listing process, interviewing and final selection
- **Terms and conditions** - This includes pay, holidays and working conditions

Direct sex discrimination involves refusing to consider somebody for a job because of their gender, for example refusing to consider a male for a job that is traditionally perceived as a female role. Indirect sex discrimination involves making it more difficult for one gender or for married people to be considered for a job, for instance if a condition of employment was willingness to regularly move home which would discriminate against married applicants as they would find this more difficult.

# Race Relations Act 1976

This Act prohibits discrimination against people based on their race, colour, nationality or ethnic origin.  It covers:

- Recruitment
- Training
- Selection
- Promotion
- Dismissal

Racial discrimination may be direct or indirect.  Direct racial discrimination could involve refusing to consider somebody for a job because of their ethnic background, for example refusing to consider an equally qualified applicant from a particular ethnic group for a job while considering others.  Indirect racial discrimination involves making it more difficult for some people to be considered for a job.  For instance, if a condition of employment was that all males had to be clean shaven, this would discriminate against members of religions that required beards to be worn.

# Disability Discrimination Act 1995

This Act prohibits discrimination against people based on their disability.  It describes a person with a disability as 'anyone with a physical or mental impairment which has a substantial and long-term adverse effect upon their ability to carry out normal day-to-day activities'.

# Employment Rights Act 1996

An example of where this Act could apply to sex discrimination is the fact that it covers the right to return to work after maternity leave.  Employers have to guarantee a woman either her job or a job of equal status on her return from her maternity leave.

# Health and Safety at Work Act 1974

An example of where this Act could apply to discrimination is a case of bullying that affects a person's health or safety.  An employee could claim constructive dismissal against an employer who failed to act when told that the bullying behaviour of a colleague was causing stress and meant that the employee was no longer able to do their job.

Other forms of discrimination may be unlawful even though no specific law prohibits them, for instance discrimination based on age or HIV infection. However, even these will be subject to new legislation by 2006.

Equal Opportunities at work come down to changing the attitude of people about colleagues who are different from themselves and making the best use of the organisation's human resources. Equal Opportunities policies have the potential to bring out the best in people.

 **What you need to know**

The definition of diversity

> What is the difference between direct and indirect discrimination?

The benefits of Equal Opportunities policies to employers

> What are the purposes of Equal Opportunities programmes?

The benefits of Equal Opportunities policies to employees

> How does harassment differ from discrimination?

The main provisions of the Sex Discrimination Acts 1975 & 1986

> How can Equal Opportunities programmes be made more successful?

The main provisions of the Race Discrimination Act 1976

> Can you think of some examples of organisations that have successfully embraced diversity?

The main provisions of the Disability Discrimination Act 1995

> Who should you tell if you feel you are being harassed?

# Maintaining security and confidentiality

Security rules are in place to protect:

- People
- Premises
- Property including stock and money
- Information
- IT systems

For your protection and the protection of your colleagues, visitors and customers security must extend to everybody who enters the building; staff, contractors, maintenance people, clients, customers and visitors. Many organisations provide their staff with badges, often containing a photograph. Some use electronic access systems which allow the staff to enter by swiping their identity card. Any genuine visitor will be carrying some form of identity which they will be willing to show when asked. All visitors should be asked to sign in and their signature checked against their identification. You must be sure everyone in the building has a right to be there. Do not leave visitors unsupervised. It is vital that everybody follows the rules. Any suspicious circumstance should be reported immediately.

A major risk to you personally is violence. If you find someone on the premises who has no right to be there:

| Do Not | Do |
|---|---|
| Put yourself at risk | Be vigilant and alert |
| Argue | Remain calm and polite |
| Give chase | Ask them their business |

There are a number of steps that can be taken to minimise the risk of violence:

- Panic buttons
- Glass screens
- Two-way radios
- Improved training
- Avoiding lone working

The main protection against violence is to know in advance what to do if you feel under threat. Violence may not necessarily come from those with no right to be on the premises. You may feel threatened by a fellow member of staff who is bullying you in order to intimidate you. The only way to deal with bullying is to report it immediately, if it starts, to your line manager.  Or, if it is your line manager bullying you, to the Human Resources Department.

A major risk to the premises is fire.  The priority must be to prevent fire, and to minimise the effect should one start.  See chapter 2 for further information on preventing fires.

The number of keys to the building issued to employees should be kept to a minimum, and a system put in place to record who has access to them.  In the event of a problem outside of working hours it will be necessary to contact a key holder to enter the building so a list of key holders should be held by the police or a private security company.  If you are a key holder make sure you know where the keys are at all times and that you are contactable in case of emergency.  Keys to internal doors and cabinets should be safely stored at night.  Safe keys also need to be locked away at night.  Safes and cabinets that contain no valuables are best left open to prevent burglars causing expensive damage forcing them open.  Internal doors need to be closed to prevent the spread of fire, but should be left unlocked if the contents of the room are not particularly valuable for the same reason.

You can help to prevent burglary by:

- Locking doors and windows
- Removing any valuable items from view
- Using any security devices available

If you are the first to enter the premises and you discover there has been a burglary:

- Telephone the police by dialling 999
- Contact your manager or the security department at Head Office
- Do not disturb any evidence

Theft is another major risk to property, stock and money, both the organisation's and the personal property of the staff:

- In offices criminals will pose as visitors or customers to steal equipment and staff's personal belongings or pose as maintenance people to remove equipment
- In hotels they will collect room keys from reception after watching the guests go out or steal equipment from conference rooms or store cupboards
- In leisure centres they will steal valuables from changing rooms or staff rooms

Some criminals may even be staff members. They may feel that stealing from a large organisation is not really theft as nobody suffers, but this is not the case. The cost of theft is passed on to the customer of the organisation through higher prices or higher charges, as well as increasing insurance premiums to cover the cost of paying compensation. A further effect of theft is that there is less profit available in the organisation to pay wages and salaries.

There are precautions that can be taken to reduce the risk of company property being stolen:

- Mark expensive equipment with the organisation's name or post code using an 'invisible' marker
- Keep a record of equipment serial numbers
- Don't turn your back on valuable equipment
- Don't assume things won't be stolen just because they are not particularly valuable
- Change the codes used to access areas regularly and especially when people who know them leave the organisation
- Sign out and sign back in again any portable equipment that is allowed to leave the building

If you see a theft taking place, or suspect that someone is stealing, there are a number of things that you can do:

- Observe their behaviour while a colleague alerts security or a manager. Try to keep them under constant observation so that they do not have the opportunity to pass on the stolen items to an accomplice
- Watch them until you are sure a theft has taken place
- Avoid confronting them if you are on your own as this leaves you vulnerable to violence
- Take a detailed description of the person in case you lose sight of them
- Above all, keep a safe distance and do not put yourself at risk

You must be aware of the limits of your authority under the law to take action against a suspected criminal. Under the Police and Criminal Evidence Act 1984 you have the power of arrest

but you do not have the authority to search people, cars or premises, only the police do.

If you search someone without their permission you are open to a charge of assault. You can request that the person empties their pockets, handbags, briefcases, etc., but you cannot insist. Always make sure you have a third person present as a witness.

Remember most criminals are opportunists, remove the opportunity and they won't be able to steal. Don't take cash or valuables to work unless you absolutely have to. If you have no choice, ask if it can be locked away somewhere safe. Keep your handbag in your sight or out of everybody else's. Don't leave your wallet in your jacket hanging on the back of a chair in an empty room. Don't leave your mobile phone on the table in the staff room. Challenge any visitors that you find in an area of the building where they are not permitted.

One of the fastest growing types of theft is the theft of information. This may be commercially sensitive information which can be stolen by one organisation from another, or personal information which can be stolen to be used fraudulently.

The information may be held on a computer, in which case it should be protected by passwords, or it may be paper copies of information, in which case care should be taken that it is not left in plain sight on desks and that it is shredded before being disposed of. Remember not to discuss confidential issues in areas where visitors or the public may be able to overhear.

Personal information about living individuals, including customers, employees, suppliers, clients or other member of the public held on computers or in some cases on paper, is covered by the Data Protection Act 1998. There are eight data protection principles which state that personal information must be:

- Fairly and lawfully processed
- Processed for specified purposes
- Adequate, relevant and not excessive
- Accurate and where necessary kept up-to-date
- Kept for no longer than necessary
- Processed in line with the rights of the individual
- Kept secure

- Not transferred to countries outside the European Economic Area unless there is adequate protection for the information

The other risk to the security of your IT system will come from viruses. These are programs that enter your computer without your knowledge and are designed to damage or delete files. Viruses infect your computer through the Internet, via e-mails or through software. There are a number of anti-virus programmes which can be purchased and will check files for viruses before you open them. The difficulty is they can usually only detect viruses which existed before the anti-virus programme was written, so need regularly updating. If you install anti-virus software and keep its virus database up-to-date you should avoid problems with viruses. You will still need to be careful about what programs you install and what files you open from the Internet.

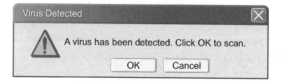

Never open files sent to you by e-mail from people you don't know, even if they appear to be harmless. Be careful if you receive an e-mail from someone you do know with an attachment which looks suspicious. Check with the sender before you open the attachment as some viruses spread by sending e-mails to everybody in the affected computer's address book.

From time-to-time you should scan your computer for viruses. The precise process for this will depend on the anti-virus software that you have running on your computer.

The other essential maintenance to undertake daily is to 'back-up' your hard disk to a removable drive, a network or the Internet. Make sure the back-up disks are kept in a fire-proof safe.

If you have any suspicions that security or confidentiality is being compromised report your concerns to someone in authority. If it transpires that there was no breach, it will be better to have checked than to have ignored the situation.

# What you need to know

The principles of the Data Protection Act
1998

What security rules are there in your
organisation?

The do's and don'ts of confronting a
trespasser

How can you help prevent burglary?

How to minimise the effect of fire

What should you do if you discover a
burglary?

How to secure money, property, premises
and information

How would you approach somebody
who is in the building that you don't
recognise?

The consequences of staff theft

What action should you take if you
suspect someone of stealing?

Your powers under the Police and Criminal
Evidence Act 1984

What type of information is most
vulnerable to theft?

The process of backing-up information

How would you scan your IT system for
viruses?

## Assessing and managing risk

Part of your job role is likely to be the assessment and
management of risks. Possibly the most important is the risk to
the health and safety of staff, customers and visitors. Other
areas that you will need to monitor are risks to the business,
business growth, projects, premises, property, equipment and
information. Risks to premises, property, equipment and
information have been covered earlier in this chapter.

In assessing the risk to health and safety it is important to understand the difference between a hazard and a risk. A hazard is a situation or an object that has the potential to cause injury, harm or ill health. A risk is the likelihood of something causing harm because the hazard, or potential hazard, exists. All organisations are required to carry out Risk Assessments which will identify where hazards exist and evaluate what the risks are. There are five steps to carrying out an efficient Risk Assessment:

- Look for the hazards
- Decide who might be harmed and how
- What are the risks, what is being done?
- Record your findings
- Review your assessment

Detailed information on identifying hazards to health and safety and how to carry out a Risk Assessment can be found in chapter 2.

The first step in assessing the risks to the business and business growth is to carry out a SWOT analysis (Strengths, Weaknesses, Opportunities and Threats). Possible threats identified might include:

- A competitor develops a new product which is better or cheaper than yours
- The patent on your product expires (patents are granted for 15 years) before you have patented an improved model
- Fashion changes. This may affect businesses beyond the obvious areas of clothing and gadgets; a fashion for

social responsibility may limit the market for cars with high fuel consumption for instance

- Changes in the demographic make-up of the population. Mass immigration or emigration or increases in the birth or death rates may change the level of demand for your products
- A rise in inflation may reduce the spending power of your customer base
- A rise in taxes may similarly reduce spending power
- A poor harvest will increase prices, which will directly affect the businesses selling those products but will indirectly affect others as customers will have less disposable income
- Changes in company law may reduce demand, for instance on-line submission of PAYE and VAT returns has reduced the demand for paper
- Changes in employment law may increase costs
- Changes in government may have wide ranging effects

Most of these threats will not appear overnight, so the way to manage them is by strategic planning; forecasting over the long term, usually at least five years ahead, in order to counter as many of the threats as possible. Ways of countering the threats identified above may include:

- Long term contracting for supply of raw materials to level out supply and price fluctuations
- Increased research and development to produce a steady flow of new products
- Diversification into products or areas of business where the risks are less
- Increased advertising to establish your business as a leading 'brand'
- Continuous pressure on costs to identify and eliminate any areas of waste

These may be seen as unavoidable risks in that the threat comes from outside the business. They have to be planned for and dealt with by utilising the expertise within the business. Some risks, however, can be insured against as the possibility of their happening can be calculated by actuaries using statistical analysis. These may include threats to:

- People from physical attack or accidents
- Premises such as fire, flood or subsidence
- Property such as theft, sabotage, accidental damage

- Stock such as theft, fraud, collusion, corruption
- Money such as theft, fraud, collusion, embezzlement
- Information such as industrial or commercial espionage, disclosure of confidential information to competitors or the media, corruption of data
- IT systems such as viruses, failure of the system

The business decision to be made is whether the risk is sufficiently great that the payment of insurance premiums is justifiable. The insurance industry, like many others, has its own terminology which it may be useful to understand. Some of its more common terms and their meanings are:

- **Actuary** - A statistician who calculates insurance premiums, risks, dividends and annuity rates
- **Adjuster** - Assesses the financial losses incurred through, for example accident, theft, fire, or natural disaster, and determines the amount of compensation
- **Assessor -** Calculates amounts to be paid or assessed for tax or insurance purposes
- **Broker** - An agent for others, for example in negotiating insurance contracts
- **Disclosure** - A prospective policy holder must tell the insurer anything that is likely to affect assessment of the risks to be insured
- **Excess** - An amount of money that a policy-holder must pay towards the cost of any insurance claim made
- **Ex gratia** - An amount of money paid by an insurer as a gesture of goodwill, rather than because it is owed
- **Fidelity guarantee** - Insurance against loss suffered as a result of acts of fraud or dishonesty by employees
- **Indemnity** - The policy holder should be put into the same position after an insurable event as he was in before the event, for instance if a fire destroys equipment which had been in use for some time the insurance payment would be less than the cost of replacing the equipment to account for its use
- **Surveyor** - Inspects buildings to determine the soundness of their construction or to assess their value for insurance purposes
- **Underwriting** - Insuring somebody or something by accepting liability for specified losses. The underwriter decides the terms and the premium to be charged
- **Warranty** - A condition in an insurance contract in which the insured person guarantees that something is the case

An area where assessment of risk is vital is as a part of the management of projects. A project is a series of activities designed to achieve a specific outcome within a set budget and timescale. Most are vital to future operations – they are often a 'test-bed' for wide-ranging changes. The risks associated with projects are:

- **They will almost always run over time** - However well you plan, people are not machines and will inevitably run into problems
- **They will run over budget** - Keeping a close eye on spending is essential to the successful management of the project
- **External factors** - The project may be your number one priority, but it won't be the number one priority of everybody else in the organisation, or of people outside the organisation. Suppliers have their own priorities and you may have to fight for your project

It is important to identify and assess anything that may be a risk to your project. You will then need to plan what action you will take if the risks come about. You will be able to identify warning signs and reduce the damage to the project by acting quickly. For instance where the project depends on the actions of someone who is not part of the project team they may have their own goals and objectives and their own ways of working. If communication has not been effective, they may not have all of the information they need. You need to keep on top of everything all the time to successfully manage the risk.

 **What you need to know**

How to identify threats to business and business growth

What threats does your organisation currently face?

How to counter threats

What is the difference between an actuary and an underwriter?

The five steps to Risk Assessment

How can you contact your First Aiders and Health and Safety Representatives?

The risks that can be insured against

Why is it important to deal with risks immediately and take steps to prevent re-occurrence?

Methods of identifying threats to projects

What is the meaning of the word 'warranty' in insurance terms?

The benefits to you of working effectively within your organisation are that you will be given more support, bigger challenges and greater opportunities. While it is important to know your employment rights it is more important to understand and fulfil your responsibilities. If you welcome the opportunity to work with as wide a range of people as possible you will learn to do things differently as other people's skills and experience will enhance your own. Keep your workplace, yourself and your colleagues safe by considering security as a priority, keep information secure by preserving confidentiality and protect the interests of the business by assessing and effectively managing risk. As a result the whole organisation will work more efficiently.

## Everyone needs the chance to realise their full potential. This will lead to economic prosperity

# Are you ready for assessment?

To achieve this unit of a Level 3 Business & Administration qualification you will need to demonstrate that you are competent in the following:

- Working in a way that supports your organisation's overall mission and your team's objectives
- Following the policies, systems and procedures that are relevant to your job
- Putting your organisation's values into practice in all aspects of your work
- Working with outside organisations and individuals in a way that protects and improves the image of your organisation
- Seeking guidance from others when you are unsure about objectives, policies, systems, procedures and values
- Contributing to improving objectives, policies, systems, procedures and values in a way that is consistent with your role
- Accessing information about your employment rights and responsibilities
- Carrying out your responsibilities to your employer in a way that is consistent with your contract of employment
- Asserting your employment rights when necessary
- Seeking guidance when you are unsure about your employments responsibilities and rights
- Interacting with other people in a way that is sensitive to their individual needs and respects their background, abilities, values, customs and beliefs
- Learning from other people and using this to improve the way you work and interact with others
- Following your organisation's procedures and legal requirements in relation to discrimination legislation
- Maintaining the security of property in a way that is consistent with your organisation's procedures and legal requirements
- Maintaining the security and confidentiality of information in a way that is consistent with your organisation's procedures and legal requirements

- Reporting any concerns about security and confidentiality to an appropriate person or agency
- Identifying and agreeing possible sources of risk
- Assessing and confirming the level of risk
- Putting in place ways of minimising risk
- Monitoring risk
- Being alert to new risks and being able to manage these when they occur
- Reviewing and learning from your experience of assessing and managing risk

(Remember that you will need the skills listed at the beginning of this chapter.  These are covered in chapter 1.)

You will need to produce evidence from a variety of sources. Carrying out the following activities will help you acquire competence at work.

**Activity 1**
If your organisation or department has a mission statement, explain in writing how this is reflected in the way that you and your team carry out your responsibilities at work.  If there is no mission statement get together with your team to design one that reflects your organisation's aims and objectives.

**Activity 2**
Write an account of your organisation's purpose and values explaining how these fit into the sector in which your organisation operates.

**Activity 3**
Make a strategic plan for your organisation (or department) for the next five years.  Assess the risks involved in carrying out this plan and suggest measures to counter the risks.

**Activity 4**
You have been asked to give a 15 minute talk at the next team meeting on 'Diversity in the Workplace'.  Prepare the notes for the talk being sure to include as many forms of diversity as possible, not just those you have personally experienced.  Rehearse the talk with a colleague and get feedback on its content.

**Activity 5**
Find out what security procedures you have at work.  Suggest improvements that could be made to offer better protection for people, premises, property, stock, money, information and IT systems.  Show these suggestions to your line manager. Your line manager can write a witness testimony on your report as it is likely to be a confidential document.

**Activity 6**
Carry out a risk assessment of the area of your workplace for which you are responsible.

**Activity 7**
Research Employment Legislation and write a report on how it impacts on your job role.

Remember:  Evidence will be generated for this unit while gathering evidence for all the other units.  Assessment should be planned alongside the appropriate optional units.

# CHAPTER 5
# UNIT 204 – Manage diary systems

One of the most important activities in an office is planning and organising schedules both for yourself and for other people.  This can be done using various types of diary depending on the information that needs to be kept.  In a busy office people's plans are constantly being changed, both by themselves and by circumstances beyond their control.  It is essential that someone co-ordinates these changes, communicating with everybody who is affected to avoid confusion and time-wasting errors.  If you are responsible for arranging meetings and appointments for somebody else, remember to leave them time for routine matters such as dealing with the post and other day-to-day responsibilities.  Also remember to allow time for them to travel from one appointment to another.

Probably the most common form of diary in use in an office is still the 'page-a-day' book.  This has the advantage of enabling you to record appointments and meetings that need to be attended during the day and on the same page recording your 'to-do' list.  As the diary can be locked away at the end of the day it is possible to enter confidential information but if you use the diary for this purpose it is important to make sure that you do lock it away if you leave your desk.  Regular events, deadlines, jobs carried forward can all be recorded but remember to keep it brief to avoid confusion and make all entries in pencil to make changes easier.  You might find it useful to divide the page into two sections, one containing appointments and the other the 'to-do' list.

Another form of diary commonly found in offices is the 'wall planner'. This usually covers a whole year with spaces for each day. Wall planners are used for long-term planning such as staff holidays, as they allow you to see at a glance whether too many people are on holiday at the same time, or if the week you want off is available. They are also useful for displaying deadlines for completion of work, and for planning promotions or events. Obviously confidential information should not be displayed on a wall planner unless it is in a room that has restricted access. They are usually laminated so that, providing the correct type of pen is used, changes can be made neatly. Alternatively coloured stickers can be attached to give a graphic display of information.

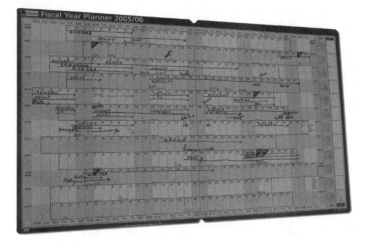

The most up-to-date form of diary is an electronic planner, this is maintained on a computer, palm top or electronic organiser. The advantages of these are that they can be set to display a reminder on screen that an appointment is imminent, they can be shared by people in different locations or alternatively password protected so that confidential information can't be seen by unauthorised people. Some more advanced electronic diaries can even invite colleagues to attend meetings by e-mail, and receive their acceptance or apologies automatically.

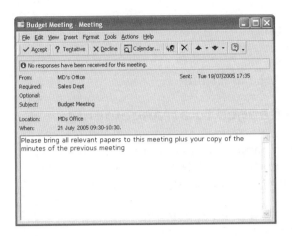

As with all innovations there are some disadvantages:

- The risk of a system failure making all of the information unavailable or, even worse, losing all of the data
- The fact that a desk top computer is not portable
- Not everybody is computer literate yet
- There is always the danger of the diary being subject to hacking

Whatever form of diary you choose to keep, be aware of the dangers of maintaining two or more versions. While this may be convenient from the point of view of being able to carry the paper version with you and still have all the advantages of the electronic system, it is vital that any changes made to one are made to the other as soon as possible to avoid confusion.

 When managing diary systems you will use the following skills:

- Questioning
- Listening
- Analysing
- Planning
- Organising
- Problem solving
- Decision making
- Negotiating

- Recording
- Communicating
- Using technology

These skills are covered in chapter 1.

## Dealing with changes to arrangements

If you are asked to change arrangements that have already been made, it is important to obtain all of the information you need about the requested changes. These may include:

- The date or time of an appointment
- The location of an intended meeting
- The names of the attendees
- The duration of the appointment

Requests for amendments may be made by telephone, fax, e-mail, letter or verbally. You will need to confirm that you have fully understood the requested changes.

You may receive a number of requests simultaneously to amend existing arrangements. These will need to be prioritised so that you can ensure that you carry these out in such an order that changes to imminent events are made first. Changes to arrangements for next week can be made after changes to tomorrow's schedule have been dealt with.

You may be keeping diaries for other people with very busy and hectic working lives. They will not have time to negotiate, so this will be your job. When changes have to be made to these diaries, you will need to be diplomatic about the way they are made. You will be responsible for negotiating with everybody involved and solving any problems that may arise due to the changes. You may be asked to make a change which on the face of it appears to be minor, for instance to change an appointment from 0900 to 1000. However the impact could be significant and have major implications for existing commitments. All other appointments for the rest of the day could be delayed. You will need to go back to your original plans to check what other arrangements will be affected by the requested change.

When you identify that a requested change will have implications for existing entries, you will need to make alternative arrangements.  It will be your responsibility to decide which changes you are prepared to accept and which arrangements cannot be altered.  To solve any possible problems you will probably have to contact a number of people to advise them that the arrangements have had to be altered, and negotiate revised schedules with them.  This may need a deal of tact and diplomacy to avoid giving the impression that something more important has come up. Once you have made a decision about a change, be prepared to back it up if need be, your boss is a very busy person and will rely on you to keep their diary up-to-date and keep them informed in advance of where they will need to be and when.

 **What you need to know**

What implications a change in arrangements might have

How might you receive amendments to a diary?

How to prioritise tasks

Why should you amend tomorrow's schedule before next week's?

How to negotiate tactfully

What are the advantages of an electronic diary?

How to use electronic diary systems

Why is it important to confirm that you have understood requested amendments?

How to use a wall planner to organise staff holidays

Whose diary are you responsible for?

What confidential information you deal with

What types of diary systems does your organisation use?

## Communicating revised arrangements

When you record agreed changes in the diary remember to amend anything that is affected by later arrangements. It is particularly important to delete appointments that have been cancelled, as it is embarrassing to turn up when you are not expected. If you are using an electronic planner this may update other people's diaries automatically. It is important to communicate agreed changes to those affected. This may be done by letter, telephone, fax, e-mail or verbally, and needs to be completed even where networked diary software is in place. You can guarantee that at least one person won't look at their diary until the alert lets them know they should have been somewhere!

Bear in mind when deciding which method of communication to use that issues of security and confidentiality need to be heeded. Arranging meetings for Royalty, politicians or celebrities, for instance, can have security implications. Meetings between people from different organisations may be confidential, as may disciplinary or grievance interviews.

If you do not keep the diary up-to-date, it is of no use to anybody. In fact it is worse than no diary at all, as people will rely on the information in the diary. Make sure all changes are made as soon as possible after they have been agreed. Check regularly and where mistakes happen, investigate the reasons and take steps to prevent them re-occurring.

 **What you need to know**

The procedures that are in place to notify attendees of schedule changes

What problems may occur when alterations are made to a schedule?

Why alterations must be updated as soon as possible

What steps would you take to deal with the problems?

The importance of ensuring that the diary
is kept up-to-date

Why should you take security
implications into account when
organising a diary?

The efficient planning and organising of diaries contributes to
the smooth running of the office and indeed, the whole
organisation.  Imagine the chaos there would be in the office
if everybody had to remember where they should be when,
and what they should be doing at any given time.  Whichever
type of diary you keep, coping with the changes to
arrangements and making sure that everybody has the latest
information is an important responsibility.

## A diary that is not kept up-to-date
## is just a book

# Are you ready for assessment?

To achieve this unit of a Level 3 Business & Administration qualification you will need to demonstrate that you are competent in the following:

- Obtaining the information you need about requested changes
- Prioritising requested changes
- Identifying the implications for existing entries
- Solving problems by negotiating alternative arrangements
- Recording agreed changes in the diary
- Communicating agreed changes to those affected
- Keeping the diary up-to-date

(Remember that you will need the skills listed at the beginning of this chapter and that these are covered in chapter 1.)

You will need to produce evidence from a variety of sources. Carrying out the following activities will help you acquire competence at work.

**Activity 1**
What are the advantages of electronic planners over a manual diary?

What is a diary alert?

If you keep a paper diary, how long are they stored after the end of the year?

**Activity 2**
The Human Resources Director has rung to say she won't be in today due to illness. She has a number of appointments in her diary. What methods would you use to re-arrange them?

**Activity 3**
Keep a work diary over the period of a month recording amendments you have made to your diary system.

**Activity 4**
Taking into account security and confidentiality, print or photocopy selected pages from your diary system.

## Activity 5

You are responsible for keeping the diary of the Sales Manager of a building contractor. The diary below is his current schedule for 21st July

**Thursday 21 July**

09 Budget meeting with MD (MD's Office)

10

11 Client Meeting at MRA

12

13 Lunch with Lydia Cluskey (Lydia's Office)

14 Finance meeting with Ben

15 Sales Dept meeting (Adam Bone's Office)

16 Disciplinary Hearing with Annabelle Hawkins

17 Drinks with Andrew & Cameron (The Rose)

At 4.00pm on 20th July, the Managing Director's secretary rings to advise that the meeting scheduled for 09.30am tomorrow has been rearranged for 11.00am.

The meeting with MRA has been organised for the past six weeks and they are a valued supplier.

How do you deal with the alteration to the schedule?

Remember: While gathering evidence for this unit, evidence **may** be generated for units 110, 301, 302, 303, 308, 311, 313 and 320

# CHAPTER 6
## UNIT 205 – Organise business travel and accommodation

When you or your colleagues are planning business trips you will need to organise the travel, accommodation and any meetings that will be attended. You will need to know when the trip is taking place, where to and how many people will be travelling. The effectiveness of a trip will be greatly enhanced if arrangements are made efficiently within the budget allowed.

There are a number of issues to take into consideration when organising business travel. To schedule the trip you will need to work in reverse from the time and date that meetings are scheduled. This will help you calculate actual travelling time. Remember that there can always be delays and you may need to allow for crossing time zones.

Depending on the destination there may be a number of alternative methods of travel available. Deciding which is the most efficient will require consideration of both cost and time constraints. For instance being driven by car allows you to work while travelling but may have added constraints. Each method will have its own challenges. Planning road travel requires you to consider:

- The type and number of vehicles to use (if several people are travelling can they share a car or would a mini bus be most efficient?)
- The most appropriate route
- Whether any long term road works affect the journey
- Parking facilities
- The effect of a long journey on the driver

The choice of rail travel depends on:

- How near to the railway station the traveller lives
- How far from the railway station the destination is
- Travelling time
- Number of changes
- Frequency and convenience of service
- Amount of luggage and equipment to be carried
- Ease of travel between station and destination

The choice of air travel depends on:

- How near to the airport the traveller lives
- How far from the airport the destination is
- Frequency and convenience of service
- Travelling and check-in times
- Ease of travel between airport and destination

The choice of sea travel depends on:

- Length of crossing
- Frequency and convenience of ferries
- How near to the port the traveller lives
- How far from the port the destination is
- Ease of travel between port and destination

The final decision will depend on comparing the above and factoring in the overall cost and the traveller's personal preferences – if they are a bad sailor they won't thank you for booking them on a ferry from Liverpool to Douglas in the Isle of Man in November, however much cheaper it might be than flying.

Also, consider the cost of the traveller's time. A saving of £50 by travelling by train instead of a flight may not be cost-effective because of the extra time the person spends travelling instead of working.

If they are staying overnight you will need to arrange accommodation, choosing this in relation to:

- Price
- Standard
- Convenience for the station, airport or port and the venue
- Car parking if travelling by road

If car hire is required you will need the following information:

- Driver's licence number
- Type of car required
- Length of hire
- Arrangements for return of vehicle
- Insurance details

Relieving colleagues of the need to worry about tickets, visas and hotel confirmations will reduce the stress involved in business travel and allow them to concentrate on the purpose of the trip. You will also be responsible for ensuring that they have the necessary credit cards, currency and traveller's cheques. You may need to deal with any problems that arise during the trip and afterwards evaluate the suppliers used for future reference.

 When organising business travel and accommodation you will need the following skills:

- Communicating
- Problem solving
- Researching
- Negotiating
- Planning
- Organising
- Checking
- Recording
- Managing time
- Managing resources
- Evaluating

These skills are covered in chapter 1.

# Planning the trip

Travel and accommodation requirements will be identified to you by the traveller or their line manager.  They will specify where they need to be, by when and for how long.  It may be a simple 'there and back' trip or a more complicated journey.

They may be travelling by car and merely require suitable accommodation or travelling by public transport and require a full itinerary.  You will need to confirm travel, accommodation and budget requirements appropriate to the traveller in order to make arrangements that are cost effective.  You will also need to identify any special requirements the traveller may have such as extra leg room on a plane, a smoking room in the hotel, assisted travel if they have a disability or special dietary requirements.

When you have identified all of the requirements it is a good idea to prepare a draft itinerary.  Where public transport is involved your arrangements are to some extent decided by the timetable.  Where road travel is planned, allow for road works, congestion, or other problems that may cause delays.

Check the draft itinerary and schedule with the traveller before making any firm bookings to be sure it meets their requirements.  They may have more experience of the actual journey than you.  It may be that they overlooked some detail in giving you their requirements which they will realise when they see the itinerary.  Checking before making the bookings will avoid possible cancellation charges.  Consider using on-line sites such as:

- www.theaa.com or www.multimap.com for road travel

- www.nationalrail.co.uk or www.scotrail.co.uk for rail travel or
- www.cheapflights.com or www.expedia.co.uk for air travel

There are many more sites to choose from. Your organisation may have their own contacts.

All forms of transport will require payment in advance of travel so you will need to know what payment facilities your organisation uses. Many organisations nowadays operate credit card accounts as this allows greater flexibility for booking on-line. If you make your bookings through a travel agent you will probably need to open an account with them. This will also be true for hotels that you use regularly.

 ## What you need to know

How to access information on available hotel rooms and their cost

> What websites would you use to look for bargain travel and accommodation?

Where to find flight times and prices

> If you were arranging for someone to catch a flight from Edinburgh to London leaving at 0930, what time would they need to check in?

How to use a railway timetable

> Where would you look for information about long-term road-works?

## Organising the trip

Now that you have agreed the itinerary, the time has come to make bookings for travel and accommodation. How you do this will depend largely on organisational policy:

- You may have arrangements with certain hotel groups that give you a special rate. In this case, telephone the reservations department and give them the details

of the number of rooms, number of nights, date of arrival and names of guests
- You may use on-line facilities to book travel and accommodation. You will need access to a credit card unless your organisation has an account with the supplier
- You may use a travel agent to make the arrangements for you. You will telephone them with the details and they will do the rest
- You may make bookings direct with the hotel or travel company by telephone or fax. You will still need the same information

However you make the bookings, you will need to get confirmation and a booking reference.

Now is the time to arrange any meetings necessary during the trip. You will need to know who is attending. If all of the attendees are from your organisation, you may be arranging all of their travel. If some of the attendees are from other organisations you may need to liaise with the person organising their travel in order to co-ordinate everybody's itinerary.

Check who is organising the room for the meeting. It may be you and nobody has told you! If it is you, think about refreshments, equipment, stationery and other resources or materials that may be needed. You can now obtain and collate documents for travel, meetings and accommodation.

Meetings may require:

- Room booking confirmations
- Agendas
- Minutes of previous meetings and directions

If foreign travel is involved you may need to obtain visas. These are usually obtained from the Embassy or Consulate of the country being visited.

They may take a while to be issued so application well in advance of travel would be advisable. There may be medical requirements that your traveller will need to be aware of in order that they can arrange any necessary inoculations or medication. Travel insurance will need to be arranged. Your organisation may have a policy which covers all members of staff when travelling, or it may be necessary to arrange individual cover for each journey. Again this may require some time to arrange. Foreign currency or traveller's cheques may also need to be arranged. This can be done through a bank, travel agent or at the post office.

All of these will need to be obtained and sorted so that each traveller has all they need in chronological order (outward journey – hotel booking – meeting documents – homeward journey).

## TRAVEL ITINERARY
**Fred Cluskey - Sales Manager**
**12-15 September 2005**

| Date | Time | Item |
|------|------|------|
| Mon 12/09/05 | 0700 | Train from Reading to Paddington arrive 0732 |
| | 0748 | Train from Paddington to Gatwick arrive 0845 |
| | 0900 | Check in Gatwick Airport |
| | 1100 | Departure to Paris |
| | 1600 | Arrival Paris |
| | | Accommodation booked at Hotel Georges V |
| | 2000 | Dinner with M. Simenon, Chief Buyer |
| Tue 13/09/05 | 0830 | Breakfast with Mme. Bardot, Designer |
| | 1000 | Meeting with clients at Rue St. Morgue |

In order to prepare for their trip, the traveller will need the information as soon as possible. Provide the traveller with an itinerary and required documents in good time. Make sure that when you have collated their visa, currency, tickets, seat reservations, hotel bookings and meeting information you pass them on immediately. A business trip can be very stressful, and having all of the information well in advance will reduce the stress. Remember how you feel when you are arranging your holidays. If you have given the traveller all of the information in good time, they will be able to confirm that their requirements have been met. If any changes are needed there will still be time to make them. Last minute changes are much more difficult and often incur additional cost. Confirm with the traveller that the itinerary and documents meet their requirements. You may need to do this in writing.

# What you need to know

Whether your organisation holds meetings
on its own premises or hires rooms

> If you were asked to arrange a meeting
> for 25 members of staff to be held in
> Brighton, where would you arrange it?

The hotel groups your organisation uses
regularly

> What inoculations/medication would
> you need for a visit to India?

Which countries require visas

> What is the quickest and most cost
> effective way to travel from Hull to
> Bristol?

The payment facilities available to you
when booking accommodation and travel

> What currency is used in Argentina?

## During and after the trip

In order to deal with any queries that may arise, you will
need to maintain records of travel, accommodation and
meetings.  Copies of all bookings made must be kept in a
'live' file for ease of reference.  When the trip has been
completed all records should be transferred to a 'dead' file.
Records should also be maintained of meetings booked and
feedback received on the accommodation, facilities and
catering for example, so that changes can be made next
time.

The list of problems that may arise in arranging travel and
accommodation is endless:

- Tickets may not be received; make sure you chase
  them up in time for replacements to be sent
- Trains and planes may be delayed; your traveller may
  need you to check whether connections will still be
  met and to re-schedule if not

- People travelling by car may be delayed by road-works or breakdowns, or may get lost in a strange town; in the case of a breakdown you may have to arrange for recovery and a hire car
- The hotel may have made a mistake with your booking; you will need to speak to them to resolve the matter or arrange alternative accommodation
- The traveller's luggage may be mislaid at the airport; they will need you to solve this for them while they get on with the purpose of their visit. If the visit is for several days they may need you to arrange financial assistance

If the problem leads to a delay you will also have to inform anybody who is waiting for the traveller to arrive that they have been delayed.

When invoices and credit card statements are received these must be checked carefully against the bookings in the dead file. Any discrepancies should be reported to the supplier immediately. Your organisation's procedures must then be followed to ensure prompt payment. This will avoid any charges for late payment and also ensure a good relationship is maintained with the supplier. If you need a favour, such as a last minute change of arrangements, a good relationship will make this much easier.

Detailed records will need to be kept of any problems that arose during the trip. Feedback from the traveller on the standard of the accommodation will be useful when considering future bookings. Positive feedback is just as important to evaluate and maintain a record of external services used. For example, you will feel more confident in booking a hotel for future use if you have had good reports on it.

Some organisations will formalise this feedback by using an evaluation report after each trip. Where this is not in place, informal feedback should be sought and recorded. When your traveller returns ask how it all went:

- Would they stay in that hotel again?
- Were the trains clean and tidy?
- Did all the taxis arrive on time?
- Was the meeting room set up the way they would have expected?
- Did all the timings go to plan?

The answers to these types of questions will help you when you have to book for the same person to go on a similar trip. You will know what sort of thing they are looking for. Many people will be much more forthcoming with criticism, you might have to ask to hear their good experiences.

 **What you need to know**

The records you need to keep on travel, accommodation and meetings

> How long do you keep information in a live file before you transfer it to a dead file?

How to obtain, analyse and record feedback from travellers

> What action do you take if a train ticket has not arrived by the morning of the trip?

Whether your organisation has roadside assistance cover

What are the possible knock-on effects of a delayed train journey?

Websites that may be useful in assisting travellers lost in a strange town

You are informed by a colleague whose trip to Istanbul you have arranged that their luggage has not arrived. What are you going to do about it?

Sometimes it may seem that everybody else is off on glamorous trips to exotic places while you're stuck in the office with the paperwork. Anybody who makes business trips regularly will tell you they are greatly over-rated. All they will see of the exotic location is the inside of a hotel room which will look exactly like the inside of every other hotel room. They will all rely heavily on your expertise in making the trip run as smoothly as possible. You are the one that can make their trip comfortable and as problem-free as possible. Who knows, they might bring you back a souvenir!

# You will feel great job satisfaction from knowing that you have got your colleagues there and back safely

# Are you ready for assessment?

To achieve this unit of a Level 3 Business & Administration qualification you will need to demonstrate that you are competent in the following:

- Confirming travel, accommodation and budget requirements
- Checking the draft itinerary and schedule with the traveller
- Arranging any meetings necessary during the trip
- Booking travel arrangements and accommodation as agreed
- Obtaining and collating documents for travel, accommodation and meetings
- Maintaining records of travel, accommodation and meetings
- Arranging credit and payment facilities
- Dealing with problems that may arise
- Providing the traveller with an itinerary and required documents in good time
- Confirming with the traveller that itinerary and documents meet requirements
- Evaluating and maintaining a record of external services used

(Remember that you will need the skills listed at the beginning of this chapter.  These are covered in chapter 1.)

You will need to produce evidence from a variety of sources. Carrying out the following activities will help you acquire competence at work.

**Activity 1**
Put together a copy of all the paperwork relating to one particular trip that you have organised.

**Activity 2**
Keep a work diary over the period of a month recording all of the travel and accommodation you have arranged and how successful the arrangements were.

## Activity 3

Your Sales Manager has asked you to arrange a trip to Australia and New Zealand for her. She has appointments in:

- Sydney on November 12th at 10.00am
- Melbourne on November 14th at 2.30pm
- Adelaide on November 16th at 9.00am and 2.30pm
- Perth on November 18th at 9.30am
- Auckland on November 21st at 10.00am
- Wellington on November 23rd at 10.30am

Flying home to London on November 25th. Research the cost and availability of:

- Flights to and from London
- Internal flights
- Hotels
- Travel insurance

Also, the necessary visas, inoculations and foreign currency requirements. Produce a draft itinerary making the Sales Manager's trip as stress free as possible. Consider different options based on a variety of available budgets

## Activity 4

True or false, organising business travel and accommodation efficiently reduces overall costs?

What is the main reason for controlling the budget for travel and accommodation?

Where would you obtain a visa for Thailand if your traveller needed one?

What documents would your colleague need before travelling to attend meetings in the USA, South Africa and Japan?

What would you need to check before passing an invoice from a national hotel group?

What will you have to do in ALL cases of delayed travel?

What one thing is absolutely essential if accurate evaluation is to be made of travel and accommodation?

Remember: While gathering evidence for this unit, evidence **may** be generated for units 110, 204, 212, 213, 216, 301, 302, 304, 308, 310, 311, 313, 314, 315, 320 and 321

# CHAPTER 7
# UNIT 212 – Use IT systems

We all work with computers every day. Even if we have chosen a career that does not directly involve working at a computer keyboard, we cannot avoid them; at the bank, at the shops, even in the home – the microwave is controlled by a computer and so is the central heating. Computers may be as small as your hand or big enough to fill a room. In this chapter we will be looking at personal computers and peripherals such as monitors, keyboards, mice, external drives, digital cameras, web cameras, scanners, speakers, printers and modems, as well as means of storing information. We will also look at linking personal computers together in networks, dealing with common problems that may arise, protecting your computer with passwords and anti-virus protection and health and safety issues surrounding personal computers.

All computers have certain things in common. They are, basically, calculating machines. Whatever their output, whether they be producing documents, controlling the traffic lights or operating a life support machine in a hospital, they are achieving all of these by manipulating numbers.

The 'brain' of the computer is the central processing unit or CPU. This device, hardly bigger than a postage stamp:

- Reads instructions
- Performs calculations
- Makes decisions
- Stores and retrieves information
- Moves information from one part of the computer to another

The computer's CPU dictates how quickly the computer works and which functions it can carry out. In a desk top computer it is located in a box commonly known as a base unit or tower.

The parts of the computer outside of the base unit are used to communicate with the CPU. They include 'input' devices which give instructions to the CPU and 'output' devices which receive information from the CPU. Input devices include:

- **Keyboard** - Used to type text and issue commands
- **Mouse** - A pointing device used to select words or objects on the screen
- **Scanner** - Used to copy photographs or images into the computer
- **Digital camera** - Transfers images directly from the camera to the computer
- **WebCam** - Transfers live moving images directly to the computer

Output devices include:

- **Monitor** - This is the screen that displays the text and images
- **Printer** - Prints hard copies of text and images
- **Speakers** - Allow sound to be transmitted by the computer

Other peripherals include networking devices, which allow computers to communicate with each other.  Probably the most common of these is the modem.  The modem converts digital information from the computer into an analogue signal that can travel over the telephone system, and back again.  Modems can be internal, situated in the base unit, or external, sitting on your desk.  The advantages of external modems are:

- Visible status lights, which help to find the cause if you have a problem
- Easy transfer to another computer
- They can be more easily re-set without switching off the computer
- They don't take up space inside the computer

Integrated Systems Digital Network (ISDN) is a system which enables data and voice communication to be carried out at up to twice the speed of standard modems.  Asymmetric Digital Subscriber Line (ADSL) is a high speed Broadband connection which operates at much greater speeds.

Another type of networking device is the network hub/router which connects PCs to one another, allowing them to share resources.  The computers are connected to the network hub/router via cables and network cards.  Alternatively the hub/router can be a wireless access point which eliminates the need for cables.

Computers can use more storage space than is available on the hard drive within the base unit.  Hard drives contain hard disks, stacked vertically inside the drive, on which data is stored.  To add storage space there are a number of options available:

- **Floppy disks** - These are used in disk drives which may be part of the base unit or may be separate peripherals
- **CD ROMs** - These hold many times more data than floppy disks.  They are also used in disk drives
- **DAT tape** - These are cassette tapes which can record up to 8GB, or more than ten CD ROMs.  They are commonly used to backup data using an external DAT tape drive
- **ZIP disks** - These hold more than a floppy disk but less than a CD ROM and have the advantage of being more robust.  They require an external ZIP drive
- **DVD disks** - These are similar to CD ROMs but hold considerably more data – typically 4.7GB
- **USB storage devices** - These include pen drives and MP3 players.  They are connected to the computer through a USB port

The information stored by your computer needs protection from people who are not authorised to access it.  This is usually achieved by the use of passwords.  In some situations you will select your own password, in others the password will be selected by a network administrator.  Either way, it is advisable to change the password regularly and when people leave your organisation.

The other risk to your computer will come from viruses. These are programs that enter your computer without your knowledge and are designed to damage or delete files. Viruses infect your computer through the Internet, via e-mails or through software. There are a number of anti-virus programs which can be purchased which will check files for viruses before you open them. The difficulty is they can usually only detect viruses which existed before the anti-virus programme was written, so need regular updating.

Many problems can be avoided if you perform regular maintenance on your computer software and hardware. There are a number of simple steps you can take:

- **Scan your hard disk** - This usually cleans up any disk errors
- **Defragment your hard drive** - Files get spread out over the hard disk, or 'fragmented'. This means the hard disk has to work harder to find the information
- **Back-up your hard disk** - In case of major problems occurring with the computer, this gives you a chance to re-create any lost data
- **Clean the keyboard** - Hold the keyboard upside down and gently shake it to remove accumulated dust. Use a cotton bud to clean between the keys
- **Clean the mouse** – With a roller-ball mouse, turn the mouse upside down and open the twist lock. Take out the ball and carefully put it to one side. Clean the rollers and the ball then put the ball back and close the twist lock

As well as risks to your computer, you need to be aware of risks *from* using computers. Computers can be a major source of health and safety problems. They can cause headaches, eye-strain, neck problems, repetitive strain injury and stress. Of course, it is not the computer that causes the problems, it is the use of the computer. To avoid some of these there are steps that you can take:

- Sit on an adjustable chair with your back supported. Your arms should be horizontal when on the keyboard and the monitor should be immediately in front of your eyes
- Make sure the screen is the right distance from your eyes to enable you to focus easily. If necessary change the zoom facility

- Consider using a wrist rest to prevent repetitive strain injury and a foot rest to improve your posture to reduce the risk of back, shoulder and neck strain
- Adjust the screen brightness to reduce glare
- Clean the screen regularly to prevent the need to squint
- Take regular short breaks

The Display Screen Equipment (DSE) Regulations apply to all who regularly use VDUs in their work, and relate to workstations as well as the equipment.  They require employers to:

- Assess all workstations for health and safety risks and lower the risks as much as possible
- Plan work activities to incorporate rest breaks at regular intervals
- Arrange and pay for eye tests and pay for spectacles or lenses if these are prescribed specifically for VDU work
- Provide health and safety training for DSE users and re-train if the workstation is changed or modified
- Provide DSE users with information on all aspects of health and safety which apply to them and measures being taken to reduce risks to their health

All of the above applies equally to laptops, personal digital assistants or hand-held computers.

 When using IT systems you will need the following skills:

- Organising
- Planning
- Using technology

These skills are covered in chapter 1.

There are a number of operating systems available.  The most commonly used is Windows XP so the examples used in this chapter relate to Windows XP.  Whether you use this system or another the principles are the same.

## Setting up hardware

Before installing any hardware it is advisable to switch off your computer.

If you are starting from a base unit the first piece of hardware to connect is the monitor. Cables connect the monitor to the PCs video port and the mains electricity. Most monitors plug into a 15 hole port. Turn the computer on and it should detect the new hardware. The computer will give you directions for installing drivers for the monitor if they are required.

You will now need a keyboard and probably a mouse. These plug into the base unit using connectors which may look identical so take care to plug the right connector into the right socket. Many computers colour code the connectors, purple for the keyboard and green for the mouse. When you turn the PC on it should automatically recognise the new hardware. Some keyboards or mice require drivers. If so follow the on screen instructions.

Next you will want to install a printer. The printer will connect to the base unit using a parallel port, a female 25 pin connection or a USB port. Make sure you connect the printer cable to the correct port, then connect the printer to the mains electricity. Check whether the printer has ink cartridges or toner cartridges already installed, if not install them, following the manufacturer's instructions. Turn on the computer, select 'My computer' from the desktop, select 'Printers', double click the 'Add Printer' icon. Follow the instructions to run the wizard. Print out a test sheet of paper to check that the printer is operating satisfactorily.

If you are going to use the computer to connect to the Internet you will want to install a modem. Modems are connected to a serial port in the base unit. These are usually 9 pin male connectors. Plug one end of a serial cable into the modem and the other into a serial port in the base unit. Connect the modem to the mains electricity using an AC adapter then plug one end of a phone line into the phone jack and the other end into the back of the modem. Turn on the modem and the computer and Windows will launch an installation wizard.

If you need to import images from hard copies into your computer you will need to install a scanner. Scanners need to be on a flat surface. They can be connected to the base unit through a parallel port, a USB port or via a SCSI (small computer system interface) connection. If you are connecting through a parallel port you will probably have to disconnect the printer. If you want to connect both the scanner and printer at the same time you will need to connect the printer to the scanner with a cable, then connect the scanner to the base unit. Connect the scanner to the mains electricity and turn on both the computer and the scanner. Windows will know that new hardware has been added and you can follow the on screen instructions.

You may decide to install a digital camera so that you can import photographs that you have taken. Cameras connect through a USB cable; the computer will recognise that you are adding a digital camera.

The next step up from a digital camera is a WebCam which enables you to videoconference, put live images onto your Website or send video to another computer. First you must install the software that came with the WebCam, then shut down the computer. Connect the WebCam to the base unit using a USB cable. When you turn on the computer Windows will detect the new hardware and launch a wizard. Follow the on screen instructions.

If you need to connect two or more computers and maybe a printer into a network there are two alternatives available; both use a device called a hub/router. The simplest method is to join the computers to the hub/router with cables. Turn off all of the computers before you turn on the hub/router. Plug an Ethernet cable into the port on the hub/router for each computer, then connect the other end of the cable to the computer before turning the computer back on. On each computer from the 'Control Panel' double click 'Network' then click 'File and Print Sharing'. Select the boxes that enable you to share files and a printer then click 'OK' twice. New drivers will be installed and the computer will ask if you want to restart. Click 'Yes'.

Alternatively you can buy a wireless access point and plug it into the uplink part of the network. Choose which computer is to be the primary and put the CD supplied into that computer. Run the installation software. Install a wireless network device on each computer. Use the software installed with the network device to test the strength of the wireless connection. You may need to move the base station or the computers until you get the best possible reception.

If you encounter any problems setting up hardware there are a number of ways of obtaining help. Your organisation may have an IT department, the manual supplied with the hardware will give help line details, or you can always use the 'Help' facility within the Windows package.

 **What you need to know**

The function of a modem

> What is meant by the term 'networking'?

The function of a scanner

> What is a CPU?

The function of a WebCam

> Why do you use passwords?

The function of a Network hub/router

> Why is it advisable to turn off the computer before attaching any peripherals?

## Accessing data

Data is held in files within the software programme in which it was first created. So a text document will be found in Word, a spreadsheet in Excel and a database in Access, for instance. To access data you must open the file that it is in, to open the file you must open the program. This can be done by clicking:

- 'Start'
- 'All Programs'
- The name of the programme that you want

Programs that you will be using regularly can be set up on the desktop so that you can open them with a double click rather than going through the above process. To do this click 'Start', click 'Programs', find the programme that you want to put onto the desktop, left click, hold and drag to the desktop. An icon will appear which represents the program. When you want to open the programme put your cursor on the icon and double click, the programme will open.

To open a file:

- Select 'File' from the toolbar
- Click 'Open'
- From the 'Look in' drop down menu browse to the correct location of the file *
- Click on the name of the file
- Click 'Open'

*The 'Look in' drop down menu will display the names of folders and storage devices containing files, such as '3½" Floppy', 'Local disk', 'CD Drive' or 'Removable disk'.

If you are opening a file on a networked computer, click on 'Start' and select 'My Network Places'. A list of all the shared folders on the network will appear. Double click on the folder containing the file that you want to open.

## Protecting data

From time-to-time you will want to change the password that allows you to log-on to your computer. To do this:

- Click 'start'
- Click 'Settings'
- Click 'Control Panel'
- Double click 'User Accounts'
- Click on the account that you want to change the password on
- Click 'Reset password'
- Type a new password in the 'type a new password' box

- Type the new password again in the 'type the new password to confirm' box
- Type something that will remind you what the password is in the 'type a word or phrase to use as a password hint' box
- Click 'change password'

Alternatively:

- Press 'Ctrl', 'Alt' and 'Delete' keys all at once
- Click 'Change Password'
- Enter the current password
- Enter your new password
- Confirm your new password
- Click 'OK'
- Click 'Cancel'

You will want to choose a password that cannot be guessed easily. It is best to avoid using names, dates or words that appear in the dictionary as these can be hacked. You may wonder what can be used. A couple of suggestions are:

- Choose a word such as 'tyrefitter'. Then instead of typing 'tyrefitter' type the character one to the right of each letter on the keyboard (yutrgoyyrt)
- Choose two four letter words and a two digit number, for instance 'blue47wall'

Either of these is easy to remember and almost impossible to guess. Be careful when choosing the hint that it doesn't mean anything to anyone else. For instance, 'tyrefitter' may be your Uncle Fred's occupation so the hint would be 'Uncle Fred'.

You may want to lock your workstation so that no-one else can use it while you are away from your desk. You can only do this on Windows XP Professional, not Windows XP Home Edition. To do this:

- Press 'Ctrl', 'Alt' and 'Delete' keys all at once
- From the Windows Security dialog box click 'Lock Computer'
- The 'Computer Locked' window appears

To unlock the computer again:

- Press 'Ctrl', 'Alt' and 'Delete' keys all at once
- The 'Unlock Computer' dialog box opens
- Type your logon password in the 'Password' box
- Click 'OK'

In case you are likely to forget to lock your workstation every time you leave it you may want to use a screen saver that is password protected. This means that as soon as the screen saver appears because the computer has not been used for a period of time, no-one can get into the programme that you were using without a password.

This is done by:

- Clicking 'start'
- Click 'Settings'
- Click 'Control Panel'
- The 'Windows Control Panel' opens
- Double click 'Display'
- The 'Display Properties' dialog box opens
- Click the 'Screen Saver' tab
- Click the 'Password protected' option

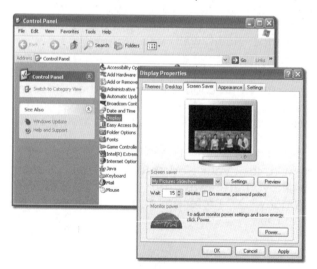

To unlock the computer again:

- Touch any key
- Enter the username and password that you use to log-on

You may share your computer and want to protect your files and folders from being opened. You can 'encrypt' them so that if anyone else opens them they appear as nonsense. To do this:

- Select the 'File' menu
- Click 'Open'
- Right click the file or folder
- Click 'Properties'. The 'Properties' dialog box opens
- Select the 'General' tab
- Click 'Advanced'. The 'Advanced Attributes' dialog box opens
- Click the 'Encrypt contents to secure data' box
- Click 'OK'
- Click 'OK'
- Choose 'Apply changes to this folder only'
- Click 'OK'

If you install anti-virus software and keep its virus database up-to-date you should avoid problems with viruses. You will still need to be careful about what programs you install and what files you open from the Internet. Never open files sent to you by e-mail from people you don't know, even if they appear to be harmless. Be careful if you receive an e-mail from someone you do know with an attachment which looks suspicious. Check with the sender before you open the attachment as some viruses spread by sending e-mails to everybody in the affected computer's address book.

From time-to-time you should scan your computer for viruses. The precise process for this will depend on the anti-virus software that you have running on your computer. On Norton AntiVirus 2002 the process is:

- Click 'start'
- Click 'All Programs'
- Click 'Norton AntiVirus'
- Click 'Norton AntiVirus 2002'
- Click 'Scan for Viruses'
- Click 'Scan my computer'. This may take over an hour
- Click 'Finished'

The other essential maintenance to undertake is to 'back up' your hard disk to a removable drive, a network or the Internet. This is simply done:

- Click 'start'
- Click 'All Programs'
- Click 'Accessories'
- Click 'System Tools'
- Click 'Backup'.  A wizard opens
- Follow the on screen instructions

 **What you need to know**

How to scan for viruses

What is a virus?

How to backup your hard disk

Why do you encrypt files?

How to encrypt files

Why should you not open e-mail attachments from unknown senders?

When to lock your work station

How do you choose a password that cannot be easily guessed?

How to open a file

How do you set up a desktop?

Take one step at a time, don't forget you can always get help from the IT department, the on screen 'Help' menu and the manuals that accompany the hardware or software you are installing and using.

## When you have mastered the basics you will be able to go on to use a whole range of programs with confidence

# Are you ready for assessment?

To achieve this unit of a Level 3 Business & Administration qualification you will need to demonstrate that you are competent in the following:

- Set up and use computer hardware
- Access files, networks and network software
- Protect hardware, software and data
- Deal with problems with computer hardware and software
- Avoid common security risks and restrict access to software and data

(Remember that you will need the skills listed at the beginning of this chapter.  These are covered in chapter 1.)

This unit is a generic unit.  The skills used to demonstrate your abilities in this unit are very specific to your organisation and as such your supervisor, team leader or manager should supervise you carrying out tasks common to your organisation.

This may involve activities such as:

- Setting up a printer
- Installing a web cam
- Locating and opening files on your network server
- Troubleshooting problems such as why a printer doesn't seem to operate correctly
- Password protecting your PC when you are away from your desk

Remember:  While gathering evidence for this unit, evidence **may** be generated for units 110, 213, 216, 217, 218, 301, 302, 314, 315, 316, 317, 320 and 321.

# CHAPTER 8
## UNIT 213 – Use IT to exchange information

One of the most exciting recent developments in the office environment has been the Internet.  This is a world wide system that stores data and is accessible by anybody with a computer, a modem and an Internet Service Provider (ISP).  It is used to access an enormous amount of diverse information via the World Wide Web (www) and to send and receive e-mails (e-mail).

The advantages of e-mail for the administrator are:

- Instant communication with people anywhere in the world, providing they have an e-mail address
- The ability to access e-mail at any time and any place
- Fast and efficient distribution of mail shots with no postage costs
- Reduced costs of paper, photocopying and postage
- An electronic record of all correspondence, incoming and outgoing
- The ability to attach documents, photographs, spreadsheets, databases and much more

Users can connect to other users wherever they may be.  An office worker can connect from a laptop anywhere in the world to their computer back in the office and have access to all the files held there.

The World Wide Web gives you access to massive amounts of information to facilitate any research project that you may be involved in.  In addition to facts that can be found on web pages it is possible to join Forums and discuss issues with other people all over the world who may have views or knowledge that you can share.  It is also possible to complete many forms and returns 'on line' for instance you can:

- Submit VAT returns and PAYE returns
- Place orders for goods and services
- Make bookings for travel, accommodation and training courses
- Place employment vacancies

Search engines such as Google, MSN and AskJeeves give you access to all of the information available on line.  Once found, this information can be e-mailed to any other computer as an attachment.

Receivers of attachments need to take great care as a number of viruses have been spread across the network in this way.  These are spread maliciously throughout the Internet and use many methods to corrupt data and 'attack' your computer.  Protection against viruses can be purchased and downloaded, but there is a continuing risk as new viruses are being developed all the time and the protection software is always catching up.

There is also an on-going problem with unsolicited e-mails (SPAM), the Internet equivalent of junk mail.  In the same way as you simply throw your junk mail in the bin, you can divert SPAM to a separate folder which will be emptied automatically.

When using IT to exchange information you will use the following skills:

- Planning
- Organising
- Researching
- Communicating
- Using technology
- Recording
- Reading
- Writing
- Problem solving

These skills are covered in chapter 1.

## Basic e-mail facilities

**Sending e-mails.** E-mail can be sent to anyone anywhere in the world as long as they have an e-mail address. To send an e-mail, open your e-mail software (usually MS Outlook or MS Outlook Express or a web-based programme such as MSN Hotmail) and click on 'New'. A template will appear.

![Monday's Meeting - Message (Plain Text)]

```
Monday's Meeting - Message (Plain Text)

File Edit View Insert Format Tools Actions Help

Send

To...    bluebirdpersonnel@msn.com
Cc...    simonthorpe@woodrowyoung.com
Bcc...
Subject: Monday's Meeting

Dear Laura

Monday's meeting has been re-scheduled and will now be held in Simon Thorpe's office at
9am on Tuesday the 25th.

Many thanks

Katie

Katie Jane
Personnel Director
Woodrow & Young
katiejane@woodrowyoung.com
```

- The cursor will be flashing in the 'To' field. Input the recipient's e-mail address (there can be more than one recipient). An e-mail address looks like bluebirdpersonnel@msn.com, for instance

- Tab to the 'Carbon copy' or 'Cc:' field.  Input the e-mail address of anybody that you want to receive a copy of the e-mail (there can be more than one)
- Tab to the 'Bcc' field.  Input the e-mail address of anybody that you want to receive a copy of the e-mail without other recipients being aware that they have had a copy (there can be more than one).  This is called a Blind Copy
- Tab to the 'Subject:' field.  Input the subject of the message
- Move the cursor to the message field and type your message

Click on the 'copy message to sent folder' box (in MS Outlook this can be found in the 'Options' menu and the message will be copied to your sent folder.  Check the content of the message for accuracy and when you are satisfied click 'Send'.  The message will be sent to all the addresses you specified.  It is possible to add a 'signature' to your e-mails containing your contact details and possibly a legal disclaimer.  Your organisation may have a signature template that you must use whenever sending e-mails.

**Receiving e-mails.**  E-mail can be received from anyone anywhere in the world as long as they have an e-mail address.  To receive an e-mail open your e-mail programme and go to your 'inbox'.  The e-mails received will be listed in chronological order.  Click on a name in the 'from' column and the e-mail will open.  After reading the message you will have a number of options.  You can click on:

- 'Reply' to send a reply to the person the e-mail came from
- 'Reply all' to send a reply to the person the e-mail came from and everybody else that it was copied to
- 'Forward' to send the e-mail on to somebody else
- 'Delete' to delete the e-mail
- 'Print' to print the e-mail
- 'Save address' to put the address of the sender or the people it was copied to into your address book

Deleted e-mails are put into a 'Deleted items folder' which can be set to automatically empty at regular intervals.  Once emptied from the folder e-mails cannot be retrieved so care must be taken when deleting messages.  Your e-mail account will have limited capacity, however, so messages can't be saved indefinitely.

## What you need to know

How to access your emails

Which email ISP system does your organisation use?

When it is necessary to keep a copy of a sent email

Can you explain the difference between 'cc' and 'bcc'?

Whether you need to print off and file received emails

What symbol is present in all email addresses?

## Advanced email facilities

The names of people that you regularly correspond with by email will have been saved in your address book. Using address books to send emails to individuals means that you do not have to type the complete email address to select that person as a recipient and that more than one recipient can be identified.

Setting up groups of email addresses can save a lot of time when sending emails to members of specific departments or grades. If you have numerous recipients that you regularly send the same email to, you can set them up as a group:

- From the 'inbox' screen click on 'contacts'. This will bring up your address book
- Click on 'Actions' and then 'New Distribution List'. Give the group a name and then select members from your existing contacts list
- When you have completed a group click on 'Save and Close' and the name of the group will be added into your address book. When you want to send an email

to all the members, simply click on the group name in the address book

An email message can have any file attached to it.  This is a convenient way of sending large amounts of information to any number of recipients.  When sending attachments, complete the email message as usual then click on 'attach' then 'file'.  You can then either enter the name of the file or use the 'browse' facility to find the file.  If you are sending more than one file click on 'OK and attach another' until all the files are attached then click on 'OK'.  You will be taken back to the message screen.  Check that the files attached are correct then send the message as usual.

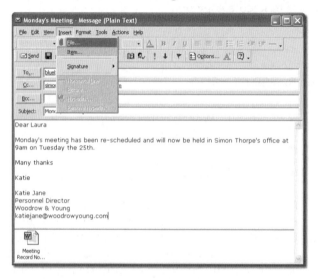

A file can be compressed or 'zipped' to reduce its size.  This can save up to 80% of hard disk space, drastically reduce email transmission time, save space in your inbox and enable you to send files as attachments that would otherwise be blocked for security reasons.  Compressing and de-compressing file attachments to send or receive zipped files requires downloaded or purchased software that facilitates this.

If you receive an email message with attachments read the message first then:

- Double click on the attachment and a screen will appear asking if you want to Open or Save the file
- Click on 'Open' to see the document in the appropriate software package

- To save the document without viewing it first, click on 'Save to disk'. You will then be shown a screen which enables you to select a location for the file

Remember to take great care before opening any attachment that comes from an unknown source. Viruses which can attack computer systems and wipe out files are often hidden in attachments. Once you have opened the attachment it is often too late.

One of the great disadvantages of electronic mail is that advertisers can flood email addresses with unwanted mail or 'SPAM'. Your ISP will almost certainly have a filter on the incoming mail to divert obvious 'SPAM' into a 'junk email' folder, but some will inevitably get through to your inbox.

If you receive an email from an unrecognised sender, or with a subject that alerts your suspicion, check with a supervisor before opening it as junk email can carry viruses which can damage your software.

Mail that is diverted to the junk email folder will be automatically deleted after a set time. It is a good idea to look in this folder regularly to check that no genuine messages have been inadvertently diverted. If there is a message in this folder that belongs in the inbox click on 'not junk' and the message will be sent to your inbox.

 **What you need to know**

How to add names to your email address book

What email group addresses does your organisation already have in place?

The value of setting up email address groups

Does your organisation already have file compression and de-compression software?

The dangers of opening attachments before they have been checked

Why should you open only emails from recognised senders?

How to recognise 'SPAM' emails

Does your organisation automatically filter 'SPAM' and junk emails?

What to do if junk emails appear in your inbox

Why should you regularly check your junk mail folder?

The potential effects of a computer virus

If you suspect that an email contains a virus, to whom should it be reported?

## Using suitable search engines effectively

There are a large number of 'search engines' available on the Internet. Their purpose is to enable you to find websites that contain the information you are looking for. Among the best known are 'Google', 'MSN' and 'AskJeeves'. Whichever search engine you choose the words you use to describe the information you are looking for will greatly affect the number of results you get. The more words you use the narrower the search. Search engines also have techniques for narrowing the search. For instance:

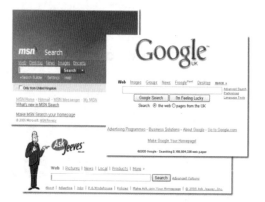

- A search for hotels in Google will produce 8,720,000 results
- Hotels in Edinburgh will produce 1,840,000 results
- Putting the "hotels in Edinburgh" in quotes will reduce the results to 67,900

- "4 star hotels in Edinburgh" will narrow the search to just 291

Having found the information you are looking for you can then send it to other people by attaching the web page to an email. If you are likely to need the information again you can 'bookmark' the page or add it to your 'favourites' so that you can return to it at a later date.

 **What you need to know**

How to select 'key' words to refine your search

> How does a search engine make using the Internet easier?

Which search engine your organisation favours

> What difference does using speech marks make in a search?

The advantages of book marking favourite websites

> If you were asked to find a flight from London to Vancouver, would you know where to look?

The World Wide Web has opened up almost all of the world's information to anybody who has access to a telephone line and a computer. Information can be shared instantly at the press of a button. As with all major advances, however, there are risks attached. If you have access to every other user in the world, they have access to you. You can be flooded with unwanted information, or receive viruses that can wipe out your work. Used with care it is certainly one of the greatest inventions of all time.

## Advances in IT have made it possible to send and receive information over vast distances in an instant

# Are you ready for assessment?

To achieve this unit of a Level 3 Business & Administration qualification you will need to demonstrate that you are competent in the following:

- Send emails to individuals and groups
- Receive, reply to and forward emails
- Send carbon copies
- Customise email formats
- Send, receive, open and store compressed and uncompressed attachments
- Manage email folders, sub-folders, address books and groups
- Send and receive instant messages
- Choose an effective search engine for the type of information you have to find
- Use efficient search techniques to find information
- Make it easy to find this information again
- Record where you have found information
- Email web pages and web links to others

(Remember that you will need the skills listed at the beginning of this chapter. These are covered in chapter 1.)

You will need to produce evidence from a variety of sources. Carrying out the following activities will help you acquire competence at work.

**Activity 1**
Find out who your Internet Service Provider is.

What command will send a received email message on to another recipient?

What is the term for a collection of email addresses in your contacts list?

When opening an attachment to an email what options are you given if you click on 'download file'?

**Activity 2**
Keep a work diary over the period of a month recording emails you have sent and received.

**Activity 3**

Keep a copy of email addresses and the groups you set up.

**Activity 4**

Search the Internet for train times from Burnley to Bristol Parkway, on Wednesday next arriving before 3.00pm. Find three trains which meet the requirements and available fares, single and return, returning the following day, leaving before 10.00am.

**Activity 5**

You have been asked to find information about Isombard Kingdom Brunel on the Internet. Search for the necessary information to write a 250-word synopsis of his life and career.

Remember: While gathering evidence for this unit, evidence **may** be generated for units 110, 301, 302 and 310.

# CHAPTER 9
# UNIT 216 – Database software

A database is an information storage system which may be held on a computer or in paper-based form. Computer databases include National Insurance records, vehicle records, criminal records and library records.

Paper-based databases include telephone directories and trade directories, for instance, although these are usually produced from computer databases these days. Databases are widely used to hold data on people. In fact there is data held on all of us on an amazing variety of databases throughout the country. Every time you use a credit or debit card to make a purchase, or visit the doctor or dentist, or fill in a form, information is added to or amended in a database.

Organisations hold data on customers that will record not only their names, addresses, telephone numbers and e-mail addresses but also their purchase history, their payment history and even personal information such as family details, vehicle ownership, dates of birth or even financial information. Different types of organisation will hold different details. An insurance company will hold different information from a retail store because they will use the information for different purposes.

The advantage of a computer database is that the information can be retrieved much more easily than it can from a paper-based system. Paper-based systems do not allow you to find all customers who have purchased a mobile phone in the last six months without searching through all the records and making a list. A computer database will provide you with a list instantly.

Database software is designed to organise and collate the related information, for instance addresses and telephone numbers or sales figures. A database programme allows data to be organised in various ways depending on the type of information stored.

These 'Relational Databases' store different types of data in separate tables within the same database. For example, a table can hold personal details about a customer including their name, address and telephone number. Another table in the database can include all of the sales made by the company. This data can then be interrogated to produce reports detailing, for example, how many washing machines have been bought by people who live in Halifax?

The features of a computer database are:

- **Form** - the interface screen where data is entered
- **Table** – where information on a particular topic is stored
- **Record** –information regarding a single item in your database. E.g. The details of one employee
- **Field** - a category for single pieces of data within a record. E.g. First name, postcode, stock number, unit price etc.
- **Data** - the information entered in a field
- **File** - a complete database

When entering and retrieving information you will need to be aware of confidentiality and legislation. The use of databases is regulated by the Data Protection Act 1998, the main points of which are:

- All companies who hold data on people must be registered with the Information Commissioner
- Any information held on computer must have been obtained legally

- Data must only be used for the purpose for which it was originally obtained
- Data must be relevant, accurate, up-to-date and not excessive
- Data must not be kept longer than necessary
- People must have access to the information held about them
- Precautions must be taken to avoid access being available to people without permission

There are organisations whose sole purpose is to collect information from various sources, collate it and sell it on to other organisations, usually for the purpose of marketing. This enables the organisation to target their marketing at the customers most likely to make purchases. As with all databases these will need to be updated regularly, to delete any out-of-date records or input any new information.

Databases are usually protected by passwords which need to be changed each time somebody who knows the password leaves the organisation. Passwords also protect the database from malicious corruption from people who may want to alter the information held.

When using database software you will use the following skills:

- Planning
- Organising
- Communicating
- Using technology
- Checking
- Problem solving

These skills are covered in chapter 1.

There are a number of database packages available. The most commonly used is Microsoft Access so the examples used in this chapter relate to Microsoft Access. Whether you use this system, or another, the principles are the same.

# Entering data

The purpose of databases is to store information in a way that allows it to be manipulated for a variety of purposes. You can obtain the data to enter into a database from a number of sources. You may be computerising existing paper-based information, or you may already have a database and be adding information to it from almost anywhere.

An existing database will constantly require updating so you will need access to the sources of information. These may hold confidential or sensitive data, and may be protected by the Data Protection Act 1998. Access to the information may be controlled by a password. If you are given the authority to setup or amend a password, use one that is easy to remember but difficult to guess. If you have to write it down, keep it somewhere that people are not likely to look for it. Be very careful that the data you enter is accurate.

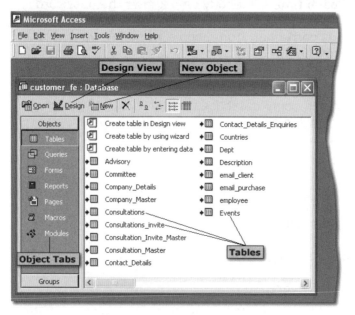

Some fields will make it difficult for you to enter the wrong sort of data, for instance you couldn't enter an address in a date of birth field, but you could enter an incorrect date of birth. This could result in someone not receiving information intended for people of their age group.

A database is made up of one or more tables. Each table is divided into 'fields' into which data is input. Each field contains one piece of information, for instance house number, road, town, county. The collected data about a person or topic forms a 'record'.

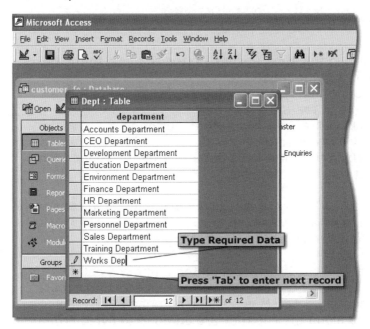

To enter data into an existing database:

- Click the 'Tables' option in the Objects bar
- Click the selected table
- Click 'Open' in the database window's toolbar
- If the table already contains records they will be visible, otherwise the table will be blank
- Type an entry into the selected field and press the 'Tab' key
- The cursor automatically moves to the next field. Type an entry into this field if required
- Continue entering data until you have completed all the necessary entries for that record
- When you have completed the record, a new blank row appears ready for the next record

In order to see all the records in a table there is a row of scroll buttons which you can use to move up and down the table quickly.

You can also use the navigation buttons to move from record to record by:

- Clicking the 'Next Record' button to move to the next record in the table
- Clicking the 'Last Record' button to move to the last record in the table
- Clicking the 'Previous Record' button to move to the previous record or
- Clicking the 'First Record' button to move back to the first record in the table

To create a new record in an existing database scroll to the end of the table and press tab or click the 'New Record' button. You are now ready to enter the new data.

It is critical that the information entered into the database is accurate, so one of the most important aspects of database work is checking data. Many people entering a list will use a ruler placed along the line they are entering to avoid errors. Some databases have cross-checking routines to prevent the input of inaccurate data. For instance age may have to be entered as well as date of birth, but these will not pick up all errors. The best check of accuracy is to check your own work as you go along and correct errors as you find them. Develop a routine for entering data that will help you avoid mistakes. Your subconscious will often alert you that you have missed a field if you are entering data in a routine fashion. If you discover a mistake in a field that you cannot amend, report it immediately. Remember the reports you get from the database will only be as accurate as the input. 'Garbage in Garbage out'.

To edit or delete an existing entry within a field move the cursor to the field that you wish to amend. If you wish to replace all of the existing data in that field simply type the new information and the original data will be replaced. If you only wish to change part of the entry, for instance if you have mis-spelt the street name in an address field, click in the field and drag the cursor across the part of the entry you wish to amend.

To delete an entire record move the cursor to the 'Record Selector' column, on the left hand side of the screen. The record will be highlighted. To select a block of records hold down the 'Shift' key and move the cursor down to the last record of those that you wish to delete. Open the 'Edit' menu and select 'Delete Record'. Click 'Yes'.

Only carry out this action if you are sure that you wish to permanently delete this record.

If the table contains more columns than can fit on the screen you may want to freeze one or more columns that you need to work on so that these columns remain on the screen at all times.

To do this:

- Click in the column that you want to freeze
- Open the 'Format' menu and select 'Freeze Columns'

As you scroll to other fields the selected frozen column remains in the same place. To unfreeze the column, open the 'Format' menu and select 'Unfreeze Columns'.

Alternatively you can hide columns that you don't need to work on, or to allow you to print only certain columns from the table. You can hide a single column or a block of columns.

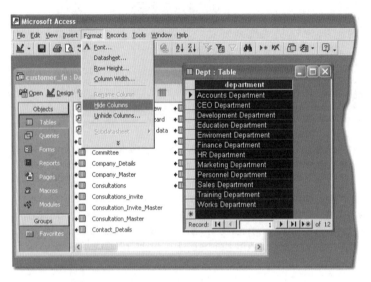

Click on the single column you wish to hide or click on the first column and drag across the other columns you wish to hide. Open the 'Format' menu and select 'Hide Columns'. To reveal hidden columns open the 'Format' menu and select 'Unhide Columns'.

When you first open a table all the columns will be the same width. You may need to vary the width of columns to suit the amount of information entered.

To do this:

- Place the cursor on the right edge of the column so that it appears like this

- Click and drag the column border to the left or right to narrow or widen the column

You may want to change the order in which columns appear. In this case place the cursor in the column title you wish to move and drag it to its new location.

If the same data is going to appear in several records in the same table you may prefer to copy an entry from one field to another.

Move the cursor to the original entry, open the 'Edit' menu and select 'Copy'. Move the cursor to the field in which you wish the information to be placed, open the 'Edit' menu and select 'Paste'. To copy an entire record move the cursor to the 'Record Selector' column for that record open the 'Edit' menu and select 'Copy', move the cursor to the next blank row, open the 'Edit' menu and select 'Paste Append'. You can also use a similar technique to move a complete record. This time open the 'Edit' menu and select 'Cut' instead of 'Copy'.

The data you enter will initially be stored in the order in which you enter it, but it is likely you will want it in some other order, alphabetical or numerical for example. You can sort the data based on any of the fields in the table.

Put the cursor in the column containing the information by which you wish to sort it. If you wish to sort the data in ascending order, i.e. A-Z or 1-100, click 'Sort Ascending' on the standard toolbar. If you wish to sort the data in descending order, i.e. Z-A or 100-1, click 'Sort Descending'.

If you want to find a particular record in an extensive table you can search for the record using any particular field.

For instance, if you were looking for the details of a customer and all the information you had was that they were in Suffolk:

- Put the cursor in the column for County

- Open the 'Edit' menu and select 'Find'
- A dialog box will open with the 'Find' tab displayed
- In the 'Find What' field, type 'Suffolk'
- Click 'Find Next'. The first entry containing the word 'Suffolk' will be located. If this is the customer you are looking for click 'Cancel'. If not, click 'Find Next' and repeat until you find the correct customer

You may want to replace all instances of an entry wherever it appears in the table. For instance if an area postcode changes you would need to change every address in that area.

Quicker than going through every address and changing them individually you can:

- Put the cursor in the postcode column
- Open the 'Edit' menu and select 'Replace'
- A dialog box opens with the 'Replace' tab displayed
- In the 'Find What' field type the existing postcode
- In the 'Replace With' field type the new postcode
- Click the 'Find Next' button and the record with first matching entry will be located

- Click the 'Replace' button. The postcode will change. The next matching entry will be located
- Repeat until the last matching entry is reached then click 'OK'

 **What you need to know**

The difference between a 'field' and a 'record'

How would you move a column?

The type of information to be entered on a database

What are the principles of The Data Protection Act?

What databases your organisation uses

Who is responsible for maintaining the databases?

Why accuracy is essential when entering data onto a database

What methods can you use for sorting information?

How to gain access to a password protected database

If your organisation had changed the specification of a product, how could you amend this in the database without having to look in every record?

The purpose of freezing columns

How do you hide unwanted columns?

How to re-size columns and rows

To sort a column alphabetically from A-Z do you use Sort Ascending or Sort Descending?

What the acronym GIGO stands for

Why is it not essential that data is entered into a database in strict alphabetical order?

# Creating database queries

The main purpose of operating a database is to enable information to be found quickly. By running database queries you can ask the computer to search through the database and find all of the records that match particular criteria. For instance, all the customers who live in Somerset or all the male customers over 18 who bought a specific make of car. You can refine the search by applying filters which specify further criteria. You may want only to highlight customers over 18, living in Somerset who bought a Ford Mondeo with cash in 2005, for instance.

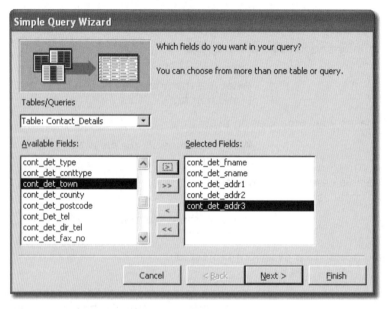

You can create a query one of two ways. You can use a Wizard and:

- Click the 'Queries' button in the Objects bar
- Double click the 'Create query by using wizard' option
- Click the 'down arrow' next to the 'Tables/Queries' field and select the table on which you want to base the query
- The 'Available Fields' list includes all the fields in the selected table. Click the first field that you want to include in your query
- Click the 'Add' button
- Repeat until all the fields you want are added, then click the 'Next' button

- In the 'What title do you want for your query' field, type the name that you want to save your query under
- Click the 'Open the query to view information' option button
- Click the 'Finish' button

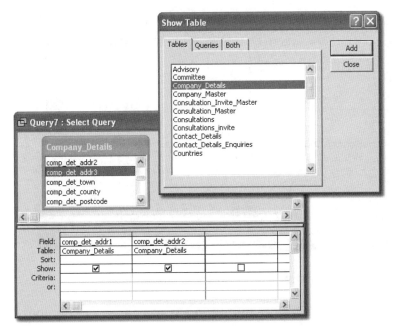

Alternatively you can start a query from scratch by:

- Clicking the 'Queries' button in the objects bar
- Double click the 'Create Query in Design view' option
- Select the table on which you want to base your query
- Click the 'Add' button to add a list of fields in the selected table to the 'Design' window
- Click the 'Close' button in the 'Show Table' dialog box
- Click in the 'Field' box in the lower half of the 'Query Design' window
- Click the down arrow in the 'Field' box and choose the first field you want to add to your query
- Repeat until the fields you want are added.  Open the 'File' menu and select 'Save'
- Type the name that you want to save your query under in the 'Query Name' field of the 'Save As' dialog box and click 'OK'

Once you have the query structure set up you will be able to enter the criteria that will enable the query to select the records you want.

Select the query that you wish to work with and:

- Click the 'Design' button in the toolbar in the database window
- The query design window will open. The top part of the window contains the tables on which the query is based. The bottom part of the window contains a grid that displays each of the fields you selected as well as the table in which each field sits
- Use the 'Sort' row to specify which field is used to sort the query in either Ascending or Descending order
- Type the value you want to match into the 'criteria' row. For instance, type 'Somerset' in the 'County' field to find all the entries for people who live in Somerset
- Click the 'Save' button on the Standard toolbar to save the query design
- Click the 'Run' button to run the query
- A table will be displayed containing only those records that match the criteria, in this case people who live in Somerset
- To close the query design window click the 'Close' button

To run a query for a range of matches (for instance, customers over 18) follow the above steps until you reach the point where you are typing in the value you want to match. Then type the criteria expression. In our example you would type >18 in the 'Age' field.

You can run a query which matches values in more than one field. For instance, you can find customers over 18 who live in Somerset. To do this you follow the above steps until you reach the stage of typing in the value. Type 'Somerset' in the 'County' field and then >18 in the 'Age' field.

When you have all the records that match your requirements you can then sort them by:

- Clicking in the 'Sort' row under the field by which you want to sort
- A down arrow appears. Click the down arrow and choose Ascending or Descending from the list
- Click the 'Save' button on the Standard toolbar
- Click the 'Run' button
- Click the 'Close' button to end the query

You can also use queries to delete records from your database more efficiently than going through them one-by-one. For instance, if you were using the database to market new cars, you might want to delete all customers who had purchased cars in 2005.

To do this:

- Open the 'Query' menu and select 'Delete Query'
- The design grid will show a 'Delete' row
- Enter the criteria for the records you want to delete, for instance, 2005 in the 'date of purchase' field
- Click the 'Save' button on the Standard toolbar
- Click the 'Run' button
- Click 'Yes' to delete the records

**Beware of this process, as you cannot undo it**

# What you need to know

How to run a database query

> If you were asked to list all the customers in the Surrey area, would you know how to?

Methods of creating a query using a wizard

> Could you enter criteria to query for an exact match?

Why it is necessary to take extreme care when deleting records

> In what circumstances would you run a database query?

How to enter criteria to query for a range of matches

> How would you enter criteria to match more than one field?

# Creating database reports

There will be times when you will be asked to produce a printed report from the information in the database. Use the techniques already described to select the range and layout of information to be printed. Once you have set up the report in the way you think is best, examine it on screen. You may want to add a heading or a date, or vary the font to emphasise certain sections. If the report is going to cover several pages, print a sample page so that you and the person you are producing the report for can have a look and check the layout. You will then be able to print off a report which contains only the information that you choose, maybe the top 100 by date of birth or those who live in a particular area. Alternatively you may be going to send the report electronically. In this case save it as a file and attach it to an e-mail.

You can create an AutoReport or create a report using a wizard. There are several AutoReports available to create simple reports with either columnar (in columns) or tabular (in tables) layouts.

To use an AutoReport:

- Open the database and click the 'Reports' option in the 'Objects' bar
- Click the 'New' button in the Toolbar
- Click either 'AutoReport:Columnar' or 'AutoReport:Tabular' in the dialog box
- Click the down arrow next to the 'Choose the table or query' field and select the table you wish to use
- Click 'OK'

A report, either columnar or tabular as chosen, will be created and the first page displayed. To look at subsequent pages use the page buttons at the bottom of the page.

To create a report using a wizard:

- Open the database and click the 'Reports' option in the 'Objects' bar
- Double click the 'Create report by using wizard' option
- Click the down arrow next to the 'Tables/Queries' field and select the table that you wish to use
- In the 'Available Fields' list click the first field you want to include in the report
- Click the 'Add' button
- Repeat until you have all the fields you want then click the 'Next' button
- A drop down list will ask you how the fields in the report should be sorted. Choose the first sort field and repeat for any additional fields you want to use to sort
- Click the 'Next' button
- In the 'Layout' area select from the 'Columnar', 'Tabular', or 'Justified' options
- In the 'Orientation' area select either 'Portrait' or 'Landscape'
- Click the 'Next' button
- Select a style from the options in the list
- Click the 'Next' button

- Type a name for the report in the 'What title do you want for your report' field
- Click the 'Finish' button

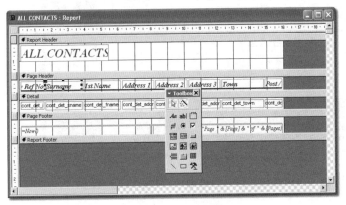

Before printing off your report you may want to make some alterations to it, such as adding labels, headers and footers, drawings or pictures.

This is done by clicking the 'Reports' option in the 'Objects' bar and selecting the report you want to amend. Click the 'Design' button in the database window's toolbar. The report opens in Design view and is divided into Report Header, Page Header, Detail Area, Page Footer and Report Footer. Items can be added to each of these sections.

At any stage during the production of a report you can amend the format of the text. There are various options available in the format menu. It is possible to format:

- **Characters** - by selecting 'font' you can change the *STYLE*, colour and size of letters, **embolden** them, *italicise* them, underline them
- **Pages** - you can change the size, orientation and margins of pages, add page numbers, headers and footers or the date and time. You can insert page breaks to indicate where a new page should begin, or columns to divide the page vertically

If you use a format for part of the report and want to use it again later, you can select 'styles and formatting' and the software will show you what you have used previously.

To add labels open the report in the Design view and:

- Click the 'Label' button in the 'Control' toolbox
- The cursor becomes '+A'. Move the cursor to the place in the report where you want a label
- Click and drag to draw a text box for the label
- Put the cursor inside the text box and type the label
- Click the 'Save' button

The placement of the label affects where it appears in the report. For instance, if the label is in the 'Details' section it will appear with the detailed information for each record in the report; if it is in the page header, it will appear at the top of every page.

Headers and footers will have been added by AutoReport or the Report Wizard. You may want to add labels or page numbers to the headers and footers, so you may need to re-size the header or footer section.

To re-size a header, put the cursor on the header section divider line, click and drag. To add page numbers click in the header or footer then open the 'Insert' menu and select 'Page Numbers'. Select the required 'Format', 'Position' and 'Alignment' options then click 'OK'. To add the date and time open the 'Insert' menu and select 'Date and Time'. Click the 'Include Date' and 'Include Time' check boxes and click 'OK'. You can add text to the header or footer by adding a new label and placing it within the header or footer, then following the instructions above.

To add a line drawing to a report, click the 'Line' button in the 'Control' toolbox, move the cursor to the area on the report where you want to draw a line, click and drag. To draw a rectangle, click the 'Rectangle' button in the 'Control' toolbox, move the cursor to where you want the rectangle, click and drag until the rectangle is the required size. To draw a straight line or a perfect square, hold down the 'Shift' key as you drag.

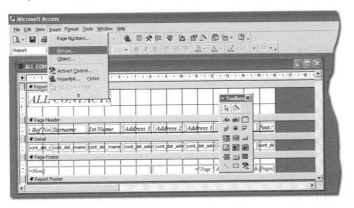

You may want to include a picture in the report such as a Company logo. Open the 'Insert' menu and select 'Picture'. The Insert Picture dialog box opens. Use the 'Look in' drop down list or the 'Places' bar and open the folder where the picture you want to add is filed. Click the picture you want. Click 'OK'. If necessary move or re-size the picture.

After making all of the required modifications it is a good idea to preview what the report will look like before printing it.

Select the report you want to preview and:

- Click the 'Preview' button
- If necessary, click the 'Maximise' button
- To look at further pages, click the 'Page' button
- To view more than one page at a time, click the 'Two Pages' or 'Multiple Pages' button
- Click the 'Close' button

Make any changes necessary then:

- Open the 'File' menu and select 'Print'
- In the 'Print Range' area enter the numbers of the pages that you want to print
- In the 'Number of Copies' field enter the number of copies that you want to print
- Click 'OK'

 **What you need to know**

How to preview a report prior to printing it

> Can you name two ways of creating a report?

Methods of adding page numbers to a report

> What is the difference between a columnar and a tabular report?

How to add labels to a report

> Could you draw a rectangle on a report?

Ways to re-size a picture that you have put into a report

> If you were asked to add the date and time to each page of a report, would you know how to?

Your organisation's protocols for naming reports

> Would you be able to add your company logo to a report?

## Managing the database

You shouldn't find many problems in actually using the system. If you do, you could be searching against criteria which the system doesn't recognise, searching for deleted or corrupted data or entering data in an inappropriate format. In this case check your manual, handbook or the program's help facility. The main problems that you may encounter are saving files with the wrong name, saving a file with a name that has already been used (which will delete the original file), or a system failure. The first two can be avoided by taking care in naming files, the last can best be prevented by backing up files regularly. This can be done by saving them onto disks and storing the disks safely, thus improving efficiency.

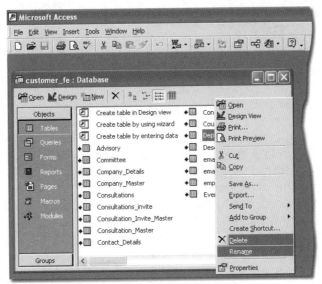

If you decide that the name you have used to save a file is wrong, click the object type in the Objects bar. For instance to rename a report click 'Reports'. From the list that will be displayed right click the report you want to rename and select 'Rename' in the shortcut menu. Type the correct name for the report and press 'Enter'.

From time-to-time you will want to delete objects from the database. Remember if you delete a table you will delete all the data in the table.

To delete an object from a database, click the object type in the Objects bar. For instance to delete a query:

- Click 'Queries'
- Right click the query you want to delete from the list that will be displayed and
- select 'Delete' in the shortcut menu
- Click 'Yes'

You may want to protect the database by giving it a password so that only certain people have access to it.

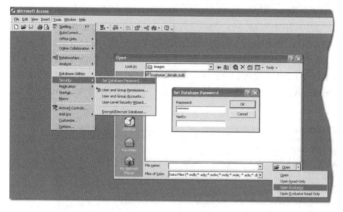

To do this:

- Select 'Open' from the 'File' menu
- Open the folder that contains the database from the 'Look in' drop down list or the 'Places' bar
- Click on the database
- Click the down arrow next to the 'Open' button
- Select 'Open Exclusive'
- Select 'Security' from the 'Tools' menu
- Select 'Set Database Password'
- Type the password in the 'Password' field
- Press 'Tab'
- Type the password in the 'Verify' field
- Click 'OK'

The worst possible disaster that could befall your database would be for all of the information held in it to be lost due to circumstances beyond your control such as a computer crash or power surge for instance. For this reason it is vital that you back up your data frequently on to an external storage device such as a floppy disk, CD Rom, memory stick or external hard drive. This creates a separate file containing all of your data which can be re-loaded should the worst happen.

**To back up a database:**

- Click the 'Save' button
- Close the database. If you are in a multi-user environment, confirm that all users have closed the database
- Using your file management system (e.g. Windows Explorer) or backup software, copy the database file to a backup medium such as a CD-Rom or memory stick

For security purposes the external storage device containing the backup files should be removed from the premises overnight or stored in a fire-proof, locked cabinet.

 **What you need to know**

Your organisation's procedures for backing up databases

Why are some databases password protected and others not?

The authority needed to access password protected databases

Does your organisation have a system for naming databases?

Why it is important to back up databases

What types of external storage devices are available within your organisation?

The maintenance of databases may appear to be one of the most routine functions of the office, but many other people depend on the database being accurate and up-to-date to carry out their tasks. Many departments could not function at all without an accurate database, and the organisation could be liable to prosecution under the Data Protection Act 1998.

**Good use of the features of databases will improve the efficiency and smooth-running of your department or organisation**

# Are you ready for assessment?

To achieve this unit of a Level 3 Business & Administration qualification you will need to demonstrate that you are competent in the following:

- Entering data
- Modifying databases
- Formatting data
- Checking data
- Database queries
- Database reports
- Improving efficiency

(Remember that you will need the skills listed at the beginning of this chapter. These are covered in chapter 1.)

You will need to produce evidence from a variety of sources. Carrying out the following activities will help you acquire competence at work.

**Activity 1**
You have been asked to create a database for a major marketing campaign in your organisation. Make assumptions about the scope and nature of the marketing campaign in line with your own organisation's needs. Design an outline database identifying the fields you are going to create. Write a brief report explaining what you have done and why.

**Activity 2**
Keep a work diary over the period of a month. Identify which databases you have been working on, the type of work you have completed and the range of database functions you have learned to use. Keep a copy of a database record you have produced.

**Activity 3**
Create a database containing at least 50 records each of at least ten fields. This can be based on any set of information of your choosing, for instance; names, addresses, telephone numbers, likes and dislikes of friends and family; the averages of your local or favourite cricket team; your CD collection; customer records not currently kept in a database. Use your imagination and see what you can come up with.

**Activity 4**

Using the database you have created set up three different database queries each matching values in at least two fields. Sort the records appropriately and print a report.

**Activity 5**

What do you understand by the following database software terms:

| | |
|---|---|
| AutoReport | Record |
| Database | Record selector |
| Field | Report |
| Label | Sort |
| Object | Table |
| Object bar | Wizard |
| Query | |

Remember: While gathering evidence for this unit, evidence **may** be generated for units 110, 212, 213, 301, 302, 320 and 321.

# CHAPTER 10
## UNIT 217 – Presentation software

Presentation software is used to produce a series of slides that can be projected or shown on a screen to be viewed by any number of people simultaneously. Slides may consist of text, images, graphs, charts, tables, video, sound and even animation. There are a number of ways of presenting slide shows. Slides can either be shown consecutively or can be merged each into the next or can be made to appear word-by-word or line-by-line.

When producing a slide show for somebody else to present it is important to listen carefully to exactly what information they want the slide show to communicate. When you feel that you have created what has been asked for it is important to check with the presenter that the slide show serves their purpose.

Slide shows can be used for a number of purposes:

- Sales promotion
- Training
- Passing on of information

The advantages include:

- The opportunity to present to a larger audience
- Reduced risk of inconsistency as the message doesn't have to be repeated a number of times to smaller groups
- Less misunderstanding as the presenter can explain the information
- The possibility of revealing information one piece at a time and checking understanding before moving on
- The ability to be delivered consistently by different presenters

It is possible to communicate far more information with the help of visual aids than simply in written form.  The detail can be covered by the addition of handouts which the software can produce.

 When using presentation software you will use the following skills:

- Planning
- Organising
- Summarising
- Writing
- Communicating
- Using technology
- Checking

These skills are covered in chapter 1.

## Before you start

You will need to sit down with the presenter and take notes so that you can remember exactly what they want.  There are several questions you will need to ask them in order to gain the information.  The first is, what is the purpose of the presentation?  It may be :

- A sales presentation aimed at customers or potential customers
- A training presentation for employees

- A presentation to management of a suggested change in procedures
- A presentation of results
- A tender for a contract
- A bid for funding
- An update on a project

The next question is, what is to be included?  It may include:

- Text
- Graphics
- Animation
- Images
- Charts
- Tables

You will then want to know how long the presentation is to last and in what order the information is to be given.  Also:

- The format of the slides
- Whether speaker notes are required
- Whether the audience needs hand outs

 **What you need to know**

The different types of presentations you
may be asked to create

What questions do you need to ask
before planning a presentation?

What questioning techniques can be
used?

What types of information may be
included in a presentation?

## Creating a presentation

In order to create a presentation you will need to use a software package.  The most commonly used package is PowerPoint, so the following instructions are based on this.

The first step to creating a presentation is to open the PowerPoint programme and familiarise yourself with the screen. On the screen you will see the Menu bar, the Standard and Formatting toolbars at the top and the Drawing toolbar at the bottom.

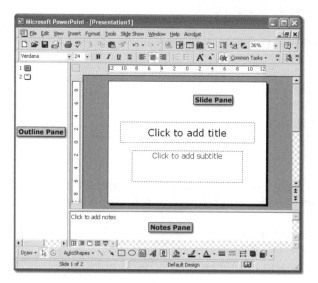

The screen shows three panes:

- The Slide Pane is where you enter the text, images, background colour etc
- The Outline Pane shows the text entered on the slides. Text can be added to or edited and new slides added
- The Notes Pane holds the notes that you may want to print for the presenter

The PowerPoint display has six views:

- Normal view where the Slide Pane dominates, the Outline Pane is open on the left hand side of the screen and the Notes Pane is open at the bottom of the screen
- Outline view where the Outline Pane dominates. This view is useful when you want to concentrate on the text
- Slide view reduces the Outline Pane to a strip showing numbered symbols for the slides. This is useful when you want to work on the layout or insert objects

- Slide Sorter view where the whole working area of the screen is used for small images (thumbnails) of the slides. This is useful when you want to re-arrange the order of the slides
- Slide Show view allows you to run the presentation
- Notes Page view shows the slide and its notes as they will appear when printed

The first five views are reached from the Status bar, Notes Page view is reached by clicking on Notes Page on the View menu.

You are now ready to start creating slides. The best way to start is to open the New Slide dialog box and select an AutoLayout. When you click OK a slide will appear on the screen. Replace the 'click to add text' with your own text. Double-click in any object frame to add an object. Text on a slide is edited and formatted exactly the same as in a word processed document, except that you cannot type on a slide. Text is entered inside a text box. These are created from the Text box tool on the Drawing toolbar, or you can start with a slide containing a text placeholder. The text box/placeholder can be moved and re-sized as required.

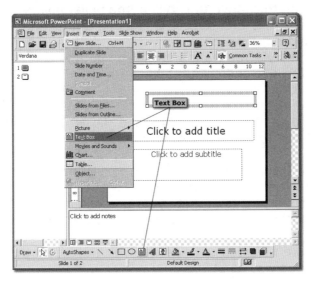

- Put your cursor on the 'Click to add text' and click, the prompt will disappear and you can type in your text
- Highlight your text using the 'click and drag' method
- Format the text by using the toolbar buttons and the font and size drop-down lists

- Drag on the outline of the box to move the box to where you want it
- Drag on a 'handle' to change the size of the box

Text placeholders come in two types – titles and subtitles, and body text. Body text initially appears as bulleted lists as this is the most likely format you will require. You can change the bullets' style, size and colour, replace them with numbers or not use them at all.

- Select a slide with a bullets placeholder
- Put your cursor inside the text box, type the first point and press 'Enter'
- This will return you to the beginning of the next line where you will find your second bullet point
- Repeat until you have entered all your points. Do not press 'Enter' after entering the last point
- Highlight all the text using the 'click and drag' method you are then ready to change the bullets
- If you don't want bullets at all, click the 'Bullets' button on the Formatting toolbar
- If you want to replace the bullets with numbers click the 'Numbering' button on the Formatting toolbar
- If you want to change the style of the bullet points, click on 'Format' and select 'Bullets and Numbering' from the drop-down menu
- Select the style you want and click on it. You can also change the size and colour if you wish
- Click on 'OK'

You may want to add images from files and clip art images to your presentation. To add an image from a file:

- Open the Insert menu, scroll down to 'Picture' this will open a further menu, select 'From File'
- Select the picture to put into your presentation
- Double click on the picture and it will be placed in the slide
- The picture will need to be re-sized or moved, do this in the same way as before

To insert an image from clip art either start from an AutoLayout containing a clip art object and double click on the object or:

- Open the Insert menu scroll down to 'Picture' this will open a further menu, select 'Clip Art'
- Select a picture from the gallery
- Right click on the picture and from the drop-down menu select 'Show Picture Toolbar'
- From this toolbar you can manipulate your picture, either by changing the colour, brightness and contrast, or by compressing, rotating or cropping your picture or by adding a border

Often you will want uniformity across all the slides in the presentation. There are a number of ways of formatting the whole presentation. The Master Slide sets the colours, text formats, images and footers that can be shown in all the slides (unless they are changed individually). You can do anything to a Master Slide that you can do to an individual slide, the difference is it will affect all the slides in the presentation. To edit the Master Slide:

- Open the View menu, point to Master and select Slide Master
- Select the title text or a bullet level
- Edit the font, style, size and colour by using the Format menu in the normal way
- If you want the same image on every slide insert it onto the Master Slide
- If you want to add a footer click into the Footer area and add your text
- Click 'Close' on the Master toolbar

You can apply a colour scheme by:

- Clicking on the Format menu and selecting Slide Colour Scheme
- Select a scheme and click Preview
- Click 'Apply to All'

You can set a background colour or design by:

- Clicking on the Format menu and selecting Background
- Select a colour from the selection on the drop-down palette
- Click 'More Colours' for a wider range

- Click 'Fill Effects' to set a gradient, textured or patterned background. You can at this point insert a picture as the background to all the slides
- Click 'Apply to All'

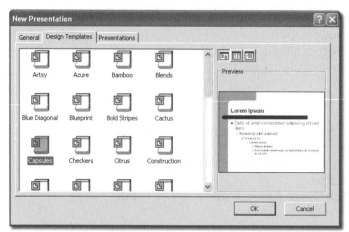

You can use a Design Template which has a background design, colour scheme and text styles. These can be used from the start of a new presentation or be applied to an existing presentation.

To start from a design template:

- Click on the File menu and select New
- Go to the Design Templates tab of the New Presentation dialog box
- Choose a template and click on it

To apply a design template to an existing presentation:

- Click on the Format menu and select Apply Design Template
- At the Apply Design Template dialog box select a template
- Click 'Apply'

It is also possible to enhance presentations by adding animation, which means that text can be made to appear word-by-word or line-by-line in a variety of interesting ways:

- Click on the Format menu and select Apply Design Template
- At the Apply Design Template dialog box select Animation Schemes
- Choose a scheme
- Click 'Apply to All Slides'

Your organisation may have a house style which they use in all documentation, stationery, leaflets and brochures. If so it is a good idea to use the house style in presentations. To set up a house style in PowerPoint create a template:

- Start a new presentation
- Edit the Master Slide adding the organisation's name and logo as required
- Open the File menu and select Save As
- At the Save As dialog box, select Design Template (*.pot) in the Save as type field
- Name the file and click 'save'

 **What you need to know**

Whether your organisation has a house style

What is the main purpose of a Master Slide?

How to change the style of bullet points

How do you use clip art?

How you can use a picture as a background

If you were asked to design a graph and insert it into a presentation, would you know how to?

## Checking and previewing the presentation

Before handing over the slide show to the presenter it is essential that you check it not only for spelling and grammar, but also for layout, continuity and that the images are of an appropriate size in comparison to the text. When you are satisfied that the slide show is technically correct and as well presented as you can make it, you will need to run it for the presenter by:

- Clicking on Slide Show
- Selecting View Show
- Clicking through the slide show

Make any alterations needed and then check with the presenter what printing is required. In PowerPoint you can print:

- The slides as they appear on the screen
- The notes by themselves
- Slides with accompanying notes as handouts
- The text of the presentation as an outline

You can select which slides to print and how many copies. If you simply want to print all the slides, click the print icon. If you want to choose what to print:

- Open the File menu and select Print
- Set the range of slides to print
- Set the number of copies
- Select the Print what option – Slides, Handouts, Notes Pages or Outline View
- For handouts set the number per page
- Set the other options as required
- Click OK

Save the presentation onto a disk and hand it over to the presenter with the printed documents requested.

 **What you need to know**

Why it is important to check the slide
show before running it for the presenter

Other than spelling and grammar what should you check a slide show for?

The printouts that are required

If you were asked to print all even numbered slides, would you know how to do it?

How to run the slide show

How can you change the order of the slides?

Modern presentation techniques have come a long way since the overhead projector or 'chalk and talk'. It is now possible to make a seamless presentation at the click of a button, rather than changing transparencies every few seconds. Most users of presentation software will use Microsoft PowerPoint, and the details above are based on this software, but there are other packages available. These will produce similar results, but the detailed pathways will be different.

## Good use of the features of presentation software will enable you to make your presentations memorable

# Are you ready for assessment?

To achieve this unit of a Level 3 Business & Administration qualification you will need to demonstrate that you are competent in the following:

- Use file handling techniques appropriate to the software
- Enter and edit presentation information
- Format slides and presentations
- Check the content, structure, style and timing of the presentation material
- Organise and present slides to achieve the required purpose and meet audience needs

(Remember that you will need the skills listed at the beginning of this chapter. These are covered in chapter 1.)

You will need to produce evidence from a variety of sources. Carrying out the following activities will help you acquire competence at work.

**Activity 1**
Keep a work diary over an agreed period of time recording which presentation software functions you have learned to use, what presentations you have prepared and for whom.

**Activity 2**
Keep a copy of the presentations you have prepared. This should include slide shows, presenters' notes and handouts for each presentation. Use this evidence as the basis of a professional discussion with your assessor.

**Activity 3**
You have been asked to produce a slide show for an important presentation. Write a report on preparing, creating and evaluating presentations. Remember to include information on how to make slide shows interesting.

**Activity 4**
Create a presentation from a design template to induct a new member
of staff to the department.  You will need slides to cover:

- Organisation mission and vision
- Terms and conditions
- Health and safety
- Job roles and responsibilities
- Working in the team
- Training and development opportunities
- Legislation and regulations

Prepare the presenter's notes and induction handouts.  Make sure the
presentation is as interesting as possible to encourage the new staff
member that this is the place that they want to spend their working life.


Remember:  While gathering evidence for this unit, evidence
**may** be generated for units 110, 301, 302, 312, 320 and
321.

# CHAPTER 11
# UNIT 218 Specialist or bespoke software

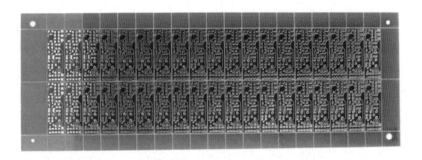

Almost all tasks that are required to be carried out within the administrative function can nowadays be carried out by computer. Some tasks such as the writing of letters, the storing and sorting of information and simple calculations can be carried out by standard software, often already on the hard drive of the computer. More complex tasks will require software specifically written to meet the needs of the business. Where the needs are fairly straightforward they can be met by specialist software; where they are specific to the organisation they will be met by bespoke software.

Specialist software includes:

- Accounts applications
- Logistics planning applications
- Computer aided design (CAD) applications
- Computer animation applications
- Digital video editing applications
- Music composition and editing applications
- Project management applications

These can be bought 'off the shelf'.

Where specialist software does not fully meet the organisation's requirements it may be necessary to develop bespoke software, that is, software which is written specifically for the organisation to meet particular requirements. As every organisation is unique it is not always possible to customise specialist software to exactly fit what is required. In this case the organisation has to commission bespoke software from a software developer. Examples of this may be:

- Customer relationship management
- Stock control
- Plan control
- Systems management
- Engineering diagnostics
- Credit management
- Sales analysis

The software developer will discuss with the organisation the exact requirements so that the software application makes the organisation more efficient and better able to provide an effective service.  Bespoke software may be used anywhere. You may find it in high volume production environments such as solicitors' offices where it supports legal case management and the production of standard documents; in local health authorities where it is used to collect and analyse data; in public authorities where it is used to manage law enforcement and debt collection; in doctors' surgeries to record data, help with referrals and provide statistical analysis.

When using specialist and bespoke software you will use the following skills:

- Planning
- Organising
- Using technology
- Checking

These skills are covered in chapter 1.

## Software application

Clearly it would be impossible to cover every conceivable application of software in the modern business and administration environment. In this section we will look at the most common applications and briefly describe their features.

### Accounts applications

These basically imitate manual accounts systems. In the same way that accounts departments used to keep a series of books, each of which had its own function, accounting software operates through a series of components which are parallels of these functions. These will include:

- Purchase ledger

- Sales ledger
- Nominal ledger
- Cash book

Transactions such as invoices raised and received, cheques raised and payments received are entered and the software completes the accounting process.  It is important to remember that every entry affects a multitude of other records.  For instance, entering a payment of a telephone bill by cheque will amend the supplier's account, the bank balance, the telephone expense code and the VAT account immediately, and have an effect on the month-end and year-end accounts.

**Computer aided designs (CAD) applications**

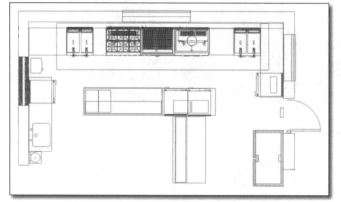

Computer aided design software greatly speeds up the whole process of design and enables testing and analysis to take place without the need to build a succession of prototypes.

Among the areas of design in which CAD has been extensively developed are:

- Architectural design
- Planning applications
- Garden design
- Engineering
- Aircraft design
- Car design

CAD helps designers to visualise their designs to scale.  This can even be in three dimensions, so that amendments can be made instantly and alternatives can be tested against each other.

The software enables you to enlarge or reduce the scale of shapes; draw circles, curves, regular and irregular shapes; select and rotate shapes; use patterns and shading and show measurements.

## Computer animation applications

Before the advent of computer animation software there were two ways to produce animated movement. Either a succession of drawings were made, in each of which the characters had made minute movements, and these were then filmed to give the illusion of continuous movement (like Mickey Mouse or The Simpsons); or physical models were filmed, then moved very slightly and filmed again until a complete film is created (like Wallace and Grommit or Chicken Run).

Both of these ways are extremely time consuming and therefore expensive. Computer animation involves drawing three dimensional models and sets on the computer. This can be done by:

- Scanning images using digital photography
- Scanning wire-frame models which can be built up into coloured and textured form
- Producing sets and furnishings using CAD

Now the finished computer animated product looks much more realistic and can actually be significantly cheaper.

## Digital video editing applications

The advantages of digital video are that it does not degrade over time and there is no generation loss. However many copies you make the quality is as good as the original. Digital video is stored in a format that can be understood by computers, which means it can be edited, manipulated, cleaned up or have special effects added.

Digital video editing software has many similarities to word processing software. It can be 'cut and pasted' without damaging the picture quality. Among the benefits of digital video editing software are:

- Improved programme finish
- Choice of programme styles
- Greater user satisfaction
- Backgrounds can be enhanced (cloudy days can look bright, for example)
- Location appearance can be improved
- People can be made to look more glamorous

Videos can be enhanced by adding text, audio, interactive menus or transition effects. This enables you to produce more interesting and effective video presentations.

## Music composition and editing applications

Music composition and editing software is a kind of musical word processing. It is used to record, edit, arrange and publish music. Generally speaking there are three types of music composition and editing software:

- **Notation programmes** - These turn compositions into printed sheet music. Music can be saved for editing or transposed to another vocal or instrumental range. Arrangements using traditional notation, guitar tablature or drum tracks can be produced
- **Sequencers** - These are used to create compositions by recording the separate parts onto individual tracks and using the sequencer to bring them together. You can start and stop at any point and change tempos or instruments at will. It is possible to produce music beyond your own ability and record it
- **Auto-accompaniment programmes** - These are basically backing tracks that you can play along with, but with the advantage of having the facility to alter the tempo. It makes practising a more fulfilling experience. You can try out different styles and harmonies, improve creativity and learn to play along with other instruments

If you are looking to create printed music you would choose a notation programme; to create CDs you would choose sequencers; to create backing tracks you would choose auto-accompaniment programmes.

## Logistics planning applications

Logistics is the management of the flow of goods either through an organisation or from an organisation to its customers.  Logistics software is used for:

- **Strategic planning** - Working out how many lorries, how many trailers and how many drivers you need, what shift patterns are needed to balance the number of drivers with the workload, the best routes to make deliveries to all the required drops in the minimum time and mileage
- **Daily planning** - Re-scheduling in response to delays, breakdowns or staff shortages.  Seasonal variations, return loads and consolidation of loads will also affect the daily plans
- **Cost minimisation** - Analysing the point at which adding further resources such as extra lorries or drivers no longer increases the profit to be made. Calculating the comparative costs of in-house servicing against out-sourcing
- **Capital expenditure planning** - Considering the impact of increased or decreased demand.  Evaluating a drop/box practice against an unload practice

Efficient use of the software enables you to see at a glance where every lorry is, what it is carrying and the drivers' hours. It enables you to react to problems such as staff sickness, road works and mechanical problems.

## Project management applications

A project is a 'series of activities designed to achieve a specific outcome within a set budget and timescale'. Prior to the development of project management software the monitoring of budgets and schedules was a time consuming activity as every variation required a number of amendments which had to be made by hand. Specialist project management software can provide:

- Gantt charts - Time is marked out in columns, with individual tasks represented as arrows or solid bars terminating at dots. The length and positions show the start date and duration of tasks
- Critical path analysis - The critical path is the longest sequence of dependent activities that lead to the completion of the plan. Any delay of a stage in the critical path will delay completion of the whole plan, unless later activities are speeded up
- Automatic or manual re-scheduling of tasks
- Cost calculations
- Time recording and task completion tracking
- Task routing to team members on completion of previous tasks
- Individual work schedules for team members

This software helps you to manage the time element of the project; the budget element is managed on either spreadsheet or accounting software.

# What you need to know

What the functions are of the various applications

>Why is the software that you are using appropriate for the task?

The advantages of using specialist software

>How do you access software?

Whether you are using specialist or bespoke software

>Is there an expert you can call on if a problem arises with the software?

# Skills and techniques

With all software packages there are certain basic skills and techniques that are required. Mastering these will enable you to produce high-quality work with whichever specialist application you use. As specialist and bespoke software covers such a vast range, it is not possible to tell you about every command in each application, but the following are basic techniques that will be found in many different packages.

## Handling files

A feature common to all software programs is the need to create, file and produce documents. Some of the general commands for these actions are:

- **New** (Ctrl+n) - This is used to open a completely blank file when you wish to start a new task
- **Open** (Ctrl+o) - This is used to open an already existing file so that you can amend it or continue working on it
- **Save** (Ctrl+s) - This is used to save the file so that the data you have input is not lost if the whole system crashes
- **Save as** - This is used when you are ready to name the file. Use a reliable file-naming system so that you can easily retrieve the file later
- **Print** (Ctrl+p) - This is used to print a hardcopy of a file or part of it

## Combining information

Documents such as reports and presentations can be enhanced with the use of other applications. Images, charts, movies and data can be imported into other documents.

- **Insert** - This is used to bring an object from one package into another, for instance a spreadsheet graph to a word processing document; text to an image file; picture to a presentation slide or simple information from a database onto a website
- **Size** - This is used to alter the size of an object
- **Position** - This is used to specify a precise location on the page

## Entering, editing and processing information

Documents and files can be easily edited by moving, deleting and copying text, images and other elements.

- **Delete** - This is used to erase data previously entered
- **Cut** (Ctrl+x) - This is also used to erase data previously entered. It can be used in combination with the 'paste' instruction to move data
- **Copy** (Ctrl+c) - This is used in combination with the 'paste' instruction to duplicate previously entered data

- **Paste** (Ctrl+v) - This is used in combination with either the 'cut' or 'copy' instruction.  Paste will add the last data selected to the file
- **Drag and drop** - This is used to move selected items from one location to another
- **Find and replace** (Ctrl+f) - This is used to replace all examples of selected text with an alternative.  For instance all references to 'motor car' with 'vehicle'

## Checking information

Whatever application you are using it is essential that you check the accuracy of the input.  Remember the acronym GIGO, 'garbage in, garbage out'.  Among the checks to be made are:

- The accuracy of text
- That figures are entered correctly
- The labeling and size of images, charts and diagrams

## What you need to know

How to choose and use appropriate tools
and functions for simple tasks

What functions can you use to move
data from one position to another?

How to select and use appropriate tools
and functions for complex tasks

What function would you use to add a
graph to a word processing document?

Techniques for handling, organising and
saving files

How would you re-name an existing
file?

The variety of specialist and bespoke software available is almost endless. Selecting the application that exactly meets the organisation's requirements will probably be the task of a technical specialist. Your role will be to learn how to make the most effective use of the packages provided. Use the manual to get the best out of the available functions.

## As with most things in life, when you buy software, you get what you pay for

# Are you ready for assessment?

To achieve this unit of a Level 3 Business & Administration qualification you will need to demonstrate that you are competent in the following:

- Use file handling techniques appropriate to the software
- Enter, edit and process information
- Combine information of different types
- Check the accuracy of information
- Save files in a format suited to the purpose
- Organise files so that they are easy to find again

(Remember that you will need the skills listed at the beginning of this chapter. These are covered in chapter 1.)

You will need to produce evidence from a variety of sources. Carrying out the following activities will help you acquire competence at work.

**Activity 1**
Write a simple 'how to' guide on a specialist or bespoke software application to help a new user.

**Activity 2**
Carry out a project that fully demonstrates the use of the specialist or bespoke software application that you use regularly.

**Activity 3**
Write a report on the project explaining the stages that you went through and the advantages of using the software application.

**Activity 4**
Keep a diary over the period of a month recording all of the specialist or bespoke software that you have used and the new functions that you have used.

**Activity 5**
For the specialist software you are using, research five commercially available alternative packages and list the advantages of your current application over each.

Remember: While gathering evidence for this unit, evidence **may** be generated for units 110, 212, 216, 217, 301, 302, 308, 314, 315, 320 and 321.

# CHAPTER 12
# UNIT 303 - Supervise an office facility

Supervising an office facility is a complex and rewarding occupation that requires the combined skills of a diplomat and a juggler – you will be expected to keep everybody happy while ensuring all targets are met.  You will have to be a diplomat to successfully handle the people involved and a juggler to successfully handle the resources.

An accomplished office supervisor will be able to talk to everybody else in the organisation from the Chief Executive Officer to the most junior staff.  You will be consulting with your line-manager, other departments, staff and suppliers on a regular basis.  Your responsibilities are likely to vary depending upon the size of office facility you supervise. Many office supervisors are responsible for keeping records of staff holidays, days off, breaks and training courses.

Clearly you will not be able to do all of this without help, so it is important that you learn to delegate.  You need to organise yourself so that you are doing your job of supervising and not doing everybody else's job for them. Your life will be much easier if you invest some of your time in developing your staff.  The more your staff can do, the more time you will have to supervise.

As office supervisor you will be required to decide which tasks are done when and who by.  The key to this will be careful planning.  How many staff do you need, doing what and by when?  Plans will need to be in place to ensure that known deadlines are achieved, and contingency plans in place to allow for the unexpected. You will need to match the existing skills of your staff to the requirements of the tasks. You will need to understand how to identify training needs and plan the training schedule.

You will also want to monitor the tasks as they are being carried out to ensure they have been done as efficiently as possible. You will need to identify any improvements that could be made to tasks in order to get them completed better, cheaper or more quickly without any loss of quality. Obviously you cannot monitor every individual task so take a representative sample. Remember the staff themselves are best placed to know how the completion of the task went, so make sure you ask them. If you discover any problems you will need to resolve them. Problems may be short term, medium term or long term. If it is necessary to offer criticism to a member of your staff make sure it is constructive, intended to improve performance not destroy confidence.

You will also be responsible for resources other than the staff. Something that many people forget to treat as a resource is time, but it is the most valuable of all resources as, although it is infinite, it is irreplaceable. Take control of your time and don't let other people's priorities steal it.

You will have a budget for resources such as office equipment, stationery and less tangible items such as telephones, postage and light and heat. Planned maintenance of office equipment may be more cost effective than regular replacement. By all means take advantage of special offers for the purchase of stationery, but don't forget the cost of storage space. It is often more difficult to manage the less tangible costs as you cannot see them accumulating, so it is much better to put controls into place to manage these before they occur than to try to cut back on them later.

If your office has equipment which is used by people from other departments, such as a photocopier, you will need to put a system in place. This system must ensure that the equipments use is controlled in a way so that jobs are carried out in order of priority and resources are not wasted by misuse.

As if all the tasks and responsibilities mentioned above were not enough, you are also likely to be responsible for the health and safety of the staff working in or visiting the office and the security of the office and all its contents.

 When supervising an office facility you will use the following skills:

- Negotiating
- Planning
- Organising
- Communicating
- Evaluating
- Checking
- Interpersonal skills
- Problem solving
- Developing others
- Prioritising
- Monitoring
- Managing time

These skills are covered in chapter 1.

# Supervising staff

Before you can start to organise other people you have to organise yourself. If you haven't already done so, instigate a tray system.

You will also need to keep a diary system, either manually or electronically, in which you can record a list of the tasks that need to be completed each day. Papers in the in-tray need to be scheduled in the diary for the day that you plan to start work on them; papers in the pending tray need to be scheduled in the diary for the day that the further information is expected.

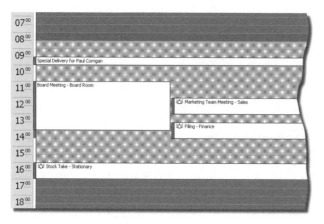

You will then be able to organise your day to deal with the tasks that are scheduled in your diary for that day. Each day should follow a routine:

- Read your incoming post and deal with each item using your tray system
- Check the list of tasks that you have to do that day
- Prioritise the tasks and decide if there are any that could be carried out by other members of your team
- Make sure you speak to every member of the team as soon after they arrive as possible; find out if they have any concerns and discuss their priorities for the day. You may find it more effective to hold a brief team meeting each day, maybe over coffee, this will depend on the number of staff and the complexity of their tasks
- During the day work on your list of tasks, but also keep an eye on how the rest of the team are coping. Experienced members of staff won't need (or

welcome) constant checking, but new or inexperienced staff will be glad of the opportunity to check that they are performing satisfactorily

- Check that you have completed everything that needs to be mailed out and it is in the out-tray before the collection deadline
- Before the staff leave for the day, check their progress against their priorities for the day
- Before you leave for the day, re-schedule any uncompleted tasks, take a brief look at tomorrow's list in case there is any preparation you need to do, then take a quick walk around the office to check that machines have been turned off and nothing confidential has been left on a desk

If you are supervising a new office, you will need to put into place systems and procedures for every task. If you are taking over the supervision of an existing office, there will almost certainly be changes that you want to make. Even if you have been in post for some time, systems and procedures may change. This could create a number of problems:

- Staff feel changes have been implemented without consultation
- Some people find it difficult to cope with change
- Changes, if not properly communicated, feel threatening

These are often caused by a lack of planning. Changes to procedures should go through three stages:

- **The idea stage** - where you, or a member of staff, come up with the idea for a new procedure or a change to an existing procedure. At this stage it will probably be a fairly vague concept but this is the point at which you should check that there are no strong organisational reasons for not pursuing the idea, whether anybody else is already in the process of developing a similar idea, or whether anybody can suggest an even better idea
- **The research and development stage -** when you explore the idea, encouraging others to offer their input and look at the costs and benefits, timescales for implementation and any impact the change will have on other procedures or departments

- **The executive stage** - when the procedure is put into place and its effectiveness evaluated

Staff will be de-motivated if they feel they have no control over changes. Their initial reaction may be to feel that they won't be able to cope with the extra work or even that the whole idea is unworkable. The most important part of implementing new procedures is communicating them to the people who will be using them. This should be a two-way process. The staff will often be able to suggest changes that you hadn't even thought of if they are encouraged to do so.

There may be a requirement for some staff training before the new procedures can be implemented. Match the present skills of the staff to the new requirements and identify any training needs. Ensure training is arranged and carried out before the start date of the new procedures. This may be a good opportunity to multi-skill members of staff, as this will have two benefits to the office:

- Trained staff will be available to cover for holidays and sickness
- Staff will feel they have benefited from the changes by receiving training in a new skill

All systems and procedures should be subject to continuous review. The attitude 'we've always done it that way' is the enemy of efficiency. You must be prepared to accept that the brilliant idea you introduced three years ago may now be hopelessly out-of-date.

Even with the best systems and procedures in place work will not be carried out effectively unless you have the right number of staff with the right skills. It will be your responsibility to prioritise the work of your staff to ensure that urgent work is completed to the required deadlines while routine work is not allowed to fall behind. At the same time you will need to bear in mind the longer term requirements of making sure staff have the skills needed to cover for each other's absence, so it is not necessarily the best idea to always give the same tasks to the same people.

It may seem in the short term advisable, or easier, to use the person who is 'best' at each task rather than bother to train other members of staff. However, other members of staff need the opportunity to gain experience too. There is also the possibility that staff will become disillusioned if they are only ever given repetitive tasks to complete and will leave. This will force you into training new staff, when it would have been easier to train the staff you had.

A multi-skilled staff will also make your life easier when it comes to organising staff holidays, days off and even lunch breaks. Wall planners allow you to see at a glance whether too many people are on holiday at the same time, or if the week you want off is available. There needs to be an agreed and understood policy on the 'hierarchy' for booking time off. This can be based on seniority, length of service or simply 'first come first served' but it must be understood by everybody. This way, people will avoid feeling aggrieved or attempting to exert pressure on others in order to get their own way. New staff will also feel the system works fairly and doesn't discriminate against them.

You will want to re-assure yourself that over a period of time tasks have been completed accurately. Before you can fairly monitor the performance of staff you must set and agree targets. As you can't monitor every individual task, you will need to take a sample that is representative of each activity. Compare the result of your monitoring with the agreed target and make sure you feedback the results to the staff. They will want to know that they have achieved their targets and, if they haven't, you will need to discuss with them what needs to be done.

Even the best managed office will have problems. Short-term problems may have to be solved immediately, without time for lengthy consideration. Medium and long-term problems should be analysed and tackled systematically. There are six stages to problem solving:

- Identify the problem
- Define the effects of the problem
- Find the cause of the problem
- Identify possible solutions
- Choose between the solutions
- Plan the way forward

Actions to correct or improve the situation must take into account all the risk factors. When action has been taken, whether the problem was short, medium or long term, check that the problem has been solved. Consider whether an alternative action may solve the problem more effectively should it reoccur. Go back to your planning and see if you could have avoided the problem in the first place.

 ## What you need to know

The office systems and procedures that apply to your job role

> Why is it important to continually review systems and procedures?

The types of problems that you are likely to encounter

> Why is good communication on systems and procedures vital?

The importance of developing staff

> What are the benefits to the office supervisor of a multi-skilled staff?

## Providing and maintaining equipment

You will need to consider what office equipment is necessary and what would simply be useful. If you decide that the equipment is necessary there will be a number of features that will influence your final purchasing decision. Your list may include:

- **Computers** - there is an enormous range of computer hardware on the market. The main factor in deciding what to purchase will be the applications that will be used, usually the more applications a computer has the more expensive it will be. You must take care that you are not paying for applications that will rarely, if ever, be used

- **Printers** - the main variables in printers are speed and quality. If you want to print high volumes and aren't too concerned about the quality, choose the printer with the highest pages per minute (ppm); if you plan to print high quality in relatively low volumes choose the printer with the highest dots per inch (dpi)
- **Photocopiers** - the features of photocopiers include speed and quality, but they also have additional features such as collating, printing back–to-back, stapling, enveloping, enlarging and reducing. Again the choice comes down to how often these features would be used

- **Telephones** - the decision is, again, likely to be based on the features of the available telephones and how many of those features you are actually going to use. You may choose to have separate lines coming in to each desk or a smaller number of incoming lines with extension handsets on each desk
- **Fax machines** - these can be thermal or plain paper machines. The disadvantage of thermal fax machines is that the fax copy will fade over time. Probably the most important decisions to make are whether to have separate fax machines or have a fax facility on

the computer and whether to have a dedicated phone line for the fax

- **Calculators** - relatively cheap to buy and fairly straightforward to choose; pocket calculators start from as little as 99p and most office functions can be carried out on a simple printing calculator costing less than £20.00

- **Shredders** - these have become much more widespread in offices in recent years as concern about identity theft and industrial espionage have increased. There are two types: straight-cut and cross-cut machines, depending on the importance of security. The resulting shredded paper can be used as packing by the despatch department or re-cycled

- **Franking machines and post scales** - the method of topping up franking machines was, until recently, to take the meter to the post office and purchase credit. Modern franking machines can be topped up electronically over a telephone line. The decision whether to have a franking machine will depend entirely on the volume of post despatched. Franking machines attract a monthly charge on top of the postage costs which only makes them  feasible for senders of relatively large amounts of post. The consideration in purchasing post scales depends on the type of post being sent. With the most up-to-date franking machines, the scales are integral

Having made your list you will need to investigate different models, different suppliers, cost and delivery dates for each item. You will also need to agree with the person responsible for the budget on how the money can best be spent. Purchases of equipment will be made from either the 'Capital' budget or the 'Revenue' budget of the organisation. Generally, Capital items are expected to be in use for more than 12 months while Revenue items will be consumed in a shorter time.

It is important to choose your suppliers with care. You will need to take a number of things into consideration including:

- Price
- Customer service
- The technical support offered

You may have difficulty finding one supplier who stands out in all of these so you will need to consider which is most important. This may differ from one piece of equipment to another. In some circumstances price will be all-important, in others service, in still others technical support may be crucial.

Remember that to the supplier, you are the customer. Long-term relationships can be beneficial to both parties, a regular customer can expect an efficient and effective service. There may appear to be short-term benefits from switching suppliers to take advantage of special offers. However, when you need urgent deliveries, you will be in a much better situation if you are known to the supplier. Similarly if your organisation operates group purchasing arrangements with suppliers, you may put their terms in jeopardy if you don't use them.

Any organisation considering purchasing or replacing office equipment will have allocated a budget for the purpose. Purchase of some Capital items may be subject to the submission of tenders by potential suppliers. Tendering is a process by which acceptable suppliers are given the opportunity to offer a price for the supply of goods or services. Each supplier completes a tender document which is returned to the purchasing organisation in a sealed envelope by a fixed date. On the agreed date all tenders are opened and compared and the successful supplier identified.

If you are responsible for placing the orders you will need to ensure that the total cost is within the budget. Remember the total cost may include delivery, insurance, VAT (if your organisation is not VAT registered), disposal of the existing equipment and the purchase of consumables. You will also need to consider maintenance costs. Some items may benefit from a planned programme of maintenance, others can be repaired as required. It is important to remember that all equipment benefits being treated carefully and as per the manufacturers instructions.

Staff will need information and training on equipment, if they have not used it before. This may be provided in-house, whether by you, an experienced member of staff, or the training department. Alternatively the supplier of the equipment or a specialised trainer may provide the training. Some employers use distance learning or web-based learning to familiarise staff with new equipment. Where incorrect use of the equipment in situ may be dangerous or expensive, off-the-job training may be necessary. Selecting a training provider should be subject to the same considerations as selecting equipment.

Staff must also be trained to consider the next user of each piece of equipment after they have finished using it. For instance, the photocopier, printer and fax machine all have ink and paper that can run out. The franking machine has credit which reduces with each run and disks need to be removed from the computer after you have finished using them. It is also important to make sure the area around the machine and the machine itself are left in a tidy manner. Keep paper clips tidy, put used paper into the recycling box and remove originals from the photocopier.

# What you need to know

The equipment required in your
organisation

> What factors do you take into account
> when deciding the technical
> specification of a new printer?

The suppliers your organisation has
contracts with

> What criteria should be taken into
> consideration when selecting a supplier
> for replacement office equipment?

The procedure for raising purchase orders
within your organisation

> Who has the authority to sign purchase
> orders in your organisation?

The budget holder for office equipment in
your organisation

> What would be the impact of failing to
> take the budget into consideration
> when making purchasing decisions?

The in-house training facilities available
within your organisation

> What criteria should be taken into
> consideration when selecting a supplier
> for training on new office equipment?

## Managing the facilities

When the facilities are in place you will be responsible for
making the best use of them. You will need to ensure that, if
training is required before the equipment can be competently
used, only fully trained staff operate it. Equipment should be
positioned so that it can be used without disrupting other
people.

There is a lot of valuable equipment in the office. It should
only be used by staff trained and authorised to use it.
Damage may be caused by untrained staff, or costs incurred

through wastage. Unauthorised use of telephones, franking machines or photocopiers, for instance, will put a strain on your budget which you may have difficulty in identifying. Unauthorised use may be personal use or staff from other departments using your facilities rather than their own. Many modern photocopiers allow for different user codes to be set up so that costs can be correctly allocated.

In order to get the best use out of equipment, it may be necessary to schedule access to it. Every user believes that their job is the most important one and that they will all want their job done now! It will take all of your tact and diplomacy to convince them that, if they have to wait, they are not being unfairly treated. The art here is to educate the user to appreciate what is possible. Make sure that your decisions are scrupulously fair, and that you can demonstrate that priority is given to the task of greatest benefit to the whole organisation. Always seek agreement rather than confrontation. This should allow for the urgency or importance of the task over the seniority of the would-be user.

Make sure you have a contingency plan for breakdowns. It is too late to say 'what do we do now?' when the breakdown occurs. You should already have decided what you are going to do if it occurs.

While everyone has a responsibility for their own personal health, safety and security you have an overall responsibility for your colleagues and visitors. There are rules for health and safety, controlling hazardous substances and the safe use of equipment. You will need to carry out a risk assessment identifying hazards and risks, particularly those arising from the installation and use of new equipment. Further information on carrying out risk assessments can be found in chapter 2.

Fires can start from small beginnings and become uncontrollable within minutes. There must be adequate means of escape. Staff must be regularly trained in fire evacuation, and visitors must be made aware of the sound of the fire alarm and position of fire exits. All accidents, no matter how small, must be entered in an accident book. Staff must know who the trained first-aiders are.

Security systems must be in place to protect the equipment, peripherals, consumables and information from theft. Equipment can be marked with the organisation's name to deter theft and increase the possibility of recovering stolen property. A system requiring staff to sign out equipment they are removing from the premises will deter the possibility of staff theft. Where large amounts of expensive consumables are stored on the premises a stock control system may be required.

To protect information from theft, paper files may be stored in locked cabinets. Electronic files may be password protected. If you are responsible for storing the files, you must be sure that only authorised people have access to them and that you follow agreed procedures and legislation for maintaining security and confidentiality. If somebody asks you to show them records that you are not sure they are allowed to see, always check before allowing them access.

Before leaving at the end of the day check that your computer is switched off, all files and papers are secured and cabinets are locked. If you are the last person to leave the office, check that everybody else's computers are switched off, there is nothing left on the desks of a confidential nature, cabinets are locked, windows are closed and lock the door behind you setting any necessary alarms.

Most crime is opportunistic – don't give criminals the opportunity.

# What you need to know

Why health and safety is important in an office environment?

Who is responsible for health and safety in the office?

The security measures in place in your organisation

Why is it important to have a contingency plan in case of breakdown?

How to diplomatically prioritise the use of office facilities

What factors need to be taken into consideration when deciding the best position for office equipment?

Having taken into consideration everything that you have now learned and put it into practice, you should have the best run office in the organisation. Your staff will be happy, well trained and content. Your equipment will be the best cared for and therefore the most efficient. The performance and productivity of your office should improve.

## Expect the unexpected and you will be ready for it and know how to deal with it successfully

# Are you ready for assessment?

To achieve this unit of a Level 3 Business & Administration qualification you will need to demonstrate that you are competent in the following:

- Identify, agree and maintain office facilities
- Co-ordinate the use of office resources
- Implement, communicate and review office systems and procedures
- Make sure office equipment is serviceable and the necessary consumables are available
- Build and maintain relationships with suppliers
- Review the office environment in line with health, safety and security policies
- Resolve problems effectively
- Provide information and guidance on office facilities
- Agree priorities with users
- Control use of office facilities
- Build and maintain relationships with other departments in your organisation
- Use a proactive rather than reactive approach to office management, think ahead
- Ensure the correct working environment for your department
- Remember your job is to support the work of the organisation, not just to run an office

(Remember that you will need the skills listed at the beginning of this chapter. These are covered in chapter 1.)

You will need to produce evidence from a variety of sources. Carrying out the following activities will help you acquire competence at work.

**Activity 1**
Review the systems and procedures for which you are responsible. Identify opportunities to make practical changes that will improve them. Draw up a plan to implement the changes. The plan needs to include the benefits you expect, total costs and the amount of time it will take for the plan to be cost neutral.

**Activity 2**
Communicate the plan that you have drawn up in Activity 1 to all affected staff and seek their feedback. Evaluate the feedback and amend the plan. Present the amended plan to your line manager. Obtain their feedback.

**Activity 3**
Carry out a review of the existing facilities in your office. Identify where there is a need to replace, upgrade or remove any equipment. Consider whether the repositioning of equipment will improve the efficiency of the office. Write a report analysing your findings and making your recommendations.

**Activity 4**
Carry out a risk assessment of the area for which you are responsible. Cover risks associated with people, equipment, space, workflow, information, security, health and safety.

**Activity 5**
Ask your line manager to suggest a realistic budget for the replacement of the equipment currently in use in your office. Research the replacement requirements. Identify the range of alternative options. Make a selection based on your budget and the functions and features needed in your office. Ask your line manager to review your findings.

Remember: While gathering evidence for this unit, evidence **may** be generated for units 110, 301, 302, 304, 319, 320 and 321.

# CHAPTER 13
# UNIT 304 – Procure products and services

The main purpose of procurement is to purchase the right quality of products and services, at the right time, in the right quantity, from the right source and at the right price. A more all-encompassing definition of the role of the procurement professional is to:

- Consistently supply products and services to meet the needs of the organisation
- Research new sources of supply to meet future requirements
- Co-operate with other departments within the organisation
- Develop policies and procedures
- Train staff
- Select the best available suppliers
- Maintain relationships with suppliers which ensure continuity of supply
- Monitor market trends
- Negotiate effectively
- Obtain the best possible value for money

The diagram on the next page shows some of the relationships between the individual activities involved in purchasing.

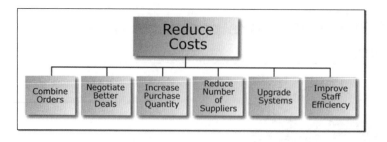

The procurement of products and services is more important in some organisations than in others. However, the contribution made to the overall profit of an organisation by improved efficiencies in purchasing is much greater than the contribution made by a similar improvement in sales.

An organisation with a profit ratio of 10% which spends 50% of its turnover on products and services aiming to increase its profit margin can achieve the same result by either increasing its turnover by 25% or by reducing its spending by 5%. This is explained by remembering that every pound not spent is a pound extra profit, but every extra pound earned incurs costs and is therefore less than a pound extra profit.

Traditionally procurement has been seen as simply purchasing. The role consisted of finding a supplier able and willing to provide goods or services in exchange for a given price. The object of the exercise was to procure the required goods or services for the best possible price

In recent years buyers have developed relationships with suppliers that are mutually beneficial. This encourages the sharing of resources such as technology with the aim of providing additional value for both parties. Overlapping interests are identified and additional efficiencies can be achieved driving down the costs to the purchaser while maintaining the profit margin of the supplier.

Purchasers will not want to enter into this kind of relationship with every supplier. According to Pareto's Law, 20% of suppliers will supply 80% of an organisation's needs. It is with this 20% that the relationship will be beneficial.

The inexperienced buyer will look at purchase price as being the most important factor in carrying out their responsibilities efficiently. However, the experienced buyer will know that their overall role involves working with others in the organisation to control, and wherever possible, reduce costs. Additional, and therefore unnecessary, costs can be incurred by:

- Over-specification
- Duplication of services
- Specifying non-standard items unnecessarily
- Over-packaging
- Increased transport costs resulting from poor design

What may appear to be a bargain purchase price can lead to a greatly increased total acquisition cost when items, such as customs duty, storage, transport, inspection, repair or replacement of faulty items are added.

The buying price is only the tip of the iceberg; all the additional costs are hidden. The effective procurer will take all the costs into account when procuring products and services.

 When procuring products and services you will use the following skills:

- Communicating
- Researching
- Problem solving
- Monitoring
- Evaluating
- Negotiating

These skills are covered in chapter 1.

# Sourcing products and services

Although every purchase order will specify what is to be supplied, by when and at what price, formal detailed specifications are not drawn up for the majority of purchases. It is likely that the required product or service is commercially available from a number of suppliers at an acceptable price. The purchasing department simply selects their requirements from those available. Some products or services are more specialised, either technically or in terms of availability. It is a part of the purchasing department's responsibility to specify exactly what is required. Where national or international standards apply to the items being purchased these are often used as the quality specification.

Obviously this is not done in isolation. The purchasing department will liaise closely with other departments to determine the final specification. If the products are for resale, for instance, the marketing and sales departments will have a major contribution to make. If the product is for use in manufacture, the production department will be heavily involved. The purchasing department's role is to provide commercial expertise, advising what is available, in what time-scale and at what price, to temper the purely technical expertise which would possibly specify the best possible product rather than the most commercially viable.

Specifications will usually state a 'tolerance', both in the quantity and quality of products to be supplied as marginal costs can have a significant effect on unit price. The purchasing department will also remain in touch with changing situations and market prices. They will be able to advise when the specification of a product or service should be amended to meet new conditions.

Having specified the products or services that are required, it is then necessary to source the product. Some products will have been supplied on a continuous basis by the same supplier, perhaps perfectly satisfactorily, but you should be constantly on the alert for alternative sources that may reduce costs without compromising quality. While the final decision may often be to remain with the same supplier for regularly purchased items, the process of sourcing products and services should still be followed.

Potential suppliers can be found through:

- **Recommendation** - Other buyers in your organisation or in your network of contacts with other organisations may be able to give you the details of suppliers that have satisfactorily supplied similar needs in the past
- **Past history** - There may be suppliers who have previously supplied you with similar products or services
- **Registration with British Standards Institute (BSI) or similar** - The BSI website gives access to certificated and kite-marked organisations
- **Catalogues and Price Lists** - Most purchasing departments maintain a library of useful material provided by potential suppliers
- **Trade Directories** - Many trades and professions publish directories containing details of suppliers
- **Agencies** - There are organisations whose sole business is to source potential suppliers for other organisations
- **The Internet** - Suppliers of just about every product and service imaginable internationally can be found on the Internet

Once a short-list of those suppliers who appear capable of meeting the specification is made, assessment of their actual strengths and weaknesses can be undertaken. There are a number of considerations:

- **Past performance** - Where you have used the supplier before, you will already know their quality
- **Reputation** - Where you have received recommendations from others you will be able to make a judgement on the supplier's potential
- **Visiting the potential supplier's premises** - This is critical when considering previously unknown suppliers for particularly expensive, or particularly important, products or services. A company that appears on its website to be well established and based in high quality premises could prove to be working from a shed in the proprietor's garden. While this should not automatically debar them from being given an order (after all some businesses which start in sheds go on to be market-leaders, and their overheads will certainly be comparatively low), you need to know the scale of organisation you are dealing with
- **Requesting and analysing samples** - Where you are planning to place an order for a large quantity, or long-term supply, of products or services, it is often useful to order (or request free of charge) a small quantity, so that you can test their suitability before committing your organisation fully

The amount of investigation you carry out into potential suppliers will depend largely on the volume and level of possible expenditure. To quote Pareto again, 80% of your budget will be spent on 20% of the products and services purchased, so the suppliers of these will obviously receive the majority of your attention.

Where you have little or no previous experience of procurement, it is obviously important to make a concentrated effort to find the right supplier. If you make a mistake there can be expensive repercussions. Similarly purchases of non-standard items which the supplier may have no experience of providing will also justify time spent in investigation.

The areas you will be investigating include:

- **Quality** - Can the potential supplier consistently deliver to a level of quality that will satisfy your organisation? Discussions to assess their understanding of the specification and their past record in achieving similar quality will help to inform your opinion

- **Quantity** - Can the potential supplier deliver the quantity of products or services that you require? One of the criteria here will be financial stability. A supplier who is unable to pay his bills on time will not be able to operate successfully. If you place an order with a supplier who ceases to trade before meeting their commitment you will be left searching desperately for a replacement at short notice

- **Timing** - Many organisations work to a 'Just-In-Time' (JIT) system which reduces the need for investing money or space in holding stock. You will need to be confident that your chosen supplier can meet the scheduled deliveries if a consistent supply is to be available

- **Service** - Obviously after-sales service is important. The availability of repairs and planned maintenance on plant and machinery or office equipment may over-ride considerations of initial price. Before-sales service is important for some products and services. Can you make contact with the person you need to talk to at the suppliers? Are quotations delivered when promised? Is technical support available? All of these will affect your view of the potential supplier's reliability

- **Price** - As mentioned earlier, the question of price is not entirely based on the purchase price. You should look at the total acquisition cost, taking into account all of the factors which add to the total cost, when comparing competing suppliers' quotations

Once you have completed the investigation of all of the suppliers identified, you will be in a position to make the decision about which supplier, or suppliers, to place an order with. The first decision to make is whether to place the order with a single supplier or to split the order across two or more. For some products and services it will clearly make sense to choose a single supplier. There may be only one able to meet your specification in an acceptable time, at an acceptable price and with an acceptable level of service. You may be placing an order for a quantity which would not be viable if split between two or more suppliers. For others it will clearly make sense to spread the order.

For those orders that fall between the two extremes, you should consider the following possibilities that could be affected by your decision:

- If you are the major purchaser of the goods and services in that particular market, placing your whole order with one supplier may lead to the closure of the other suppliers and creates a monopoly
- If you place your order with a single supplier you may get a better price based on quantity. If you place your order with several suppliers you could get a better price based on competition
- If you place your order with a single supplier you may be able to schedule deliveries easily as you only have one supplier to deal with. If you place your order with several suppliers you will be protected from the risk of disruption of supply should something go wrong with one supplier's distribution
- If you place your order with a single supplier they will be motivated to go out of their way to fulfil your requirements. On the other hand, they may become complacent and begin to fail to fulfil your requirements

Having reduced your list of potential suppliers to one (or maybe more) you will then want to negotiate with the selected suppliers to ensure that you obtain the best value for your organisation's money. Negotiations may be based on one issue or many, held on a one-to-one basis or between teams. The negotiation may be conducted over the telephone and concluded in a matter of minutes or they may be conducted face-to-face over a prolonged period.

Negotiation takes place in three phases, preparation, discussion and implementation. Any failures mainly occur in the preparation and implementation stages. The amount of time allocated to preparation will depend upon the complexity and importance of the negotiation. There are four key issues to be identified when preparing to negotiate:

- What is it you want to achieve?
- How important is each of your identified wants in relation to each of the others?
- What is your opening bid?
- What is your walk-away position?

There will be a number of things you want to achieve. Unless you are extremely lucky (or in a position of extreme relative strength) you will not achieve all of the things you want. You will, therefore, need to identify (for yourself) the relative importance of each and decide which you are prepared to concede to achieve the others. You will also need to identify your starting position. As this is going to be the best you can hope to achieve you will need to give this serious consideration before disclosing it. This applies to all of the conditions of the purchase, quality, quantity, timing, service and price. Once you have stated what you are willing to accept, you will be negotiating towards less acceptable terms not better. You must also have decided (but not revealed) the point on each of these conditions beyond which you will not negotiate. This is the least you are willing to accept.

The second part of the preparation stage is to try to establish what the other side's position is likely to be on the same issues and to establish some common ground from which negotiation can start. Negotiations are best carried out in an atmosphere which encourages agreement. If negotiations are taking place face-to-face:

- Make sure you arrive on time
- Start the negotiation by confirming those areas that are already agreed
- Be seen to be listening to the other party
- Avoid making quick decisions

You will be trying to find out what the other side is looking for and encouraging them to state their opening bid before you are put in a position of stating yours. This is because you will be hoping that their opening bid offers you a better deal than you were going to ask for. The normal situation, however, will be that your opening bid and theirs will leave a gap to be negotiated.

The discussion stage should not start with an argument. Arguments do not move negotiations forward. Both sides should be suggesting solutions to overcome problems. This will move the negotiation into the bargaining stage where one side offers to give up one of their wants in exchange for a concession from the other side. For instance, the supplier may offer to reduce the unit price in exchange for a longer delivery time. You will have already decided during the preparation stage the relative importance of price and delivery and will be able to respond to this offer accordingly.

There are recognised ploys used by experienced negotiators. The problem with ploys is other experienced negotiators recognise them for what they are and have developed counters to them. Examples of well known ploys and their counters are:

- **Good cop/bad cop** - Two members of a team operate as one difficult to negotiate with, the other looking for an agreement. Their plan is to make you accept the offer put forward by the 'good cop' because it is so much better than that being insisted on by the 'bad cop'. The counter is to adopt a similar strategy
- **The builder strategy** - You want to negotiate a price that includes everything. They want to negotiate a price for the basic job and advise you of extra costs as they are incurred. The counter is to make your specification extremely detailed
- **The double-glazing salesman ploy** - They put forward what sounds like an attractive offer but impose a strict deadline on your acceptance. The counter is to make it clear from the beginning what your time frame is for making the decision
- **The lesser of two evils** - They give you a choice between two offers, one of which is so terrible that you will accept the other which, although bad, is not as bad. The counter is to refuse to accept either and offer to go elsewhere
- **The 'shirt off my back' approach** - They try to convince you that even your best offer is so unreasonable that they would be left in an impossible

position if they accepted it. The counter is to make your best offer and stick to it

The end of the discussion stage is agreement. It is possible that the agreement will be that you can't come to an agreement. Both of you will have to walk away and the process begins again. Hopefully though, you will reach a stage where both sides have a deal which is better than their walk-away position and as near as possible to their opening bid. Make sure the agreement is put in writing and signed by both parties so there can be no confusion over what was agreed.

The negotiation then moves to its final phase, implementation. No negotiation is complete until the agreement has been fulfilled. Until you have taken delivery of the products or services which you have negotiated at the price, time, quantity, quality and with the service agreed, negotiations are not complete. Any failure to meet the agreed terms will require the re-opening of negotiations. A wise procurer will ensure that penalties for failure to meet the obligations on the part of the supplier are included in the contract or purchase order.

 **What you need to know**

The role of a professional procurer

> Why is the contribution from improved efficiency in purchasing greater than that from an equivalent improvement in sales?

How to develop mutually beneficial relationships with suppliers

> How does purchase price differ from total acquisition cost?

How to specify products and services

> Why should you consider changing suppliers whenever a new order is raised?

Who to liaise with when specifying
products and services?

> Within your organisation, what sources
> are used to identify potential new
> suppliers and how are they assessed?

The phases of negotiation

> How may you investigate potential new
> suppliers?

Common negotiation ploys and their
counters

> Why negotiations are not complete
> until agreements are implemented?

## Purchasing products and services

Except in very small organisations or particularly minor
transactions you will want to raise paperwork to officially
place a purchase order with a supplier. This may not, in
practice, be a piece of paper with 'Purchase Order' written
across the top as it once would have been. In more recent
times orders are often placed electronically over the Internet,
but some form of agreement must be raised between the
purchaser and the supplier. In cases of high-value or
complex purchases a contract may be used as the purchase
order. Sam Goldwyn famously said, 'a verbal contract is not
worth the paper it's written on' and while that is not legally
accurate, as a verbal contract is as binding as a written one,
it is not advisable to rely on a handshake as a confirmation of
agreement.

The purpose of the purchase order is to define what the
purchaser is committed to accept and pay for. The goods
receiving department will be given a copy of all purchase
orders and instructed only to accept deliveries against an
outstanding order. A copy is also often sent to the Purchase
Ledger department with instructions that invoices should only
be paid against an official order and delivery note.

**PG Corrigan Associates**          **Purchase Order**

Treacle Mine
21 Humber Ave
London
SW17 3NW

PO Number - Date
000200619713 - 09/01/2006

Any Queries please contact
Isobel Randall

Our Ref
Treacle Mine Web

Please deliver to:

Isobel Randall
PG Corrigan Associates
10-11 Corporation Rd
Leeds
LS1 3NT

Invoices should quote the PO number and be sent to:
Accounts payable Department
PG Corrigan Associates
10-11 Corporation Rd
Leeds
LS1 3NT

Please supply the undermentioned goos or services to the specified address in accordance with
instructions below and conditions of purchase overleaf.

A delivery note must accompany the goods.

| Description | Delivery Date | Order Qty | Unit | Price per unit | Net Value |
|---|---|---|---|---|---|
| Promo Mini-Site | 10/02/06 | 1 | N/A | £750.00 | £750.00 |

| | |
|---|---|
| Total net item excl VAT GBP | £750.00 |

A contract may cover a number of orders over a period of time or a geographical area. Contracts are often made renewable annually to allow the purchasing department to review the supplier's performance. It is a good idea to stagger the renewal dates of annual contracts to avoid being faced with renewing all contracts every December.

Signatures on contracts and orders are binding on the organisation. In most organisations different levels of staff will have authority to sign based on the value of the agreement. It is your responsibility to know what the limit of your authority to sign documents is and to ensure that you do not exceed it.

The purchase of products and services is not complete until delivery has been satisfactorily made. The purchasing department will need to be advised of deliveries received against orders to track the supplier's performance against the original agreement. Deliveries are checked against the purchase order and some form of goods received note produced. Often this will be raised electronically rather than on paper. Where goods do not meet the purchaser's specification this will be noted by the receiving department and arrangements will need to be made with the supplier for their disposal. The method of disposal will depend on the agreement made between the purchaser and the supplier at the time of the order.  Methods will include:

- Return to the supplier for credit
- Acceptance at a reduced price
- The goods being scrapped by the receiver and a credit note raised by the supplier

The next step in the procedure is the arrival of the invoice. This will be checked against the purchase order and the delivery note and, if everything is satisfactory, payment arranged.  Invoice authorisation may be carried out by the accounts department or the purchase department.

There are circumstances in which the normal purchasing procedures will not apply.  Processing large numbers of small orders is often not an efficient system as the administration cost may be disproportionate to the value of the order.  An organisation that operates from a large number of sites may place a blanket order with a supplier for an unspecified quantity of an item to be delivered as and when requested by any of the sites.  Invoices will then be raised against the deliveries made quoting the blanket order number.

Large or complex projects may have a procedure designed especially to cover the purchasing of all the products and services required.  For instance, if your department was responsible for placing the order to design and build a hospital you will need technical support to produce specifications before you can source suppliers.  The process often used in this situation is called two-stage tendering. The first stage is to invite un-priced technical bids.  Based on these, a technical specification is prepared and used for the second stage in which complete priced bids are invited.

In many procurement situations your supplier will rely on other organisations to supply them while your customer will, in turn, have their own customers.  This produces a continuum of supply sometimes known as a supply chain or value stream.  It is in the interests of all involved in the continuum that the goods or services flow efficiently from one end to the other and that payment flows equally efficiently in the opposite direction.

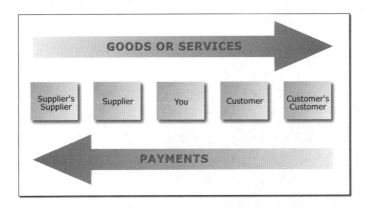

Co-operation between all those involved in the chain is to their mutual benefit. The Japanese conceived the theory of working closely with their suppliers to remove conflicts and tension. This idea was developed further in the UK with the concept of partnership sourcing. This is defined as 'a commitment by customers and suppliers, regardless of size, to a long-term relationship based on clear mutually agreed objectives to strive for world-class capability and competitiveness'.

Another form of customer-supplier relationship you will need to be aware of is known as 'reciprocity'. This is a system where organisation A buys from organisation B on the understanding that B will in turn buy from A. This has benefits in that both organisations have a market for their product, but the drawback is that it limits their choice of suppliers. It may make good sense from the sales department's point of view but is unlikely to be the best solution from the purchasing department's.

A form of customer-supplier relationship which may appear on the face of it to be relatively simple but, in reality, is often complex, is the relationship between two companies within the same group of companies. The decision whether to purchase from an associated company rather than on the open market complicates the supplier selection process. On one hand inter-company purchases are beneficial to the group as a whole as all of the profit from the transaction remains within the group. On the other hand the relationship between the two companies can skew the competitiveness of the supply. Unless it is group policy that purchases are to be made from associated companies whenever possible, the purchasing department will probably treat them in the same way as any external supplier.

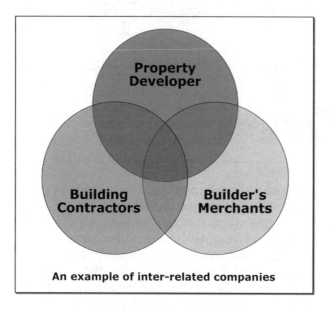

**An example of inter-related companies**

Associated with the question of inter-company purchasing is the whole issue of out-sourcing. In the same way that the purchaser will look at external suppliers in competition with potential suppliers from within the group, you should also be considering whether services provided by other departments in the organisation could be supplied more efficiently from external sources. As mentioned at the beginning of this chapter it is the purchasing department's responsibility to purchase the right quality of products and services, at the right time, in the right quantity, from the right source, at the right price.

An area where problems can arise is securing the products and services at the right time. The purchase order will have stated a delivery date. This will have been the subject of negotiation and agreement between the purchaser and the supplier. The problems arise when the delivery date is not met. Purchasers will ordinarily blame the supplier for failing to carry out the agreement, but it is not always that simple.

Sometimes the problem may be with the purchaser who has allowed insufficient time for delivery, sometimes with the supplier who has quoted an unachievable delivery date in order to secure the order. Sometimes, of course, the problem is beyond the control of either party. There may be transport difficulties, industrial action, weather conditions or difficulties further along the supply chain.

The first step to avoiding problems associated with late delivery is to ensure that the user department appreciate the lead time involved. Lead time is the minimum delay between placing the order and receiving the goods. It depends on the supply position - whether goods have to be manufactured specially to meet the specification and the distance the goods have to travel.

If the delivery date has taken into account the lead time, then it is reasonable to judge the supplier's performance on their ability to deliver the products or services on time. The supplier can then be advised that their performance will be taken into account when the selection of suppliers, to meet future requirements, is considered. There are two ways of measuring supplier performance in this area. The number of overdue deliveries as a percentage of total deliveries will give a simple ranking. A slightly more complicated measure is to consider how late deliveries are and weight the ranking accordingly. The choice between the two measures depends on whether you would rather have a number of slightly late deliveries or most deliveries on time and occasional deliveries very late.

Some organisations will have a section within the purchasing department whose responsibility is to expedite the receipt of products and services. Expediting should be a proactive task rather than a reactive, fire-fighting exercise. Those responsible for expediting should be in regular contact with suppliers between the placing of the order and the due date for delivery to continually check on the order's progress. This will allow the supplier to advise in advance where a problem has arisen which puts the delivery date in jeopardy. Action can then be taken either to assist the supplier to overcome the problem or to source the requirements elsewhere before the delay becomes critical.

The true aim of the expediting section should be to make their work unnecessary. If the following standards can be regularly achieved the need to expedite will have been considerably reduced:

- User departments accept lead times
- Specifications are unambiguous
- Specifications are considered sacrosanct by purchasers
- The ability of suppliers to meet contracts is effectively checked prior to placing orders
- Suppliers do not offer what they know is unachievable
- Delivery dates are specified not implied
- Delivery dates are considered sacrosanct by purchasers
- Purchasers and suppliers understand and respect each other's needs

The purchasing of products and services is an area which requires constant monitoring in order to ensure that all possible areas of inefficiency are eliminated. This includes internal systems and procedures as well as the selection and performance monitoring of suppliers.

 **What you need to know**

The authorisation levels for purchase ordering in your organisation

What is the purpose of a purchase order?

The differences between purchase orders and contracts

When is a purchase completed?

Your organisation's arrangements for
dealing with unsatisfactory products

In what circumstances would blanket-
orders be raised?

The concept of partnership sourcing

How does a supply chain work?

Whether your organisation has a policy on
inter-company purchasing

What do you understand by the term
'lead time'?

How to measure supplier performance

What is the true aim of expediting section?

The role of the procurer has increased in status over the last few years. This is because of its strategic importance in both the reduction of costs and improvements to quality have been recognised. What was once a predominantly clerical function is now seen as a proactive management role involved in supply chain management and concerned with the total cost of acquisition.

# Avoid specifying a high-tech pen which can write upside down in zero gravity when what you need is a pencil

# Are you ready for assessment?

To achieve this unit of a Level 3 Business & Administration qualification you will need to demonstrate that you are competent in the following:

- Agree a specification for product or service
- Source quality products and services that meet your specification
- Select the product or service which represents best value for money
- Procure products or services following your organisation's procedure
- Create and maintain partnerships with suppliers to improve quality and cut costs
- Deal effectively with problems as they occur, seeking support from others where necessary
- Continually monitor and evaluate procurement procedures
- Take action to improve efficiency and obtain better value for money

(Remember that you will need the skills listed at the beginning of this chapter. These are covered in chapter 1.)

You will need to produce evidence from a variety of sources. Carrying out the following activities will help you acquire competence at work.

### Activity 1
Evaluate the performance of a selection of your organisation's current suppliers. Write a report indicating where better value for money can be achieved through improving efficiency.

### Activity 2
Your line manager has decided to replace all the office furniture in your department. You have been given the task of writing a specification for the replacement furniture covering the quantity, quality and features required. Liaise with the users to produce a specification.

**Activity 3**

Source potential suppliers to meet the specification produced in Activity 2. Compare their relative strengths and weaknesses. Obtain prices from each supplier. Consider whether one supplier or a number of suppliers would best suit your requirements. Write a recommendation on the supplier(s) to be used, justifying your reasons for selection.

**Activity 4**

Raise dummy purchase orders for the supply of the office furniture. Consider whether staged deliveries or a one-hit move would be least disruptive for the department and take into account comparative total acquisition costs. Schedule delivery accordingly.

**Activity 5**

Your organisation has reviewed the financial services it receives. It has decided to evaluate alternative products and services with a view to implementing changes in the future. Identify the range of financial products and services that are needed in your organisation. Carry out research to identify and cost alternative solutions for your organisation, making sure you point out the benefits for each recommendation.

Remember: While gathering evidence for this unit, evidence **may** be generated for units 110, 301, 302, 303, 310 and 320.

# CHAPTER 14
# UNIT 305 – Manage and evaluate customer relations

Customers come in many shapes and sizes. Some are internal to your business; that is people inside your organisation who get a service from you. Others are external to your business. You may know the people who use your organisation's products and services as pupils, students, patients or clients. The important thing is they are your customers and you need to provide them with the best service you possibly can.

The management of customer relations is about knowing your customers and meeting their needs. Customers will judge the organisation on the care they receive from everybody that they interact with. Many activities will influence your customers' impression of your organisation. It is important you and your staff realise the importance of customer service standards. Even though your team may not be directly involved with customer, everyone in your organisation is working towards meeting customers' needs:

- The sales department must make it easy for a customer to make a purchase or place an order. Confirmation of receipt of order must be prompt and the customer kept informed of any delays in despatch
- The accounts department must provide suitable acceptable methods of payment, send out prompt

and accurate invoices, provide an accessible system for querying invoices and customer-friendly credit facilities
- The despatch department must provide a flexible delivery service, contact the customer promptly in case of any changes to delivery arrangements and check the quality of the goods before despatch
- The after-sales department must be available when customers need them and provide a prompt and reliable service in the event of problems
- The complaints department must make it easy for customers to complain, respond promptly to complaints, keep records to identify trends and take action to reduce recurring problems
- The administration team must provide the business support function required by their organisation. This may be an internal service where customers are colleagues, or an external service to customers or members of the public

Hopefully most of your customers will be happy with the service your organisation provides, but from time-to-time some may be unhappy, disappointed or even angry about a situation. The way you deal with these customers will reflect on the organisation you work for. The Supply of Goods and Services Act 1982 sets a minimum that the customer is entitled to, but many organisations will go further to keep their customers happy. Other legislation that may affect your dealings with customers includes:

- The Consumer Credit Act 1974 which regulates the way that credit can be offered to customers
- The Consumer Protection Act 1987 which prohibits the sale of dangerous goods
- The Estate Agents Act 1979 which governs accounts in respect of clients' money
- The Property Mis-descriptions Act 1991 which prohibits false or misleading statements of property by estate agents or builders
- The Trade Descriptions Act 1988 which regulates the description of goods and false claims for services
- The Unsolicited Goods and Services (Amendment) Act 1975 which controls the supply of unsolicited goods and demands for payment
- The Unfair Contract Terms Act 1977 which makes unfair contract terms void

There is also a variety of legislation specific to different occupations. You need to make yourself aware of the legislation that applies to your particular organisation. Personally, you must be vigilant in your dealings with your customers in offering a solution. There will be a limit to how far you will be prepared to go to satisfy your customer, even the most customer-friendly organisation can only be reasonably expected to go so far.

 When managing and evaluating customer relations you will use the following skills:

- Interpersonal skills
- Questioning
- Listening
- Negotiating
- Managing time
- Monitoring
- Evaluating
- Problem solving

These skills are covered in chapter 1.

## Know your customer

One of the most common questions asked within an organisation is 'who are my customers?' The answer is, usually, 'anybody you supply goods or services to'. Customers may be internal to the organisation or external. Customers are the reason for your work, not an interruption to it. They are the life-blood of the organisation, and without them there would be no organisation.

Remember it is far easier to lose a customer than to gain a new one. Many organisations spend a great deal more time, effort and money in attracting new customers than they do in retaining the ones they have already. This can be a serious mistake.

It is your responsibility to build positive working relationships with your organisation's customers which will ensure that they remain loyal. Get to know them, how they would like to be addressed, what products or services they regularly need and how often.  When a customer is unsure of their needs, use open questions to help them clarify exactly what they want.  Remember, open questions usually begin with:

- How
- Why
- Where
- What
- When
- Who

Use 'active listening' to make sure you fully understand their requirements.  Remember the aim is to reach a 'win win' situation that satisfies the organisation's needs as well as the customer's needs.  When you feel you have reached an agreement summarise the conversation you have had and confirm the agreement by repeating it back to the customer. If the customer feels valued they will give you the opportunity to put right any problems that may occur.

# What you need to know

Who your customers are, both internal
and external

> Do you have a list of your
> organisation's regular customers?

What you can offer potential customers:

    Products and services

    Terms and conditions

> Could you explain to a new member of
> staff how to build positive working
> relationships with customers?

Ways to make customers feel valued

> Do you know your organisation's policy
> on discounts?

How to address your customers

> What would happen if your
> organisation's customer service was
> not efficient?

The customer service legislation that
applies to your organisation

> What specific legislation impacts on the
> level of customer care provided by your
> organisation?

The impact other departments have
on customer care

> Do you know what products or services
> your regular customers order?

## Meet your customers' needs

'The customer is always right'. Despite this customers will
not always know what they want, (even if they do they may
not find it easy to explain). You will have to listen carefully
to what they say and ask intelligent questions such as:

- How many?
- What colour?

- For delivery by when?
- Smoking or non-smoking?
- Single or return?
- What denominations would you like the money in?
- When did you buy it?
- How long would you like the warranty for?

In order to identify and confirm your customer's needs it is important to listen actively to the customer's responses, and take note of what they *don't* say. There is a risk that they will see you as the expert and not want to disagree with you although your suggested solution may not actually match their needs. They may not want to give the real reason if they are dissatisfied.

Your job is to provide the information, goods or services to your customers at the agreed time. Summarise the outcome of any conversation you may have and give them the opportunity to confirm or deny your understanding of what has been agreed. Make sure they are satisfied with the service you offer. It will probably be a good idea to write down the details of the agreement either as you go along or immediately afterwards.

When you believe you have met the customer's needs and the service has been delivered on time, you will still need to follow up with the customer to check customer needs and expectations are met. It is possible that despite your best efforts to ensure that everybody understood what had been agreed, the customer is still not happy with the service you provided. Your organisation may have a formal method for obtaining the customer's confirmation that they are satisfied. If not, a verbal check may be sufficient.

# What you need to know

Whether your organisation has a formal method for obtaining confirmation that the customer is satisfied

> How do you deal with a situation where you have checked that the customer is satisfied and they have surprised you by saying 'no'?

The consequences of failing to check that the customer is satisfied

> If your department were to produce 40,000 copies of a 500 page book, at what stage would you check that the customer's requirements were being accurately met?

What the limit of your authority is when negotiating with customers

> What would you do if nothing you suggested was acceptable to the customer?

How to summarise a conversation to confirm agreement

> How can you tell if somebody is actively listening to you?

## Systems and procedures

When you know what will satisfy the customer, agree with them exactly what is going to happen and when. This may require you to liaise with other departments in order to agree the timescales and procedures that need to be followed and the quality standards to be achieved. Make sure you have the commitment of everybody involved that they will play their part in achieving the target of meeting the agreement.

The customer has placed an order with your organisation in preference to others who could have supplied their needs.

If you don't keep your side of the bargain the customer will feel disappointed with the service your organisation has provided.  Having agreed what is to happen next, you will have to take the necessary steps to ensure that you meet your commitments.  Agree milestones along the way to completion so that you can check whether the process is falling behind.

It is often counter-productive to continually check progress as this can alienate colleagues who are actually carrying out the task, so clearly agreed stages at which progress will be checked will allow you to be aware of potential delays before the final deadline is reached.  Where problems arise that put the timescales or quality agreed at risk, action needs to be taken to make every effort to get back on target.  It may be necessary to consider:

- Employing extra people to complete the job
- Utilising existing people for longer hours
- Buying-in other resources to increase productivity

Where, despite your best efforts, it is clear that the deadline is not going to be met, this is the time to advise the customer.  This will involve phoning them, apologising for the problem, explaining the effect this will have on the agreement and re-negotiating the agreement.  They aren't going to be happy, but they are going to be even more unhappy, if you wait until the deadline arrives and then tell them that it's not going to be met.

 **What you need to know**

The functions of other departments that will be involved in delivering the promised service to the customer

Why is it important to agree milestones?

The quality standards your organisation works to

What extra resources are likely to be useful in achieving a deadline?

How to obtain the commitment of other departments to the achievement of customer satisfaction

Who do you have to liaise with to authorise extra resources?

What action to take if deadlines aren't going to be met

If you find you are unable to meet an agreed deadline, when should you tell your customer?

How to set practical milestones

Why is it important to inform your customer that you can't meet the deadline agreed?

## Dealing with complaints

Customer care is about the systems, procedures and the whole organisation's approach to the customers. This will include:

- Openness, honesty and respect for your customers
- Sales and order systems
- Accounts and invoice systems
- Delivery systems
- After sales service
- The customer complaints process

You will need to know how to resolve a complaint. Failing to carry out the solution within the agreed timescales may be the final straw in the eyes of your customer. To reduce the effect of this it will be necessary to agree with the customer at this stage what will happen if you fail to carry out the agreed service. You must always bear in mind the limits of your authority.

How you handle complaints will decide whether it is the last time you ever see the customer or if they are happy to return regularly in the future. There are some important 'do's and don'ts':

- Do listen to what they say
- Don't try to have the last word
- Do empathise with how they feel
- Don't show you are annoyed
- Do apologise for the inconvenience
- Don't raise your voice
- Do tell the customer what action you are taking
- Don't say you are unable to do anything
- Do learn to value complaints
- Don't EVER turn your back on a customer

Aim to resolve the complaint promptly in order that the customer feels important. Accept responsibility for the problem. To the customer, you represent the organisation. Remember to leave the customer feeling that they were right. Never argue with a customer, you can't win.

Every organisation will have its own individual procedures for dealing with customer complaints. It is important that you fully understand those procedures and follow them as failure to do so may have serious consequences. What may seem a minor problem at the time may have serious consequences at a later date, and the fact that you can show that you have followed the organisation's procedures may be important in your defence of your actions.

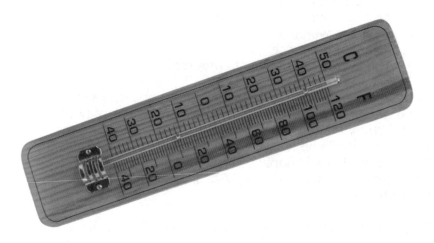

# What you need to know

The legal implications of dealing with
customer problems

What are your organisation's
procedures for dealing with formal
complaints?

The types of problems that could arise in
the future

Why should an organisation welcome
complaints?

## Monitoring and evaluating services

Probably the best way to reduce the number of complaints
that you have to deal with is to effectively monitor the
service that you are giving to your customers. This will help
you to recognise where problems arise and what you can do
to improve your service and prevent the complaints from
happening.

The most effective method of monitoring your service is
actively to seek feedback from your customers. The benefits
of customer feedback are:

- Understanding your customers' present needs and potential requirements allows you to meet their needs more effectively. You may need to develop new products, increase the range of services that you offer or improve the products or services you already offer. If you know what your customer is going to need you can make the necessary improvements before they are asked for
- The opportunity to get a customers' eye view of the business. Long standing organisations can sometimes lose sight of their overall purpose in the pursuit of internal goals
- Understanding the service level your customer expects so that you meet actual expectations rather than aiming to provide a level of service that isn't required
- If you don't ask customers how you are doing, they won't tell you. Many dissatisfied customers will simply take their business elsewhere rather than complain to you about the service they have received. If you regularly ask for feedback you may learn of problems in time to take action before the customer has gone elsewhere
- You find out just how many dissatisfied customers you actually have. It is said that only one in every 20 commercial customers who is dissatisfied actually complains, but each one tells 11 other people that they are unhappy. This means if you get ten complaints, 200 customers are actually unhappy and they will have told 2,200 people. Don't think if you have no complaints that you have no dissatisfied customers; it just means you haven't reached the twentieth yet
- You will learn what your competitors are offering. Often it would be difficult for you to get detailed information on the service being provided by your direct competitors, but your customers will happily let you know if they are being offered a better service elsewhere
- Your customers' perception of your organisation will improve. They will feel able to trust you as you are seeking their opinion in order to improve your service to them. A study found that twice as many people who complained and did not get satisfaction bought again from the same supplier as those who were dissatisfied but didn't complain

Organisations may feel there are reasons for not actively seeking customer feedback, but these reasons are usually a reflection of the organisation's fear that the feedback will uncover problems.  Looked at positively these fears usually prove to be groundless as any problems exposed can, and indeed must, be dealt with:

- Organisations are afraid they will only get negative feedback.  There are two possible ways of looking at this.  Either they are right, in which case they clearly have a customer service problem and they need feedback to help them solve it.  Or they are wrong, in which case they will be pleasantly surprised by the amount of positive feedback they receive
- Organisations are afraid seeking feedback will raise their customers' expectations.  While no organisation will satisfy every customer every time, every organisation need to know what it is their customers want and how best they can meet most of their customers' needs most of the time
- Organisations are afraid they won't get sufficient useful information.  The solution to this is to ask the right people the right questions in the right way

There are a number of formal ways to collect customer feedback:

- **Questionnaires** - Usually multiple choice questions sent to selected customers
- **Customer interviews** - Face-to-face or by telephone
- **Customer panels** - A group of customers meet regularly to give consensus feedback
- **Customer focus groups** - A group of customers is brought together to give feedback on a particular aspect of customer service
- **Customer comment cards** - Available at reception for customers to complete if they wish
- **Customer free-phone** - Allows customers to telephone if they have any feedback to give

Feedback can also be collected informally by:

- Listening actively to customers
- Asking for comments from customers

Seeking feedback from customers must be an on-going process, but unless the responses are recorded and analysed there is no point in collecting them. In all but the smallest organisations feedback will be recorded using computer software, either a database or spreadsheet package.

Some forms of feedback will readily provide information in a way that can be directly entered into a package and provide statistical information, other forms will have to be interpreted. The design of questionnaires for instance should take into account the fact that if faced with an odd number of choices many people will select the middle option rather than giving a considered answer. Information should allow you to make positive statements about the feedback received, for instance '87% of customers were satisfied or very satisfied with delivery times' rather than 'most customers had no complaints to make'.

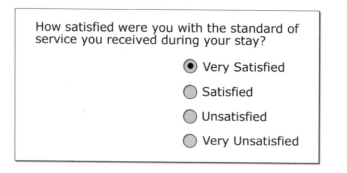

How satisfied were you with the standard of service you received during your stay?

⦿ Very Satisfied

◯ Satisfied

◯ Unsatisfied

◯ Very Unsatisfied

The computer software should be used to analyse the information gathered and produce reports that graphically represent the opinions given. The actual form of presentation used will depend on the information being analysed but may be tabular, line graphs, bar charts, pie charts etc., which makes it easy to see where a problem lies.

Having uncovered a problem it is important that action be taken to resolve the issue. If the resolution of the issue is likely to be very expensive or time consuming it may be worth considering extending the research before making any changes. If your initial sample was quite small there may be a statistical anomaly in the results. For instance if you asked ten people whether they were satisfied with your delivery times and eight said they weren't, it would be worth asking another 100 people for their views before investing in additional delivery vehicles. You may find the only eight people who are dissatisfied happened to be in the first ten you asked!

Once you have identified a genuine area of concern, you should consult with all the interested parties to agree a set of objectives to improve the situation. Remember to make the objectives SMART:

- **Specific** - 'Improve delivery times' is an objective, but it is not specific, whereas 'improve delivery times by 10%' is
- **Measurable** - There must be a system in place to record the achievement of the specific objective. For instance, to measure whether delivery times have improved by 10% there must be a record of delivery times prior to the objective being set as well as afterwards
- **Achievable** - The objective must be capable of being reached, without being too easy. If there is no possibility of improving delivery times by 10%, setting it as an objective will achieve absolutely nothing. Nobody will make any attempt to achieve it. Much better to set an achievable objective of 5%
- **Relevant** - The objective has to be meaningful to the organisation but also relevant to what the person being set the objective is able to control. There is no point in telling the accounts department that we need to improve delivery times by 10% as there is nothing they can do about it
- **Time based** - There has to be a date by which the objective is to be achieved. If you set an objective of improving delivery times by 10% without saying by when, how will you know if it has been achieved?

At the end of the time specified for achieving the objective, review not only whether the objective has been achieved (e.g. delivery times have improved by 10%) but also whether achieving the objective has had the desired effect on customer feedback. Check that the action has actually improved customers' satisfaction levels.

Even if all the feedback indicates that there are no serious problems it is important to continue to collect feedback and not to allow complacency to set in, assuming that there will continue to be no problems in the future. The sooner a problem is identified the easier it is to take remedial action.

# What you need to know

Why it is important to continually monitor customer satisfaction

What are the benefits of collecting effective customer feedback?

The different ways of collecting customer feedback

Why is it preferable to have an even number of options in a customer questionnaire?

How to analyse customer feedback

What does the acronym SMART stand for?

Why some organisations are reluctant to seek feedback from customers

How can this reluctance be overcome?

In conclusion every customer, whether internal or external, must be treated as if they were the most important person in the organisation. Your purpose must be to satisfy their requirements as vital business can be lost if your organisation doesn't have the correct relationship with its customers. Make sure your team knows and follows your organisation's procedures for dealing with both orders and complaints. If every customer request is dealt with efficiently and effectively there will be no cause for complaint; while it may not be possible to achieve this fully, the successful management of customer relations will go a long way towards reducing complaints. Actively seeking customer feedback will enable you to recognise areas for improvement and take the necessary action at an early stage. It is a lot cheaper and less stressful to prevent problems than it is to deal with them.

## The first step to dealing with a problem is acknowledging the problem exists

# Are you ready for assessment?

To achieve this unit of a Level 3 Business & Administration qualification you will need to demonstrate that you are competent in the following:

- Build positive working relationships with customers
- Identify and confirm customer needs
- Agree timescales and quality standards with customers, and the procedures to follow if these aren't achieved
- Provide services to agreed timescales and quality standards
- Check customer needs and expectations are met
- Resolve or refer complaints in a professional manner and to a given timescale
- Obtain and record customer feedback
- Analyse and evaluate customer feedback
- Take action to improve customer relations

(Remember that you will need the skills listed at the beginning of this chapter. These are covered in chapter 1.)

You will need to produce evidence from a variety of sources. Carrying out the following activities will help you acquire competence at work.

### Activity 1

You are the General Manager at a hotel and the receptionist is working alone on the reception desk. It's 9.00am and she has been on duty since 4.00am without a break. There is a queue of guests, some wanting to check out, others seeking directions to a function being held in the hotel conference room that morning. There is an atmosphere of discontent spreading through the queue. Suddenly a customer pushes their way to the front and starts demanding to see the manager. They begin shouting about the poor service, the lack of hot water in their room, the poor quality of the breakfast, the litter in the car park and the disgraceful price charged for drinks in the bar. You feel that none of this is your fault, but you have to deal with the irate customer. At the same time you must avoid holding up the other guests who are still waiting in the queue and placate the receptionist who is feeling she hasn't had sufficient support from you.

How do you deal with the situation?

## Activity 2

Compile a customer questionnaire to collect feedback on customer satisfaction in your organisation. State the reasons for the number of questions used and the range of options given.

## Activity 3

Write a report detailing the methods you would use to record and analyse the feedback from the above questionnaire.

## Activity 4

Design a method of collecting information from your organisation's customers which will enable you to evaluate their opinion of your customer service. Collect the information from a substantial proportion of your customers. Analyse the results and make recommendations for changes to systems and procedures which address any challenges identified. Present your findings and your recommendations to your line manager in either a written report or as a PowerPoint presentation.

## Activity 5

Research the legislation that is relevant to customer service in your job role. Write a report on how it affects the solutions you can offer to customers' requests.

Remember: While gathering evidence for this unit, evidence **may** be generated for units 110, 212, 213, 216, 301, 302, 314, 315, 318, 320 and 321.

# CHAPTER 15
# UNIT 306 – Managing the payroll function

The function of the payroll department is to administer the payment of wages and salaries to employees and directors. It is extremely important to ensure accurate calculation of pay and deductions. Comprehensive records must be kept to satisfy the requirements of HM Revenue and Customs and to enable queries to be dealt with efficiently.

Only payments to employees and directors are normally actioned through the payroll system. Your organisation may 'employ' people such as consultants or sub-contractors, but they will submit invoices and be paid through the Purchase Ledger system. It is important, therefore, to understand the distinction between employees and directors on the one hand and self-employed people on the other as this will affect the way they are taxed, the National Insurance Contributions (NICs) they make and whether they are entitled to any contractual benefits such as sick pay, maternity pay, entry to the company pension scheme, employment protection or holiday pay.

The characteristics of employment include:

- A hierarchical relationship, where the employer can instruct the employee on what to do, when and how
- Payment by the hour, week or month

- Entitlement to a Contract of Employment
- Contracted hours of employment

The characteristics of self-employment include:

- The option to decide what to do when and how
- Payment on completion of the job
- No entitlement to a Contract of Employment, often a contract is issued for each job
- No regular hours, no overtime paid if additional time is spent completing tasks or for holiday taken

In principle directors are employees as far as the payroll is concerned. Certain additional conditions apply when calculating the tax and National Insurance deductions of directors, which are explained later in this chapter.

Tax and National Insurance are deducted from employees' pay by their employer, and it is the employer who will be held responsible for any deductions that have not been made. Self-employed people are responsible for paying their own tax and National Insurance. There is an exception in the building industry where the main contractor is required to deduct basic rate tax from the labour element of the pay of self-employed sub-contractors.

Special rules apply to certain types of employment including:

- Students
- Employees involved in a trade dispute
- Young people on a training scheme
- People who work gang squad systems
- Married women entitled to pay reduced rate National Insurance Contributions

The above list is not exhaustive and is subject to change, so it is advisable to look in the 'Employer's Further Guide to PAYE and NICs, CWG2' available from HM Revenue and Customs (HMRC) for the current situation.

The legislation which requires employers to deduct Income Tax and National Insurance from the pay of employees is the Finance Act which is amended every year by the budget. The budget is introduced by the Chancellor of the Exchequer, usually in March, and sets the tax rules for the tax year which runs from 6 April to 5 April.

Under the Finance Act organisations are required to make returns to HM Revenue and Customs. This Government Department was formed by the amalgamation of the Inland Revenue and Customs and Excise Departments and is responsible for:

- Income, Corporation, Capital Gains, Inheritance, Insurance Premium, Stamp, Land and Petroleum Revenue Taxes
- Environmental taxes: climate change and aggregates levy and landfill tax
- VAT
- Customs Duties and frontier protection
- Excise Duties
- National Insurance
- Tax Credits
- Child Benefit and the Child Trust Fund
- Enforcement of the National Minimum Wage
- Recovery of Student Loan repayments
- Developing Lorry Road User Charging

It is important to understand what constitutes 'pay'. From the point of view of HM Revenue and Customs taxable pay includes:

- Basic wages or salary
- Overtime
- Bonuses
- Pensions
- Sick pay
- Maternity pay
- Tips
- Luncheon Vouchers over 15p per day

The above list is not exhaustive and advice should be sought if employees are receiving any other form of benefit.

Directors and employees earning more than £8,500 per year are also taxed on other benefits, full details of which can be found in the 'Employer's Further Guide to PAYE and NICs, CWG2'.

Under the Employment Protection (Consolidation) Act 1978 every employee is entitled to be told how their pay has been calculated, including gross pay, deductions and net pay. This is usually done in writing using a pay slip. Deductions will normally include Income Tax and NICs, although there are a variety of other deductions which can be made, most of which require the employee's authority.

Income Tax is collected from employees through the Pay As You Earn (PAYE) system. Until the 1940s Income Tax was collected annually, which meant the Treasury received all of its Income Tax revenue at one time rather than spread over the year and people found difficulty in paying tax on income which they had probably already spent. PAYE ensures that tax is collected every time an employee is paid, which avoids both the difficulties above.

NICs are not, strictly speaking, a tax as they were introduced to pay for benefits such as pensions, the NHS, unemployment pay and sick pay. In more recent times all government revenue has been consolidated and NICs are no longer used to pay directly for benefits. National Insurance is calculated on gross income above the lower earnings limit, which is fixed each year in the Finance Act. NICs are paid by both the employee and the employer.

Other adjustments to the pay of employees may include:

- Statutory Sick Pay (SSP)
- Statutory Maternity Pay (SMP)
- Statutory Paternity Pay (SPP)
- Statutory Adoption Pay (SAP)
- Company pension contributions
- Additional Voluntary Contributions (AVCs)
- Charitable donations
- Attachment of Earnings

Employers are required by law to maintain records of pay and deductions. These records include:

- Form P11 which records gross pay and PAYE deductions and must be kept for three years
- Form P14 which summarises each employee's P11 and is completed in triplicate. The top two copies are submitted to HM Revenue and Customs and the third copy forms the 'P60' which is given to the employee
- Form P35 is the Employer's Annual Return which summarises Income Tax and NICs deducted and SSP, SMP, SPP and SAP recovered
- Form P11D which records expenses and benefits in kind paid to directors and employees earning over £8,500 per year
- Form P9D which records expenses and benefits in kind paid to employees earning less than £8,500 per year
- Details of the make and model of company cars, types of fuel and business mileage

In the case of SSP you must keep:

- All dates of employee sickness lasting for four or more days in a row
- All payments of SSP you make during each Period of Incapacity for Work (PIW)

This is so that the Inland Revenue can check that your employees are receiving their proper SSP entitlement.
All SSP that you pay must be included in gross pay. Any deductions you can lawfully make from pay can also be made from SSP.

In the case of SMP you must keep:
- The medical evidence of the pregnancy, form MAT B1, Maternity Certificate
- A record of the payment dates and the amount paid
- The date the pay period began
- A record of any weeks in the 26 week period when SMP wasn't paid, with reasons

In the case of SPP you must keep:
- The declaration of family commitment, form SC3
- A record of the payment dates and the amounts paid
- The date the pay period began
- A record of any unpaid SPP with reasons

In the case of SAP you must keep:
- The evidence the adoption agency gave your employee and they gave you
- A record of the payment dates and the amount paid
- The date the pay period began
- A record of any weeks in the 26 week period when SAP wasn't paid, with reasons

Duplicate pay slips should be retained in order to record all deductions made from pay, whether statutory or voluntary, as these would be required by HM Revenue and Customs investigating employees' deductions, checking the tax implications. Records of appraisals, performance reviews and disciplinary procedures must be retained in order to justify dismissal of employees, or selection for redundancy based on performance.

Records are subject to the Data Protection Act 1998. If your organisation is registered under this Act you will need to ensure that all the records you keep comply with its principles.

There may be occasions when the organisation finds it necessary to make staff redundant. Redundancy is defined as dismissal due solely or mainly to:

- The fact that the employer has stopped, or intends to stop, that part of the business for which the employee was employed; or has stopped, or intends to stop, operating the business in the place where the employee was so employed, or
- The fact that the business no longer requires the employee to carry out work of a particular kind, in a

particular place. This can relate to the work having stopped altogether, or being diminished, or expected to stop or diminish

In the case of a reduction in the requirements for employees to carry out work, choices must be made as to which employees stay and which are made redundant. There are a number of options available to organisations in the way that selection for redundancy is carried out. The critical issue is that selection must be shown to be fair:

- **First in, last out (FILO)** - Selection is on the basis of length of service
- **Performance** - Selection is based on the employees' ability to carry out their role
- **Volunteers** - The option of redundancy is offered to everyone and volunteers are sought
- **Retirement** - All staff over the normal retirement age and those approaching it are selected

The employer may want to use a mixture of the above selection methods as each has drawbacks. Care must be taken to ensure that selection can be shown to have been made on a fair basis, as employees made redundant may claim unfair dismissal at an Industrial Tribunal.

When managing the payroll function you will use the following skills:

- Planning
- Organising
- Researching
- Checking
- Communicating
- Using technology
- Reading
- Recording
- Problem solving
- Using number
- Managing time

These skills are covered in chapter 1.

# Managing the payroll function

The beginning of the payroll function is the calculation of the employees' and directors' gross pay. There are a number of different ways in which an employee's gross pay may be calculated:

- Fixed monthly salary, i.e. annual salary divided by 12
- Four-weekly salary, i.e. annual salary divided by 13
- Hourly pay, i.e. number of contracted hours worked multiplied by hourly rate

In addition there may be overtime payments, bonuses, holiday pay or benefits such as SSP, SMP, SPP or SAP. There is also the option for employees to have regular charitable donations deducted from their pay. In order to increase the value of these donations to the recipient charity, they are deducted after the calculation of NICs but before the deduction of PAYE.

From this gross pay it will be necessary to make deductions for Income Tax, NICs, pensions, AVCs, charitable donations and Attachments of Earnings. Some employees may be entitled to payments of Working Tax Credits which are added to their net pay.

**Week 1**  Apr 6 to Apr 12          **Tables A** - Pay Adjustment Tables

| Code | Total pay adjustment to date | Code | Total pay adjustment to date | Code | Total pay adjustment to date | Code | Total pay adjustment to date | Code | Total pay adjustment to date | Code | Total pay adjustment to date | Code | Total pay adjustment to date | Code | Total pay adjustment to date | Code | Total pay adjustment to date |
|---|---|---|---|---|---|---|---|---|---|---|---|---|---|---|---|---|---|
| | £ | | £ | | £ | | £ | | £ | | £ | | £ | | £ | | £ |
| 0 | NIL | | | | | | | | | | | | | | | | |
| 1 | 0.37 | 61 | 11.91 | 121 | 23.45 | 181 | 34.99 | 241 | 46.52 | 301 | 58.06 | 351 | 67.68 | 401 | 77.29 | 451 | 86.91 |
| 2 | 0.56 | 62 | 12.10 | 122 | 23.64 | 182 | 35.18 | 242 | 46.72 | 302 | 58.25 | 352 | 67.87 | 402 | 77.49 | 452 | 87.10 |
| 3 | 0.75 | 63 | 12.29 | 123 | 23.83 | 183 | 35.37 | 243 | 46.91 | 303 | 58.45 | 353 | 68.06 | 403 | 77.68 | 453 | 87.29 |
| 4 | 0.95 | 64 | 12.49 | 124 | 24.02 | 184 | 35.56 | 244 | 47.10 | 304 | 58.64 | 354 | 68.25 | 404 | 77.87 | 454 | 87.49 |
| 5 | 1.14 | 65 | 12.68 | 125 | 24.22 | 185 | 35.75 | 245 | 47.29 | 305 | 58.83 | 355 | 68.45 | 405 | 78.06 | 455 | 87.68 |
| 6 | 1.33 | 66 | 12.87 | 126 | 24.41 | 186 | 35.95 | 246 | 47.49 | 306 | 59.02 | 356 | 68.64 | 406 | 78.25 | 456 | 87.87 |
| 7 | 1.52 | 67 | 13.06 | 127 | 24.60 | 187 | 36.14 | 247 | 47.68 | 307 | 59.22 | 357 | 68.83 | 407 | 78.45 | 457 | 88.06 |
| 8 | 1.72 | 68 | 13.25 | 128 | 24.79 | 188 | 36.33 | 248 | 47.87 | 308 | 59.41 | 358 | 69.02 | 408 | 78.64 | 458 | 88.25 |
| 9 | 1.91 | 69 | 13.45 | 129 | 24.99 | 189 | 36.52 | 249 | 48.06 | 309 | 59.60 | 359 | 69.22 | 409 | 78.83 | 459 | 88.45 |
| 10 | 2.10 | 70 | 13.64 | 130 | 25.18 | 190 | 36.72 | 250 | 48.25 | 310 | 59.79 | 360 | 69.41 | 410 | 79.02 | 460 | 88.64 |
| 11 | 2.29 | 71 | 13.83 | 131 | 25.37 | 191 | 36.91 | 251 | 48.45 | 311 | 59.99 | 361 | 69.60 | 411 | 79.22 | 461 | 88.83 |
| 12 | 2.49 | 72 | 14.02 | 132 | 25.56 | 192 | 37.10 | 252 | 48.64 | 312 | 60.18 | 362 | 69.79 | 412 | 79.41 | 462 | 89.02 |
| 13 | 2.68 | 73 | 14.22 | 133 | 25.75 | 193 | 37.29 | 253 | 48.83 | 313 | 60.37 | 363 | 69.99 | 413 | 79.60 | 463 | 89.22 |
| 14 | 2.87 | 74 | 14.41 | 134 | 25.95 | 194 | 37.49 | 254 | 49.02 | 314 | 60.56 | 364 | 70.18 | 414 | 79.79 | 464 | 89.41 |
| 15 | 3.06 | 75 | 14.60 | 135 | 26.14 | 195 | 37.68 | 255 | 49.22 | 315 | 60.75 | 365 | 70.37 | 415 | 79.99 | 465 | 89.60 |
| 16 | 3.25 | 76 | 14.79 | 136 | 26.33 | 196 | 37.87 | 256 | 49.41 | 316 | 60.95 | 366 | 70.56 | 416 | 80.18 | 466 | 89.79 |
| 17 | 3.45 | 77 | 14.99 | 137 | 26.52 | 197 | 38.06 | 257 | 49.60 | 317 | 61.14 | 367 | 70.75 | 417 | 80.37 | 467 | 89.99 |
| 18 | 3.64 | 78 | 15.18 | 138 | 26.72 | 198 | 38.25 | 258 | 49.79 | 318 | 61.33 | 368 | 70.95 | 418 | 80.56 | 468 | 90.18 |
| 19 | 3.83 | 79 | 15.37 | 139 | 26.91 | 199 | 38.45 | 259 | 49.99 | 319 | 61.52 | 369 | 71.14 | 419 | 80.75 | 469 | 90.37 |
| 20 | 4.02 | 80 | 15.56 | 140 | 27.10 | 200 | 38.64 | 260 | 50.18 | 320 | 61.72 | 370 | 71.33 | 420 | 80.95 | 470 | 90.56 |
| 21 | 4.22 | 81 | 15.75 | 141 | 27.29 | 201 | 38.83 | 261 | 50.37 | 321 | 61.91 | 371 | 71.52 | 421 | 81.14 | 471 | 90.75 |
| 22 | 4.41 | 82 | 15.95 | 142 | 27.49 | 202 | 39.02 | 262 | 50.56 | 322 | 62.10 | 372 | 71.72 | 422 | 81.33 | 472 | 90.95 |
| 23 | 4.60 | 83 | 16.14 | 143 | 27.68 | 203 | 39.22 | 263 | 50.75 | 323 | 62.29 | 373 | 71.91 | 423 | 81.52 | 473 | 91.14 |
| 24 | 4.79 | 84 | 16.33 | 144 | 27.87 | 204 | 39.41 | 264 | 50.95 | 324 | 62.49 | 374 | 72.10 | 424 | 81.72 | 474 | 91.33 |
| 25 | 4.99 | 85 | 16.52 | 145 | 28.06 | 205 | 39.60 | 265 | 51.14 | 325 | 62.68 | 375 | 72.29 | 425 | 81.91 | 475 | 91.52 |
| 26 | 5.18 | 86 | 16.72 | 146 | 28.25 | | 39.79 | 266 | | | | 376 | 72.49 | 426 | 82.10 | 476 | 91.72 |
| 27 | 5.37 | 87 | 16.91 | 147 | 28.45 | | | | | | | | | | | 477 | 91.91 |

Income Tax deductions are calculated under the PAYE system. The amount to be paid depends on the employee's gross pay to date in the tax year and their Tax Code. Each employee will have been given a Tax Code by the HMRC at the beginning of the tax year. This will be based on information held on that employee and will be calculated taking into account the personal allowance (the amount of money each of us is allowed to earn each year before we pay any Income Tax) and any other allowances the individual is entitled to. Where the information alters during the course of a tax year an amended Tax Code will be issued. It is important that you are using the current Tax Code for each individual employee when calculating their tax deduction.

Tax tables are supplied by HMRC in both electronic and paper formats. These enable you to look up the employee's gross pay to date in the relevant week or month and their current Tax Code and read off the total tax due to date. By deducting the tax paid previously, the tax due in this week or month can be calculated. There may be occasions when the result is a negative figure. In this case the employee is due a Tax Refund and this should be added to the employee's pay rather than a deduction being made. Tax Refunds should always be double-checked before being paid as an error in calculations can lead to major problems.

National Insurance Contributions are paid by both the employee and the employer and are based on the gross earnings in the week or month, unlike PAYE they are not based on cumulative earnings over the tax year to date. This can have the effect of increasing contributions disproportionately in pay periods when bonuses or awards are paid. HMRC provide National Insurance tables covering:

- **Table A** - Contracted In Rates for employees who are not contracted out of the state pension
- **Table B** - Reduced Rates for married women and widows who elected to pay less National Insurance in exchange for reduced benefits. This option was withdrawn in 1977, but some employees will still be subject to Table B
- **Table C** - Pension Rates for employees over the state retirement age
- **Table D** - Contracted Out Rates for employees who are contracted out of the state pension

- **Table E** - Reduced Rates and Contracted Out for contracted out women who pay reduced rates

**Weekly table**

Table letter **B**

| Employee's Earnings up to and including the UEL | Earnings at the LEL (where earnings are equal to or exceed the LEL) | Earnings above the LEL, up to and including the ET | Earnings above the ET, up to and including the UEL | Total of employee's and employer's contributions | Employee's contributions due on all earnings above the ET | Employer's contributions |
|---|---|---|---|---|---|---|
| | | 1b | 1c | 1d | 1e | |
| 1a | | | | | | |
| £ | £ | £ P | £ P | £ P | £ P | £ P |
| 447 | 82 | 12.00 | 353.00 | 62.39 | 17.14 | 45.25 |
| 448 | 82 | 12.00 | 354.00 | 62.57 | 17.19 | 45.38 |
| 449 | 82 | 12.00 | 355.00 | 62.74 | 17.24 | 45.50 |
| 450 | 82 | 12.00 | 356.00 | 62.92 | 17.29 | 45.63 |
| 451 | 82 | 12.00 | 357.00 | 63.10 | 17.34 | 45.76 |
| 452 | 82 | 12.00 | 358.00 | 63.28 | 17.39 | 45.89 |
| 453 | 82 | 12.00 | 359.00 | 63.45 | 17.43 | 46.02 |
| 454 | 82 | 12.00 | 360.00 | 63.62 | 17.48 | 46.14 |
| 455 | 82 | 12.00 | 361.00 | 63.80 | 17.53 | 46.27 |
| 456 | 82 | 12.00 | 362.00 | 63.98 | 17.58 | 46.40 |
| 457 | 82 | 12.00 | 363.00 | 64.16 | 17.63 | 46.53 |
| 458 | 82 | 12.00 | 364.00 | 64.34 | 17.68 | 46.66 |
| 459 | 82 | 12.00 | 365.00 | 64.51 | 17.73 | 46.78 |
| 460 | 82 | 12.00 | 366.00 | 64.68 | 17.77 | 46.91 |
| 461 | 82 | 12.00 | 367.00 | 64.86 | 17.82 | 47.04 |
| 462 | 82 | 12.00 | 368.00 | 65.04 | 17.87 | 47.17 |
| 463 | 82 | 12.00 | 369.00 | 65.22 | 17.92 | 47.30 |
| 464 | 82 | 12.00 | 370.00 | 65.39 | 17.97 | 47.42 |
| 465 | 82 | 12.00 | 371.00 | 65.57 | 18.02 | 47.55 |
| 466 | 82 | 12.00 | 372.00 | 65.75 | 18.07 | 47.68 |
| 467 | 82 | 12.00 | 373.00 | 65.92 | 18.11 | 47.81 |
| 468 | 82 | 12.00 | 374.00 | 66.10 | 18.16 | 47.94 |
| 469 | 82 | 12.00 | | | | 48.06 |

To calculate the NICs to be deducted, check the employee's NI Table and read off the contributions due from the gross pay for the week or month ignoring any pence. Remember at this stage to also calculate the employer's contribution as this will be needed later.

Information on the level of **pension contributions** and any **AVCs** to be deducted will be provided by the pensions administrator who may be internal to the organisation if the pension is operated by the organisation, or external if the pension is operated by a pensions company.

An **Attachment of Earnings Order** (AEO) is made by a court to recover a debt from an employee. This tells the employer

- The total debt owed by the judgment debtor
- The amount of the weekly or monthly deductions to be made by the employer ('the normal deduction rate')
- The amount below which the court considers that the judgment debtor's earnings should not be reduced, in order to allow judgment debtors to support

themselves and any dependants ('the protected earnings rate')

At each payday the employer is ordered to:

- Set aside the employee's protected earnings
- Calculate the employee's attachable earnings
- Deduct the amount specified in the order
- Pay the remainder to the employee

Remember the protected earnings are calculated from net pay after deduction of PAYE and NICs.

**Working Tax Credits** are paid when the employer receives the Start notice, form TC700 which tells you when to start and how much to pay.

When starting payments:

- Pay the Working Tax Credit every pay day unless you have no wages to pay. If you have no wages to pay, see below
- Pay the daily rate shown on the Start Notice multiplied by the number of calendar days in the pay period. The start and finish periods probably won't be a full week or month but otherwise you will pay 7 days to weekly paid employees; for monthly paid employees it will be 28 (29) days for February, 30 or 31 days for other months
- Pay Working Tax Credit in advance if you pay your employee in advance
- Pay the full amount even if your employee hasn't worked for you every day of the pay period
- Pay the full amount even if you are only paying
  - Statutory Sick Pay (SSP)
  - Statutory Maternity Pay (SMP)
  - Statutory Paternity Pay (SPP)
  - Statutory Adoption Pay (SAP)
  - Sickness, maternity, paternity or adoption payments under your own scheme
- Show the Working Tax Credit as a separate entry on the employee's pay slip as an addition to net pay
- Keep a record of the Working Tax Credit paid on the form P11 Deductions Working Sheet, or equivalent

**Do not:**

- Add Working Tax Credit to wages before you work out tax and NICs. It's not liable to PAYE tax and NICs
- Add Working Tax Credit to wages when working out pension contributions.  It's not treated as earnings
- Deduct Working Tax Credit from your employee's individual PAYE tax

To make changes to amounts paid you will receive an Amendment Notice, form TC701 if there is a change to the daily rate and you will be given 42 days notice.  You won't be asked to deal with more than two amendments in the employee's pay period (weekly/monthly/other).  If you do get a third amendment call the Employer's Helpline on 0845 7 143 143.

Do not stop paying the tax credit to an employee just because you suspect that they are not entitled to it or should be getting a smaller amount.  Employees (claimants), not you (the employer) are responsible for telling HMRC about changes in their circumstances which could affect their tax credit entitlement.  However, if you are particularly concerned, please telephone the Employer's Helpline.  The matter will then be reported to the Tax Credit Office who will, if necessary, contact the employee to see if there has been a change in their circumstances.

In the case that no wage, or salary, is due as a general rule you can make up a pay packet for an employee just to pay the Working Tax Credit but you don't have to.  If you prefer not to, please call the Employer's Helpline for advice.  This is especially relevant in cases where:

- An employee to whom you pay Working Tax Credit is not due to receive any wages, SSP, SMP, SPP or SAP in a pay period and
- You don't know if or when, that employee will start work again, even though they remain on your payroll (for example, casual workers who may have long gaps between periods of working)

You may in such cases wish to remind your employees that they should report changes of circumstances (e.g. reduced working hours, unpaid leave lasting for more than 4 weeks etc) that may affect their entitlement.

Provided you have paid tax credit in accordance with the instructions, you will not be responsible for any overpayment resulting from your employees' failure to give information that affects their tax credit award.

You can only stop payment if:

- You are told to on either
    - A form TC702 Stop notice, (you will have 42 days' notice), or
    - A form TC703 Emergency stop notice, (a date will have been agreed with you)
- You have no wages, SSP, SMP, SPP or SAP to pay on pay day. If this is the case, please call the Employer's Helpline for advice (see section 'No wages/salary due' above)
- Your employee
    - Leaves, or
    - Dies

**Starters and leavers**

Slightly different procedures apply when employees start or leave during the pay period. A new starter will bring with them a form P45 which will state their gross pay and tax deducted to date. This information will need to be entered onto a P11 and used to calculate their PAYE deductions. If they don't have a form P45 you must ask them why. This could be for a number of reasons:

- Their former employer didn't give them one. In this case they must ask their former employer to supply a P45. The employer has the statutory obligation to issue a P45 when employment ends
- The employee has lost their P45. It is not allowed by law for their previous employer to issue a duplicate so you must treat the employee as if they had never had a P45
- They were previously self-employed or were working abroad
- They were previously claiming unemployment benefit

If they are unable to supply a P45 you must complete a form P46. On this form the employee is asked to sign one of three statements:

Inland **Revenue**

**Details of employee leaving work** | **P45**
Copy for Inland Revenue office | Part 1

1 PAYE Reference

Office number    Reference number

2 Employee's National Insurance number

(Mr Mrs Miss Ms Other)

3 Surname (in CAPITALS)

First name(s) (in CAPITALS)

4 Leaving date (in figures)    Day    Month    Year

5 Continue Student Loan Deductions(Y)

6 Tax Code at leaving date. If Week 1 or Month 1 basis applies, write 'X' in the box marked Week 1 or Month 1.    Code    Week 1 or Month 1

7 Last entries on Deductions Working Sheet (P11). Complete only if Tax Code is cumulative. Make no entry here if Week 1 or Month 1 basis applies. Go to item 8.
Week or month number    Week    Month

Total pay to date    £    p

Total tax to date    £    p

8 This employment pay and tax. ∎No entry is needed if Tax Code is cumulative and amounts
Total pay in this employment    £    p

- **Statement A** - This is my first regular job since leaving full time education. I have not claimed Jobseekers Allowance or received Income Support because of unemployment since then
- **Statement B** - This is my only or main job
- **Statement C** - I receive a pension as well as the income from this job

If the employee signs Statement A or Statement B and the level of pay is above the NI threshold, the P46 should be sent to HMRC immediately, a form P11 prepared and tax deducted using the emergency tax code. If the level of pay is less than the PAYE threshold but more than the NIC lower earnings limit, keep the P46 and prepare a form P11. Enter 'NI' in the tax code space. If the pay is less than the PAYE threshold and less than the NIC lower earnings limit, keep the P46 and record the employee's name and address and amount of pay.

If Statement C is signed the P46 should be sent to HMRC immediately, a form P11 prepared and tax deducted at the basic rate using tax code BR. NICs should be deducted if earnings are above the lower earnings limit and the employee is below the state pension age.

If the employee doesn't sign any of the statements you must assume they have more than one job, send the P46 to HMRC immediately and deduct tax at the basic rate.

PAYE – notice of new employee

**Inland Revenue**

Send in on the first pay day for employees who
- do not have a form P45, or
- were previously paid below the PAYE threshold.

**Section 1 - to be completed by the EMPLOYEE**

Read each statement carefully. Tick **each one** that applies to you. **Only sign this form if you have ticked one or more of the boxes for Statement A, Statement B or Statement C.**

**Statement A**
This is my first regular job since leaving full-time education. I have not claimed Jobseekers Allowance, or income support paid because of unemployment since then.

**Statement B**
This is my only or main job.

**Statement C**
I receive a pension as well as the income from this job.

I confirm that I have ticked the statements that apply to me.

Signed _____    Date ___ / ___ / ___

**Section 2 - to be completed by the EMPLOYER**
Your Employer's Help Book *Day-to-day payroll, E13* tells you how to complete this form.
See Part 4 under 'A new employee doesn't give you a form P45'

Employee's details                Coding information

National Insurance                                    PAYE threshold

The P46 also requires the employee's National Insurance number. If the employee can't remember or find their NI number check any documentation you may have for the employee which shows the NI number.

If you are unable to find your employee's NI number:

- Keep a record of their full name - surname and first name(s) - address, date of birth, gender
- If you have to send a form P46 to your HMRC office take no further action as they will automatically trace the employee's NI number and tell you what it is. If the NI number cannot be traced, your Inland Revenue office will ask the Inland Revenue National Insurance Contributions Office to carry out a clerical trace, which may involve writing to your employee

If the NI number is traced the Inland Revenue National Insurance Contributions Office will confirm to you what it is on form P46-5, and confirm to your employee what it is on form P217.

It is important that form P46 is completed even in the circumstances where it is only to be kept on file as HMRC may carry out a PAYE compliance visit and will want to see a completed form P46 for every employee who has not provided a P45 regardless of the level of earnings. Where form P46 is not available they may assume that all employees have other jobs and deem all wages to be subject to PAYE and NICs. The employer can be held responsible for payment not only for the year in which P46s have not been completed, but for up to six years previously unless the employer can prove that a form P46 was not necessary.

When an employee leaves during a pay period it is important to remember to accurately calculate their pay up to their date of leaving, taking into account any pay in lieu of notice or any accrued holiday pay owing or to be deducted. A P45 must be completed and part 1 sent to HMRC immediately, while the employee is given parts 1a, 2 and 3. If the employee has died write 'D' in the box on the P45 and send all four parts to HMRC.

**Directors**

Many directors will receive a fixed monthly salary, but sometimes their total package includes performance bonuses or awards and this can complicate the calculation of their PAYE deductions. There may also be occasions when directors are provided with loans by the organisation as an advance against their salary or bonus.

Care needs to be taken over the pay period in which directors' pay is taxed. Complete guidance is given in the 'Employer's Further Guide to PAYE and NICs, CWG2' but, in general, pay is taxed when the director is entitled to receive payment even if it is not taken until later. Tax is payable on the earliest of the following dates:

- The date payment is made
- The date the director is entitled to be paid
- The date payment is credited to an account the director can draw on
- The date remuneration is decided on

Loans are liable to PAYE as soon as the advance is made. Directors are also treated differently for National Insurance purposes. Because their pay may vary considerably from one pay period to another, directors' NICs are based on their cumulative earnings for the tax year.

When all of the above deductions and additions to gross pay have been calculated and carried out, you will have calculated the employee's net pay. This amount will then have to be paid to the employees according to the arrangement the organisation has with its staff. Payment may be made by cash, cheque or directly into the employee's bank account.

The employees' forms P11 and SSP, SMP, SPP and SAP records must then be updated and the amounts due to HMRC in respect of PAYE, NICs, employer's NICs less any recoverable benefits calculated. These amounts are paid over to HMRC monthly or quarterly depending on the organisation's arrangements with HMRC. Amounts due to the pensions administrator and in respect of Attachments of Earnings are also calculated and the payments arranged.

The total amounts paid out in respect of wages, tax, National Insurance and pensions must then be input into the Nominal Ledger system in order to update the bank balance and expense codes. Management information can then be produced comparing these costs to the budgeted costs by week or month and by year to date. The content and format of the information provided will have been agreed with the management that requested it. Some levels of management will require detailed information while others will require an overview.

| Dept | This Month | | | | Year to date | | | |
|------|--------|--------|-------|--------|--------|--------|--------|--------|
| | Actual | Budget | +/- | % | Actual | Budget | +/- | % |
| Sales | 12427 | 11000 | 1427 | 12.97 | 72562 | 66000 | 6562 | 9.94 |
| Admin | 7312 | 8000 | (688) | (8.60) | 43943 | 48000 | (4057) | (8.45) |
| Purchasing | 8319 | 9000 | (681) | (7.57) | 53151 | 54000 | (849) | (1.57) |
| Despatch | 5369 | 4000 | 1369 | 34.23 | 26294 | 24000 | 2294 | 9.56 |
| Total | 33427 | 32000 | 1427 | 4.46 | 195950 | 192000 | 3950 | 2.06 |

The above table is a simplified example of the management information that can be produced. From this information you can see that the sales and despatch departments are significantly overspent against their budgets while the administration and purchasing departments have made significant savings. There may, of course, be legitimate reasons for the overspend; despatch may have had an unplanned workload to meet demand generated by the extra efforts of the sales department. It is not the function of the payroll department to make judgments on the information, merely to provide the information for operational management to base decisions upon.

Other departments may seek clarification from you on the management information provided. In the example shown, for instance, the manager of the despatch department may ask for further information on the monthly overspend which has taken his department over budget for the year to date. By providing a breakdown of the total monthly spend and the equivalent figures for previous months the reason for the variation may be found. It may be, for instance, that one or more members of the despatch department have received payments of accrued holiday pay or overtime payments.

Individuals may query items on their pay slip, most often querying the calculation of gross pay or amounts deducted. Their concerns must be dealt with sympathetically, providing them with as much information as possible to satisfy their query. Where you are unable to fully answer the query because, for instance, you have received notification of a change in their Tax Code, you should advise them how to contact the people who can fully explain the situation.

It may be that on investigation you discover an error has been made. Where this has resulted in the employee being disadvantaged there are two alternatives open to you. Either an adjustment can be made in the next pay period or an advance can be paid immediately and the adjustment made in the next pay period. The decision will probably depend on the amount involved and the wishes of the employee. Whichever option is followed, detailed notes must be kept of the cause of the discrepancy and the action taken so that accurate adjustments can be made.

Having resolved the error to the satisfaction of the employee it is necessary to investigate the cause of the error to prevent re-occurrence. The investigation may reveal the need for staff training or a security problem. Unfortunately staff working in payroll have opportunities to defraud an organisation. Some of the security areas to check are:

- Creation of dummy employees or casual workers
- Continuing to pay employees after they have left
- Payments of unauthorised overtime, bonus or holiday pay
- Different deductions entered on pay slips and P11s

Random checks may uncover security problems but a more reliable method is to check sections of the payroll from start to finish on a rolling basis.

To preserve confidentiality of payroll information, queries from individuals should be dealt with face-to-face or, if the size or geographical spread of the organisation makes this difficult, in writing. Telephone queries should be discouraged both because of the risk of impersonation and because of potential difficulties arising from unrecorded agreements.

Other queries may be received from government bodies such as HMRC or the Department of Work and Pensions or such organisations as the Child Support Agency or mortgage lenders. In general, while government bodies have the authority to ask for information on individuals' circumstances, any other organisation seeking such information will need the authority of the individual. Such requests for information should, therefore, be referred to the individual involved before any confidential facts are disclosed.

# What you need to know

How to calculate gross pay

What is pay?

The characteristics of employment and self-employment

What information **must** appear on a pay slip?

The deductions that may be made from gross pay

What do the terms 'SMP', 'SSP', 'SPP' and 'SAP' mean?

The employee records that must be retained

How does the calculation of NICs for directors differ from other employees?

How to calculate Income Tax and NICs due

How often does your organisation make payments to HMRC?

Your organisation's pay periods and payment methods

How are the amounts due to HMRC calculated?

The importance of receiving form P45 from new starters

What action should you take if there is no National Insurance number given on a new starter's form P46?

The distribution of the copies of a P45 for a leaver

Who are you obliged to supply with information on an individual's circumstances?

The level of management information required in your organisation

Why would you not give confidential information over the telephone?

## Managing redundancy situations

When an organisation finds it necessary to make employees redundant, you will receive a list of the affected employees and the date their employment is to be terminated. Check the list to ensure that there are no apparent breaches of employment legislation. If you have any concerns in this area raise them with the department responsible for selecting the redundancies.

Once any queries have been resolved and the list is finalised, liaise with the pensions administrator in order that they can organise any necessary abatement of pensions contributions or payment of any pensions benefits due.

Employees fulfilling the following criteria are entitled to statutory redundancy pay under the Employment Rights Act 1996:

- Employees continuously employed for a period of two years, excluding any period before the employee attained the age of 18
- Employees made redundant, broadly speaking, because the business is ceasing or the requirements of the business have altered in such a way that the kind of work carried out by the employee is no longer needed

Employees may be disqualified from claiming redundancy payments if:

- The business has undergone a change of ownership, but the business has continued to operate as before. Only if the change of ownership leads to cessation of the business or some other alteration, as a result of which the employee is dismissed, can they claim redundancy
- They have attained the normal retirement age for a person in the employee's position or, if there is no normal retirement age, the age of 65
- They are working under a fixed-term contract agreed, renewed or extended since 1 October 2002

- They are members of the armed forces, Parliamentary staff or Crown servants

Although directors are not specifically excluded, it is arguable whether they are in fact covered by the Employment Rights Act. Where a company ceases to trade, statutory payments are in practice made to directors in relation to services performed as employees under contracts of service (whether written or not).

A statutory redundancy payment is due where the employee is dismissed (as compared with resignation). For this purpose, an employee volunteering for redundancy is dismissed. If the employee leaves before the redundancy date by agreement, payment remains due.

Statutory redundancy pay is calculated as the total of:

| For each complete year of service between 18 and 21 | ½ a week's pay |
|---|---|
| For each complete year of service between 22 and 40 | 1 week's pay |
| For each complete year of service between 41 and 65 | 1½ weeks' pay |

For the purpose of calculation:

- The minimum is one week per year of service up to a maximum of 12 weeks
- A 'week's pay' is the amount due under the employment contract on the date that the minimum notice of termination was or should have been given, but
- A week's pay can't exceed a specified figure which is uprated annually by HMRC

Some organisations will pay higher levels of redundancy pay than those required by legislation (non-statutory). These may be part of a redundancy package which includes payments made for reasons other than redundancy. Provided these non-statutory redundancy payments are made in a genuine redundancy situation then they too are considered by HMRC as compensatory and free from Income Tax (unless they exceed £30,000) and NICs. The general conditions that must be satisfied are:

- The employee must have at least two years' continuous service

- Payment must be made to all employees being made redundant
- Payment must not be excessively large in relation to earnings and length of service

The table below shows examples of payments that may form part of the redundancy package and where tax and National Insurance are payable.

| Payment | Tax payable? | NICs payable? |
|---|---|---|
| Redundancy payment | Only on the amount over £30,000 | NO |
| Unpaid wages | YES | YES |
| Bonus payment | YES | YES |
| Accrued holiday pay | YES | YES |
| Occupational pension | YES | NO |

Having calculated the effect on the employees' gross pay and deductions, input the figures into the payroll system so that the employees receive a payment on their termination date that includes all the monies due to them.  Organise the production of a P45 for every employee.

As redundancy will not occur regularly, you will need to exercise care in dealing with what will probably be an unfamiliar situation.  Ensure that all calculations are double-checked before they are actioned, and that all communication regarding redundancy is subject to absolute confidentiality.

 **What you need to know**

The impact of the Employment Rights Act
1996 on redundancy

How can employers ensure their
selection for redundancy complies with
Employment Legislation?

The elements of a redundancy package
that are liable for tax and National
Insurance

What is the basis for the calculation of statutory redundancy pay?

Who to refer queries on redundancy selection to

What are the criteria for non-statutory redundancy payments to be exempt from Income Tax and NICs?

How to investigate apparent security problems within the payroll department

What regular checks should be made on the payroll system to prevent embezzlement?

For many organisations wages and salaries are the largest expense item in the budget. The payroll department is responsible for administering the payment of monies due to both employees and Her Majesty's Revenue and Customs. The calculation of deductions can be extremely complicated. Many organisations operate their payroll through a computerised package, but it is essential that at least the manager of the payroll function understands how to calculate tax and National Insurance manually.

## The accurate calculation of payments due to employees is critical both to the efficient operation of the organisation and the morale of the staff

# Are you ready for assessment?

To achieve this unit of a Level 3 Business & Administration qualification you will need to demonstrate that you are competent in the following:

- Ensure the treatment of all allowances and enhancements is correctly identified with respect to tax, National Insurance and pensions deductions
- Update rates for permanent and temporary payments and deductions against agreed scales for each type of employee affected
- Calculate exceptional payments in accordance with organisational requirements, to the deadlines agreed
- Reconcile the National Insurance liability for directors against the National Insurance actually paid
- Monitor compliance with attachments to earnings legislation
- Ensure termination payments are processed accurately and in accordance with legislative requirements
- Reconcile total charges to organisational budgets against aggregate payroll totals and correctly code them for allocation
- Seek clarification or additional information from employees or managers where the nature of their queries is not clear
- Check that individuals raising queries are authorised to receive the information they are requesting
- Agree all requests for information for content, and the medium in which data is to be presented, together with the format of the information and deadlines for the despatch of information
- Produce accurate information that meets the requirements agreed with the intended recipients
- Respond to telephone or face-to-face enquiries accurately and in accordance with the organisation's customer care requirements
- Refer enquiries to the appropriate person when you do not have the authority or expertise to resolve them

- Ensure all documentation relating to the redundancy is checked for compliance with statutory and organisational requirements
- Refer documentation that does not comply with statutory and organisational requirements to the appropriate person for resolution
- Calculate the length of reckonable service, age and value of a week's pay in accordance with statutory rules
- Calculate the amount of any statutory redundancy payment accurately
- Apply the terms of any local, non-statutory scheme to enhance the statutory payment correctly
- Inform the relevant pensions administrator where the redundancy is linked to pensionable retirement; calculate any abatement correctly and apply it to the final payment
- Input to the payroll system all sums due in respect of the redundancy in ways that ensure that payments will be made at the correct time and will receive the appropriate tax treatment
- Ensure all communications relating to redundancy are conducted at an appropriate level of confidentiality

(Remember that you will need the skills listed at the beginning of this chapter. These are covered in chapter 1.)

You will need to produce evidence from a variety of sources. Carrying out the following activities will help you acquire competence at work.

**Activity 1**

You work as the payroll manager at Pickings Distribution Ltd. You are informed confidentially by the Human Resources manager that five employees are to be made redundant on 30 August 2006. From the information supplied, calculate the gross redundancy payment due to each employee, deductions to be made, and net redundancy payments due.

| Name | Date of birth | Start date | Annual salary |
|------|---------------|------------|---------------|
| Margaret Buckland | 16.05.46 | 15.04.64 | £30,000 |
| Catherine Christian | 16.04.82 | 29.04.98 | £17,500 |
| Arthur Bellamy | 22.10.62 | 13.06.03 | £26,450 |
| Clive Akabusi | 30.08.87 | 23.07.04 | £12,650 |
| Mohammed Saladin | 01.01.77 | 17.06.05 | £15,525 |

The organisation has decided to make non-statutory payments amounting to 5% of annual salary in addition to the statutory redundancy payments.

## Activity 2
Research the Employment Rights Act, the Data Protection Act and Industrial Tribunals legislation and write a report stating how they impact on your job role.

## Activity 3
A new starter to your organisation commences work on 1 June. They present you with a P45 showing their total pay to date as £4,000.00, their tax to date as £294.35 and their Tax Code as 600H. Their annual salary in their new job is to be £30,000.00 paid in 12 equal payments on the last day of each month. Calculate their tax and National Insurance deductions using the Tax Tables available from HRMC for their first three pay periods.

## Activity 4
Complete a form P11 for the following employees for the tax year 2005-2006 taking into account the increases in salary during the tax year

| Name | NI No. | DOB | Tax Code | NI Table | Salary at 6 Apr | % Increase in salary | Date of increase |
|------|--------|-----|----------|----------|-----------------|----------------------|------------------|
| J Willis | FH788990A | 15.04.71 | 549H | A | 19,000 | 3.2 | 01.08.05 |
| D Smith | GA769702A | 30.03.73 | 532H | A | 16,500 | 3.5 | 01.07.05 |
| A Lui | HD563864A | 27.05.67 | 682H | A | 20,555 | 3.1 | 01.10.05 |
| S West | JL984595L | 13.10.51 | 556L | A | 36,268 | 2.95 | 13.09.05 |
| V Hunt | LJ948502L | 06.08.49 | 546H | A | 27,959 | 4.6 | 06.08.05 |
| I S Pratt | LG385036H | 15.03.82 | 246L | A | 16,500 | 5.5 | 31.12.05 |
| V Deep | AH468154H | 26.09.81 | 493H | A | 14,035 | 5.1 | 05.02.06 |

## Activity 5
Keep a work diary over three pay periods showing the queries you have received and how you have dealt with them.

Remember:  While gathering evidence for this unit, evidence **may** be generated for units 110, 212, 213, 216, 218, 301, 302, 307, 310, 315, 320 and 321.

# CHAPTER 16
# UNIT 307 – Complete year-end procedures

Every employer is required to deduct Income Tax and National Insurance Contributions (NICs) from their employees' pay. In turn these deductions have to be paid to Her Majesty's Revenue and Customs (HMRC). Returns have to be completed and forwarded to HMRC annually to report on the amounts deducted or withheld from employees and paid to HMRC during the tax year, which runs from 6 April – 5 April. At the end of every tax year each employee has to be given a form P60 advising them of their total pay and deductions. Unless you have a dispensation from HMRC excusing you from completing them, employers must also complete either a form P11D or a form P9D if their employees have received expenses or benefits during the tax year.

There are substantial financial penalties for organisations who fail to submit their returns by the deadlines laid down by HMRC so it is important that tax year-end procedures are well organised and carried out efficiently to a planned timetable. The deadline dates and penalties for failure to comply are currently as follows:

| Deadline | | Penalty |
|---|---|---|
| 19 April | Pay all outstanding tax and Class 1 NICs | Automatic interest charge |
| 19 May | Forms P35 submitted | Automatic penalties |
| 31 May | Forms P60 given to employees | Penalties |
| 6 July | Forms P11D and P9D submitted | Up to £300 per return |
| 6 July | Forms P11D and P9D given to employees | Penalties |
| 19 July | Pay all outstanding Class 1A NICs | Automatic interest charge |
| 19 July | Forms P11D(b) submitted | Penalties |
| 19 October | Pay Income Tax and Class 1B NICs on any PAYE Settlement Agreement | Automatic interest charge |

With effect from 2003 organisations have been able, and in some cases required, to submit their returns electronically. The timetable for electronic filing becoming obligatory depends on the number of people employed by an organisation, but there are incentives available to encourage employers who are not yet required to use this communication method.  The timetable is as follows:

| No. of employees | First electronic return | Deadline for submission |
|---|---|---|
| 250 or more | 2004-2005 | 19 May 2005 |
| 50 - 249 | 2005-2006 | 19 May 2006 |
| 1 - 49 | 2009-2010 | 19 May 2010 |

You can send your Return online using:
- The online services of an agent or payroll bureau
- The Inland Revenue's free Online service (recommended for up to 50 P14s)
- 3rd party payroll software
- Electronic data exchange (EDI) - more suitable for large employers

Year-end summaries of salaries and wages paid, tax and NICs deducted and amounts outstanding to be paid to HMRC must be produced to supply management information and to ensure an organisation's accounts can be completed.

When completing year-end procedures you will use the following skills:

- Planning
- Organising
- Researching
- Checking
- Communicating
- Using technology
- Reading
- Recording
- Problem solving
- Using number
- Managing time

These skills are covered in chapter 1.

## Payroll year-end returns

By the dates shown in the table above, every organisation has to supply HMRC with a summary of their payroll information.  A number of forms are supplied for this purpose, although most can be completed online.

### Form P14

During the year a form P11 will have been completed for every employee who has had tax and/or NICs deducted. Form P14 summarises the figures from each employee's form P11.

Fill in a form P14 for each employee employed during the tax year (including those who have left during the tax year) using totals from the form P11.

| Section on form P14 | Advice |
|---|---|
| Employer's name and address | • Show your full address, including the postcode<br>• Don't use sticky labels or a rubber stamp in this box |
| Inland Revenue office name and Employer's PAYE reference | • Enter your Inland Revenue office name and Employer's PAYE reference from the front of form P35. You will also find this on the front of your P30BC, Payslip Booklet |
| Tax Year to 5 April | If you are using a form P14 that does not have the year pre-printed:<br>• Make sure the forms are for the right year<br>• Enter all four numbers of the year, for example: 2005 |
| Employee's details<br>National Insurance number | Copy this from the front of form P11.<br>• It will be two letters, six numbers, followed by one letter (for example, AB123456C)<br>• Ensure that the full and correct number is quoted and can be read clearly |
| Date of birth | • Enter the day and month as well as all four numbers of the year your employee was born |
| Surname and first two forenames | • If you don't know the employee's full forename(s), put their initial - or initials - at the start of each forename box<br>• Don't put titles (like Mr, Mrs or Ms) or nicknames |

| | |
|---|---|
| **National Insurance contributions in this employment**<br><br>NIC Table letter<br>Columns 1a to 1c | • Copy this from the End of Year Summary section on the back of form P11<br><br>• Copy these amounts from the End of Year Summary section of form P11<br><br>• Make entries in whole pounds only. For example, in column 1a 3773 - not 3773.00<br><br>• The entries in these boxes must be 'right justified'. For example, in column 1b, '£572' is shown as, 5 7 2<br><br>• If the employee is normally weekly or monthly paid - and earned consistently above the earnings threshold - the amounts in columns 1a and 1b inclusive should always be<br><br>    1a - a multiple of the Lower Earnings Limit (LEL)<br><br>    1b - a multiple of Earnings Threshold (ET) minus LEL<br><br>• If there is an entry in column 1a, you must still send in form P14 - even though no NICs may be payable<br><br>NB. If you are sending your P14s online you must complete columns 1a to 1c. Where there are no earnings or no NICs to report, complete form P14 to show contribution category letter X and zero fill columns 1a to 1c. |
| Columns 1d and 1e | • Copy these amounts from the End of Year Summary section on form P11<br><br>• The amounts in these columns must be in pounds and pence<br><br>• Where you operate a contracted-out occupational |

| | |
|---|---|
| | pension scheme, and the column 1d total to be carried forward from the P11 is a minus figure, enter 'R' in the corresponding box immediately to the right of the column 1d total boxes on the P14<br><br>NB. If you are sending your P14s online you must complete columns 1d and 1e. Where there are no earnings or no NICs to report, complete form P14 to show contribution category letter X and zero fill columns 1d and 1e. |
| **Statutory payments in this employment**<br><br>Box 1f | • Insert here the total amount of SSP paid to the employee in those tax months for which an amount has been recovered under the Percentage Threshold Scheme |
| Boxes 1g to 1i | • Copy these amounts from the corresponding columns on form P11 |
| Scheme Contracted-out Number | • Only fill in this box if the employee is a member of a Contracted-out Money Purchase (COMP), COMP Stakeholder Pension scheme (COMPSHP) or the COMP part of the Contracted-out Mixed Benefit (COMB) scheme that you operate<br><br>• You can find this number on your Contracting-out Certificate. If you can't find your Certificate, telephone the Contracted-out Pensions Helpline on **0115 974 1444**<br><br>• Please leave blank if the employee is part of a Contracted-Out Salary Related (COSR) scheme or the COSR part of a COMB scheme |

| | |
|---|---|
| | From 6 April 1997 members of a COMP or COMPSHP scheme, including the COMP part of a COMB scheme, receive a rebate of their NICs based on their age. This is known as an Age Related Rebate (ARR). When completing the employee's form P14, End of Year Summary, you must ensure that the correct Scheme Contracted-out Number (SCON) is entered on form P14 against the relevant earnings. |
| | Failure to enter the correct SCON, where contribution Table letter F or G applies, will result in non-payment of the ARR. |
| Student Loan Deductions | • Copy this amount from the totals box at the bottom of column 1j on form P11 <br><br> • Enter total £s only on form P14 |
| Tax Credits | • Copy this amount from the totals box below the bottom of column 9 on form P11 <br><br> • If there is an entry in this box you must send in form P14, even if the employee paid no tax or NICs in the tax year <br><br> • NB. See above, Columns 1a to 1c and Columns 1d and 1e. |
| Date of starting and Date of leaving | • Only make an entry in these boxes if the employee starts and/or leaves your employment during the tax year <br><br> • Please use figures only, for example 10 05 2004 |
| **Pay and Income Tax details** <br> In previous employment(s) | Enter here details you have of pay and tax deducted for employments earlier in the year. <br><br> • Enter '0.00' if there was no previous employment |
| In this employment | • Always fill in these boxes. The amount must be in pounds and |

| | pence |
|---|---|
| Total for year | • Only fill in these boxes if the employee was working for you at 5 April **and** you know the pay and tax figures for the year, including those for any previous employments |
| Employee's Widows & Orphans/ Life Assurance contributions in this employment | • Where an employee is legally obliged to pay contributions to a Widows/Widowers and Orphans, or Life Assurance fund, that qualify for tax relief but are not authorised under 'net pay arrangements' for tax relief, enter the amount of contributions paid up to a maximum of £100.  For further information on 'net pay arrangements' see the Employer's Further Guide to PAYE and NICs, CWG2, under 'pensions contributions paid by employee' |
| Final tax code | • Fill these boxes from the left-hand side<br><br>• Always show here the tax code you were using at 5 April, or when you last paid your employee<br><br>• Only enter the tax code. Do not include any other characters like asterisks or leading zeros<br><br>• If you operated the tax code on a week 1/month 1 basis, enter 'W1' or 'M1' after the code. Do not use any other abbreviations<br><br>• Where form P11 shows 'NI' in the tax code box, leave the tax code box on form P14 blank<br><br>• Change any suffix A or H code to a T code to avoid rejection of your return |
| Payment in week 53 | • If Payment in Week 53 is included in the Pay and Tax |

| | totals, put one of the following notations in this box '53' if there were 53 weekly paydays in the year. '54' if there were 27 fortnightly paydays in the year. '56' if there were 14 four weekly paydays in the year |
|---|---|

Put the forms into alphabetical order of surname, or in the order you list your employees on the P35.

- If you use **both** forms P14 and approved substitutes, list and bundle them separately
- If you are sending in both landscape and portrait P14s, arrange your P35 listing and P14 bundles in this order: landscape first, portrait second. This will speed up the processing of the forms

## Form P35

Form P35 is the 'Employer's Annual Return'. It summarises Income Tax and NICs deducted from employees and Statutory Sick Pay (SSP), Statutory Maternity Pay (SMP), Statutory Paternity Pay (SPP) and Statutory Adoption Pay (SAP) recovered.

Paper forms P35 are issued by HMRC towards the end of each tax year. If you haven't received yours by the end of March contact your Inland Revenue office.

The paper P35 is a 4-page form.
- Page 1 tells you what your obligations are, and where to get further help
- Pages 2 and 3 require you to list the details of your employees and summarise your payments for the year
- Page 4 contains several 'tick box' questions for you to complete before signing and dating the form

If you previously filed online using the Internet, and are currently registered to do so, then you will not receive a paper form. Instead a P35N (Notification to File) will be sent to your Secure Mailbox.

**Filling in Pages 2 and 3 of form P35**
**Part 1 Summary of payments for the year**

You must list each employee for whom you have completed a form P11, Deductions Working Sheet or equivalent record. NB: If some or all of your forms P14 are being sent by Internet, Electronic Data Interchange (EDI) or Magnetic Media, there is no need complete the Part 1, Summary of employees and directors, section of the return.

If there are more than 10 entries you will have to use forms P35(CS), Continuation Sheets (or equivalents). If you didn't receive any with your form P35, or did but want some more, they are available on the Employer's CD-ROM or by logging on to the HMRC website at the Employers Home Page.

Alternatively you can call the Employer's Orderline on **0845 7 646 646** or use your own equivalent record as long as it contains the same information.

You will need to list:
- For limited companies, directors first and mark their entries with an asterisk (*)
- Your employees in alphabetical order, or in the same order as you have collated the P14s
- For each employee, the total of employee's and employer's NICs recorded in column 1d of the 'End of Year Summary' box on form P11
- For each employee, the tax deducted or refunded, recorded in the 'In this employment' box on form P11

If you make a mistake and record the wrong entry:
- Draw a line through the entry so that it can still be read, and
- Record the correct detail alongside

## Part 2 Summary of payments for the year

Complete boxes 1 to 32 as applicable and check that your payments to the Accounts Office are correct. NB: If you were not required to complete boxes 1, 2, 4 and 5 in Part 1 (see above notes) you must begin by entering the respective NICs and Income Tax totals for all your employees for whom you have completed a form P11 (or equivalent record) regardless of how your forms P14 have been submitted.

| | |
|---|---|
| Box 1 | Add up the entries from the NICs column (on form P35). Enter the total in Box 1. Mark minus amounts 'R'. |
| Box 2 | You will only use this box if you prepare more than 10 forms P14. Enter the total amount(s) of NICs brought forward from any form P35(CS), Continuation Sheets (or equivalents) used. Mark minus amounts 'R'. |
| Box 3 | Add Box 1 and Box 2 together, and enter the total in Box 3. This gives you the total amount of NICs deducted. Mark minus amounts 'R'. |
| Box 4 | Add up the entries from the Income Tax column above (on form P35). Enter the total in Box 4. Mark minus amounts 'R'. |
| Box 5 | You will only use this box if you prepare more than 10 forms P14. Enter the total amount(s) of Income Tax brought forward from any form P35(CS), Continuation Sheets (or equivalents) used. Mark minus amounts 'R'. |
| Box 6 | Add Box 4 and Box 5 together, and enter the total in Box 6. This gives you the total amount of tax deducted. Mark minus amounts 'R'. |
| Box 7 | You will only use this box if you asked your Accounts Office for an advance. Enter the amount you received in Box 7.<br><br>You would have asked for an advance if you had to make tax refunds to employees but didn't have enough deductions in hand from which to pay them.<br><br>You need to pay back these amounts because you received credit for paying them in Boxes 4 and 5. You may have recorded these payments on form P32, Employer's Payment Record (or equivalent), or your P30BC, Payslip Booklet. |

| | |
|---|---|
| Box 8 | You will only use this box if you deducted tax from subcontractors during the year. Refer to your CIS36, Contractor's Annual Return. Copy the amount from Box F of the CIS36 to Box 8 of the P35. |
| Box 9 | Add Boxes 6 + 7 + 8 and enter the total in Box 9. |
| Box 10 | Add Box 3 to Box 9, and enter the total in Box 10. |
| Box 11 | You will only use this box if you made any Student Loan Deductions this year. Add together the total amounts shown in column 1j on all the forms P11 and enter this new total in Box 11 (whole pounds only). |
| Box 12 | Add Box 10 to Box 11, and enter the total in Box 12. This gives you the total deductions made, including NICs, Income Tax and Student Loan Deductions. |
| Box 13 | If you have paid SSP to your employees during the year, enter in Box 13 the amount you are entitled to recover under the Percentage Threshold Scheme (PTS). Include any payments received directly from your Accounts Office to cover the recovery of SSP, which you have also shown at Box 22. For further details see the Employer's Help Book, E14, What to do if your employee is sick. |
| Box 14 | If you have paid SMP to your employees during the year, enter in Box 14 the amount you are entitled to recover. Include any payments received directly from your Accounts Office to cover the recovery of SMP, which you have also shown at Box 22. For further details see the Employer's Help Book, E15, Pay and time off work for parents. |
| Box 15 | Enter in Box 15 any compensation you are entitled to claim in addition to the SMP recovered. For further details see the Employer's Help Book, E15, Pay and time off work for parents. |
| Box 16 | If you have paid SPP to your employees during the year, enter in Box 16 the amount you are entitled to recover. Include any payments received directly from your Accounts Office to cover the recovery of SPP, which you have also shown at Box 22. For further details see the Employer's Help Book, E15, Pay and time off work for parents. |
| Box 17 | Enter in Box 17 any compensation you are entitled to claim in addition to the SPP recovered. For further details see the Employer's Help Book, E15, Pay and time off work for parents. |

| | |
|---|---|
| Box 18 | If you have paid SAP to your employees during the year, enter in Box 18 the amount you are entitled to recover. Include any payments received directly from your Accounts Office to cover the recovery of SAP, which you have also shown at Box 22. For further details see the Employer's Help Book, E16, Pay and time off work for adoptive parents. |
| Box 19 | Enter in Box 19 any compensation you are entitled to claim in addition to the SAP recovered. For further details see the Employer's Help Book, E16, Pay and time off work for adoptive parents. |
| Box 20 | You will only use this box if you applied for an NIC Holiday and are entitled to your share of the NIC back. Enter the amount in Box 20. You may have recorded this information on your form P32, Employer's Payment Record (or equivalent), or your P30BC, Payslip Booklet. |
| Box 21 | Add all Boxes from 13 to 20 together, and enter the total in Box 21. |
| Box 22 | You will only use this box if you received funding from your Accounts Office to pay SSP/SMP/ SPP/SAP or to recover the amounts of SSP/SMP/SPP/SAP you have paid. Enter the total amount of funding received in Box 22. You may have recorded this information on your form P32, Employer's Payment Record (or equivalent), or your P30BC, Payslip Booklet. |
| Box 23 | Calculate Box 21 minus Box 22, to get the net amount of statutory payments recovered. Enter the total in Box 23. |
| Box 24 | You will only use this box if you have received form TC700, Employer notification to start paying tax credits and have paid tax credits to your employees. Add together the total amounts shown in column 9 on all the forms P11, and enter this new total in Box 24. |
| Box 25 | You will only use this box if you received funding from your Accounts Office to pay tax credits. Enter the total funding received in Box 25. Refer to your final form TC712, Tax credits - Funding Notice, for this year. |
| Box 26 | Calculate Box 24 minus Box 25 to get the net amount of tax credits. Enter the total in Box 26. |
| Box 27 | Add Box 23 to Box 26 and enter the total in Box 27. This is the total amount of statutory payments recovered and net tax credits. |

| | |
|---|---|
| Box 28 | To check the total amount payable by you for the year:<br>• Calculate Box 12 minus Box 27, but<br>• If Box 27 is a minus figure – add Box 27 to Box 12 |
| Box 29 | Enter the total of NICs and Tax that you have paid to your Accounts Office during the year.  Remember to include any overpayment from the previous year transferred to this account by the Inland Revenue.  You may have recorded your payments on form P32, Employer's Payment Record (or equivalent), or your P30BC, Payslip Booklet. |
| Box 30 | Enter in Box 30 the amount in Box 28 minus the amount in Box 29.  If the figure in Box 29 is less than the figure in Box 28, the figure you enter in Box 30 is the amount still to be paid to the Inland Revenue.  Send the balance to the Accounts Office immediately - do not send it with your form P35.  See your P30BC, Payslip Booklet for instructions on how to make payment.  Interest will be charged if the balance is paid after 19 April 2005.  If the figure in Box 29 is more than the figure in Box 28, you may have overpaid and should enter the amount in Box 30 with the letter 'M' (for minus) in front.  Your Inland Revenue office will be in touch in due course about any overpayment shown in Box 30. |

Only fill in Boxes 31 and 32 if you are a limited company and CIS deductions have been taken from payments received for work in the construction industry.

| | |
|---|---|
| Box 31 | CIS deductions are recorded on forms CIS25.  Refer to form CIS132, column E, for the total deductions suffered and copy this amount to Box 31. |
| Box 32 | Enter in Box 32 the amount in Box 30 minus the amount in Box 31.  If the figure in Box 31 is less than the figure in Box 30, the figure you enter in Box 32 is the amount still to be paid to the Inland Revenue.  Send the balance to the Accounts Office immediately - do not send it with your form P35.  See your P30BC, Payslip Booklet for instructions on how to make payment.  Interest will be charged if the balance is paid after 19 April.  If the figure in Box 31 is more than the figure in Box 30, you may have overpaid and should enter the amount in Box 32 with the letter 'M' (for minus) in front.  Your Inland Revenue office will be in touch in due course about any overpayment shown in Box 32. |

## Filling in Page 4 of form P35

Now turn to Page 4 of the form and use the prompts below to help you complete it.

### Part 3 Checklist

#### Question 1
If you have employees for whom you have not completed a form P14, or P38(S), tick 'No'.

These employees are likely to be part-time or casual staff. If you tick 'No' you must complete a form P38A, Employer's Supplementary Return, which you can get from the Employer's Orderline on **0845 7 646 646**.

#### Question 2
A 'free of tax payment' is a payment where the employer (rather than the employee) bears any tax due.

#### Question 3
Has someone other than you paid expenses or provided benefits to any of your employees during the year as a result of the employee working for you?

#### Question 4
This question is in two parts. If the answer to the first part of this question is 'Yes', you will have to complete and enclose a form P14 for each employee concerned.

#### Question 5
Did you pay any part of the employee's pay direct to anyone else, for example, paying school fees direct to a school?
If you did, was the payment included in the employee's pay for tax and NICs purposes and in the pay shown on the employee's form P14?

This does not include Attachment of Earnings Orders or payments to the Child Support Agency.

#### Question 6
The rules referred to, also known as IR35 rules, may apply to anyone supplying their services to a client through an intermediary, such as a service company or partnership.
For further guidance about the IR35 rules:

- Visit the HMRC website
- Call the IR35 Helpline on **0845 303 3535**
- Obtain the leaflet IR175, Supplying services through a limited company or partnership, from any Inland Revenue office or from the Employer's Orderline

The only engagements affected by the IR35 rules are those in which the worker would be classed as an employee of the client if it were not for the service company or partnership involvement.

Where the rules apply the intermediary may have to account for an additional amount of PAYE and NICs, based upon the income from the engagements, after an allowance for certain expenses and pension contributions.

If you had anyone who worked through an intermediary such as a service company or partnership in the year to 5 April, tick the first 'Yes' box under this question.

If you included any PAYE and NICs deducted from the deemed remuneration on this form P35, Employer's Annual Return, tick the second 'Yes' box under this question.

If you tick the second 'Yes' box but the amount of the deemed payment is provisional, confirm on a separate sheet and send it with the form P35, Employer's Annual Return.

Under the current arrangements if you can't finalise the amounts by 19 May, you will not have to pay a penalty so long as you send in your form P35, Employer's Annual Return by that date, and you pay all of the PAYE and NICs due in respect of the deemed payment by 31 January. If these arrangements are withdrawn, or changed, notification will be given in a Press Release.

You will still be charged interest from 19 April until the date when the PAYE and NICs are paid.

### Part 4 Contracted-out pension schemes

If you operated a pension scheme that was contracted-out of the State Second pension, enter the employer's contracted-out number from your Contracting-out Certificate in this box.

## Part 5 Employer's certificate and declaration
## It is very important that you complete and sign this section.

This section consists of several statements covering the return of forms P14, P38A, P11D, P11D(b) and P9D.
The appropriate boxes need to be ticked to indicate that forms are enclosed, will be sent later, or are not due.
The person signing the form must say who they are, for example, company secretary, payroll manager, proprietor and so on.
If you are sending your Return in parts **you must**:
  • Use a P14 Cover sheet, available from the Employer's Orderline, for any part containing paper P14s, or your Return will be rejected
  • Choose a unique identifier for each P14 part being sent
  • Show in the box provided the number of P14 parts being sent (not including the P35 itself)

NB: If you intend to send your Employer's Annual Return (P14s and P35) solely on paper you must continue to send your form P35 and all your forms P14 together in full to your Inland Revenue office.

Online Return and Forms - PAYE, or 3rd party software, which lets you send your Employer's Annual Return in parts will ask you for a unique identifier, which you must provide prior to the submission of each P14 part. The unique identifier can be anything that you find easy to remember, up to 12 characters. Whoever sends the P35 must know exactly how many P14 parts are being sent in total.

HMRC will only tell you that a Return sent in parts has been accepted when all the parts have been checked to make sure that they meet their quality standards.

If you want to send your Return in parts, see your Employer's CD-ROM.

## Form P38(S) and P38A

For any student employed by you during their holidays you will need to complete a form P38(S) which states the amount of pay they earned. For any employee for whom you did not complete a form P14 or a form P38(S) you will need to complete a form P38A.

On the front of form P38A complete:

- The employer's name
- Tax Office
- Tax District reference
- Collection reference

If you hold a form P46 completed at either statement A or statement B for each employee and each employee was paid less than the Lower Earnings Limit (LEL) you can sign a declaration to that effect and you don't need to complete the back of the form.

On the back of form P38A complete Section A for any employee who was paid more than the LEL in any pay period or who was taken on for more than a week unless they are a harvest worker:

- The full name of the employee
- The last known address of the employee
- The National Insurance Number

- The type of work done
- The dates employed if less than a full year
- The total pay for the year ended 5<sup>th</sup> April

Complete in Section B the same details for:

- Any worker who was paid more than £100.00 in total in the year ended 5<sup>th</sup> April who has not already listed in Section A and
- Harvest workers

You must then sign a declaration that either:

- You have made no payments that need to be listed or
- That the details given above, and on the attached sheets, are correct and complete

After you have filled in your P14s, P35 and where appropriate P38(S) and P38A:

- Remove any pins or staples
- Detach any stubs or sprocket holes
- Separate the three parts of each form P14, or the individual copies if you use continuous stationery
- Make separate bundles of the top and second copies
- Don't fold forms P14

By 19 May, send your P35, the top two copies of forms P14 and any forms P38A, to your Inland Revenue office, even if your payments of PAYE and NICs are not up-to-date.

Do not send in photocopies or forms P38(S). Remember penalties are chargeable if forms P14 or P35 arrive late.

Pay any outstanding amounts of monthly or quarterly PAYE and NICs for the tax year directly to your Accounts Office. Do not send payments with forms P14 and P35.

By 31 May give a form P60 to each employee who was working for you at 5 April and for whom you have completed a form P11 or equivalent record:

- Scrap forms P60 for those employees no longer working for you at 5 April
- Give only one form P60 to an employee, even if that employee has had more than one period of employment with you in the tax year - this P60 should only be for the period that covers 5 April
- If an employee asks for another copy, you may issue a duplicate.  Any duplicate must be clearly marked with the word 'DUPLICATE'

You must keep the following forms for at least three years after the end of the tax year to which they relate:

- Forms P11 and pay records.  This applies even if an employee does not pay any PAYE or NICs in the tax year but you have completed a form P11 to keep records of earnings and/or tax credits
- Forms P38(S) including those relating to students for whom a form P14 has been prepared

If you operate a pension scheme for your employees that is contracted-out of the State Second Pension, keep these records for as long as the employment lasts and three years after that.

# What you need to know

Which forms to return to HMRC

What penalties are there for failing to return forms by the due date?

How to complete form P14

Where do you obtain form P60?

How to complete form P35

What payroll records have to be kept?

How to complete form P38(S)

How long do payroll records have to be kept?

How to complete form P38A

Does your organisation complete its payroll returns electronically?

The deadlines by which organisations of different sizes have to complete their payroll returns electronically

What are the dates by which payroll returns have to be made?

## Reportable benefits and expenses

Unless you have a dispensation for all of your employees you will need to fill in forms P11D, P11D(b) and P9D to give information about employees' expenses and benefits in the tax year. In certain circumstances it is possible to apply for a dispensation from HMRC that relieves you from reporting expenses payments and benefits in kind on form P11D because they are satisfied that no tax is payable on them. Payments which can be covered by a dispensation include:

- Qualifying travel expenses
- Entertaining
- Subscriptions to professional bodies or learned societies
- Non-cash vouchers and credit tokens provided to cover expenses

Payments which can't be covered by a dispensation include:

- Business mileage payments
- Company cars and vans that are taxable
- Private medical insurance
- Cheap loans

Also, the Inland Revenue normally accepts that expenses payments which are covered by a dispensation don't count as earnings for NICs purposes. Where an employer has a dispensation the items listed will not be treated as a benefit in kind and liable to Class 1A NICs.

Employees whose expenses payments and benefits in kind are covered by a dispensation don't have to include them on their tax returns. Also, they are not included in their tax assessments or PAYE codes.

Any type of expenses payments (apart from round sum allowances) and most benefits in kind can be included, for example:

- Qualifying travel expenses
- Entertaining
- Subscriptions to professional bodies or learned societies
- Non-cash vouchers and credit tokens provided to cover expenses

The following are examples of benefits in kind that can't be included:

- Company cars and vans that are taxable
- Private medical insurance
- Cheap loans
- Payments made in connection with an employee's use of his or her own vehicle for business travel can't be included because payments below a certain amount are exempt from tax

However, you may still be able to save yourself some work by sending P11D information on lists to your Tax Office. Ask your Inspector for more information about this.

HMRC must be sure that:

- No tax would be payable by your employees on expenses paid or benefits provided, and
- Expenses claims are independently checked and authorised within the firm and, where possible, are supported by receipts

A dispensation only covers:

- The circumstances for which it was issued, and
- The type and amounts of expenses payments and benefits in kind it specifically mentions

You should tell HMRC of any changes, for example, if you modify your system for controlling expenses payments or you alter your scale rates for expenses. If your scale rates simply keep pace with prices, HMRC will normally be able to agree them without asking further questions. Until advised you should not use the dispensation from the date the change occurred.

HMRC will review the dispensation from time-to-time, but will only withdraw it if the above conditions are no longer satisfied. Employees or directors who authorise their own expenses payments may have to be excluded. HMRC will say in the dispensation which employees and which kinds of expenses payments and benefits in kind are covered.

A dispensation can start from any date during the tax year, and you can apply at any time. Complete the application form and send it to HMRC. If you have any notes for guidance on employees' expenses, enclose a copy with the form. HMRC will tell you if any further information is needed.

New rules took effect from 6 April 2002 for expenses payments to staff when they use their own cars for business travel. You can find further information in booklet 490 'Employee travel. A tax and NICs guide for employers'. Each year tax-free mileage rates are published by HMRC. If your mileage payments are equal to or below these rates there will be no tax or NICs due so there will be no need to report this information and no basis for including them in a dispensation. Any amounts that you pay over the published rates are taxable and must be entered on the P11D. Your Tax Office will be able to advise you of the current rates.

## Forms P11D and P9D

You can find copies of forms P11D, P11D(b) and P9D, and help on how to fill them in, on the Employer's CD-ROM. Using the CD-ROM you can also fill in the forms on screen.

You will need to fill in forms P11D and P11D(b) if you have paid or provided taxable benefits or expenses to:

- Directors
- Employees paid at a rate of more than £8,500 a year
- Members of the families or households of the above, including spouses, children and their spouses, parents, dependants, servants and guests

Where you have completed a P11D for the taxable benefits or expenses paid or provided to an employee, give the employee a copy.

**Return of Class 1A National Insurance contributions due**
**Return of expenses and benefits - Employer's declaration**

**Year ended 5 April 2005**

Employer's PAYE reference

Accounts Office reference

Please return this form to the address shown below ▼ ▼

Employer's name and address

If this form has not been issued automatically it may not show all your details. If this is so, please fill in the top of the form before you send it to your Inland Revenue office.
Please read the notes overleaf before completing the return.
Do not declare any amounts already reported under the Taxed Award Scheme arrangements.

**1 Class 1A National Insurance contributions (NICs) due**

Enter the total benefits liable to Class 1A NICs from forms P11D. (This is the total of the brown Class 1A NICs boxes on forms P11D. There is a quick guide on page 5 of CWG5 if you are not sure.) **A** £

If you need to adjust the figures entered in box A, do not complete box C below, tick this box ☐ and complete Section 4 overleaf.

Multiply by Class 1A NICs rate **B** 12.8%

Class 1A NICs payable by 19 July 2005 **C** £ (box A x rate in box B)

**2 Employer's declaration**

Tick the relevant box(es) and fill in the appropriate details

No expenses payments or benefits of the type to be r... ...been or will be provided for the

You will need to fill in form P9D if you have paid or provided taxable benefits to employees, but have not completed form P11D because they earned at a rate of less than £8,500 a year.

**Revenue P9D** Expenses payments and income from which tax cannot be deducted 2004-05

**Note to employer**
Complete this return if you made expenses payments or provided benefits to an employee but you have not completed a form P11D because he or she earned at a rate of less than £8,500 during the year 6 April 2004 to 5 April 2005.

Brief notes are included on this form. Our booklet 480 'Expenses and Benefits – A Tax Guide' gives more detailed information.

Send the completed P9D to your Inland Revenue office by 6 July 2005. You must give a copy of this information to the employee by the same date.

You do not need to include the information shown on this form in any return on form P11D(b). Class 1A National Insurance contributions are not due on benefits reported on form P9D. See our leaflet CWG5(2005) Class 1A National Insurance contributions on Benefits in Kind.

**Note to employee**
Your employer has filled in this form. Keep it in a safe place as you may not be able to get a duplicate. You will need it for your tax records and to complete your 2004-05 Tax Return if you get one.

The box numbers on this P9D have the same numbering as the Employment Pages of the Tax Return, for example, 1.12. Include the total figures in the corresponding box on the Tax Return, unless you think some other figure is more appropriate.

Your tax code may need to be adjusted to take account of the information given on this P9D.

**Employer's details**
Employer's name

Employer's PAYE reference

**Employee's details**
Employee's name

Works number or department

National Insurance number

**A(1) Expenses payments**

If the employee paid expenses solely and necessarily in the performance of his or her duties and/or business travelling expenses and you repaid the amount of those expenses, you do not need to include them here. Total all other expenses payments including
 • payments that included Value Added Tax (VAT), even if the VAT was later recovered from HM Customs and Excise
 • round sum allowances
 • all relocation expenses payments and benefits (see note below).
Some relocation expenses qualify for relief (see booklet 480, Chapter 5 and Appendix 7). The maximum amount that can be paid for any one move is £8,000. You should total all the qualifying payments made for each move including
 • any payments made in 2003-04, and
 • any benefits provided under the relocation package in 2004-05 or 2003-04.
The excess over £8,000 of any qualifying expenses payments and benefits for each move should be included in the total expenses payments figure entered below.

By 6 July, completed forms should reach your Inland Revenue office. Penalties are chargeable if forms arrive late.

For more detailed information about benefits and expenses and Class 1A NICs see:

- Booklet CWG5, Class 1A National Insurance contributions on benefits in kind - a guide for employers, a reference guide covering all aspects of Class 1A NICs
- Booklet CA33, Class 1A National Insurance contributions on Car and Fuel Benefits - a guide for employers, a guide if you provide employees with a company car and/or fuel which is available for their private use
- Booklet 480(2004), Expenses and benefits - a tax guide, a comprehensive guide to the tax law relating to expenses payments and benefits
- Booklet 490, Employee travel - a tax and NICs guide for employers, a guide setting out the approach which the Inland Revenue will normally take in applying legislation on employee travel
- P11D Guide, a guide to the completion of forms P11D Return of expenses and benefits
- P11D Working Sheets, optional working sheets for calculating the cash equivalent of certain benefits

You can get any of these forms or booklets from the Employer's Orderline on **08457 646 646** or they are available from your Employer's CD-ROM.

 **What you need to know**

How to apply for dispensation from completing form P11D

What expenses and benefits in kind can be included in a dispensation?

How to complete form P11D

What expenses and benefits in kind can't be included in a dispensation?

How to complete form P11D(b)

What is the deadline for returning forms P11D, P11D(b) and P9D?

How to complete form P9D

Where can you obtain forms and guidance on their completion?

The accurate completion of year-end payroll procedures is absolutely vital to the reporting of correct management accounts for the organisation.  They form part of the annual returns the organisation is required to make to shareholders, Companies House, the Charities Commission or the National Audit Office.

## There are only two things certain in this life – death and taxes

# Are you ready for assessment?

To achieve this unit of a Level 3 Business & Administration qualification you will need to demonstrate that you are competent in the following:

- Reconcile cumulative pay records to year-end balances
- Reconcile totals of tax and NICs deducted with payments made to the Collector of Taxes, taking into account recoverable sums
- Reconcile the total value of basic and supplementary pension contributions and Additional Voluntary Contributions from each employee with cumulative net taxable pay prior to completion of year-end returns to the Revenue
- Complete all statutory and non-statutory year-end returns accurately
- Despatch all statutory and non-statutory year-end returns by the agreed media and due dates
- Distribute employee year-end information for employees by the applicable statutory date
- Prepare internal year-end summaries for accounting purposes in an accurate and timely manner
- Identify the existence of a tax and National Insurance liability for benefits and expenses
- Identify statutory and non-statutory exemptions from liability to tax and National Insurance
- Ensure that dispensations are up-to-date and are applicable to current organisational procedures
- Identify the relevant statutory return to be submitted for each employee
- Identify the correct method of calculating the tax and National Insurance liability of benefits and expenses
- Correctly calculate the value of taxable benefits
- Report the value of taxable benefits and expenses accurately, taking into account non-reportable items
- Calculate the Class 1A National Insurance liability accurately in accordance with statutory timescales
- Calculate the tax and Class 1B National Insurance liability on benefits where the organisation has agreed to meet the liability

- Complete all statutory and non-statutory year-end returns accurately
- Despatch all statutory and non-statutory year-end returns by the due dates
- Ensure all year-end information for employees is made available by the applicable statutory date
- Produce internal year-end summaries for management accounting purposes in an accurate and timely manner

(Remember that you will need the skills listed at the beginning of this chapter. These are covered in chapter 1.)

You will need to produce evidence from a variety of sources. Carrying out the following activities will help you acquire competence at work.

### Activity 1

You are the payroll manager for an organisation which has six employees paid on the PAYE system. Their P11s show the following information at the end of the tax year.

Complete forms P14, P60 and P35 using the above information.

| Name | NI Table | 1a | 1b | 1c | 1d | 1e | Total pay | Tax deducted |
|------|----------|------|------|------|------|------|-----------|--------------|
| Jim Smith | A | 4272 | 624 | 3504 | 839 | 388 | 8400 | 542 |
| Alan Welsh | A | 4272 | 624 | 3492 | 831 | 384 | 8388 | 540 |
| Peter Carter | A | 4272 | 624 | 5400 | 1285 | 594 | 10296 | 959 |
| Alice White | B | 4272 | 624 | 3330 | 522 | 72 | 8226 | 504 |
| Ali Mahmood | A | 4272 | 624 | 5040 | 1199 | 554 | 9936 | 880 |
| Yousaf Yahana | A | 4272 | 624 | 3600 | 856 | 356 | 8496 | 563 |

### Activity 2

Obtain and research all the relevant end of year payroll forms and guides and familiarise yourself with the completion of the forms.

Remember: While gathering evidence for this unit, evidence **may** be generated for units 110, 212, 213, 216, 218, 301, 302, 306, 310, 315, 320 and 321.

# CHAPTER 17
# UNIT 308 – Monitor information systems

All organisations have a need to store and manage information. Producing information is a cost to the business. Costs are incurred in collecting the information, processing and storing it. If this cost is to be acceptable, the information must be of value to the organisation. The value of some information can be quantified. Information which accelerates the decision making process or reduces uncertainty has a measurable value.

In most circumstances, however, the availability of information will provide benefits which it will not be possible to place a specific value on. Information provided to customers on product availability and prices may well sway their decision to purchase. However, it is not usually possible to separate the effect of the information from other influences. Similarly information which builds up a background understanding of a situation has value, but it is impossible to quantify.

An organisation will store information on a variety of subjects including:

- Sales
- Purchasing

- Accounts
- Personnel
- Payroll
- Stock
- Customers
- Suppliers
- Technical specifications
- Legislation
- Competitors
- Production
- Despatch
- Transport
- Company assets
- Insurance
- Archived records

Information systems store data in a form that enables it to be retrieved on demand and used to produce targeted information for a variety of purposes. If storage of data were all that is required, a simple filing cabinet would suffice. Modern organisations require an information system that can:

- **Classify data** - e.g. name, address and National Insurance number
- **Sort data** - e.g. into male employees and female employees
- **Summarise data** - e.g. number of full time and part time employees
- **Manipulate data** - e.g. calculate the total wage cost
- **Identify appropriate data** - e.g. provide a list of employees earning over a selected figure

While these systems may be manual or electronic, electronic systems have the advantage of being more easily updated and the information more quickly retrieved. The raw material for information systems is data. All types of computerised transactions produce data. This is a resource which can be utilised to produce management information. To make this resource available it is important that the data is retrievable from the application in which it is created.

Your organisation probably uses a variety of database programmes. Each database will have been purchased to meet the needs of the individual user department. The dilemma is that the data produced by one database may not be compatible with that produced by others. The solution is to create an information system which is able to download data from all the databases and manipulate it to produce the required management information.

A relatively simple organisation may be able to buy an information system 'off the shelf' which will meet its requirements, or which can be adapted to do so. A larger or more complex organisation will need to have a tailored bespoke system designed. In designing the system the needs of the end users must be identified. Specialist system analysts will be involved in designing the necessary programme. A specification will be written listing the hardware, software and data storage requirements. The future needs for information should be predicted and allowed for as far as possible to delay the obsolescence of the system.

When the information system has been designed and installed, the data will be loaded. Tests will be carried out and the necessary adjustments made. Problems may be identified with the manipulation of the data. The system must be capable of analysing the data and producing usable results. You will then need to organise staff training in the use of the system. This may be carried out in-house, by distance learning or by staff attending external courses. You will also need to arrange continuous monitoring of the system to ensure that the required level of accuracy and accessibility is being obtained. The requirements for information will evolve as time passes and it is important that the system is capable of continuous improvement to meet changing demands.

When monitoring information systems you will use the following skills:

- Researching
- Analysing
- Negotiating
- Planning
- Organising
- Developing others
- Monitoring
- Evaluating
- Problem solving
- Managing resources
- Using technology

These skills are covered in chapter 1.

In a small organisation it is feasible to develop information systems by identifying the application areas in which systems are needed and purchasing individual database applications for each. It is unlikely that this will satisfy the needs of a medium or large organisation which require a more complex information system. These systems will need to integrate the information from various application areas.

You will need to identify the requirements of the users of the system. For instance, the marketing department may need information on all previous purchasers of a product in order to target a mail shot. The accounts department may need information on all outstanding sales invoices more than three months overdue.

Once these are understood you can design and specify a suitable system. There are a number of reasons that you may decide to specify an electronic information system:

- Your present system cannot cope. Either the requirements of the business have changed, or the sheer volume of data to be processed has increased beyond the current system's capabilities

- You have identified potential cost savings. Your current manual system is labour intensive, and an electronic system will produce the same results with a significant saving in wage costs. The electronic system will also free-up office space currently used by the additional clerical staff
- Senior management have identified a need for better or faster management information in order to enable more effective decisions to be made
- Your organisation is losing its competitive edge to other organisations who have installed electronic information systems. Your competitors are able to react more quickly to changes in the market and provide more efficient customer service
- You are aware that better, more efficient systems have become available. While your present system may be delivering adequate results you believe that investment in more up-to-date technology will benefit the organisation
- Your organisation wishes to portray itself as being at the cutting edge of technology. This will be particularly relevant if you are in a market sector where your systems are on show to your customers
- There have been significant changes in legislation requiring your organisation to produce greater amounts of information for the operation of the payroll or submission of company accounts

Having decided that the potential benefits of installing a new electronic information system appear to justify the cost, you will now need to investigate exactly what system you need and exactly what the cost will be. There will be three groups of people involved in this study:

- The users of the existing system. They will be able to explain exactly what the current system is able to provide and the input involved. They will also be able to define what it is they would like the new system to provide and where they see the opportunity for reduction in the input
- Computer programmers take that information from the users and turn it into applications that will produce the outputs sought. But beware, there can be a communication gap between the users and the programmers as they think in different languages
- System analysts are the interpreters between the users and the computer programmers. They are able to understand the needs of the users and explain them in terms that the programmers can recognise. The relationship between system analysts and computer programmers is similar to that between a solicitor and barrister, where the solicitor instructs a barrister on the client's needs in legal terms which the client would be unable to express

The responsibilities of the systems analyst are to:

- Analyse the existing system to determine its information use and its requirements
- Assess the feasibility of replacing the existing system with an electronic system (or upgrading the existing electronic system)
- Design a new system specifying the programmes, hardware, data, structures and controls required
- Test the new system to ensure it delivers the requirements
- Oversee the installation of the new system
- Create the necessary user manuals and technical guides
- Evaluate the system

You may want to form a steering committee consisting of representatives of management, users, programmers and systems analysts to guide the project. The project will have to be managed through a number of stages if it is to be successfully implemented. The first stage is to agree the overall scope of the project. At this stage terms of reference are agreed:

- Which departments of the organisation need the system?
- What are the problems that the system is required to address?
- When is the feasibility report to be delivered?
- What is the budget for producing the feasibility report?

The second stage is for the systems analyst to investigate the current system. He or she will need to interview the users of the system and look at the documentation currently in use. The users will have the opportunity to explain how the current system actually works in practice, as opposed to how it is supposed to work in theory. A feasibility report will then be produced which indicates:

- A number of alternative solutions to the problems that the system is required to address
- The benefits and feasibility of each alternative and a broad estimate of the costs involved

The third stage is for management to review the feasibility report and make a decision whether to authorise more detailed analysis of the proposed solutions. If the go-ahead is given the systems analyst looks in detail at the process necessary to satisfy the objectives and functions of the system. This is called 'process analysis'. The systems analyst will then look at the data required to feed the process. This is called 'data analysis'. The result of stage three will be a logic model of the system, not in any way a physical representation.

Stage four starts with the users reviewing the logic model and agreeing that it is capable of resolving the problems identified in stage one. The systems analyst then designs the physical aspects of the system and suggests alternative designs. At this stage these will often represent low, medium and high cost solutions with corresponding levels of benefit. These alternatives will be presented to management who will decide between them and commission one of them.

Stage five is the point at which the system begins to take physical shape. A detailed specification is written which provides a more accurate estimate of total costs. Management can now sign off this estimate and purchase orders can be raised for hardware and software and contracts written for programmers' time. Programmes are commissioned, hardware is specified, the structure of the databases are specified and a schedule of implementation created. The systems analyst will be particularly concerned at this stage with:

- **Making the system secure** - Security of the system involves ensuring that it is protected from corruption, that it is complete in that it delivers all of the stated requirements, that the data it produces is accurate and that it can deliver continuous outputs
- **Ensuring that the system is user-friendly** - At each point at which the users come into contact with the system it needs to be easy to use

Then you will be ready for the system to come together:

- Hardware is purchased and installed
- Programmes are written and tested
- Databases are created
- Historic data is loaded onto the databases
- Procedures are drafted
- Paperwork is designed
- Staff are trained in the requirements of the new procedures
- Security of the existing files is maintained
- The new system is tested
- The system is handed over to management

Once the system has been handed over by the systems analyst it is time to put it to use. Few organisations will be in a position to completely shut down one system and start up

another overnight.  There will have to be a transitional stage.
This may involve parallel running of the two systems.  The
advantage of this is that if the new system fails the old
system is still in place.  The disadvantage is that it is
expensive in terms of labour costs.  An alternative is to run a
pilot of the new system.  This may involve only operating the
system over a reduced volume of input.  The object is to
identify any teething problems.  These may be technical and
require re-programming or identify training needs that can
be addressed before the system goes fully live.

The next stage is to evaluate the system.  Hardware and
software will require maintenance to ensure continuous
satisfactory performance.  Hardware maintenance will be
arranged through a maintenance contract either with the
supplier or with a specialist hardware maintenance company.
Maintenance of the software will involve ironing out faults
which have become apparent with use or making alterations
to the programme to improve efficiency or to meet amended
system requirements.  After the system has had a chance to
settle down an evaluation report will be compiled comparing
the actual performance of the system with the original aims
and objectives of the project.  Where the evaluation report
identifies minor discrepancies between the two, maintenance
can be used to resolve them.  Where major differences are
identified a decision will have to be taken whether to re-
programme the system or to identify where improvements
can be incorporated into a future system specification.

When this has been completed, it will be necessary to
instigate a system that continually monitors the processes.
It will not be possible for you to monitor every task carried
out by the system so you will need to design some form of
sampling.  There are a number of methods of sampling:

- **Random sample** - You pick a process to check
  completely at random.  The advantage is that nobody

can predict what will be sampled and make a special effort to ensure that particular process is carried out correctly

- **Structured sample** - A grid of processes and time is drawn up and a pattern of sampling established.  The advantage is that everything is checked over a period of time.  The disadvantage is that people can predict when checks will be carried out
- **Informed structured sample** - Starting from a grid as in the structured sample the level of sampling is adjusted over time to reflect the results of the sampling.  Processes which regularly indicate problems are sampled more often than those which are always up-to-date.  The advantage is that your resource is directed towards areas that require attention.  The disadvantage is that processes that have historically been no problem may develop problems unnoticed

And finally, the last stage is to carry out a post implementation audit.  This will usually be carried out by a team who are completely independent of both the users and the analysts.  This may be an internal audit department or an external organisation.  The purpose of this audit is to:

- Consider the adequacy of the system documentation
- Judge the effectiveness of staff training
- Review the reliability of outputs
- Compare the actual costs with the estimate

- Compare the actual response times with the specification

The auditors will produce a report which comprehensively assesses the system against the initial requirements.

## What you need to know

Why it is important that information is managed effectively and efficiently

What are the criteria for selecting an information system?

The information which your organisation requires to be managed

Why is it important to involve the users when specifying an information system?

How to develop a system specification

What problems may occur with information systems?

The stages of implementing an information system

Why is it important to continuously improve information systems?

Methods of identifying training needs

What are the advantages of electronic information systems over manual information systems?

Alternative ways of monitoring processes

How can problems with information systems be dealt with?

The information systems currently in use in your organisation

What is the purpose of forming a steering committee?

The role of the systems analyst

What does your organisation require an information system to do?

The reason for commissioning a feasibility study

What different methods are available to train staff in the use of a new information system?

Information systems recognise that data is an important resource which requires management. They have been developed to replace file-based systems of information storage. Where information is held in files which are the responsibility of different departments, there is a risk of inconsistency where one department is more efficient than another in updating the information. Organisations require more flexible retrieval and reporting facilities to simplify decision making. Information systems can meet these organisational needs.

# Information systems are the heart of the organisation. They pump the life-blood around the system

# Are you ready for assessment?

To achieve this unit of a Level 3 Business & Administration qualification you will need to demonstrate that you are competent in the following:

- Identify the information to be managed and the resources available
- Design a system specification that meets identified needs and an agreed budget
- Develop an information system to meet the specification
- Provide training on use of information system to users
- Monitor the use of the information system
- Resolve problems when they occur
- Review and further develop the information system to meet users' needs

(Remember that you will need the skills listed at the beginning of this chapter.  These are covered in chapter 1.)

You will need to produce evidence from a variety of sources.  Carrying out the following activities will help you acquire competence at work.

**Activity 1**
Monitor an existing information system in your organisation for an agreed period.  If possible select a manual system or a computerised system that has limited functions.  Evaluate the effectiveness of the processes to achieve the objectives of the system.

**Activity 2**
Identify where the system that you have been monitoring doesn't adequately achieve its objectives.  Write a report indicating the problems that need to be addressed.  Identify what actions need to be taken to review appropriate organisational needs.

**Activity 3**
Investigate the system by interviewing the users and examining the documentation.  Consider benefits that could be gained by replacing or updating the current system.

**Activity 4**

Produce a feasibility report containing possible solutions to the problems identified in Activity 2. Compare the relative costs, benefits and feasibility of each solution.

Remember: While gathering evidence for this unit, evidence **may** be generated for units 110, 212, 213, 217, 218, 301, 302, 310, 312, 314, 315, 318, 319, 320 and 321.

# CHAPTER 18
# UNIT 309 – Run projects

A project is, by definition, a series of activities designed to achieve a specific outcome within a set budget and timescale.  Projects will generally fall into one of four groups:

- **Manufacturing projects** - The final result is a piece of equipment, a ship, an aircraft or an oilrig
- **Construction projects** - The final result is a road, a bridge, a railway or a building
- **Management projects** - These may not produce a tangible result.  The project could be the relocation of the organisation or the introduction of a new system
- **Research projects** - The objectives may be tenuous and the results unpredictable.  Columbus, for example, did not intend to discover America when he started his project

Project Management is sometimes seen as a peripheral role, outside the main activity of the organisation, but most projects are vital to future operations – they are often a 'test-bed' for wide-ranging changes.  No two projects are ever exactly alike, and you can never predict the course of any project or guarantee its final outcome.  You may manage projects using a computerised or manual system.  Either way, you will be following the same basic principles.

Before embarking on a project it is important to define its purpose, aims and objectives. You then need to analyse any risk either to the project or to the organisation caused by the decision to go ahead with it. Risks to the organisation may include:

- Interruption of normal business to facilitate the project
- Diversion of resources, including people, to the project
- By-passing organisational procedures as the project doesn't fit into the normal structure
- A change in the prevailing financial situation. This may arise from the project itself or from external influences such as interest rates, government policy or stock market fluctuation
- The effect on the organisation's reputation if the project is unsuccessful

A major risk to the project is that it will run over budget. For a project to be successful the resources must be in place and available when needed. Check that you have a sufficient budget and a realistic timescale before you begin. You must be ready to adapt your plans, since circumstances and requirements will almost certainly change as the project goes on. Remember to include a contingency plan to cover the unknown or unexpected. You may think that keeping a close eye on spending is boring, but it is essential to successful project management.

Before the project begins you will need to work out what resources are needed. Remember to include everything in your initial estimate, as you are likely to be held to it later. Be realistic in your estimates and remember that people are a resource, and their time has to be paid for. Decide on a costing method at the beginning and apply it consistently. If a person has to work on the project everyday for ten days, but only for two hours a day, the cost is twenty hours at their hourly rate, not ten days. If a photocopier is needed for the project, the total cost of purchase should be charged to the project only if the photocopier will be used solely for the project. In that case, would it be more cost effective to hire one? Make sure you keep accurate records of all project-related expenditure. If you find you are over spending in one area you may have to reduce your budget in another area.

Projects almost always run over time which is a risk you have to take very seriously. However well you plan, people are not machines and will inevitably run into problems. It is unlikely that all of the activities involved in the project will start at the same time. Breaking the project down into its component activities, and then grouping the activities, will show you how they fit into a logical sequence. This will help you to work out how many people you need and what skills they will be required to have. If everyone understands their role there will be fewer misunderstandings.

You will need to know how much time each activity is likely to take. A poor estimate at the beginning can cause serious problems as the project develops. Involve team members in the initial estimates. If there are serious differences of opinion over the time required for a particular activity, estimate in the middle. Make a note of the maximum and minimum times estimated as these may be useful if flexibility is needed later. Remember that some activities can't start until others are finished. Keep a careful track of progress against the original plan, as slippage will need to be communicated to those waiting to start their involvement.

The project is also at risk from external factors. You will need to consult with a number of others in managing a project. These will include the client, other stakeholders, team members and suppliers. The project may be your number one priority, but it won't be the number one priority of everybody else in the organisation, or of people outside the organisation. Suppliers have their own priorities and you may have to fight for your project.

It is important to identify and assess anything that may be a risk to your project. You will then need to plan what action you will take if the risks come about. The purpose of project management is to minimise, contain or counter the risks and organise resources. To evaluate risks, one method is to multiply the probability of the risk occurring by the cost of correcting the resulting problem. When you have evaluated the risks you can manage them. Remember it is not cost effective to spend more eliminating a risk than the cost of dealing with the problem.

The manager of a project team has direct line responsibility for the project team members. It is your role to guide the team in the right direction. The purpose of the project must be agreed by everybody involved so that everyone has the same aims. There should be no need to make significant changes to the project. Everybody involved must be committed and their commitment will be gained most effectively through continuous good communication. Tell everybody about any changes as soon as they are agreed. It is extremely frustrating to be working on a remote part of the project only to find the 'goalposts' have been moved without your knowledge.

You have no other work to distract you from the project's goals. Successful teams consist of people with a common goal. The project manager needs to recognise the good performance of team members in front of the whole team, but deliver any necessary criticism or feedback in private. You must also remember to praise the team as a whole so that everyone feels a part of the success. The team will develop through the stages of:

- **Forming** - Each member asking the question 'why am I here?'
- **Storming** - Each member asking the question 'what is my status in the team?'
- **Norming** - Each member asking the question 'how will we work together?'
- **Performing** - Each member asking the question 'what can I do now?'

If the project continues long term the team will go through two more stages, boring and mourning. Team members may stop looking for new challenges or ways of doing things. At this point you will need to encourage innovation, possibly adopting a change for its own sake to prevent stagnation. If a member of the team leaves, the rest may miss their presence in the team. Give the team an opportunity to get involved in the selection and induction of the replacement. This will have the added benefit of helping the newcomer to integrate into the team.

During the lifetime of the project you will need to be amenable to the probability that the client's needs may change, and you will have to be prepared to adapt your plans accordingly. Your client will expect you to bring in the project within the agreed timescales and to budget. Regular communication with the client to inform them of the project's progress is essential. This is best done in writing to avoid any misunderstandings.

 When running projects you will use the following skills:

- Planning
- Organising
- Communicating
- Managing resources
- Managing time
- Problem solving
- Prioritising
- Monitoring

These skills are covered in chapter 1.

## Planning the project

It is important to identify the differences between a project and everyday work. A project has a clear start and a clear end while everyday work is usually ongoing and process driven. The other main features of projects are that they have an organised plan, separate resources, a dedicated team and established goals. It is possible that the aims and objectives will have been set for you before you take on the management of the project. You will need to be clear that everybody involved understands what these are.

The project's objectives will fall into the following three categories:

- **Performance** - The user's needs must be met
- **Budget** - The user's needs must be met within the agreed costs
- **Time** - The user's needs must be met within the agreed time

The client, whether external or internal to the organisation, will know what they want. They will not know exactly what is possible – if they did, they would not need a project manager. To successfully manage a project you will need to be able to define your goals and be sure they are achievable. You must be able to answer with confidence how much the project will cost; how many people will it need; how long will it take and will it be cost effective.

If the project manager is to meet the objectives in all three categories, those objectives must be clearly defined. The client and the project manager will discuss the client's requirements and a preferred solution will be agreed. This solution forms the basis of the project specification. This specification must cover all the requirements of the project.

The specification is a statement of what the end result of the project will be, the timescales and the budget. It is based on the requirements of the customer and must contain the following:

- **Start date** - This is the date on which the customer and the project manager agree that the project is to take place. From this point the customer is responsible for the costs involved
- **End date** - This is the date by which the customer requires the project to be completed. There may be penalty clauses inserted into the contract if you fail to achieve the objectives by the end date
- **Budget available** - This is an agreed total amount that the customer is prepared to invest in the project. You may well find the customer unwilling to fund any overruns on the original budget

- **Completion criteria** - This tells you how you know when the project is finished.  If the project is for an external customer, this states exactly what must be achieved if the customer is to accept responsibility for paying for the project.  If for an internal customer, this states the point at which the project can be handed over to the user
- **Terms and conditions** - This is a basic definition of who is responsible for what and when.  It may include staged handover of parts of the project, staged payments and the parameters for later amendments
- **Legal and safety requirements** - This will specify who is responsible for ensuring that all legislation that may be appropriate to the project is met
- **Quality measurements** - This will define the standard to which the work involved must be carried out

A detailed project specification will make running and monitoring the project much easier.  This can be produced manually or using specialist project management software.  The project specification must then be agreed with the customer.  This is where you compare what is possible with what the customer originally wanted.  The customer must then agree that what you propose is acceptable.  If the customer is internal the agreement will need to cover what resources will be required from within the organisation, and how they will be made available.  It may be necessary to obtain the agreement of others within the organisation affected by your use of resources for the project.

One of the most important things to plan is who does what.  Members of the team need to be given specific tasks.  The skills of each team member need to be taken into account.  Once roles and responsibilities are established each individual must be given terms of reference stating what they have to do, who they report to, who reports to them and what they are expected to deliver.  Teams must be briefed so that everyone knows what everyone else is responsible for and how that affects their role.

Another important consideration is accurate estimation of the time activities will take.  If you are not familiar with the tasks to be carried out you can greatly underestimate the amount of time needed.  You may forget to take unexpected events

or high-priority unscheduled work into account, or fail to
allow for how complex the overall job is.

To properly estimate how long each activity will take, you
must consider all the components that will make it up.  Allow
time for any:

- Liaison with outside bodies
- Meetings
- Quality assurance
- Accidents and emergencies
- Staff holidays
- Staff sickness
- Equipment breakdowns
- Late deliveries
- Interruptions

In any project there will be activities that can't start until
another is completed.  These are known as dependencies.
They exist both within the project and between the project
and external influences.  Dependencies dictate the timescale
of the whole project.  The overall length of the project can be
determined by the use of:

- **Gantt charts** - These help you to plan out tasks to be
  completed, give you a basis for scheduling those
  tasks, help to allocate resources and work out the
  critical path to complete the project.  To draw a Gantt
  chart first list all the activities in the project.  For each
  activity show the earliest start date, an estimate of
  how long it will take and whether it is parallel (can be
  carried out at the same time as another activity) or
  sequential (depends on another activity being
  completed).  If the activity is sequential indicate
  which other activities it depends on

The following is a list of activities for creating an information
system.  The resources for all activities are available from
week 1 but many of the activities are dependent on each
other.

| | Activity | Resources available | Length | Type | Dependent on |
|---|---|---|---|---|---|
| 1 | Write programs | Week 1 | 3 weeks | Parallel | |
| 2 | Test programs | Week 1 | 1 week | Sequential | Activity 1 |
| 3 | Create databases | Week 1 | 2 weeks | Sequential | Activities 1 & 2 |
| 4 | Load data | Week 1 | 2 weeks | Sequential | Activities 1, 2, 3, & 7 |
| 5 | Draft procedures | Week 1 | 2 weeks | Sequential | Activity 1 |
| 6 | Design paperwork | Week 1 | 1 week | Sequential | Activities 1 & 5 |
| 7 | Train staff | Week 1 | 3 weeks | Sequential | Activities 1 & 2 |
| 8 | Test system | Week 1 | 1 week | Sequential | Activities 1, 2, 3, 4 & 7 |
| 9 | Hand over | | | Sequential | Activities 1 - 8 |

Plot the tasks on graph paper. Next, schedule actions so that sequential actions are carried out in the required sequence. Dependent activities cannot start until the activities they depend on are complete.

**Critical path analysis (CPA)** - This is a method of assessing:

- The tasks to be carried out
- Areas where tasks can be performed in parallel
- The resources needed for the project
- Priorities within the project
- The correct sequence of activities
- How to schedule and time activities
- The shortest time in which a project can be completed
- Ways of shortening urgent projects

To draw a critical path analysis chart, first list all the activities in the project. For each activity show the earliest start date, an estimate of how long it will take and whether it is parallel (can be carried out at the same time as another activity) or sequential (depends on another activity being completed). If the activity is sequential indicate which other activities it depends on.

Once you have listed the activities create a circle and arrow diagram in which circles show events, i.e. the start and finish of an activity and an arrow running between two circles shows the activity. A description of the activity is written below the arrow and the length of the task above it. All arrows run left to right.

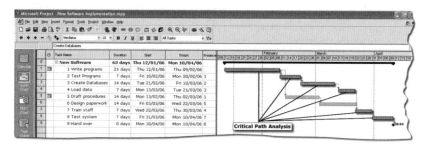

Where one activity can't start until another has been completed, the arrow for the dependent activity starts at the completion event circle of the previous activity. The diagram above shows that the earliest the system can be handed over is at the end of week 9. This depends on all of the estimates of the length of activities being met. It may be that having created your critical path analysis the total time from start to finish is not acceptable. The critical path (the longest route from start to finish) shows you where allocating additional resources will be effective. Having extra staff drafting procedures and designing paperwork will not reduce the overall project length. If by allocating additional resource you can reduce the time needed to create databases and load data, you can reduce the critical path.

The benefit of critical path analysis over Gantt charts is that it helps identify the minimum length of time needed to complete a project. It also helps identify where projects can be accelerated to reduce this minimum time.

- **Program Evaluation and Review Technique (PERT)** - This is a variation of critical path analysis that takes a more sceptical view of the time activities will take. To use PERT take the shortest time an activity can take, the most likely time and the longest time. Use the following formula to calculate the actual time each activity will take. Shortest time + 4 x likely time + longest time ÷ 6.

While all of the above methods can be carried out using pen and paper, there are software programs such as Microsoft Project available which greatly reduce the time needed to calculate the critical path.

Having calculated the overall time that the project will take to complete, get the agreement of the client. Whether the client is internal to the organisation or external, it is worth getting their acceptance of your timescale in writing to avoid conflict later.

 **What you need to know**

The projects your organisation is involved in currently

What risks are involved in managing projects?

How to calculate the resources needed

What different methods are there of determining the critical path of a project?

How to estimate the time needed

What are the project manager's responsibilities to team members?

The stages of development teams go through

What objectives must all projects meet?

The differences between projects and every day work

What are the standard contents of a project specification?

# Running the project

Many projects are implemented and managed using milestones. These are simply identifiable points in the life of the project. They are useful when monitoring progress in terms of time and cost. You can compare progress towards a milestone with the plan using the percentage of the work completed and cost incurred to date as a basis. This can be illustrated on a milestone chart. Using the horizontal axis to illustrate time and the vertical axis to illustrate cost, milestones can be plotted. A line can be drawn joining the milestones to illustrate the planned progress in terms of time and cost. As each milestone is achieved it can be plotted on the chart and a line drawn to illustrate actual progress. The horizontal difference between the two lines indicates time slippage, the vertical difference cost slippage.

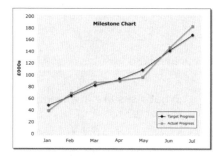

Remember, however, that milestones are not activities in themselves. Team members responsible for activities or milestones must report to you, as the project manager, regularly. Reports should include:

- The current position
- Achievements since the last report
- Potential problems
- Opportunities or threats to milestones

Problems are usually caused by events outside your control. If you are aware of the risks you will be able to identify warning signs and reduce the damage they may do to the project by acting quickly. A common area of risk is where the project depends on the actions of someone who is not part of the project team. They do not report to you or the team directly. They will have their own goals and objectives and their own ways of working. If communication has not been effective, they may not have all of the information they need. You need to keep on top of everything all the time to successfully manage risk.

It will be easier to deal with the unexpected if you expect it to happen. It may not be possible to plan for every contingency but the more you have considered the less threat it will pose to the project. If you are inexperienced at project management, seek advice from colleagues who may have more experience. They may be able to give you advice on dealing with potential problems. You may then have to change your plans to take these into account. Remember that planning is an ongoing event and that you must remain flexible enough to react to the unexpected. Make sure this is allowed for in your arrangements with your client.

You can then collate the information into a project management report which summarises the current position. Your milestone chart will enable you to draw some conclusions:

- A project on time but over budget suggests extra effort is being put in to overcome problems
- A project on budget but behind time suggests a lack of priority being given to the project
- A project which is behind and over budget suggests there are problems which are not being overcome

If everything has gone well, or everything that has gone wrong has been managed, the project will end on time and on budget. Probably the most effective way of judging the success of this is from the client's point of view. If the client is happy, you have achieved your main goal. You will still want to look at the project's success from other angles, however. Even if the project was completed on time and to budget it is likely that there will be areas where improvement could be made.

Throughout the life of the project you will have been gathering information. When the project is complete this information will be useful in analysing every part of the project. As well as using this statistical evidence, a series of de-briefing meetings should be held with the project team to evaluate the project. At these meetings you should discuss:

- What do we know about the individuals, the team and the organisation as a result of the project?

- What would we do differently if we were to carry out a similar project?
- Did we get the planning right, or if not, where did we get it wrong?
- What have we learned about processes or management from the project?

Record everybody's thoughts and input so that your evaluation can be as thorough as possible.

You should complete a comprehensive report detailing the strengths and weaknesses identified by the evaluation of the project. If the project was internal, this should be made available to all the stakeholders so that it can inform decisions on future projects. Be objective in your report, don't use it to attach blame or deflect criticism. Emphasise the positive aspects, but do not attempt to whitewash the shortcomings of the team. Improvement will only follow from honest evaluation.

 **What you need to know**

How to create a milestone chart

> Why is it helpful to plot milestones in the progress of a project?

The purpose of a milestone chart

> How can you reduce risks to a project?

Measures of success in project management

> Who can you seek advice from internal or external to your organisation?

The structure of a final project report

> How is a project evaluated?

The project manager needs the following skills in order to be successful:

- Perception in order that they can spot potential problems before they become too damaging
- Be prepared to question all information they are given without supporting evidence
- Be familiar with project management techniques, including appropriate software applications
- Be 'hands on', projects can't be managed solely from behind a desk
- Excellent motivators, both of members of the team and others who can affect the success of the project
- Good organisers
- Ability to control meetings
- Most of all they need to be excellent communicators
- Gain co-operation with management and colleagues at all levels, contacts in other organisations and, of course, the client

## The success of the project will almost entirely rely on the skills of the manager

# Are you ready for assessment?

To achieve this unit of a Level 3 Business & Administration qualification you will need to demonstrate that you are competent in the following:

- Confirm the purpose, aims and objectives of the project
- Agree the project specification
- Confirm resources for the project
- Plan the project and agree use of resources
- Agree timescales for the project
- Implement and monitor the project
- Seek advice in response to unexpected events
- Achieve required outcomes on time and to budget
- Report on project outcomes

(Remember that you will need the skills listed at the beginning of this chapter. These are covered in chapter 1.)

You will need to produce evidence from a variety of sources. Carrying out the following activities will help you acquire competence at work.

**Activity 1**
You have been given the task of organising for your office to be re-carpeted and redecorated. Treat this task as a project and write a specification for it.

**Activity 2**
Carry out a critical path analysis for the specification you have written for Activity 1. You can use a GANTT chart, PERT or CPA. You can create the path manually or using a software application.

**Activity 3**
You have been given the task of organising the relocation of your organisation to new premises which have been leased six miles away from your current location. The existing staff will all be re-locating. Write a project specification estimating time and budget requirements. Include all aspects of the move including furniture and equipment, connection of utilities and advising customers and suppliers of the move.

**Activity 4**
Carry out a critical path analysis for the specification you have written for Activity 3. You can use a GANTT chart, PERT or CPA. You can create the path manually or using a software application.

**Activity 5**
Agree with your line manager the purpose, aims and objectives of a project that you will be responsible for carrying out. Plan and prepare for the project, carrying out a risk assessment to identify possible problems or risks. Implement and evaluate the project. Prepare a project report for your line manager. (The project can be simple, e.g. sourcing a new stationery supplier, or complex e.g. arranging an international conference in New York.)

Remember: While gathering evidence for this unit, evidence **may** be generated for units 110, 212, 213, 217, 218, 301, 302, 304, 310, 311, 312, 314, 315, 319, 320 and 321.

# CHAPTER 19
## UNIT 310 – Research, analyse and report information

All organisations depend to a greater or lesser extent on information. This may be information on products, customers, competitors, sales, purchases, staff or legislation. The list is endless. This information can be obtained from a wide variety of different sources. It is important that you research efficiently, analyse the results carefully and present your findings appropriately.

There are, of course, some organisations whose main purpose is the storage and processing of information. Others will store information which they feel is needed on a regular basis and research information that is only needed occasionally.

Once the information has been sourced it needs to be organised, analysed and presented in a way that meets the requirements of the user. Research will usually provide quantitative or qualitative information. In robust research projects you may want to find out both quantitative and qualitative information.

Quantitative research works best with large numbers of people. It provides data in numeric terms. Data is usually obtained by doing some desk research or asking people to complete a carefully planned questionnaire, either directly by telephone or face-to-face, or indirectly by post or e-mail. Qualitative research is used to explore less easily defined objectives, such as opinions. It is usually carried out with small groups of people to investigate their views or behaviour.

There are five main research methods. The first four involve you doing the research with people and are known as primary research methods:

- **Observation** - Where the researcher observes practices and activities, without joining in, to identify what's happening and why. Observation is usually a qualitative method of research but last century there were mass observations designed to provide policy makers with quantitative data
- **Experiment** - When a test or tests are specially designed to see what happens under controlled conditions. This type of research is commonly used in the pharmaceutical industry
- **Interviews** - Which can be planned and carried out face-to-face, over the phone or via a video facility. A small series of in-depth interviews will provide qualitative information while a larger series of small interviews can provide quantitative information
- **Questionnaires** - Which are usually designed to collect information from a variety of sources. The most sophisticated questionnaires are designed to collect and analyse returned data using a computer programme. Initially, this costs more to design and implement but relatively little to analyse

The last method is secondary research:

- **Desk research** - In which as much as possible is learned from existing sources. This can be as simple as getting information about a competitor's product to a complex activity where many different sources may have to be researched to gather lots of information

Try not to overlook trends which your research uncovers. For instance, if you had researched the sale of word processors and discovered a 50% increase in the last two years, you might have deduced that there was no future in typewriter ribbons, carbon paper or correcting fluid.

Information, once collected, needs to be organised in order that it can be analysed to extract trends and comparisons. These can then be used to predict future events or to draw conclusions. Comparing information on your organisation with information from similar or competitor organisations on subjects such as rates of pay, market share, staff numbers or sales growth can be invaluable. It can help your organisation formulate future plans. Analysis also involves evaluating the information to determine its accuracy and to eliminate any possible bias.

Having carried out sufficient analysis to enable appropriate conclusions to be drawn the information will need to be presented in such a way that it satisfies the requirements of its intended audience. This may be in the form of a spreadsheet, memo, report or a slide show. The critical factor in making this decision is the nature of the audience rather than the nature of the information. Consider the use of charts and graphs to present statistical information as many people find numerical tabulation difficult to follow.

When researching, analysing and reporting information you will use the following skills:

- Planning
- Researching
- Analysing
- Organising
- Decision making
- Reading
- Writing
- Using number
- Problem solving
- Communicating
- Using technology
- Presenting information

These skills are covered in chapter 1.

# Research information

When you research information there are a number of things that you need to know. Obviously you will need to know what information is required but also how much, by when, in what format, from what sources and in what depth.

It may be necessary to liaise with other departments to obtain information which they may hold in databases, or to go to internal or public libraries to research in reference books, magazines, newspapers and brochures. You may find the necessary information on the computer, either the organisation's own systems or the Internet.

Once you have decided exactly what information is needed, consider all the possible sources and decide which ones to use. Think about the following:

- What information you are going to need
- What information you already have
- What past research might provide information
- What information is available within the organisation
- What information is available on the Internet or other external sources
- By when the information is required

The purpose of the research you are going to undertake may be relatively simple, such as listing all the outstanding invoices more than three months overdue, or may be a major research project, such as gathering information on the comparative advantages and disadvantages of computerising the accounts system. In either case the process of carrying out the research remains the same.

Start with information you may already have. In a relatively simple task there is a good chance that you already have most, if not all, of the information. This may be held in a database or spreadsheet programme for instance. To list all the outstanding invoices more than three months overdue only requires you to sort those invoices out from all the others.

A major research project will involve much more time and much wider research.

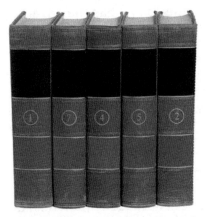

In a simple task it is possible that the information asked for is a regular requirement. Reference to the previous time that the information was provided will often mean that all that is needed is an up-date. In a more major project it may be that research has been carried out in the past which may be a good starting point.

Having looked at past research, look at information within the organisation that may be relevant. Obviously if the task is wholly internal then all of the information will be found within the organisation. In a major project you will need to gather information from both inside and outside. Discuss your project with everybody you can think of who may have helpful knowledge. You may well be surprised at how much your contacts already know. You could find that someone has experience from a previous job of carrying out the very project that you are researching.

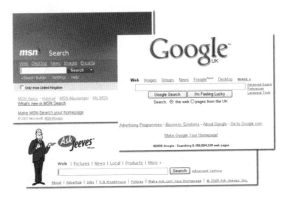

Once you have exhausted internal sources you will have to broaden your horizons. One of the greatest advances of our time is the Internet, which holds information about a comprehensive range of subjects and has the advantage of being free. You can accelerate your research by the use of 'search engines' whose purpose is to help you to find relevant websites. Among the best known are 'Google', 'MSN' and 'AskJeeves'. Whichever search engine you choose the keywords you use will greatly affect the number of results you get. For instance if you were searching for a word processor in South Kensington, London on 'MSN' and you used the keywords:

- Word processors you would get 400,261 results
- Word processors prices 200,387 results
- Word processors prices reduced 54,539 results
- Word processors prices reduced UK 20,686 results
- Word processors prices reduced UK London 11,755 results
- Word processors prices reduced UK London Kensington 402 results
- Word processors prices reduced UK London Kensington south 349 results

If you are unable to find what you are looking for on the Internet there are a number of other sources:

- Telephone directories
- Trade directories
- Suppliers
- Libraries
- Catalogues
- Reference books
- Magazines
- Newspapers
- Leaflets
- Brochures

These will be of varying relevance depending on the research.

In all searches for information bear in mind the questions of copyright and confidentiality. Any published work is likely to be subject to copyright and you will need to check carefully whether you are entitled to use it. Any personal data will be subject to the Data Protection Act 1998.

Most commercial information will be confidential and you would certainly need the approval of the organisation to publish it anywhere outside of the organisation.

The breadth and depth of research will be partly informed by the deadline. Clearly if you have a fairly distant deadline you will be able to research more sources of information than if the information is required at short notice. The way you undertake your research is called 'research methodology'. It is often important to outline your research methodology so that it is clear you have understood the terms of reference.

At this stage you are gathering information and not necessarily being selective about it. If there is time, take on board all current information which appears to be relevant rather than choosing the most important and discarding the rest. The detail which appears to be fairly unimportant can prove to be the critical factor in the analysis.

Use a method of recording the information that will allow you to retrieve it easily and analyse it when you have completed the research. Either print off all of the Internet-based information so that you have everything in hard copy, or, if you have the facility, scan in the paper-based information to the computer so you have everything electronically.

Whichever way you choose to record the information it will be useful to keep a record of the sources used. These can be put together at the end of a report in alphabetical order, often referred to as a bibliography. If asked to justify any conclusions drawn from the information, or if similar information is required in the future, it will be easier to refer to the previous search than to go through the whole process again. Records may be kept on paper or electronically, but either way will need to be cross-referenced so that they can be retrieved.

# What you need to know

The type of information your organisation has available

Do you know how to use search engines?

Previous research carried out by your organisation

What sources of information are available to you?

The difference between quantitative and qualitative research

What are the five main research methods?

The difference between primary and secondary research

What is meant by research methodology?

The deadline to complete the search for information

Why should you record the sources of information used?

Exactly what information is required

What would you find in a bibliography?

## Analyse and report information

When you have analysed all the information you will need to organise it into a format which matches the purpose of the research.  If all that is required is a list of outstanding invoices, produce a list, not a pile of invoices.

If the information is numeric, you may choose to present it in the form of a spreadsheet:

| | This year | Last year | Inc/dec |
|---|---|---|---|
| Sales | 15552 | 20353 | -4801 |
| | | | |
| Maintenance | 205 | 584 | -379 |
| Telephone | 315 | 263 | 52 |
| Stationery | 504 | 72 | 432 |
| Total expenses | 1024 | 919 | 105 |
| Sales - Expenses | 14528 | 19434 | -4906 |

Alternatively, the same information could be presented in the form of a pie chart:

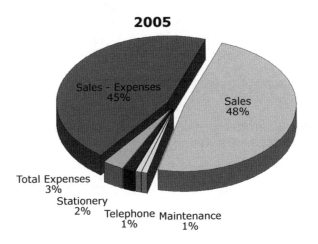

or a line graph:

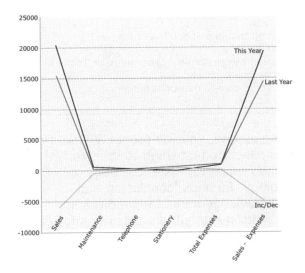

or a bar chart:

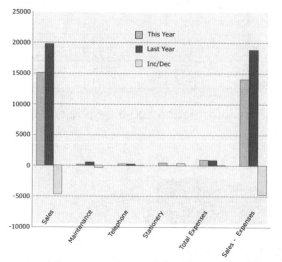

If you are asked for a summary of customer contact you could supply it in the form of a memo:

**MEMO**

| To: | Sales Manager |
|---|---|
| **From:** | William Weston |
| **Date:** | 15th August 2005 |

**Subject:** Preston Works – Customer contact summary

| 01.04.05 | Request for catalogue |
|---|---|
| 02.04.05 | Catalogue sent |
| 05.04.05 | Telephone call to make appointment for rep |
| 06.04.05 | Visit by rep |
| 14.04.05 | Order received by telephone – order number 2546448 |
| 17.04.05 | Order despatched by post |
| 18.04.05 | Invoice raised – invoice number 886654 |
| 19.05.05 | Payment received |

If the project is a complex one, you will probably need to write a report. In this case the first thing to do is to write an outline structure for the report, for instance: title, introduction, methodology, findings, conclusion and recommendations, acknowledgements, appendices and bibliography. Having written the outline, sort the information under these headings. You will then be able to organise the information within each heading to produce a report that delivers the information in a logical order. Remember, if your project has included desk research, put your sources at the back of your report in a bibliography.

TITLE: DRAFT REPORT ON THE ADVANTAGES AND DISADVANTAGES
OF COMPUTERISING THE ACCOUNTS SYSTEM

**INTRODUCTION:** This report is to consider the advantages and
disadvantages of computerising the accounts system taking into account the
cost of purchasing software, training needs, the requirement to operate
parallel running and the timescales involved.

**MAIN BODY:** Information on:
- Available software
- Cost
- Training needs analysis of staff
- Case study from a similar organisation

Check the draft to confirm that the final report is likely to
meet your requirements before completing the report.

Having confirmed that the outline of the report meets your
requirements, produce a final copy. In this copy the report
will contain:

- **The Title**
- **The Introduction** - The background to the report
  and an overview of what the report contains
- **The Methodology** - Report what methods you used
  to collect information, for example Internet research
  and telephone interviews
- **The Main Body** - Display all the information that you
  have gathered, set out in a logical form so that the
  reader is led towards the conclusion
- **The Conclusion** - Analyse your findings and state
  what your research has led you to, and how. Be
  careful to draw your conclusion from the information
  that you have included in the report, not from any
  previously held opinions of your own
- **Recommendations** - State any action that you feel
  should be taken as a result of the conclusions
- **Acknowledgements** - If you have received help
  from others in compiling the report acknowledge their
  contribution in this section
- **Bibliography** - Source material should be referred to.
  This should be listed alphabetically by author and the
  date of publication given
- **Appendices** - There may be information which you
  have referred to in the main body which is too
  detailed to be given in the report. In that case it may
  be useful to give the whole of the information in an
  appendix

When you have completed the report it is essential that you proof read it before printing and distributing copies. Most word processing packages contain spell checking and grammar checking facilities. Use these first to correct the more glaring errors, but don't rely on them entirely. They tend to use American spelling and grammar, so will accept 'color' and reject 'colour', for instance. When the automatic checking is complete, **read** the document carefully to look for missed errors, and also for correct use of paragraphs, headings and sub-headings, style and formatting. Be particularly careful to proof read numbers, dates, times and amounts. Check for errors between similar words such as 'affect' and 'effect' or 'less' and 'fewer'.

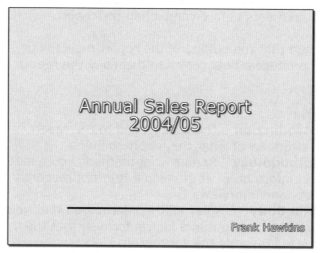

If the information is to be provided to a group of people you may choose to present it as a slide show. In this case you would transfer the main points, probably the title, the conclusion and the recommendations onto slides and show it to the group, talking through the full information and providing hand outs for them to consider.

The hand outs should contain the full text of the report and also an outline of the slides. You may also want to leave room for notes beside each slide on the handout.

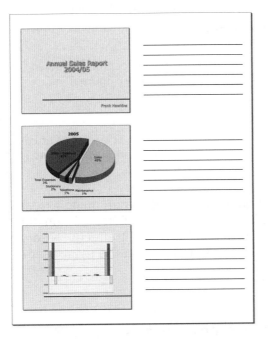

When the report has been presented, review the information and decide whether it is worth keeping for future reference. If so, make sure that you review it from time-to-time and discard anything that has become out of date. Out of date information is less useful than a blank sheet of paper.

## What you need to know

How to structure a report

Why is it important to agree aims, objectives and deadlines?

The different formats that can be used to present information

Why should you match the information produced to the initial requirements?

How to organise information so that you can analyse it

How would you record the sources of information in order that it may be retrieved at a later date?

When the use of charts and graphs is appropriate for presenting information

What trends can be extracted from staff turn-over figures?

The problems with allowing bias to affect the analysis of information

What are the advantages of comparing your organisation with others in the same sector?

The most important thing to consider when doing research is to planning., Use all available sources of information, select the most relevant information, analyse it effectively, organise it to your requirements and present it in the most user-friendly way.

# Are you ready for assessment?

To achieve this unit of a Level 3 Business & Administration qualification you will need to demonstrate that you are competent in the following:

- Agree aims and objectives and deadlines for the information search
- Identify relevant sources of information
- Search for and obtain information to meet deadlines
- Record the information
- Maintain a record of sources used
- Organise the information in a way that will help you analyse it
- Examine, interpret and extract the information required
- If necessary, get feedback on what you have found
- Present information in the most appropriate format, accurately and on time

(Remember that you will need the skills listed at the beginning of this chapter. These are covered in chapter 1.)

You will need to produce evidence from a variety of sources. Carrying out the following activities will help you acquire competence at work.

## Activity 1
Your sales manager is planning a trip to the following cities; Sofia, Prague, Kiev and Budapest. You have been asked to research relevant information on the countries to be visited, for instance currency, whether visas are needed, the security situation, inoculations required, suitable hotels, travel arrangements and any other information you think may be useful. Produce a concise report on each country.

## Activity 2
You are working for a local newspaper. Your editor asks you to research the life of a local celebrity and produce a resumé.

## Activity 3
Whatever sort of organisation you work in, there will be a certain amount of waste produced. This may include paper, printer cartridges, cardboard, drinks cans, disposable cups from the water dispenser. Research the cost of disposing of the waste and the possibility of re-cycling some or all of it; perhaps selling the paper or having the printer cartridges re-filled. Calculate the savings that could be made over the course of a year taking into account storage space and any additional staff costs.

## Activity 4
You have just got a new job as an administrator in a small company producing components. These components range from small, relatively light weight parts to bulky, heavy items. The components are distributed world-wide and you are concerned that the organisation is not using the most cost-effective methods of distribution. Research the alternatives and produce a report.

## Activity 5
Select one share from each of the following sectors of the Stock Market:
- Construction and Building
- General Retailers
- Software and Computer Services
- Telecommunication Services
- Utilities
- Banks

Your research should show rises and falls in profit over the period of a month. Imagine you purchase 500 shares in each at the current price. Over the period of a month record the value of each holding once a week. At the end of the month produce a graph which shows how the value of each has increased or decreased, and the change in the total value.

Analyse your findings and record what you intend to do with each block of shares.

**Activity 6**
Negotiate a research project at work with your line manager. Agree the aims and objectives of the research, the time you can take to carry out the research and the way you are going to report the findings and recommendations to your line manager.

Remember: While gathering evidence for this unit, evidence **may** be generated for units 110, 212, 213, 216, 217, 301, 302, 312, 314, 315, 320 and 321.

# CHAPTER 20
# UNIT 311 – Plan, organise and support meetings

All businesses get involved in meetings. Some have a wide variety of meetings while others, like small businesses, may only participate in a few meetings.

Meetings can be formal or informal but if they are to have any significant effect, they will need to be recorded. A meeting that is **not** organised before it happens, structured while it is happening and the main points of agreement recorded and followed up after it has happened, is only a discussion.

When arranging a meeting it is necessary to decide what sort of meeting it is going to be and its purpose. Meetings are held for several different reasons, for instance:

- **Annual General Meetings** - All companies with shareholders are obliged to hold a meeting at least once a year where all shareholders are entitled to attend. Their purpose is to give shareholders the opportunity to question directors and vote on resolutions

- **Extraordinary General Meetings** - Additional meetings can be called if the holders of at least 10% of the shares require them. Their purpose is to discuss issues that have arisen since the last Annual General Meeting that won't wait until the next e.g. dismissal of CEO or Management
- **Board meetings** - The directors of the company meet regularly to discuss the general running of the organisation
- **Management meetings** - The managers meet to discuss the day-to-day running of the organisation. The purpose of the meeting is to decide how the strategy agreed by the Board is to be implemented
- **Team meetings** - These may include the sales team, the production team, the customer service team, the design team or the accounts team each discussing the issues that affect them directly. At these meetings team leaders will 'cascade' information from the management
- **Staff meetings** - These are held less often than team meetings. Their purpose is to inform all of the staff simultaneously of major issues that will affect everybody
- **Committee meetings** - These range from official public committees such as Parish Councils to less formal bodies like Social Club committees or the Health and Safety committee within the organisation

It is not always necessary for all the participants in a meeting to be in the same place. Modern technology allows for video conferencing, where people can see and hear each other via cameras and microphones, and teleconferencing where any number of people can be connected by telephone simultaneously. These can save travelling time and costs, especially if some of the participants are overseas. These should be arranged with care as some people find the technology intimidating, and the lack of physical interaction can reduce the effectiveness of the meeting.

Meetings require organising, to ensure that all attendees know the time, place and purpose of the meeting. As far in advance of the meeting as possible, send out invitations to attend. This will give time for people to diarise the meeting and advise whether or not they are able to attend. They can also advise if they have any special requirements so that you have plenty of time to make the necessary arrangements.

At this time also send a map showing the location of the meeting, car parks and the nearest railway station together with directions to the venue.

A week before the meeting send an agenda and copies of any meeting papers to those who indicated they would be attending.

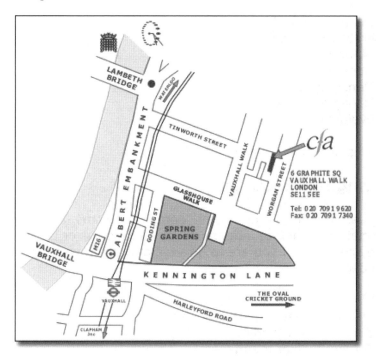

The agenda of a meeting sets out in a logical order what is to be discussed at the meeting. Ask people to confirm their attendance and make a note of replies so that you can prepare the apologies for absence.

Meetings also require recording, so that attendees and others can be sure what future actions were agreed, who is to carry them out and to what timescales. The record of the meeting is known as the 'minutes', which must then be circulated to all those who were present and those who sent their apologies.

When planning, organising and supporting meetings you will use the following skills:

- Negotiating
- Planning
- Organising
- Communicating
- Checking
- Interpersonal skills
- Problem solving
- Writing
- Monitoring
- Managing time
- Managing resources
- Evaluating

These skills are covered in chapter 1.

## Preparing for meetings

Meetings are held to discuss ideas, identify problems, pass on information, generate interest, reach conclusions or co-ordinate activities.  If you are to arrange a meeting you will need to decide:

- Where the meeting is to be held
- When the meeting is to be held
- Who will be attending
- The purpose of the meeting
- What resources are required
- Whether any catering arrangements need to be made
- The special requirements of the people attending

The decision on the venue will depend on factors such as:

- The purpose of the meeting
- The number of attendees
- The seniority of the attendees
- The geographic location of the attendees
- Whether your organisation has in-house facilities for such a meeting
- Potential disruption to the business

Selecting a venue within your own premises or nearby has the advantage of saving travelling time and cost for people based on the premises, as well as the convenience of being able to refer to any information held on the premises. Having decided on the venue you will need to arrange for the availability of the meeting room, any necessary equipment and catering requirements. If not in-house, then obtain quotes from suitable venues and, if possible, contact other people who have used the venue previously, this will give you an idea of the standards you can expect. It is important to ensure that the standard of hospitality and catering is appropriate. Make sure it is clear exactly what is being provided. Is equipment and catering included or does that need to be organised separately? Regular contact with the venue is important so that you are aware of any potential problems that may arise and can inform them of any changes in the number of attendees.

The layout of the room will depend on the purpose of the meeting. There are three common layouts for meeting rooms:

- **Classroom** - This is where a speaker stands in front of an audience seated round a number of tables. This layout is useful if people are to take part in 'workshops'
- **Boardroom** - This is where the whole group sit round a table. If people attending are to discuss ideas, reach conclusions or co-ordinate activities this layout may be most appropriate
- **Theatre** - This is where a speaker stands in front of an audience seated in rows of seats. This layout may prove more suitable if information is to be passed on

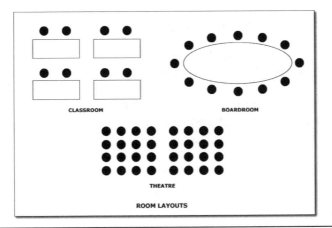

CLASSROOM                BOARDROOM

THEATRE

ROOM LAYOUTS

Where a screen or flipchart is being used it is essential that everyone can see it without too much movement. If you are arranging a meeting for a large number of people consider whether microphones are necessary to enable everybody to hear what is being said, but remember not to place speakers where people will be deafened by the sound.

Other equipment you may need to have available includes:

- A laptop, to allow a PowerPoint presentation to be shown
- A multi-media projector
- Whiteboards and dry-wipe markers, for brainstorming sessions
- An easel, to put the flip chart on

Don't forget the small stuff; pencils, paper and maybe a dish of sweets to keep the speaker's voice box lubricated.

Laptops and multi-media projectors have virtually replaced the use of overhead projectors in recent times. The opportunities to include sound, animation and video clips, as well as the ease with which the presenter can move from one slide to the next by remote control make overhead projectors obsolete.

Having organised the venue you will need to prepare and agree an agenda and meeting papers. In a regular formal meeting the first three items of the agenda are usually:

- Apologies for absence
- The minutes of the last meeting
- Matters arising

The last two items are always:

- Any other business (A.O.B.)
- The date of the next meeting

The actual business of the meeting is sandwiched between the first three and the last two items.

**Social Club Meeting held on 19<sup>th</sup> May 2004**
**West Hotel, Pendleton. 2.30pm.**

# Agenda

1. Apologies

2. Minutes of the last meeting

3. Matters arising

4. Chair's report

5. Treasurer's report

6. Recruitment of Chair discussions

7. A.O.B.

8. Date of the next meeting

Copies of any documents the people attending will need in advance of the meeting will have to be produced and sent to them with the agenda, as this will give them time to read and consider them. If they are to discuss the content of the papers they will need to receive them well before the meeting in order to prepare.

The person chairing the meeting (the Chair) will need to know before the meeting what the desired outcomes are, so ask the attendees to also let you know if there are any major issues that they wish to discuss. In many cases the Chair will have been involved in the initial planning of the meeting and will be well aware of its purpose, but there will be occasions when they will need to be briefed on the particular stances or viewpoints of the attendees.

Also ask people to advise if they have any special requirements. These may include dietary, mobility, hearing or vision impairment or travel and accommodation. If you are advised that anybody has a particular need, liaise with the venue organiser to ensure that it can be met. You will also need to ensure that all Health and Safety and security requirements have been taken into consideration.

# What you need to know

The differences between various types of meetings

What five items are on every agenda?

The Chair's needs prior to the meeting

Why do you need replies confirming intention to attend?

The types of equipment that may be needed for a meeting

What are the advantages of holding a meeting on your own premises?

Before arranging a meeting you need to know where it will be, when it will take place, who will attend and the purpose of the meeting

What would be the best room layout for an Annual General Meeting?

What attendees will need prior to a meeting

How would you arrange a venue for a national sales conference?

# On the day of the meeting

- Arrive well before the start time of the meeting.  This will allow you to check that all the arrangements are in place
- Check that the catering is organised for the times that the agenda states it will be available
- Check that all of the equipment is in place and that it works
- If the meeting is not on your premises:
    - make sure you know where the toilets are
    - whether there is a fire alarm test arranged that day
    - where the fire exits are
    - where the assembly point is
    - where lunch is going to be served
    - if there are facilities for smokers
    - if there is disabled access
    - who is responsible for first aid and how to raise the alarm if you need to

Make sure that you have spare copies of the papers you sent prior to the meeting available for those who have lost them, forgotten them or claim never to have received them.  There may be other items for discussion at the meeting, which were not included on the agenda.  If this happens, make sure you have sufficient copies of relevant papers for the meeting, because these have not been circulated in advance.  These should be collated into the order in which they will be discussed and placed in position on the tables.  Sorting the papers into order will enable people to follow the agenda more easily and reduce the distraction that searching through piles of paper causes.  Make sure everyone has a full set of papers.

When people start to arrive make sure someone is on hand to greet them, sign them in and give them a delegate's badge if necessary, tell them where the cloakroom is, where refreshments can be found, the location of the meeting room and answer any questions they may have.

The level of recording of the meeting will depend on the type of meeting.  The more formal the meeting, the more detailed the notes that must be kept.  Notes of all meetings, however, must be accurate as they may be used later in a variety of circumstances.  The most formal meetings will require minutes to be taken and signed by the Chair as a true record. There are various ways in which minutes can be taken including:

- **Verbatim** - Everything is recorded word for word
- **Narrative** - A summary of the meeting including discussions and conclusions. Formal resolutions are recorded verbatim
- **Resolution** - A resolution is a motion which has been voted on and passed. Details of the 'proposer' and 'seconder' are recorded with a verbatim recording of the resolution

Minutes are a written record of what took place at a meeting, and whichever form is used they must contain everything of importance. They must be written in a neutral fashion and always in the past tense. For instance, if Mr. McTavish says, "I am pleased to report that sales are up by 25% this year compared to last", the minutes would record, 'Mr. McTavish reported that sales in the current year were 25% up compared to the previous year'. The words 'I' and 'we' are not used in minute taking.

While taking the minutes:

- It is better to write too much than too little
- Record what is said and agreed in the order that it happens, not necessarily in the order the items appeared on the agenda
- Try to persuade the Chair to stick to the agenda
- If you are uncertain what someone has said, ask them to repeat it and read it back to them before you record it to check that you have it right
- Where someone refers to something that has been discussed at a previous meeting, cross-refer this in the minutes
- Record names and times of late arrivals and early departures
- If formal resolutions are being voted on, record the names of the proposer and seconder
- If asked, record details of any opposing view to the majority
- Make sure all agreed actions state who is responsible for carrying them out and the target date
- If necessary record the agreed date, time and place of the next meeting

- Include a list of all attendees
- Ensure that all attendees and those whose apologies for absence were noted receive a copy

---

Minutes of Social Club Meeting held on 19th May 2004 West Hotel, Pendleton. 2.30pm.

Those present

Bill Banstow        Chair
Mike Willis         Secretary
Pete Axty           Treasurer
Carol Carter
Brian Williams
Kevin Bissle
Janet Hewitt

Apologies for absence were received from: Michael Ford

Late Arrivals were Kevin Bissle and Janet Hewitt

Minutes of the last meeting were approved.

The Chair reported that discussion with management started with regard to the possibility of using the staff canteen for future events.

The Treasurer reported that there were 7 subscriptions still outstanding. It was agreed that letters be written to the appropriate members advising them that if payment was not received by 6th June their membership would be terminated.

Kevin Bissle proposed that Bill Banstow should remain Chair for a the next 12 month period. Seconded by Janet Hewitt.

Bill Banstow accepted the extension of his period as chair.

A.O.B.

Carol Carter suggested that a staff outing to the seaside in August could be arranged.

It was agreed that she would look into the costings of such an event.

The next meeting will be on 16th June 2004 at 2.30pm at the West Hotel, Pendleton.

As well as taking minutes it will probably be your responsibility to:

- Make sure everybody knows where the toilets are
- What to do in case of a fire alarm
- Where and when refreshments are available

If it is a formal meeting you may need to:

- Advise the Chair on legal issues or matters of convention
- You may have to arrange for the photocopying of papers during the meeting
- Deal with failures of power, equipment or caterers

If the meeting is not being held on your own premises you will need to have checked who to contact in any given set of circumstances. If the fire alarm should sound you will need to guide everyone to a place of safety.

Less formal meetings will still require that notes be taken of the actions agreed action. The item discussed, the outcome or action required and the name of the person or persons responsible for carrying out the action are recorded. The discussions are not recorded.

| ITEM No. | ACTION REQUIRED | BY WHOM | BY WHEN |
|----------|-----------------|---------|---------|
| 1 | New office furniture to be ordered | Bill Welch | 30.04.06 |
| 2 | Year end procedures to be completed | Everybody | 28.05.06 |
| 3 | Office junior to be recruited | Karin Begum | 28.05.06 |
| 4 | Invoicing to be brought up to date | Mark Lennon | 28.05.06 |
| 5 | Filing to be brought up to date | Rachel Starr | 30.06.06 |
| 6 | Quarterly newsletter to be produced | Pete Biggs Samantha Wilson | 13.10.06 |

# What you need to know

The different types of minutes required

> Why is it necessary to record late arrivals and early departures?

Who should receive copies of the minutes

> What duties other than recording the minutes might you have during the meeting?

What to include in and what to exclude from the minutes

> What is meant by the terms 'proposer' and 'seconder'?

The importance of recording who is responsible for carrying out agreed actions and by when

> In what circumstances would you record an opposing view to a majority decision?

## After the meeting

When you have typed-up the minutes take them to the Chair and ask their approval of the content. Make any amendments that are necessary to ensure that the minutes are an accurate record of the meeting and agreed action points. Distribute the minutes to the attendees and those who submitted apologies for absence as soon as possible and before the agreed deadline. Some organisations have particular ways of highlighting action points to be completed before the next meeting as it is important to ensure everyone understands who's doing what and by when. Don't forget to keep a copy for the file. Check through the action points to see if there were any papers to be forwarded following the meeting and make sure these are enclosed. You may also need to send copies of papers distributed at the meeting to those who submitted their apologies.

# Minutes of Social Club Meeting held on 19<sup>th</sup> May 2004
## West Hotel, Pendleton. 2.30pm

1.0 Those present

| | |
|---|---|
| Bill Banstow | Chair |
| Mike Willis | Secretary |
| Pete Axty | Treasurer |
| Carol Carter | |
| Brian Williams | |
| Kevin Bissle | |
| Janet Hewitt | |

1.1 Apologies for absence were received from: Michael Ford

1.2 Late Arrivals were Kevin Bissle and Janet Hewitt

1.3 Minutes of the last meeting were approved.

2.0 The Chairman reported that discussions with management had started with regard to the possibility of using the staff canteen for future events.

3.0 The Treasurer reported that there were seven subscriptions still outstanding. It was agreed that letters be written to the appropriate members advising them that if payment was not received by 6$^{th}$ June their membership would be terminated.

4.0 Kevin Bissle proposed that Bill Banstow should remain Chair for the next 12-month period. Seconded by Janet Hewitt.

4.1 Bill Banstow accepted the extension of his period as Chair.

5.0 A.O.B.

5.1 Carol Carter suggested that a staff outing to the seaside in August could be arranged.

5.2 It was agreed that she would look into the costings of such an event.

6.0 The next meeting will be on 16$^{th}$ June 2004 at 2.30pm at the West Hotel, Pendleton.

You may receive requests to alter the contents of the minutes after you have distributed them. These must always be referred to the Chair. If they agree that the amendment will produce a more accurate record of the meeting, an amended set of minutes will need to be produced and circulated. If the Chair is unwilling to have the minutes amended, you will need to advise the attendee accordingly and they will have to raise the matter at the next meeting.

You may need to diarise the action points so that you can contact the person responsible for taking the actions and check what progress has been made. Where there appears to be a potential problem, you may need to report this to the Chair or ask if there is any assistance that you can give to help achieve the desired result.

 ## What you need to know

Whose approval of the minutes is necessary before they are distributed

> Why is it essential to keep a file copy of the minutes?

The actions to take if you are asked to amend minutes after they have been distributed

> What might have to be sent to people who submitted their apologies?

Whose responsibility it is to follow up action points between meetings

> Why is accuracy vital in minute taking?

Whether any documents will need to be distributed to enable action points to be completed

> When should minutes of meetings be distributed?

The efficient planning, organisation and accurate recording of meetings is essential to the effective running of a business. Meetings do not just happen, they require a great deal of work before, during and after the event. You will need to know and be able to spell the names of everybody at the meeting, as well as having at least a passing knowledge of the business being discussed.  You must be able to concentrate throughout the meeting, remaining alert and being organised so that you can record what is happening without missing anything.

**To be a successful meetings organiser requires the organisational ability of a general and the patience of a saint**

# Are you ready for assessment?

To achieve this unit of a Level 3 Business & Administration qualification you will need to demonstrate that you are competent in the following:

- Plan and agree the meeting brief
- Organise and confirm the venue, equipment and catering requirements
- Prepare and agree an agenda and meeting papers
- Invite attendees and confirm attendance
- Make sure attendees' needs are met
- Collate and dispatch papers for the meeting within agreed timescales
- Make sure the Chair receives a necessary briefing
- Produce spare copies of meeting papers
- Arrange the equipment and layout of the room
- Make sure attendees have a full set of papers
- Take accurate notes of the meeting, including attendance
- Provide information, advice and support when required
- Produce a record of the meeting
- Seek approval and amend the meeting record as necessary
- Circulate the meeting record to agreed timescales
- Respond to requests for amendments and re-circulate amended copies
- Follow up action points
- Evaluate and maintain a record of external services

(Remember that you will need the skills listed at the beginning of this chapter. These are covered in chapter 1.)

You will need to produce evidence from a variety of sources. Carrying out the following activities will help you acquire competence at work.

## Activity 1

You have been appointed the secretary of your organisation's Social Club. They are holding a committee meeting next Wednesday, September 6th to discuss future events. Produce an agenda for the meeting and the notice you would send to the committee.

## Activity 2

The following action points were recorded at the above Social Club meeting.

Bill Grates is to organise the firework display for November 5th.
Sharon Sloane is to make arrangements for the visit of Father Christmas to the local hospice on Christmas Eve.
Michael Fisher is to purchase the masks for the Halloween Ball.
Victoria Ashman has agreed to hire the Father Christmas outfit for the staff Christmas party.
Brian Graham has offered to arrange the transport home for people attending the New Year's Eve party.
Matthew Christian is going to buy the prizes for the Christmas Party raffle.

As secretary it is your responsibility to follow up the action points. Create an action plan and diarise the actions that you need to take.

## Activity 3

Minutes must not be written in the first person and must always be in the past tense. Re-write the following statements to make them acceptable as minutes.

Bill Rich said, 'I will have that report ready by Wednesday'.
Anthony Banks feels that Wednesday will be too late.
The sales figures were produced yesterday.
It is essential that the work is carried out today.
Tomorrow is the deadline for completing the agreed action.
We have all agreed that the deadline needs to be extended.
Point six on the agenda will be carried forward to the next meeting.
Our prices have not increased over the last twelve months.
Rachel Matthews said, 'I will be on holiday when the next meeting is held'.
The Treasurer intends to resign at the next meeting.

## Activity 4

You have been asked to organise a sales meeting to be held at work. Identify who should be invited to attend, the most suitable location, how long the meeting should last and the agenda items. Calculate the cost of refreshments and list the resources that will be required. Locate a suitable external venue and get quotes for holding the meeting there. Compare the costs of holding the meeting internally and externally.

**Activity 5**

You have been asked to arrange an all day meeting for 40 people with lunch and coffee/tea included.  The purpose is to inform them of a new product that your organisation is about to launch onto the market.  Research local venues for the meeting, obtain quotes and suggested room layouts.  Two of the attendees are in wheelchairs and one is a vegetarian.  Take their needs into account.

**Activity 6**

Attend a meeting (this could be a team meeting at work, a social club meeting, a meeting at college) and take notes of what is said.  Produce minutes from your notes.  Ask someone else who attended the meeting to review the minutes and check that you have included all the important points (if there are official minutes produced you could check yours against them).

**Remember:**  While gathering evidence for this unit, evidence **may** be generated for units 110, 212, 213, 216, 301, 302, 314, 320 and 321.

# CHAPTER 21
## UNIT 312 – Make a presentation

For many people having to make a presentation is one of the most daunting prospects of their working life. Very few of us would claim to be natural presenters. Even people who speak in public for a living have had to learn the necessary skills before they can appear completely at ease. Beginners in this field can often make basic mistakes in their preparation which lead them to make a poor presentation. Their awareness that the presentation went badly reinforces their perception that this is a skill you are either born with or will never be able to learn. However, nothing is further from the truth: you can learn these skills.

Often the first advice you will be given when preparing to make your first presentation is to 'be yourself'. This advice is not particularly helpful if you are either lacking in self confidence and convinced that no one will be interested in listening to what you have to say or sufficiently self confident that you believe you will be able to sustain a full day's presentation without any preparation whatsoever. The presenters we admire in public or on the television appear to have the ability to simply be themselves. But as you know, they often have totally different personality traits when they are not in front of an audience.

Before you can start to put together a presentation you will need to ask yourself a number of questions.

**What is the presentation about?** It may be:

- A sales presentation aimed at customers or potential customers
- A training presentation for employees
- A presentation to management about a suggested change in operations or procedures
- A presentation about results
- A research presentation
- A tender for a contract
- A bid for funding
- An up-date on a project

**Do you have all the necessary information or do you need to find out further facts?**

It is important that you know at least as much as, and preferably more than, your audience about the subject you are making a presentation on. If you have any doubt about the depth of your knowledge, explore all possible sources of information before preparing your presentation.

**Who is your audience?**

The size and membership of the group that you will be presenting to will have a major impact on the way you present:

- A small audience (less than ten people) requires you to talk to the group as if you are speaking to each person individually. The presentation can be given sitting down if this makes you feel more comfortable
- An audience of between ten and 25 needs a stand up presentation, probably with visual aids, but you will still be able to deal with individual questions and relate to individual members of the audience
- An audience of over 25 people requires careful management, you will need to check that everybody can hear you and see the visual aids. It will be much more difficult to handle questions without the risk of disengaging the rest of the audience

**How long are you going to speak for?**

There may be two parameters to the duration of your presentation. How long will it take to say what you have to say and how much time is available. If the time available is less than the time you think you need, make sure you are going to get across the main points and include the detail in handouts which the audience can read later. If the time available is more than the time you think you need, consider adding workshop activities, but only where these will genuinely add to the value of the presentation.

## Where is the presentation to be given?

If you are unfamiliar with the venue try to visit it before the event to check that there are no problems such as health and safety issues, access to electricity or internet connections or insufficient space for the size of the audience. On the day of the presentation arrive at least half an hour before you are due to start so that you can check the room is not cold or over hot, the layout is as you wanted it and that the equipment is all working.

## What style of presentation are you going to give?

You may plan a simple 'chalk and talk' where you stand in front of your audience and speak with only the aid of a white board or flip chart to write on. You may decide to add an overhead projector (OHP) so that you can prepare simple visual aids. You may need to produce a slide show using software such as PowerPoint so that you can present more complex visual aids, perhaps adding graphics and sound. The decision on the style will probably be informed by the answers to the other questions, a presentation lasting five minutes to an audience of three people is unlikely to warrant a PowerPoint slide show.

It may help to remember these five steps to making an impressive presentation:

- **P**urpose - Know why you are making the presentation
- **R**esearch - Know what you are going to say
- **I**ndividual - Make the presentation memorable
- **M**eaningful - Tell them something they didn't know
- **E**nthusiasm - If you don't care why should they?

Keep the acronym '**PRIME**' in mind and you will haven taken the first step towards becoming a competent presenter. It is also necessary to take steps to avoid the pitfalls that blight the presenter's life.  The most common obstacles you will encounter as a new presenter are:

- **S**cript - Don't be tempted to simply read your notes
- **H**andouts - These can disrupt your flow
- **E**nnui - Don't reveal your lack of interest
- **L**ack of belief - Don't let them know you don't believe
- **F**lannel - Don't waffle to fill the time

Always remember the five Ps: planning and preparation prevent poor performance.  The most difficult presentation you will ever make will be the first one.  You will not know what to expect, what will work well or what to avoid.  After making your first presentation ensure you have given the audience the opportunity to evaluate your performance and, most importantly, act on their comments.  You will then have some data to use when preparing your subsequent presentations.  Always gather feedback from your audience so you can go on improving your skills.

 When making a presentation you will use the following skills:

- Negotiating
- Researching
- Summarising
- Planning
- Organising
- Writing
- Communicating to groups
- Managing time
- Using technology
- Evaluating

These skills are covered in chapter 1.

# Preparing the presentation

You will be making a presentation for one of two reasons; either someone has asked (or told) you to or you feel you have something that needs to be said. In either case you would not be making the presentation unless there was some information that needed to be passed on to an audience. The difference between the two situations is that where you feel you have something that needs to be said you will usually know what it is you want to say. If you have been asked to give a presentation you may feel less sure that you have all the facts.

The key is to research the subject thoroughly. Even if it is a topic that you are considered to be an expert on, there will still be areas where you can learn, so gather as much information as you can. Collect any information related to the subject of your presentation and you will be surprised how many ideas will present themselves which will expand the boundaries of what you have to say. Be creative in your research, go off at a tangent and you will discover fascinating facts that will enliven your presentation.

Once you have collected as much information as possible it is time to structure the information so that your presentation has a beginning, a middle and an end. You may want to tell the audience the background to the information you are giving them, follow this with the situation as it stands, then the reason for changing the situation and finish with the suggested changes.

One of the difficulties of this structure is that they may already know the background and the situation as it stands and you may lose their attention before you get to the information that they really need. This can be overcome by a technique which is sometimes described as:

- Tell them what you are going to tell them
- Tell them
- Tell them what you have told them

To an inexperienced presenter this appears to mean that you have to say everything three times but, in reality, it is a structure that is widely used. Next time you watch a documentary on television try to spot the structure. At the beginning the narrator will tell you what the programme is about, then they will tell you about it, then at the end they will recap what you have seen. This is particularly noticeable in programmes with commercial breaks as they will often go through the whole process before and after each break.

A deciding factor in your structure will be the time available for the presentation. If you are responsible for organising the talk you may be able to set the limit yourself. If you are presenting at somebody else's request you may be given a time limit. You will probably find when you start to structure your information that you have too much rather than too little. What may appear to be a shortage of information will often expand to fill the time available once you have allowed time for an introduction, your presentation, questions and a conclusion. If you try to give your audience too much information they will remember very little of it.

Aim for a maximum of seven points that you want your audience to remember. If your accumulated material can't be divided into a maximum of seven subjects, try ranking the information and discarding any that comes below seventh place. You will almost certainly find that this information is not really necessary to your presentation.

When you have decided what you are going to include in your presentation you will need to give some thought to the make up of the audience. If your talk is on a technical subject, the existing level of knowledge will influence the amount of jargon that you will be able to include. If only one member of the audience does not understand a technical term that you intend to use you will have to either remove it from your speech or explain it in non-technical language. The difficulty there, of course, is that all the other members of the audience who understood it will lose interest while you explain it.

You always need to consider the resources you will need:

- **Venue** - This is critical to the presentation's success. Too small a room will make the audience feel uncomfortable and make it difficult for them to concentrate. Too large a room will make interaction with the audience difficult. If the room is too warm or too cold your audience will become distracted. If the room is an awkward shape the audience will find it difficult to see or hear you. When you know what venue you will be using, practice standing at one end of the room and speaking to someone standing at the opposite end. If they can't hear you clearly you will have a problem when you make your presentation. Consider using a microphone to overcome this
- **Room layout** - There are a number of different room layouts available to suit different styles of presentation. Details of these can be found in chapter 22
- **Housekeeping** - You need to know where the fire exits are, whether a fire drill is due and where the toilets are. Arrange for flowers to be placed in the room to create a pleasant atmosphere. Background music playing while delegates are arriving and leaving makes for a more relaxed mood. Remember to switch the music off before you begin your presentation
- **Refreshments** - Make sure refreshments are available. Decide whether you will provide tea, coffee, water, juice, sweets, biscuits, continental breakfast etc. for the audience before the presentation or during breaks. Make sure there is a glass of water for the speaker throughout the presentation
- **Equipment** - Decide what you will need. Make sure it can be provided. Find out who is responsible for providing the equipment. Arrive early on the day of the presentation to ensure all the equipment is in place and working properly. Consider whether you will need any of the following items:
  - Laptop, projector or screen
  - Internet access
  - Overhead projector or screen
  - Flip chart and pens
  - White board and pens
  - Delegate packs, writing paper and pens/pencils

Try to avoid interruptions such as phone calls or members of the audience being contacted during the presentation. Ask your audience to switch off their mobile phones before you begin your presentation.

Once you are confident that you know:

- What you are going to be talking about
- Who to
- For how long
- Where
- When
- That you will have all the equipment you need

You will be able to turn your mind to how you are going to deliver the information. The longer and more complex the presentation the more need there is for visual aids. A simple, short briefing may be given by a presenter standing in front of the audience and merely speaking to them. A technical or all-day presentation will certainly need some visual aids and audience participation. The type and amount of technology you introduce into your presentation will depend on your own confidence in using it. If you attempt to use advanced technology that you are not fully conversant with, this could detract from your ability to present the information. However, many presentations are enhanced when information technology is used. If you feel unable to deal with the technology and presentation at the same time, why not ask a colleague to help control the equipment and press the buttons for you.

Whatever form of presentation you decide to give, it is vital that you rehearse it and check your timings. What looks on paper like a good hour's material may prove to last only 20 minutes in practice. Give yourself milestones that will warn you if you are in danger of over running or finishing early. You will then be able to tailor devices such as encouraging or discouraging questions or debate amongst the audience to extend or contract the time.

Prepare handouts containing all of the information that you have included in your presentation, as these will act as an aide-memoire to the audience, along with handouts covering any more detailed information which you were not able to include in the presentation. The distribution of the handouts will very much depend on their content and purpose. If they provide:

- Background information which the audience will need if they are to understand the presentation they should be sent to the audience in advance
- Information which the audience needs during the presentation they should be given to the audience on arrival
- Materials for workshops or discussions they should be given to the audience when that part of the presentation is reached
- Information to reflect or act upon after the presentation they should be given to the audience as they leave the presentation

Your organisation may use standard evaluation sheets to obtain feedback from the audience on the presentation. In this case make sure there will be sufficient available on the day for everyone in the audience. If there is no standard form it is well worth while compiling one of your own, as the best way to improve your presentation technique for the future is to obtain constructive feedback each time you present. The feedback should cover:

- An overall rating of the presentation
- Whether the attendee's aims were met
- What the attendee learnt from attending
- Which areas of the presentation were particularly useful and which not particularly worth while
- Any way in which the presentation could be improved in the future

More specific feedback will depend on the type and purpose of the presentation and the audience.

The final thing to prepare is a way of remembering everything you wanted to say. Inexperienced presenters sometimes try to write down everything they want to say. This is a mistake as you will find yourself either reading the script, which is extremely boring for the audience. When this happens you will find yourself unable to engage with them, or you will find yourself constantly searching for your place in your notes. The trick is to write as little as possible while covering everything you need to say.

If you are using a PowerPoint Presentation, your key words will be on the slides and you can use these to remind yourself of the points you want to get across. If you are presenting without any visual aids you will need the key words written down. Write them on A6 plain cards, two or three to a card. This way you can easily find your place and maintain eye contact with your audience all at once. Cards are preferable to paper as they don't betray your nerves as much as a piece of paper shaking in your hands!

 **What you need to know**

The situations in which you may be involved in giving presentations in your organisation

What is meant by the acronym PRIME?

How to structure a presentation to engage the audience

What is meant by the acronym SHELF?

The checks to be carried out at the venue prior to the time of presentation

Why is it important to make presentations interesting?

The types of equipment available for giving presentations and how to use them

Can you give two reasons why card is better than paper for writing key words?

When to distribute handouts

Why is it important to rehearse
presentations and practise timings?

## Giving the presentation

On the day of the presentation arrive at the venue at least
half an hour before you are due to present. Check that
everything that you need is available and that everything is
working. Check that the layout and ambient conditions of
the room are as you requested. Run through the
presentation in your mind and reassure yourself that you are
well prepared. Remember that first impressions are lasting
impressions so use positive body language:

- If possible, be in the room before your audience
  arrives. This will put you 'in charge' from the start
- If you can't be in the room first, make sure you have
  familiarised yourself with the room so that you can
  enter it confidently
- Stand up straight and keep your head up as this will
  make you appear confident
- Don't hold your arms across the front of your body as
  this will be seen as defensive
- Don't stand behind a table or desk as this will create a
  barrier. If you feel the need for support stand in front
  of a piece of furniture and lean against it without
  slouching

Start your presentation by introducing yourself (if you are
not already known to all of the audience) and if you are using
a technical assistant, introduce them as well. Tell the
audience what you are going to tell them, how long it is
going to take and the protocol for answering questions, i.e.
whether you welcome questions throughout the presentation
or will have a plenary session at the end. The response you
receive from the audience at this stage will set the tone for
the whole presentation so it is important that you get into
your stride straight away.

Don't let the thought of your body language distract you, but
at the same time don't let your body language distract your
audience. If you are normally expressive and use hand
gestures in everyday conversation, they will generally appear
natural if you use them during your presentation. Try to

avoid hand to face gestures such as rubbing your nose, as these are seen as indicators that you are unsure of your subject or even being less than honest.

Telling the audience what you are going to tell them will have reinforced in your mind the points you need to cover. You now need to move on to giving them the information that is the purpose of their attendance. There are a number of techniques which will help you to deliver your points:

- Short sentences are easier to absorb
- Simple sentences containing only one idea are better than complex sentences
- Be precise but avoid sounding too prepared
- Use metaphors to illustrate ideas
- Maintain eye contact with everyone in the room. Don't direct your delivery to one person or group

Don't attempt to put all of the information onto one slide. Use the slide to list the main points you are aiming to cover, and expand on the points verbally. Avoid using too much animation or colour as this will distract the audience from listening to what you have to say. Don't walk between the projector and the screen while the projector is operating. Speak clearly and loudly enough to be heard at the back of the room without being uncomfortably loud for those close to you or close to the speakers if you are using a microphone.

Throughout the presentation keep one eye on the clock. If you have placed milestones in your notes you will be able to judge whether you need to accelerate or decelerate your delivery. Avoid the temptation to do this by speaking more quickly or more slowly as either will risk losing the audience's attention. Have a contingency plan in mind so that you know which areas you can reduce or remove completely from the presentation if you need to save time and which areas you can expand on if you have too much time. Unless you are a natural, it is probably safest to avoid humour. This doesn't mean you can't add a light touch to the proceedings but jokes have a nasty habit of either not being funny, which will embarrass you, or being found offensive by at least one member of the audience, which will embarrass them.

At some point in the presentation, or in the session at the end, you will have to deal with questions. It is important that you are prepared in advance. Although you can't anticipate every question you may be asked, you can be ready for certain types of question:

- The question that tests your expertise. The questioner asks you to explain in greater depth
- The question that demonstrates the questioner's expertise. No real response is required, the purpose of the question is to 'show off'
- The question that aims to correct an assertion that you have made. The questioner is, in essence, saying that you are wrong
- The question that seeks justification. The questioner doesn't want to believe what you are saying

- The question that comes too early. The questioner is raising a point that you fully intend to answer later in the presentation

Obviously the way that you deal with each question will depend on the circumstances. Generally, however, if you don't know the answer or don't have the information available, say so and offer to come back to the questioner later. If answering the question at that stage would seriously disrupt your plan for the presentation offer to 'park' the question and come back to it at the end if it still hasn't been answered. If you have made an honest mistake and the questioner has spotted it, own up, apologise and move on.

Bring the presentation to a close by 'telling them what you have told them'. Review the main points that you want the audience to remember, but avoid the temptation to go through all the arguments again. Thank your audience for attending and listening and, if they are leaving at this point, wish them a safe journey. Remember to ask them to complete the evaluation form and, preferably, leave them at the end of the event.

On receiving the evaluation forms look at the feedback objectively. If a single member of the audience is critical of an aspect of your presentation which the rest of the audience found satisfactory or better, you probably don't need to take too much notice. If, on the other hand, most of the audience is critical the chances are you need to reconsider the way you handle that aspect in the future.

 **What you need to know**

How to control your natural gestures

> Why is it important to arrive at the venue early?

Techniques for delivering information

> How much information should be included on visual aids?

The use of milestones in timing a presentation

How do you bring a presentation to a successful close?

The importance of having a contingency plan for adjusting the timing

What feedback are you looking for from the audience?

How to handle difficult questions

How do you evaluate the feedback objectively?

Remember you will always be nervous before giving a presentation.  Nerves are a positive thing, without them your presentation could be flat and uninteresting.  The key is to control your nerves and make them work for you.  Go into the presentation with a positive attitude, if they have asked you to make the presentation it is because they believe you are the best person for the job.  After the presentation evaluate the feedback objectively, be honest with yourself without being overly self critical and your presentation skills will improve with each presentation.

## It's natural to have butterflies in your stomach – getting them to fly in the right direction is the art

# Are you ready for assessment?

To achieve this unit of a Level 3 Business & Administration qualification you will need to demonstrate that you are competent in the following:

- Agree the purpose, content, style and timing of the presentation
- Research and plan the presentation
- Prepare the presentation to achieve its purpose
- If appropriate, obtain feedback on the presentation
- Practise and time the presentation
- Produce presentation handouts
- Check equipment and resources
- Circulate presentation handouts and materials
- Address the audience and make the presentation, summarising your key points
- Provide the audience with the opportunity to ask questions
- Respond to questions in a way that meets the audience's needs
- Collect feedback on the presentation
- Evaluate the presentation and identify improvements

(Remember that you will need the skills listed at the beginning of this chapter. These are covered in chapter 1.)

You will need to produce evidence from a variety of sources. Carrying out the following activities will help you acquire competence at work.

**Activity 1**
Prepare a presentation on a subject that you feel confident about, e.g. advising your team of the department's performance over the last period or plans for the future. Select an appropriate method of delivery to a group of between ten and 25 people

**Activity 2**
Design an evaluation form that will enable you to collect relevant feedback on your presentation skills

## Activity 3
Give the presentation that you have prepared in Activity 1. This can be to the target audience or to an assessor or colleague. Ask the audience to complete an evaluation form.

## Activity 4
Evaluate the feedback and write a statement explaining how you would amend the presentation in light of the comments made.

## Activity 5
Attend a professionally delivered presentation. This could be a public lecture at the Town Hall, a sales presentation for overseas property or a lecture at your local college, for instance. Make notes on what the presenter did so you can start to improve your own presentation skills.

## Activity 6
Negotiate with your line manager a presentation that you can give to colleagues or members of staff. Prepare the presentation and make plans to present it in an agreed location. Once your line manager has approved your draft presentation and plans, invite your audience and deliver the presentation. Obtain feedback from your audience using your own or your organisation's feedback form. Evaluate the feedback.


Remember: While gathering evidence for this unit, evidence **may** be generated for units 110, 212, 213, 217, 301, 302, 310, 314, 315, 320 and 321.

# CHAPTER 22
# UNIT 313 – Organise and co-ordinate events

Events are, according to the dictionary, 'important incidents, occurrences, especially ones that are particularly significant, interesting, exciting, or unusual'. They differ from meetings which are 'gatherings of people for discussion, occasions when people gather together to discuss something'.

When arranging an event it is necessary to decide what sort of event it is going to be and its purpose. Events take many different forms, for instance:

- **Conferences** - Events which may last for more than one day in which delegates meet to discuss issues of common interest. Delegates may be internal to the organisation, external or both
- **Exhibitions** - Events arranged to display your organisation's products or services to existing customers, potential customers or the public
- **Product launches** - Events arranged to make potential customers aware of a new product or service your organisation is making available
- **Presentations** - Events arranged to award members of staff or customers with honours for their efforts on behalf of the organisation
- **Seminars** - Similar to conferences but usually one-day events dedicated to a particular topic

- **Briefing sessions** - Events arranged to provide information to delegates on a topic

Events require organising, to ensure that all delegates know the time, place and purpose of the event. Many events, particularly those involving large numbers of delegates will have a dedicated event organiser. Their role includes:

- **Agreeing the event brief** - Your 'client' will know the type of event they want, when and for roughly how many people
- **Negotiating a budget** - There may be a fixed sum available and specific criteria to meet
- **Locating suitable venues** - Size, location, resources, facilities for delegates with special requirements and price need to be considered
- **Arranging the hire of the venue** - Give the venue co-ordinator provisional numbers of delegates initially and confirm actual numbers when known
- **Organising the necessary resources** - What can the venue co-ordinator supply and what has to be sourced elsewhere?
- **Arranging the attendance of delegates** - Send out invitations and collate responses
- **Helping with the running of the event** - Being on hand throughout the event
- **Helping to vacate the venue at the end of the event** - Removing all equipment and resources that don't belong to the venue
- **Evaluating the event** - Collating feedback from delegates and presenters
- **Preparing accounts comparing actual cost with budget** - Keeping track of how the budget was spent
- **Providing delegates with any follow-up material** - Hand outs, sales brochures, order acknowledgements or appointments

Different types of events will require different resources. These will often include accommodation, equipment, catering and even car parking facilities. Delegates may have special requirements including wheelchair access or induction loops. Your responsibilities will also cover Health and Safety and security during the event, legislation surrounding any contracts that you enter into with the venue or suppliers of hired equipment and coping with problems that arise during the event.

As the organiser of the event you will probably delegate many of the tasks involved. Your overall responsibility is to co-ordinate the completion of all the tasks before, during and after the event to ensure everything runs smoothly.

 When organising and co-ordinating events you will use the following skills:

- Negotiating
- Planning
- Organising
- Communicating
- Checking
- Interpersonal skills
- Problem solving
- Monitoring
- Managing time
- Managing resources
- Evaluating

These skills are covered in chapter 1.

## Before the event

As the organiser of the event you will be working with a client who may be internal to the organisation or external. The client will be able to advise what kind of event they require, when it is to take place and approximately how many people will attend. This information will form the basis of an event brief. As organiser you will need to get this brief agreed in writing and as much detail as possible.

You will also need to agree an overall budget for the event. This may be arrived at in one of two ways:

- The client has a maximum sum of money available to pay for the whole event. Your role is to provide the best event within that budget
- The client has specific requirements for the location, standard of accommodation, levels of equipment, duration and season for the event. Your role is to provide the best price to meet the requirements

The decision on the venue will depend on factors such as:

- The purpose of the event
- The number of delegates
- The standard of venue required to suit the delegates
- The geographic location of the delegates
- Whether your organisation has in-house facilities for such an event
- Potential disruption to the business

Selecting a venue within your own premises or nearby has the advantage of saving travelling time and cost for people based on the premises. If the venue is external to the organisation obtain quotes from suitable suppliers. To identify potential venues find out if your organisation has a database of venues that they have used previously. If they have, look at the evaluations that have been carried out. Look on the Internet, in directories and trade magazines.

It is important to ensure that the standard of hospitality and catering is appropriate. Make sure it is clear exactly what is being provided. Many venues will offer a choice between:

- A daily delegate rate which includes meeting room, equipment, lunch and refreshments at a price per delegate
- A 24hour delegate rate which includes meeting room, equipment, lunch and refreshments, dinner, accommodation and breakfast at a price per delegate
- An executive rate which includes all of the above plus superior accommodation and meals at a price per delegate

Alternatively meeting rooms and equipment can be hired at a daily rate and meals, refreshments and accommodation paid for at a price per delegate. There will also be a choice of room layout to be decided.

When you have collected information from potential venues, make a short-list. Visit as many short-listed venues as possible and contact other people who have used the venues previously. This will give you an idea of the standards you can expect.

If you have been given an overall budget you will be able to select venues that provide the best value within the budget.

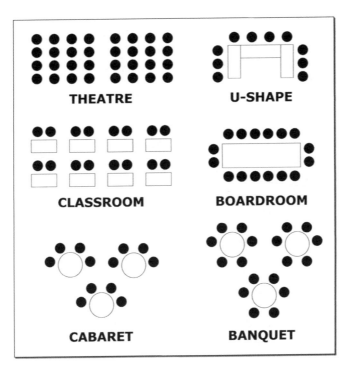

THEATRE

U-SHAPE

CLASSROOM

BOARDROOM

CABARET

BANQUET

If you have been given specific requirements to meet, you will be able to select venues that meet those requirements. This information must then be discussed with the client who will make the final decision.

Once a final decision on venue has been taken, you can start to organise the event. Major events can take up to a year to organise. The following is an outline timetable for the 12 months prior to the event:

**12 months before:**
- Select the venue
- Book the venue
- Invite speakers
- Compile a to-do list
- Advise venue estimated number of delegates and accommodation required

**6 months before:**
- Finalise programme of activities
- Send out invitations to delegates
- Agree menus and refreshments
- Confirm room layouts
- Book equipment

**4 months before:**
- Order any complimentary items for delegates
- Follow up unanswered invitations
- Acknowledge responses and provide details of venue

**2 months before:**
- Re-confirm in writing all arrangements made at four and six month stages
- Visit venue to finalise arrangements
- Send reminders to invited speakers
- Print delegate badges, place cards and menus

**1 month before:**
- Re-check all arrangements made
- Assemble all items needed for event

**2 weeks before:**
- Confirm final details

**1 week before:**
- Re-confirm numbers to venue
- Draft seating plans

**On the day:**
- Arrive early and run through arrangements with the venue co-ordinator
- Rehearse speakers
- Relax and enjoy the event
- Collect evaluation forms

0930  Registration
      T+C Muffins x 75
1000  Opening Presentations

1030  Break
      T+c Biscuits x 80
1045  Workshop 1
      Frances Hawkins - CEO

1215  Lunch
      Restaurant Buffet x 80
1315  Software Demo
      Fred Cluskey
1330  Workshop 2
      Hannah Randall
1445  Break
      T+c 80
1500  Workshop 3
      Abigail Inskip
1630  Close

Your client may want guest speakers to appear at the event. They will either have specific individuals in mind or they may know the subject they want covered and leave you to find a suitable speaker. It is important that you contact potential speakers at the earliest possible opportunity. Good speakers can be booked up months in advance.

As far in advance as possible, send out invitations to attend. This will give time for people to diarise the event and advise whether or not they are able to attend. They can also advise if they have any special requirements so that you have plenty of time to make the necessary arrangements.

Copies of any documents the delegates will need in advance of the event will have to be produced and sent to them. This will give them time to read and consider them. If they are to prepare to discuss the content of the papers they will need to receive them well before the event.

Where a screen or flipchart is being used it is essential that everyone can see it without too much movement. If you are arranging an event for a large number of people consider whether microphones are necessary to enable everybody to hear what is being said, but remember not to place loud-speakers where people will be deafened by the sound.

Other equipment you may need to have available includes:

- Laptop and multi-media projector
- Overhead projector and screen
- VHS and monitor
- Flip chart and easel
- Free standing lectern
- PA system

Don't forget the small stuff; pencils, paper and maybe a dish of sweets to keep the voice box lubricated.

Laptops and multi-media projectors have virtually replaced the use of overhead projectors in recent times. The opportunities to include sound, animation and video clips, as well as the ease with which the speaker can move from one slide to the next by remote control make overhead projectors obsolete.

When you receive responses from invited delegates to confirm their attendance make a note of any special requirements. These may include dietary, mobility, hearing or vision impairment or travel and accommodation. If you are advised that anybody has a particular need, liaise with the venue co-ordinator to ensure that it can be met. You will also need to ensure that all Health and Safety and security requirements have been taken into consideration.

Prepare a delegate pack to be given to the delegates on the day of the event. Include any papers they will need during the event, claim forms for expenses if relevant and an evaluation form so that they can give feedback on the event itself and the arrangements for accommodation, refreshments etc.

Write to the delegates who have confirmed attendance and send a map showing the location of the event, car parks and the nearest railway station together with directions to the venue.

The venue co-ordinator will require a purchase order from your organisation confirming your agreement to their booking terms and conditions. This will form the basis of a contract between your organisation and the venue which will be subject to contract law. This will cover charges for cancellations or changes to arrangements subsequent to confirmation. There will usually be a sliding scale of charges depending on the time of cancellation.

# What you need to know

The types of resources required by
different events

> What is the role of the event organiser?

The types of event your organisation
holds

> What is included in an event brief?

Sources of potential venues

> What different methods may be used to
> arrive at an overall budget for an
> event?

How to short-list possible venues

> What special requirements may
> delegates have?

The different layouts available for events

> What equipment may be needed for
> different types of events?

The timetable for organising major events

> What legislation applies to contracts?

## During the event

Arrive well before the start time of the event. This will allow you
to check that all the arrangements are in place. Check that:

- The catering is organised for the times agreed
- All of the equipment is in place and that it works
- You know where the toilets are, if the event is not on
  your premises
- There is no fire alarm test arranged for that day
- You know where the fire exits are
- You know where the assembly point is
- You know where lunch is going to be served
- There are facilities for smokers
- There is disabled access
- You know who is responsible for first aid
- You know how to raise the alarm if you need to

If guest speakers are taking part it is advisable to run through the arrangements for their slot with them before delegates arrive.  They may bring with them computer disks which need checking for compatibility with the venue's equipment, OHP slides or other visual aids which need positioning in the room.  If they are to use equipment with which they are not familiar they will need to be given the opportunity to make themselves comfortable with its use.

If your event involves overnight accommodation, the main problems on arrival are likely to be overload of reception facilities.  If check-in is not available until later in the day, storage for delegates' luggage will be necessary.  It may be worth considering arranging pre-registration where the venue is supplied with a list of delegates and completes registration forms for each prior to their arrival.  Then the delegate will only have to give their name at reception to be given their key.  If their accommodation will not be available at the time of arrival it is essential that a luggage storage room is provided for delegates arriving by public transport or taxi.

As the delegates arrive for the event:

- Be on hand to greet them
- Check whether they have any additional needs
- Show them where to sign in, if necessary
- Tell them where the cloakroom is
- Tell them where refreshments can be found
- Tell them the location of the event
- Tell them where they can store luggage
- Answer any questions they may have
- Distribute any identity badges
- If delegate packs are to be supplied, either hand them out as the delegates arrive or advise them where they are to be collected
- If there is a seating plan, show the delegates where to find it

Once the event is under way, you will need to be available to everybody. Arrange with reception to advise you as late arriving delegates turn up so that you can greet them and escort them into the event. Through the day you need to keep one step ahead of everything that is happening. Before the morning coffee break, check refreshments are available. Before lunch, check arrangements are in hand. Before each speaker, check everything is ready and working that that speaker requires.

You will also be responsible for dealing with any problems that arise. Potential problems to be prepared for include:

- Speakers failing to arrive. Hopefully you will have had some warning. If booked speakers are suffering travel difficulties they will be able to phone ahead and let you know. If they are able to give you some estimate of the delay you may be able to re-schedule other activities
- Refreshments not being on time or to an acceptable standard. You will need to liaise with the venue co-ordinator or the caterer to deal with the problem. It may be that an individual delegate has not advised you in advance of a special dietary requirement. In this case you can only do the best you can to provide them with an acceptable alternative
- Equipment failure. Even though you have checked the equipment before the event, it is quite likely that something will fail to work when it is needed. If the equipment has been supplied by the venue, call the venue co-ordinator to deal with the problem. If you have supplied the equipment, you may have to fall back on an alternative method of presenting
- Heating, lighting or air conditioning problems. You will never satisfy all of the delegates where these are concerned. Some will always be too hot, some will always be too cold. All you can do is make sure the equipment is functioning efficiently and try to keep the majority happy

You will need to follow up any delegates that do not arrive at all. If accommodation has been booked in their name, the venue will need to know that they will not be using it. If they are able to re-use the accommodation, there will be a reduction in the cancellation charge.

# What you need to know

Issues to be checked on your arrival at
the venue

> Why is it important that you arrive well
> before the start of the event?

The problems that may arise at reception
from delegates arriving en masse

> What problems may you have to deal
> with during the event?

The advantages of arranging pre-
registration

> Why should you run through
> presentations with speakers before the
> event?

Your responsibilities when delegates
arrive

> What issues may arise around non-
> arrival of delegates?

Your responsibilities during the event

> When should you check refreshments?

## After the event

At the successful conclusion of the event, there are still a
number of responsibilities for the event organiser.  If the
event has been work-related consider giving each delegate a
Certificate of Attendance.  This will remind them of the event
and also be useful if they are maintaining a record of
Continuous Professional Development.  Collect together any
evaluation forms that delegates have left and keep them
carefully to analyse later.

If the delegates have stayed overnight, you will need to be on hand at reception when they check out. Each delegate will be responsible for ensuring their keys are returned and any extras paid for. The joining instructions will have made clear what costs are included in the accommodation and which are the responsibility of the delegate. If delegates leave the venue without settling their bill, the venue will hold the organisation responsible and you will need to chase them up. It is much easier to deal with this situation before the delegate leaves.

You will also be responsible for dealing with the equipment. If it has been supplied by the venue, you will only need to hand it back in the same condition in which you received it. If has been hired from elsewhere, you will need to supervise its return or collection. If you have brought it with you, you will need to pack it up safely to take it back with you.

Confirm with the venue co-ordinator that everything is OK before you leave.

When you get back to the office, analyse the evaluation forms that you have collected and any others that have arrived in the post. It is human nature to concentrate on the criticism contained in evaluation forms and overlook the praise. It is important to look at the feedback objectively. Where individuals were less satisfied with aspects of the event than other delegates you will need to consider whether this is simply a matter of being unable to please all of the people all of the time.

Where common issues are raised you will need to formulate an action plan to deal with them. If they relate to your own performance, take on board the matters raised and resolve to do better next time. If they relate to the performance of invited speakers, you should pass on the feedback to the speaker as they will be interested. If they relate to aspects of the venue which can be improved, pass on the feedback to the venue co-ordinator. If they relate to issues which can't be changed, such as the location of the venue, make a note to take them into account when considering the venue for future events.

If there are any documents which need to be circulated to delegates following the event, arrange for them to be copied and distributed. Send copies to delegates who were unable to attend and indicated that they would like details forwarded.

The final responsibility is to settle the accounts. Authorise payment of invoices for the venue, hire of equipment, catering, expenses for the delegates, speakers' fees and expenses, etc. Add to these the cost of preparation of papers, postage of invitations and post event documentation, your time spent on the whole event, not forgetting travel costs in selecting the venue. This will give you the total cost of the event, which you will need to reconcile with the original budget.

Analyse the actual costs against your original estimates and identify where any over-spend has arisen. Where there is an under-spend, this is not necessarily a good thing. Where you have had a successful event, and achieved genuine savings against the budget by successful negotiation, congratulations. Where feedback from the delegates has been less than favourable, look at where you have made savings against the budget and consider whether the event deserved the full budget being used.

# What you need to know

The purpose of collecting evaluation forms
from delegates

> Why should you give a Certificate of
> Attendance to delegates?

How to ensure that the venue is
successfully vacated

> Why is it important to be available at
> reception during delegates' check-out?

Methods of analysing evaluation forms

> How would you pass on negative
> feedback to speakers or the venue?

How to deal with negative feedback

> Why should you always confirm that all
> is well with the venue co-ordinator
> before leaving?

The costs to be included in the total for
comparison with the original budget

> Why is a saving against the original
> budget not necessarily a good thing?

Throughout the event there will be endless calls on your time
and initiative.  Use all your reserves of cheerfulness and
patience and the event will be a major success, enjoyed by
everybody, even you.

## A well organised event appears runs smoothly – an event without planning appears disorganised

# Are you ready for assessment?

To achieve this unit of a Level 3 Business & Administration qualification you will need to demonstrate that you are competent in the following:

- Agree the event brief and budget
- Identify and cost suitable venues
- Prepare and send out invitations to delegates
- Identify and co-ordinate resources and the production of event materials
- Co-ordinate delegate responses
- Confirm venue and event requirements
- Agree contracts if required
- Provide delegates with joining instructions and event materials
- Prepare the venue
- Co-ordinate activities and resources during the event
- Help delegates to feel welcome
- Respond to delegates' needs throughout the event
- Resolve problems
- Clear and vacate the venue
- Co-ordinate the event evaluation and identify action points for the future
- If necessary, prepare and circulate papers
- Reconcile account to budget

(Remember that you will need the skills listed at the beginning of this chapter.  These are covered in chapter 1.)

You will need to produce evidence from a variety of sources. Carrying out the following activities will help you acquire competence at work.

**Activity 1**
Your organisation has decided to hold a sales promotional event, to which the public are to be invited.  Source suitable venues and obtain estimates of cost.  Consider issues of health, safety and security, and whether refreshments are to be offered or made available.  Write a report with recommendations to your line manager.

## Activity 2

You have been asked to find suitable speakers on the following subjects for a conference to be held in 12 months' time:

- Company law
- Executive health
- Recruitment and selection
- Strategic planning
- Time management
- Motivation

Source at least two speakers for each subject and investigate the costs involved.

## Activity 3

You have been asked to organise an event in six months' time. Write an outline timetable for the organisation. Identify who should be invited to attend, the most suitable location, how long the event should last and suitable speakers. Locate three suitable external venues and request quotes for holding the event at each. Compare the costs and facilities and make a recommendation for which venue to use and why.

## Activity 4

After you have arranged the sales event in Activity 3, the Human Resources Director asks you to arrange a presentation to, and leaving party for, a senior member of the management team. You have three months to prepare for this activity. A leaving present needs to be purchased and the party can follow immediately after the event at the same location. As a result many of the delegates will need overnight accommodation. Amend the outline timetable to take this change of plan into account.

## Activity 5

You have been asked to arrange a three-day event for 120 people with accommodation, meals and refreshments included. The purpose is to inform the delegates of a new information system that your organisation is about to commission. The delegates are staff located at premises throughout the UK, including six in Northern Ireland. Research suitable venues for the event, obtain quotes and suggested room layouts. Two of the attendees have hearing difficulties, one is in a wheelchair and one is allergic to dairy products. Take their needs into account.

## Activity 6

Negotiate with your line manager to run an event for your organisation. Agree your terms of reference with your line manager including aims, objectives, budget and target audience. Agree milestones with your line manager, so each stage of the event is approved by them before you move on to the next phase. Plan the event. Implement the plan. Evaluate the event. Report on the event to your line manager.

Remember: While gathering evidence for this unit, evidence **may** be generated for units 110, 212, 213, 216, 301, 302, 314, 315, 320 and 321.

# CHAPTER 23
## UNIT 314 – Word processing software

Improvements in word processing software over the last few years have revolutionised the production of documents. Modern packages can be used to create, edit and produce documents including newsletters, journals, complex reports, form letters, form envelopes and form address labels to a much higher standard than was previously possible.

While technology has expanded upon the skill of the typist, it now involves much more than typing letters. Although the skill of 'touch-typing' is still very useful, a wider knowledge of the various functions of the keyboard is now necessary. The arrow keys and the 'Home' and 'End' keys allow you to move around the screen easily. There are a range of commands available from the keyboard:

- Text commands
- Format commands
- Editing commands
- Print commands

Using available software, a wide range of simple but effective modifications can be made. Text can be amended, moved, enhanced, deleted and then saved. Numerous different typefaces are available such as *Monotype Corsiva* or Comic Sans MS each of which can be changed to include colour, shadowing, emboldening, italics and underlining for emphasis and impact.

Other features available include:

- Word count, which as well as counting the number of words in a document will count pages, characters, paragraphs and lines
- Pagination, which numbers the pages
- Headers and Footers, which repeats text at the top (header) or bottom (footer) of each page
- Footnotes, which numbers and positions footnotes where they are required
- Switch screens, which lets you work on two documents at once
- Thesaurus, which gives you a list of synonyms (words which have the same or similar meaning)

Become familiar with those you use regularly. Set up directories and save documents according to their type. Learning to use the full power of word processing software will enable you to produce documents more quickly, more accurately and to a higher standard of presentation.

 When using word processing software you will use the following skills:

- Presentation
- Planning
- Organising
- Communicating
- Using technology
- Reading
- Checking

These skills are covered in chapter 1.

There are a number of word processing packages available. The most commonly used is Microsoft Word so the examples used in this chapter relate to Microsoft Word. Whether you use this system, or another, the principles are the same.

## Basic word processing

When you start a new document you will need to create a new file. In word processing terms a file may be a single document, or a collection of connected documents. The common feature is that a file has a single file name. Click on the file menu, then on 'new'. Input the text and click on 'save'. At this point the programme will name the file for you, probably 'document 1' or something similar.

To name the file click on 'file' then 'save as' and give the file a name which enables you to find it again at a later date. Your organisation may have a system for naming files such as the originator's initials followed by the date, for example.

- When you want to find a file again click on 'open' and a list of file names will appear. Click on the file name and the file will open
- You may want to print a hard copy of the file. To do this click 'file' and 'print' or the 'print' icon. You will be given a number of options including changing the number of copies required
- If you want to send the file to another computer, you will need to know the recipient is using the same software as you. If they are not, their computer will not be able to read the file. You may have to convert the file to a format that can be read by them. Alternatively many word processors can automatically convert documents received in other formats

Probably the greatest advantage that word processing has over typing is the opportunity for editing text. Functions available include:

- **Delete** - This key enables you to remove single characters
- **Cut** (Ctrl+x) - This is on the edit menu and enables you to remove blocks of text you have highlighted
- **Copy** (Ctrl+c) - This is on the edit menu and enables you to highlight a block of text and repeat it somewhere else
- **Paste** (Ctrl+v) - This is on the edit menu and enables you to insert the block of text which you cut or copied to a new location
- **Find and replace** (Ctrl+f) - This is on the edit menu and enables you to locate one or all examples of a word or phrase and replace them with an alternative
- **Inserting special characters and symbols** - This is on the insert menu and enables you to use a wide range of non-Arabic letters and other signs

- **Mail merge** - This is on the tools menu and enables you to combine addresses from a database with the text in letters, mailing labels and envelope templates
- **Track changes** (Ctrl+Shift+e) - This is on the tools menu and enables you to indicate on a document where changes have been made for reviewing purposes

When you have completed a document, it is essential to check your work. Most word processing packages contain facilities for checking text such as spell checking and grammar checking. Use these first to correct the more glaring errors, but do not rely on them. They may not be able to distinguish between words which are spelt correctly but misused in context, such as 'there' and 'their'. Also, they tend to use American spelling and grammar, so will accept 'color' and reject 'colour', for instance. When the automatic checking is complete, **read** the document carefully to look for any missed errors, and also for correct use of paragraphs, breaks, headings and sub-headings, style and formatting.

 **What you need to know**

How to open an existing document

What word processing applications does your organisation use?

To be able to identify Americanised spelling

Do you know the functions of the edit menu?

How to save and name a document

Could you set up a mail merge for a marketing mail shot?

Which documents require the use of the mail merge facility

Do you know how the word processor differentiates in its indication of a spelling or grammatical error?

The uses of the word count function

What is the rationale behind your organisation's standard format for naming documents?

# More advanced word processing

There are a number of more advanced functions available in the word processing package. These are used to help you to produce better quality documents more quickly and efficiently.

## Converting files

You may want to open files that were created in a different format and save them in Word format. For instance if the original document is in Microsoft Works:

- On the File menu, click 'Open'
- In the 'Files of type' list, select 'Works 6.0 & 7.0'
- In the 'File name' box, enter the name of the file that you want to convert, then click 'Open'
- On the File menu, click 'Save As'
- In the Save As dialog box, make any changes that you want in the 'File name' box, click the file format that you want in the 'Save as type' list, and then click 'Save'

The Portable Document Format (PDF) file format is commonly used. This format preserves the documents' layout and prevents them being edited in Word. Word does not provide a direct way to save documents in PDF, additional software is required to convert Word documents to PDF or vice-versa.

## Linking and embedding objects

You may want to insert objects into a Word document to include information from files created in other programs. For example, a monthly sales report might contain information from a Microsoft Excel worksheet. If you link the report to the worksheet, the data in the report can be updated whenever the worksheet is updated; if you embed the worksheet in the report, the report contains a static copy of the data.

When an object is linked, information is updated when the source file is modified. Linking is useful when you want to include information that is maintained independently or when the information needs to be kept up-to-date in the Word document.

When an object is embedded, information in the destination file doesn't change if the source file is modified.

To create a linked or embedded object from an existing Microsoft Excel file into a Word document:

- Open both the Word document and the Excel worksheet
- Switch to Excel and select the object you want
- Click 'Copy'
- Switch to Word and click where you want the information
- In the Edit menu, click 'Paste Special'
- Click 'Paste link' to link or 'Paste' to embed
- In the 'As' box, click the entry with the word 'object' in its name

When the information in the source document changes, if you wish to update the information in the linked document, in the Edit menu click 'Update link'.

**Bookmarking text**

You may want to identify a location or selection of text that you want to revise at a later point. Instead of scrolling through the document to locate the passage, you can go to it by using the 'Bookmark' dialog box. To add a bookmark:

- Click where you want to insert a bookmark
- On the Insert menu, click 'Bookmark'
- Under 'Bookmark name', type or select a name. Bookmark names must begin with a letter, can contain numbers but must not include spaces. You can separate words using the underscore character
- Click 'Add'

To go to the selected text:

- On the Insert menu, click 'Bookmark'
- Select the bookmark name
- Click 'Go to'

## Captioning

You may want to add a numbered label such as 'Figure 1' to a table, figure or equation. Word can automatically add captions when you insert items into the document or you can add the captions manually. You can vary the caption label and number format for different types of items for instance, 'Table II' and 'Equation 1-A' or you can change the label for one or more captions, for instance, 'Table 2' to 'Figure 2'. To create a new caption label:

- On the Insert menu, point to 'Reference'
- Click 'Caption'
- Click 'New Label'
- In the 'Label' box, type the label you want
- Click 'OK'
- Click 'OK'

## Paragraph numbering

You may want to add numbers to items in the body text of a paragraph. Click in front of the first item you want to number in the paragraph:

- On the Insert menu, click 'Field'
- In the 'Categories' box, click 'Numbering'
- In the 'Field names' box, click 'ListNum'
- In the 'List name' box, select the format you want
- Click 'OK'

Click in front of the next item you want to number and press Ctrl+Y.

## Indexing

You may want to index the document. An index lists the terms and topics discussed in the document and the pages they appear on. To create an index you must first mark the index entries in the document. Word adds an Index Entry field to the document. After you have marked all the entries you choose an index design. Word then collects the index entries, sorts them alphabetically, references their page numbers, finds and removes duplicate entries from the same page and displays the index.

To use existing text as an index entry, select the text:

- Press ALT+SHIFT+X
- Click 'Mark All'
- Click 'Close'
- Click where you want to insert the finished index
- If the Index Entry field is visible click 'Show/Hide' on the Standard toolbar
- On the Insert menu, point to 'Reference', click 'Index and Tables'
- Click the Index tab
- Click a design in the 'Formats' box
- Select any other index options you want
- Click 'OK'

## Tables of contents

You may want to create a table of contents.  Select the first section of text you want to include:

- Press ALT+SHIFT+O
- In the 'Level' box, select the level and click 'Mark'
- Click 'Close'
- Select the next section of text and repeat until all required text is added
- Click where you want to insert the Table of contents
- On the Insert menu, point to 'Reference'
- Click 'Index and Tables'
- Click the 'Table of Contents' tab
- Click the 'Options' button
- In the 'Table of Contents Options' box, select the 'Table entry fields' check box
- Clear the 'Styles' and 'Outline levels' check boxes
- Click 'OK'

## Importing information

You may want to introduce information from outside of the document.  This may be from other files in the same software, from other software, through a scanner or digital camera, or from the Internet.  This can be done from the Insert menu using:

- **File** - Any file already held on your hard drive or on a disk can be imported.  If your computer is Internet enabled you can import pages from the World Wide Web

- **Picture** - Any picture already held on your hard drive or on a disk can be imported. You can also import pictures from other software on your computer, or through a connected scanner or digital camera, or from the Internet. There is a facility to create charts, diagrams or drawings
- **Autotext** - This inserts a selection of common phrases such as 'Yours sincerely' or 'Dear Sir or Madam'
- **Object** - This enables you to insert items from other software installed on your computer
- **Hyperlink** - This enables you to take shortcuts to other parts of the document, other files, even to a website such as www.ask.com or www.msn.com. By right clicking on the hyperlink and selecting 'open hyperlink' or by pressing the Ctrl key and left clicking you will be taken straight to the website or shortcut you have inserted

The possibilities are endless when you start to import material into documents. The whole world of published material is available to you, subject to copyright laws. Care will need to be taken when importing non-text objects. In a letter 'less is more' where pictures and diagrams are concerned. In a report pictures and diagrams can certainly add to the impact, but you must take care that they are used only when they are relevant and can add to the content. Their positioning and size must also be carefully considered. Beware the use of images for their own sake.

**Watermarks**

You may want to use a picture as a watermark that appears behind the text in a document. To create a watermark:

- On the Format menu, point to 'Background'
- Click 'Printed Watermark'
- Click 'Picture Watermark'
- Click 'Select Picture'
- Select the picture you want
- Click 'Insert'
- Select any additional options you want
- Click 'Apply'
- Click 'Close'

If the document contains a large amount of text you may want to choose a simple picture so that the reader's eyes aren't distracted from the text.

# What you need to know

How to import images from a scanner or digital camera

> Where would you find a suitable image for a sales brochure?

What types of files can be imported into a word processed document

> What is the process to insert a spreadsheet into a report?

How to create a Table of Contents

> How would you add an additional column to an existing table?

Techniques for inserting tables and using borders and shading

> Can a PDF document be converted to Word?

How to convert a Microsoft Works document into Word

> What is the process for linking objects?

The differences between linking and embedding objects

> How would you create a caption label?

How to bookmark sections of text

> How are duplicate entries from the same page removed from an index?

The process to follow when creating an index

> In what circumstances would you create a Table of Contents?

How to add numbers to text within paragraphs

> When would you use a Watermark?

## Formatting

Having gathered all of the information into the document, you will need to consider laying out the document in the appropriate format. If you are producing a letter or fax, you can use a pre-formed layout from the tools menu or create a template so that you can use a consistent layout in the future. If there is text that would be more easily read in the form of a table, this can be created using the table menu.

From this menu you can:

- Create, insert or delete columns, rows or cells
- Amend the height or width of cells
- Sort alphabetically
- Convert text to tables
- Add borders and shading

At any stage during the production of a document, formatting text may be necessary. There are various options available in the format menu. It is possible to format:

- **Characters** - By selecting 'font' you can change the **STYLE**, colour and size of letters, **embolden** them, *italicise* them, underline them, change the s p a c i n g , or add various text effects
- **Paragraphs** - You can align text using the centre or justify options, or by selecting 'bullets and numbering' add bullet points or numbers. You can make other amendments by selecting 'borders and shading', or by altering the line spacing, tabs and indents

- **Pages** - You can change the size, orientation and margins of pages, or add page numbers, headers and footers or the date and time. You can insert page breaks to indicate where a new page should begin, or columns to divide the page vertically
- **Sections** - As you will see from the examples above it is not necessary for the whole of a document to be in the same format. By highlighting individual sections of a document you can apply different formats.

## Mail Merging

You may want to create a set of documents that are essentially the same but where each document contains unique elements, such as a letter that contains standard text but different addresses and greeting lines. To do this you can use Mail Merge. Mail Merge can create:

- A set of labels or envelopes with the same return address on each but unique destination addresses
- A set of form letters, e-mail messages and faxes with the same basic content but each with specific names or addresses
- A set of numbered coupons identical except each contains a unique number

All you have to do is create one document that contains the common information and add placeholders for the information that is unique to each. Open a blank document in Word and leave it open then:

- In the 'Tools' menu, click 'Mail Merge'
- Click Create and then select 'Form Letters' to create a mail merged letter
- Click 'Active window'
- Next, click 'Get Data' and then 'Open data source' to select an existing contacts list. Make sure you select the correct option in the 'Files of type' drop-down list

If you have not already done so, in the main document complete the letter by typing the text you want to appear in every letter and then add merge fields by:

- In the main document, click where you want to insert the field and click on the 'Insert merge field' button which will have appeared in the top left corner
- Insert any of the following:
  - address block with name address and any other information
  - greeting line
  - other fields of information
  - electronic postage
  - postal bar code

Repeat for all the fields you want to insert. Then click 'Save As' on the File menu. Name the document and click 'Save'.

## Passwords

Having created a complex document which may have taken you some time you will want to protect it from being amended by anybody else. The best way to protect your work is to control access to files on your computer by the use of a password.

Passwords should be easy to remember but difficult to guess. It is probably obvious that you should avoid using consecutive numbers or letters such as '12345678' or 'abcdefgh' or letters adjacent on the keyboard such as 'qwerty'; it is also dangerous to choose your name, relatives' names or dates of birth as these can be guessed. What is not so obvious, perhaps, is that hackers can find any password that is a word in a dictionary, even in a foreign language or spelled backwards. It also doesn't work to change letters for symbols such as 'Adm1n1$tr@t10n' as this is also a known format.

You could come up with a completely random combination of numbers and letters, but how would you remember it? You would probably write it down somewhere. A strong password contains at least eight characters including letters numbers and symbols and is easy to remember but difficult to guess. The easiest way to create a strong password is to come up with a phrase that you can remember such as 'My grandson was born on Friday 2$^{nd}$ May'. You could make a strong password by using the first letter of each word 'MgwboF2M'.

However strong the password you come up with it is of no use if you don't keep it secret. Don't write it down, tell anyone else or keep it in an unprotected file on the computer.

## What you need to know

How to format characters

> Could you produce a newsletter with two columns?

What formats are suitable for different documents

> Would you be able to insert a footer with automatic page numbering?

When to use colour and highlighting

> If asked to produce a sales brochure, what text effects would you use?

Why standard formats are used within organisations

> Why should you not use words that can be found in a dictionary as passwords?

How to produce high quality Mail Merged letters

> What menu would you find 'borders and shading' in?

## Using the keyboard effectively

There are a variety of Short-cut key functions available on the keyboard to reduce the number of keystrokes necessary. These include:

- **Ctrl+B** - switches the bold function on and off
- **Ctrl+C** - copies selected text or images into the clipboard
- **Ctrl+I** - switches the Italics on and off
- **Ctrl+O** - takes you to the file directory
- **Ctrl+P** - takes you to the print menu
- **Ctrl+S** - saves the document that you are working on

- **Ctrl+V** - pastes into the document the last text that was cut or copied
- **Ctrl+X** - cuts selected text

Learn to use as many of these as possible. Different packages and different keyboards will have different functions available. You can also set up short-cuts thereby improving efficiency.

For instance, to set up your word processing programme as an icon on the desktop, so that you can access the programme with a double-click rather than going through a series of menus:

- Left click on 'start'
- Left click on 'Programs'
- Find the word processing programme, left click and drag it onto the desk top

Another short-cut is to customise your toolbars. For instance, if you use cut and paste often it would be easier to have these functions on the toolbar so that you do not have to go into the edit menu every time you want to use them.

- Go to a blank area of your toolbar and right click
- Make sure your standard toolbar is switched on
- Left click on the toolbar arrow at the right of your standard toolbar
- Click on 'add or remove buttons'
- Highlight the standard toolbar on the drop down menu
- Left click 'cut' and 'paste'
- Left click 'reset toolbar'

An advanced shortcut is to set up 'macros'. If you repeat a task regularly, you can automate the task so that a single command will carry out the whole task. For instance, if you always produce one copy of letters on headed paper and a second on plain paper, you can set up a macro to produce the two copies on one command.

- Go to 'tools' menu
- Highlight macro and click on 'record new macro'
- Click on keyboard
- Press the 'ctrl' key and 'Q' simultaneously
- Click on 'assign'

- Click 'close' this opens a small toolbar on the screen
- From that point on you are recording everything you do until you tell it to stop. Carry out the complete function that you wish to assign to the macro (set up print functions etc)
- Press the stop button in the new toolbar
- From then on use your shortcut whenever you want to use the function it is set up to do

## What you need to know

How to create strong passwords

> Can you set up a macro to print out a document on a variety of paper types?

How to use short-cuts and macros

> When would it be necessary to add a short-cut to your desk top?

Which icons you need to have on your toolbars

> If asked, would you be able to show someone how to change the toolbars?

The functions available on the keyboard to reduce key strokes

> Why is it important to improve efficiency?

Early word processors were just glorified electric typewriters with a screen. Word processing software has advanced over recent decades and the technology is still developing rapidly. New and exciting word processing packages and features are coming on to the market all the time but the results achieved are only as good as the person operating them. Keeping up-to-date with current trends in software is a continuous challenge, but an exciting one.

## Good use of word processing features will improve the quality and impact of your documents

# Are you ready for assessment?

To achieve this unit of a Level 3 Business & Administration qualification you will need to demonstrate that you are competent in the following:

- Use file handling techniques appropriate to the software
- Combine information of different types
- Enter and edit text
- Format and layout documents
- Produce and check the accuracy of the document
- Make use of software tools and techniques to improve word processing efficiency

(Remember that you will need the skills listed at the beginning of this chapter and that these are covered in chapter 1.)

You will need to produce evidence from a variety of sources. Carrying out the following activities will help you acquire competence at work.

**Activity 1**
Produce a mail merge document that contains common information and placeholders for names, addresses and the greeting line.

**Activity 2**
Prepare a report on word processing documents in your organisation. Use the following functions:
- Linking and embedding objects
- Bookmarking
- Captioning
- Paragraph numbering
- Watermarking
- Indexing
- Table of contents

**Activity 3**
Create either a macro or a short-cut to carry out each of the functions in Activity 2.

**Activity 4**

Produce a newsletter about your area of work importing information from at least two different software packages in use on your computer. Use the following enhancements:

- Paragraph numbering
- Columns
- Importing pictures and spreadsheets

**Activity 5**

Produce an information brochure for a new product or service using the following enhancements:

- Linking
- Embedding
- Captioning
- Table of Contents
- Importing pictures and objects
- Watermarking
- Using various fonts and text effects

Remember:  While gathering evidence for this unit, evidence **may** be generated for units 110, 212, 301, 302, 318, 320 and 321.

# CHAPTER 24
# UNIT 315 – Spreadsheet software

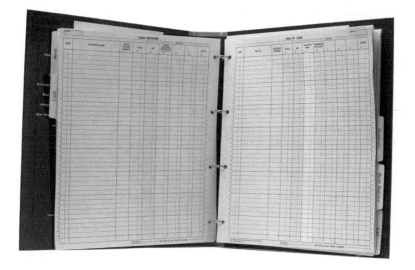

Spreadsheets existed long before spreadsheet software. Originally they were simply sheets of paper divided into columns and rows by hand. Figures were entered into the columns and rows and calculations carried out using mental arithmetic or abacuses. The main drawbacks to this were if you made an error in entering or calculating data, it was difficult to make corrections and when data changed, there was no alternative but to create a completely new spreadsheet.

This gave no opportunity to use the spreadsheet as a 'model' to predict the result of variations. Spreadsheet software is designed to record data and perform calculations. It can be used for such tasks as:

- **Budgeting** - For example budgeting for wages. Before the year begins you input the number of staff you expect to employ, the number of hours you expect them to work and the hourly rates. The spreadsheet calculates the total planned cost of wages. As the year progresses you input the actual number of staff employed, the actual number of hours they work and the hourly rates. The spreadsheet calculates the total actual cost of wages and compares this to the plan. You are then able to adjust the number of staff, the number of hours and the hourly rates accordingly

- **Calculating costs** - For example the cost of producing items for sale. Fixed costs are entered at the beginning of the year and variable costs are entered as they occur. The spreadsheet calculates the total cost of production
- **Comparing costs** - For example if a number of employees are entitled to claim expenses, these can be entered on a spreadsheet as they are claimed, the spreadsheet will total the expenses for each employee enabling you to compare them
- **Management accounts** - Income and expenses are entered and the spreadsheet calculates profit or loss. If previous months or years are also input the spreadsheet will calculate increase or decrease against the previous period. If planned income and expenses are entered the spreadsheet will calculate increase or decrease against plan

The calculations can be shown as plain data, in a table or in the form of graphs or charts. There are a number of different styles available including:

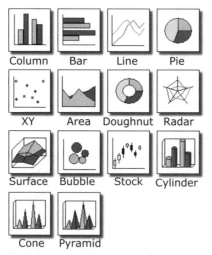

Spreadsheets are usually protected by passwords which need to be changed each time somebody who knows the password leaves the organisation. Passwords also protect the spreadsheet from malicious corruption from people who may want to alter the information held.

When using spreadsheet software you will use the following skills:

- Analysing
- Interpreting
- Planning
- Organising
- Communicating
- Using technology
- Using number
- Checking

These skills are covered in chapter 1.

There are a number of spreadsheet packages available. The most commonly used is Microsoft Excel so the examples used in this chapter relate to Microsoft Excel. Whether you use this system, or another, the principles are the same.

It is possible to convert data held in one spreadsheet package to allow it to be manipulated in another. If you have an existing Lotus 123 spreadsheet for instance, and you want to work on it in Microsoft Excel you can:

- Open the file in Lotus 123
- Click 'File'
- Select 'Save As'
- Select the relevant Microsoft Excel file type from the 'Save as type' drop down menu
- Click 'Save'

The file can then be opened in Microsoft Excel and worked on as normal.

## Entering data

When using spreadsheet software you will be working in 'workbooks' which consist of a number of 'worksheets'. A worksheet consists of a grid of 'cells' made up of columns and rows. Columns are vertical and rows are horizontal. Cells are named by referring to the column and row that each cell is found in (for instance the cell that is in the third column from the left and the eighth row from the top is cell C8). You may be used to the term 'cursor' to mean the position pointer that is used when using word processing software, in spreadsheet software this position pointer is called a cell pointer and is a white cross shape.

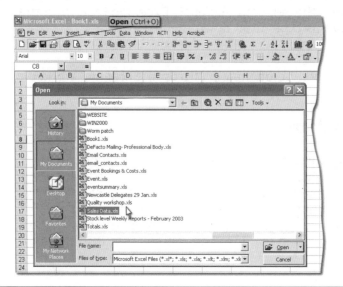

The cell in which the cell pointer is positioned is called the active cell. There is always at least one active cell at all times. The active cell can be identified by its black border. It is possible for more than one cell to be active. A range of connected cells can be active at the same time, for instance the range A12:C14 includes the cells A12, A13, A14, B12, B13, B14, C12, C13 and C14.

To open an existing workbook:

- Click the 'Open' button on the 'Standard' toolbar
- Select the 'My Documents' icon in the 'Open' dialog box or find the file you want in the 'Look In' drop down list
- Double click the file you want to open in the 'Open' dialog box

You can enter either text or numbers into a worksheet. In any cell there can be text, numbers or a combination of both.

To enter data:

- Put the cell pointer in the cell that you wish to add data to
- Type the data required in that cell
- Press 'Enter' (on the right of the keyboard) if you wish to enter data in columns or 'Tab' (on the left) if you wish to enter data in rows
- The cell pointer automatically moves to the next cell down or the next cell to the right
- Repeat until you have entered all the required data

If you type text into a cell, when you enter text that starts with the same letter into another cell, the software will assume that you are going to type the same word. The word will automatically be entered; if you don't want to use it keep typing and the new word will be typed in.

You may want to enter a series of data, for instance Monday, Tuesday, Wednesday etc. If you type Monday into cell A1, Tuesday into cell B1, Wednesday into cell C1 you can then click and drag the cell pointer over cells A1:C1 move the cell pointer to the lower right corner of the range until it changes to a thin black cross and continue to drag over D1:G1, release the mouse and Thursday, Friday, Saturday will automatically be entered. This also works for numbers and months of the year.

You will need to save your work regularly so that you don't lose your data in the event of a power failure or computer crash. If you have saved your work regularly when you re-start your computer after a disaster such as this you will have lost only the data you have input since your last save. There is nothing more annoying than to input data for four hours only to lose it all because you have neglected to save. To do this, click on the 'Save' icon on the 'Standard' toolbar.

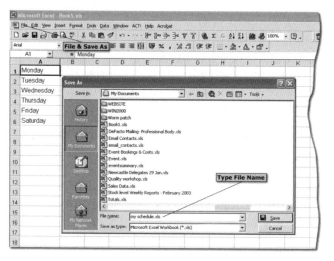

When you have entered all the data that you require:

- Open the 'File' menu and select 'Save As'
- Click the 'My Documents' icon or find the folder you want to save the file in from the 'Save In' drop down list
- Type the file name in the 'File Name' field
- Click 'Save'

# What you need to know

Your organisation's file naming systems

Do you know the difference between a workbook and a worksheet?

How to open an existing workbook

What is a horizontal series of cells called?

Methods of inserting a series of data

Where would you find cell Y93?

How to select a range of cells

Why is it important to save worksheets regularly?

How to convert a spreadsheet to a different package

Why would you need to convert a spreadsheet?

## Formulas and functions

A great advantage of using electronic spreadsheets is that you can add, delete or amend entries and the spreadsheet will automatically re-calculate the results. This works using formulas and functions. A formula calculates a value from the values in other cells. A function is an abbreviated formula that performs a specific operation on a group of values. For instance the SUM function automatically adds entries within a range.

The way the formula is affected when it is copied into another cell depends on the way cells in the formula are referred to. There are three types of cell references:

- **Relative cell references -** When a formula is copied from one cell to another, the cell references within the formula change to reflect the new location

- **Absolute cell references** - When a formula is copied from one cell to another, the cell references within the formula remain the same
- **Mixed cell references** - A single cell entry in a formula that contains both a relative and an absolute cell reference

In all of the instructions that follow we will be using relative cell references only.

One way to use a formula is to type it directly into the cell. Any cells can be included in the formula, they don't need to be next to each other. Different arithmetical operations can be combined within the same formula, for instance you can enter B2+B3-B5.

To enter a formula into a cell:

- Put the cell pointer into the cell where you want the result of the formula to appear (the resultant cell) and click
- Type = followed by the cells you want to calculate, for instance B2+B3-B5
- Press 'Enter'

There are more than 250 functions available which can be used to perform calculations for you. To find the function you are looking for:

- Click the 'down arrow' next to the 'AutoSum' button on the 'Standard' toolbar
- From the list that appears select 'More Functions'

- Either type a description of what you want to do (for instance, 'I want to find the highest number') in the 'Search for a function' text box and click the 'Go' button or
- Scroll through the list in the 'Select a function' box and click 'OK' when you find the one you want

The following functions, which can be found by clicking the 'down arrow' next to the 'AutoSum' button, are among the most useful.

AutoSum (SUM) adds numbers in a range of cells.

To use this function:

- Click in the resultant cell
- Click the 'AutoSum' button on the 'Standard' toolbar
- A dotted line will appear around a range of cells
- To accept this range of cells press 'Enter'
- To alter this range of cells click and drag on the cells that you want to calculate
- Press 'Enter'

(AVERAGE) works out the average of a number of cells.

To use this function:

- Click in the resultant cell
- Click the 'down arrow' next to the 'AutoSum' button on the 'Standard' toolbar and select 'Average'
- A dotted line will appear around a range of cells
- To accept this range of cells press 'Enter'
- To alter this range of cells click and drag on the cells that you want to find the average of
- Press 'Enter'

(MAX) finds the largest of a number of cells.

To use this function:

- Click in the resultant cell
- Click the 'down arrow' next to the 'AutoSum' button on the 'Standard' toolbar and select 'Max'
- A dotted line will appear around a range of cells
- To accept this range of cells press 'Enter'
- To alter this range of cells click and drag on the cells that you want to find the largest of
- Press 'Enter'

(COUNT) counts the number of cells.

To use this function:

- Click in the resultant cell
- Click the 'down arrow' next to the 'AutoSum' button on the 'Standard' toolbar and select 'Count'
- A dotted line will appear around a range of cells
- To accept this range of cells press 'Enter'
- To alter this range of cells click and drag on the cells that you want to find the number of
- Press 'Enter'

(MIN) finds the smallest of a number of cells.

Note: This function recognises negative numbers, so -46 will be smaller than 0.

To use this function:

- Click in the resultant cell
- Click the 'down arrow' next to the 'AutoSum' button on the 'Standard' toolbar and select 'Min'
- A dotted line will appear around a range of cells
- To accept this range of cells press 'Enter'
- To alter this range of cells click and drag on the cells that you want to find the smallest of
- Press 'Enter'

After you have entered a function or a formula you may want to alter it.

There are three ways of doing this, click in the cell that you want to alter then:

- Press 'F2', edit the formula in the cell or
- Put your cell pointer onto the 'Formula' bar and edit the formula or
- Click the 'Insert Function' button on the 'Formula' bar, the 'Function Arguments' dialog box will open. Change the function in the dialog box and click 'OK'

A formula or a function can be copied from one cell to another by:

- Click the cell that you want to copy
- Click the 'Copy' button on the 'Standard' toolbar
- Click the cell into which you want to paste the function or formula
- Press 'Enter'

Remember the formula will change after copying, for instance if the formula in cell A11 is =AVERAGE(A1:A10) and you copy it to cell D11, the formula in D11 will become =AVERAGE(D1:D10).

AutoCalculate will carry out any of the functions described above and display the answer in the 'Status' bar rather than in a cell.

To use AutoCalculate:

- Select the cells that you want to calculate
- Right click the 'Status' bar and select the required option (e.g. Count)

From time-to-time you will see symbols appearing in cells. These are used to indicate where errors have occurred. You will need to recognise which symbol indicates which error in order to correct them.

If you see the following symbols in a cell this is what each means:

- '####' means the cell is not wide enough to contain the information
- '#DIV/O!' means the formula is trying to divide a number by 0 or by an empty cell
- '#NAME?' means the formula contains an incorrectly spelled cell or function name
- '#VALUE!' means the formula contains text
- '#REF!' means the formula contains reference to a cell that isn't valid

 **What you need to know**

The difference between a formula and a function

Can you copy a formula to another cell?

How to find the function that you want to use

When would you use AutoCalculate?

What the following symbols mean

'#####'

'#DIV/O!'

'#NAME?'

'#VALUE!'

'#REF!'

What would you use the following functions for?

> 'AutoSum'
>
> 'AVERAGE'
>
> 'MAX'
>
> 'COUNT'

## Editing and formatting worksheets

One of the major advantages of an electronic spreadsheet is the ease with which you can correct any errors or omissions. You can insert a cell, column or row; delete entries; change values or find and replace data.

To insert a cell:

- Click on the worksheet where you want to insert a cell
- Select 'Cells' from the 'Insert' menu
- A dialog box will open.  Select what you want to happen to the existing cells, for instance 'Shift cells Right' and click 'OK'
- The existing cells in the row shift to the right and a new cell is inserted

To delete a cell:

- Select the cell or cells you want to delete
- Select 'Delete' from the 'Edit' menu
- A dialog box will open.  Select what you want to happen to the existing cells, for instance 'Shift cells Left' and click 'OK'

- The existing cells in the row shift to the left and the unwanted cells disappear

To insert rows and columns:

- Click on the cell above which you want to add a row or to the right of were you want to add a column
- Select 'Rows' or 'Columns' from the 'Insert' menu
- A new row or column is inserted

To delete rows and columns:

- Right click on the row header or column header
- Select 'Delete' from the shortcut menu that appears
- The row or column is deleted

There will be times when you want to change the values within a cell.  There are three ways to do this:

either:

- Click the cell that you want to change
- Type the correct data into the cell
- Press 'Enter'

or:

- Click the cell that you want to change
- Press 'F2'
- Using the 'Backspace' key delete the incorrect content and type in the correct content
- Press 'Enter'

or:

- Double click the cell that you want to change
- Using the 'Backspace' or 'Delete' key delete the incorrect content and type in the correct content
- Press 'Enter'

There will be times when you want to find specific information in a large spreadsheet more quickly than by scanning through until you come across it.

This can be done by:

- Selecting 'Find' in the 'Edit' menu
- A dialog box will open. Type the data you want to find in the 'Find what' text box
- Click the 'Find next' button
- The first cell containing the data will be indicated. If you want to find further examples continue to click 'Find Next' until you find the one you are looking for
- Alternatively click 'Find All' and all examples will be listed in a text box
- Click 'Close'

You may find that you have to change the same data in a number of cells throughout the worksheet. For instance, you may want to replace all references to 2005 with 2006. This can be done by:

- Selecting 'Replace' from the 'Edit' menu
- A dialog box will open. Type the data you would like to replace in the 'Find what' text box
- Press the 'Tab' key
- Type the new data into the 'Replace with' textbox
- Click 'Replace All'
- A dialog box will open telling you how many replacements have been made. Click 'OK'
- Click 'Close'

You can also format the worksheet to make its appearance more interesting or the information easier to read. You can increase and decrease the width of columns and the height of rows; change the colour of the data or the cell background; change the way numbers appear; choose from a variety of fonts and font sizes or the placement of the data in the cell.

To change the width of columns or the height of rows move the cell pointer to one side of the column header or the bottom edge of the row header.  Click and drag the edge to the desired width or height.

To change the colour of the data or cell background:

- Select the cells that you want to change
- To change the colour of the data select the 'font colour' down arrow on the formatting toolbar
- Select a colour from the palette
- To change the colour of the background select the 'fill colour' down arrow on the formatting toolbar
- Select a colour from the palette

Numbers can appear in a variety of ways. They can be simple numbers, decimals, currency or dates for instance.

To format numbers:

- Select the cells you want to format
- Right click and select 'Format Cells' from the shortcut menu
- A dialog box opens. Click the 'Number' tab
- Select the 'Category' you require
- Click 'OK'

The most common formats for numbers are:

- **General** - for instance 143809
- **Number** - for instance 143,809.00
- **Currency** - for instance £143,809.00
- **Accounting** - for instance £143,809.00
- **Percentage** - for instance 14380900.00% what does this mean in terms of percentage? Surely 14.3809%

To add emphasis or to differentiate between different types of data you may want to change the font and font size. This is done by:

- Selecting the cells you want to change
- Click the font field down arrow in the 'Standard' toolbar
- Select the font that you want to use
- Click the 'font size' field down arrow
- Select the font size you want to use

Finally, you may want to position the data within the cell either horizontally or vertically. To do this:

- Right click on the cells you want to align
- Select 'Format Cells' from the shortcut menu
- Click the 'Alignment' tab
- Click the down arrow next to the 'Horizontal' field
- Select your preference
- Click the down arrow next to the 'Vertical' field
- Select your preference
- Click 'OK'

# What you need to know

How to insert rows, cells and columns

How do you delete a row from a worksheet?

The three ways to change the value in a cell

How would you find all the references to similar data in a worksheet?

How to replace data

How many different ways are there to format numbers?

The procedure for changing the width and height of columns and rows

If you want to change the alignment of data in a cell, what process would you use?

## Presenting data

When you have completed the editing and formatting of your worksheets you will want to print off the results. There are a number of ways of enhancing the presentation of the data including the addition of charts which allow the reader to see the data presented graphically; headers and footers which allow you to title the report and include the date and time; choose between landscape and portrait; number the pages and add or remove the gridlines for clarity.

Before starting to print you will need to use 'Print Preview' so that you can decide which of the above enhancements you wish to make.

Open the worksheet that you want to print then:

- Click the 'Print Preview' button on the 'Standard' toolbar
- The worksheet will be displayed. Click the 'Zoom' button to make the worksheet on the screen larger

- Click 'Margins' and drag the margins to set the print area
- Click 'Close'
- Select the cells you want to print
- Select 'Print Area' from the 'File' menu
- Select 'Set Print Area'
- If the print area you have selected covers more than one page click the 'Print Preview' button
- Select 'Setup'
- Select 'Fit to 1 page(s) wide by 1 tall'
- Select 'Landscape' or 'Portrait'
- Click on the 'Header/Footer' tab
- Click the down arrow next to the 'Header' field
- Scroll through the header options and select one
- Click the down arrow next to the 'Footer' field
- Scroll through the footer options and select one
- Click on the 'Sheet' tab
- Click the 'Gridlines' checkbox
- Click 'OK'

You can create a selection of charts to help people understand the significance of the data.

To create a chart:

- Select the cells you want to include
- Click the 'Chart Wizard' button on the 'Standard' toolbar
- Select the chosen 'Chart Type'
- Select the chosen 'Chart Sub-type'
- Click 'Next'

- Select 'Rows' or 'Columns' in the 'Series in' area
- Type the name of the chart in the 'Chart title' field
- Type values for the x-axis and y-axis in the 'Category (X) axis' and the 'Category (Y) axis' fields
- Click 'Next'
- Click the 'As Object in' option
- Click 'Finish'

To change the chart type:

- Right click on the plot area and select 'Chart Type' from the shortcut menu
- Select the new 'Chart Type'
- Select the new 'Chart Sub-type'
- Click 'OK'

When you are completely satisfied with the look of the worksheet and any chart that you have decided to use you are ready to print.

To do this:

- Select 'Print' from the 'File' menu
- Click the down arrow next to the 'Printer Name' field to choose the printer that you are going to use
- In the 'Print range' area click 'Page(s) From and To' and type the pages you want to include or click 'All'
- In the 'Number of Copies' field type the number of copies that you want
- Select 'Collate' if appropriate
- Select from 'Selection', 'Active Sheet(s)' and 'Entire workbook'
- Click 'OK'

Remember the purpose of spreadsheet software is to enable you to perform calculations much more quickly than you would be able to using a pen and paper. When you first start you may think that you could actually achieve your ends more efficiently using a pen and an accounts pad; but if you persevere and master the intricacies of the software, you will soon find that you can produce spreadsheets not only in a fraction of the time, but also in a much more interesting way.

## Spreadsheet software can make even the driest set of figures look interesting

# Are you ready for assessment?

To achieve this unit of a Level 3 Business & Administration qualification you will need to demonstrate that you are competent in the following:

- Handle and convert files
- Combine information of different types
- Enter and edit spreadsheet data
- Format spreadsheets
- Select and use appropriate functions and formulas
- Check information
- Analyse and interpret data
- Present data
- Improve your efficiency in working with spreadsheets

(Remember that you will need the skills listed at the beginning of this chapter.  These are covered in chapter 1.)

You will need to produce evidence from a variety of sources. Carrying out the following activities will help you acquire competence at work.

### Activity 1
Create a spreadsheet containing at least 10 columns and least 20 rows. This can be based on any set of information of your choosing, for instance sales figures for each department over 10 weeks; daily temperatures of different cities over a period of time; your own expenditure over a period of time; hours worked over a period of time. Use your imagination and see what you can come up with.

Find the average
Find the total number
Find the highest number
Find the lowest number

### Activity 2
Having completed the above task present the information as:

A column chart
A bar chart
A line chart
A pie chart

An XY (scatter) chart
An area chart
A doughnut chart
A radar chart

## Activity 3

Compare the results and write a report explaining which type of chart you would use to present this information and why.

## Activity 4

What do you understand by the following spreadsheet software terms:

| | |
|---|---|
| AutoFill | Axis |
| Cell | Chart |
| Column | Data range |
| Dialog box | Drop down list |
| Field | Format |
| Formula | Function |
| Mixed cell reference | Objects |
| Row | Sort |
| Wizard | Worksheet |

## Activity 5

Create a spreadsheet based on your personal budget for one year. The spreadsheet needs to include all income and expenditure items. A list of possible cell titles is included in the example below:

| | Jan | Feb | Mar | — | Nov | Dec |
|---|---|---|---|---|---|---|
| **Income** | | | | | | |
| Salary (Gross) | | | | | | |
| Deductions | | | | | | |
| Salary (Net) | | | | | | |
| Other Income | | | | | | |
| **Total** | | | | | | |
| **Expenditure** | | | | | | |
| Rent/Mortgage | | | | | | |
| Heating | | | | | | |
| Electricity | | | | | | |
| Telephone | | | | | | |
| Food | | | | | | |
| Travel | | | | | | |
| Other | | | | | | |
| **Total** | | | | | | |
| **Balance** | | | | | | |

Devise a formula that:

- Adds up all the income and expenditure items using the appropriate formula
- Calculates the difference between income and expenditure and put this in the balance cell
- Your income increases by 3% in June. Devise a formula that increases the gross salary cell by 3%. The other cells should change automatically.

Create a chart or graph covering the whole year.

Remember: While gathering evidence for this unit, evidence **may** be generated for units 110, 212, 213, 301, 302, 320 and 321.

# CHAPTER 25
# UNIT 316 – Website software

The Internet began in the late 1960s when the American Government created a network of computers which, being located over a large area, would be able to withstand a nuclear attack. Even if some of the computers were destroyed the remainder would function and would still contain all of the information and capability of the original network. The network expanded to include non-military Websites (often known as 'sites') across America and eventually the world.

There are now many thousands of networks around the world, each maintained by an individual government or organisation and each connected to every other network within the Internet. The Internet includes electronic mail (email) which enables any user to contact any other user, and the World Wide Web (web) which consists of massive collections of information stored on computers connected to the Internet.

To connect to the web you will need a software programme known as a Web Browser such as Internet Explorer, Mozilla or Safari and an Internet Service Provider (ISP). An ISP is the organisation with which you subscribe in order to be able to access the web E.g. BT Openworld, Telewest Broadband, Tiscali, Wanadoo and many more.

Each document on the web is situated on a web page which can include text, pictures, sound, animation and video. Collections of web pages form a website which is made available to users of the Internet via a Web Server. Each web page is given a unique address or Uniform Resource Locator (URL) which enables users to find the page they are looking for. The most common form for this would be www.thenameofmycompany.com. However, it is not always necessary to include the 'www' and there are many types of domain codes such as co.uk, .biz, .tv, uk.com and many others.

Web pages often contain <u>highlighted text</u> (hyperlinks) which, when clicked on, connect to other web pages so that the user can navigate from one web page to another without having to type out the URL every time. When your mouse pointer hovers over a hyperlink, its appearance changes to a hand pointer like this.

Web pages are placed on the Web by individuals, often to share information on hobbies or pastimes, and by organisations either for commercial or altruistic reasons. Commercial purposes include:

- Promoting organisation brand or vision
- Advertising new products and services
- Informing potential customers of business locations
- Research
- Carrying out electronic transactions including ordering, making payments, transferring money
- Recruitment
- Technical support
- Timetables

Non-commercial web pages are published by individuals and organisations to share information that they feel should be freely available to everybody. This may include information on health, charities, politics, education and even the weather forecast.

The first consideration when planning a website is who the website is aimed at. Is it intended for general use or for an identified audience? If it is for a specific audience you will need to make sure that the content is designed to be of interest to that group of people. Decide what you want the website to achieve before you plan the design of the pages.

It is a good idea to look at a number of existing web pages and decide what aspects of the pages you like, and what aspects you are less impressed by, as a guide to determining the layout. You will probably find the pages that most impress contain some information which is both useful and interesting.

Collect together the information that you want your website to contain. Remember that you may need diagrams, images, company logos and the addresses of other related websites. Some of the content will already exist, some you will have to create. Organise the content into sections each of which will form a separate web page. Each page should have enough content to fill at least a single screen and no more than five screens.

Your website should start with a home page as this is usually the first page readers will access. The home page should contain a brief summary of the other pages and an outline of their contents. Always put the most important information at the top of the page. Use tools such as headings and formatting to make the important information stand out. Headings are used to indicate main topics and help the reader to find the information they are interested in more quickly. Paragraphs also help with this and short paragraphs are more easily read than long ones.

There are four basic layouts that you can choose from:

- Slide show layouts organise the pages in a straight line. This is suitable for pages that need to be read in order, such as step-by-step instructions
- Hierarchical layouts organise all the pages off the home page. The home page acts as a contents page directing the reader to the relevant page
- Web layouts are much less structured. The reader can move from any page either back to the home page or to a map linking them to any other page
- Combination layouts combine the benefits of hierarchical and web layouts and allow readers to move freely between the pages

Whichever layout you choose, don't be tempted to over-use images. On a website, images can affect the speed at which pages can be downloaded. Although with faster and faster broadband connections this is becoming less of a problem.

However, some readers will deliberately turn off the display of images because of this, so it is important that your page can get its message across without the images. Images are used as:

- **Dividers** - An image can visually separate sections of a web page
- **Clarification** - An image can expand on the text, for instance a map is better than directions, a graph is better than a table
- **Background** - An image repeated over the whole page can create interest and texture
- **Navigation** - Images of arrows can help the reader move between pages

Images can be obtained from collections purchased on CD-ROMs such as Clip Art, imported using a scanner or digital camera, copied from the Internet or created using a paint programme such as Microsoft Paint. You may want to create a small version of the image known as a 'thumbnail' which allows readers to decide whether they want to view the full size image. Remember to check the position regarding copyright before using any imported images on your web pages. There are websites that provide royalty free graphics and photographs including:

- www.freefoto.com
- www.freegraphics.com
- www.animation-central.com
- www.cooltext.com

These may be useful for practicing your image importing and manipulation techniques.

The feature of web pages which makes them really powerful is the fact that you can link any web page to any other web page anywhere on the Web by creating a 'hyperlink'. Simply set the text as a hyperlink by entering the complete URL for the page you want to link your page to. The reader can click on the hyperlink and be immediately connected. You can also include a link on your web page that allows the reader to send comments to you by email.

When producing web pages you will need to check a number of issues prior to completing the task:

- As you will probably be using images imported from other files and the Internet, make sure you check that they are suitable for your use
- Check the text to ensure that it is accurate. This means not only grammatically correct but also correct in its content. Check that it is consistent throughout in terms of tense as well as substance and that the layout is as intended
- Confirm with the person who the information has been created for that you have understood where it is to be used, when it is required and that it is suitable for the purpose

You will also need to check that the work does not infringe upon any legislation. The Acts most likely to be involved are:

- **The Copyright, Designs and Patents Act 1988** - This protects the authors of any literary work, including computer programs, from having their work copied for 70 years from the end of the calendar year in which the last remaining author of the work dies
- **The Data Protection Act 1998** - This prevents you from using any personal information you may hold on any individual for any purpose other than that for which it was obtained
- **The Computer Misuse Act 1990** - This makes illegal unauthorised access to computer material and unauthorised modification of computer material

Finally ask a colleague to review your work and give you feedback on how clearly and accurately it will communicate the information to the intended audience.

 **What you need to know**

The websites your organisation operates

What is the function of an Internet Service Provider?

The legislation that affects website production and use

What is a Web Server?

The maximum number of screens suitable
to create one web page

What should a Home page contain?

The basic layouts of websites

What is a URL?

The sources of images, sound, animation
and video

Why is it important to check the
accuracy of the content of your
website?

 When using website software you will use the
following skills:

- Planning
- Organising
- Communicating
- Using technology
- Checking

These skills are covered in chapter 1.

There are a number of website packages available. One of
the most commonly used is Macromedia Dreamweaver, so
the examples used in this chapter relate to Dreamweaver.
Whether you use this system, or another, the principles are
the same.

## Creating a website

Dreamweaver offers a choice of three views in the Main
window. These are the Design View, the Split Screen View
and the Code View. For the purposes of this book we will be
using the Design View only as it requires no previous
knowledge of HTML (HyperText Markup Language) coding.
Working with the Design View is similar to working in a word
processing package.

The Document toolbar is situated towards the top left of the window and is used to toggle between the various view options and to set the page title.

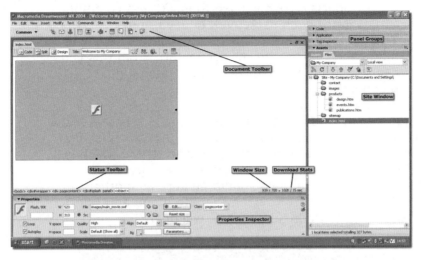

The Status bar is situated along the bottom of the window and displays the tag selector (which you will only use if you are using HTML) the Window size drop-down menu which tells you the size of the window, the estimated download speed and a Launcher Bar which contains shortcuts.

A number of panels can be opened by opening the Window menu, including:

- **The Properties inspector** - This enables you to edit text, layout and images
- **The Objects panel** - This contains seven button categories which allow you to insert objects:
  - Common - This includes images, table and layers
  - Character - This includes special characters such as accents or copyright symbol ©
  - Forms - This contains the necessary elements to create response forms
  - Frames - This provides pre-formatted framesets
  - Head - This is used for adding background information written in META tags such as a website description which will be recognised by Search Engines

- Invisible - This contains common objects such as anchor tags and scripts that don't appear in the browser window
- Special - This is used to insert less common items such as ActiveX or Java Applets
- **The History panel** - This records all the steps you have taken in the current document. From this you can select any previous step and undo all the steps taken since

The first step towards creating a website is to create a folder for all your website files. This should contain only files that are going to be part of the final website i.e. those which will be uploaded to the Web Server. Other files such as photographs and documents should be kept in another folder. To set up a website open the Site menu and select 'New Site'. A Site Definition window will open:

- Enter a name for your website
- Select 'Yes' or 'No' for whether you wish to use server technology. This is an advanced feature so 'No' will be OK for now
- Click on the folder icon and select the folder you have set up for your website files
- Select the method with which you will upload your site to the Internet. You can add these details at a later date so click 'None' for the time being
- Click 'OK'

The website that you have named will now appear in the Local Site area of the Site window. To open the Site window press (F8) on your keyboard.

Files and folders can be created and deleted from within the Site window. To create a new file:

- Open the File menu
- Select New File
- Enter a name for the file
- Double click on the file icon

To create a new folder:

- Open the File menu
- Select New Folder
- Enter a name for the folder

To delete files and folders:

- Highlight the file or folder in the Site window
- Press Delete or Backspace
- Click 'OK' in the dialog box which will open

You can view the structure of your website by clicking on 'Site Map'. Linked files are shown in the order in which the links appear in each page. To print the Site Map:

- Open the File menu
- Select Save Site Map

- Enter a name and file type (.bmp or .png)
- Choose where to save the file
- Click 'OK'
- Open the programme in which you have saved your Site Map and print it

The next step is to actually build a web page. To open a new page, open the File menu and select New. To open an existing page open the File menu, select Open, select the file you want to open and click Open.

Access Page Properties by opening the Modify menu and selecting Page Properties (Ctrl+J). From the Page Properties dialog box you can select:

- **Page title** - This will appear at the top of the browser window, not in the web page. Do not confuse the page title with the file name
- **Background image** - This is selected using 'Browse' and will be automatically tiled or repeated to fit the browser window
- **Background** - Click on the Colour picker box and select a background colour for the page
- **Text** - Click on the Colour picker box and select a text colour for the page
- **Links** - Click on the Colour picker box and select a link colour for the page
- **Visited Links** - Click on the Colour picker box and select a visited link colour for the page. This will show which links have been visited in a different colour
- **Active Links** - Click on the Colour picker box and select an active link colour for the page. This colour appears when the user clicks on the link

To create text on the page, simply type directly into the Design View window. You can then use the **Properties inspector** to format the text and select font type, colour, size and style. To format text, highlight the text and open the Properties inspector.

To create a heading open the Format drop down menu and choose from the Heading options between Heading 1, the largest and Heading 6, the smallest. The text will appear in bold and be followed by a paragraph break.

To choose a font open the font drop down menu and select from the fonts displayed.  As the web page can only appear in a font that the user has on their system, the fonts appear in strings.  You should select the string that has your first choice of font at the beginning.  The web page will appear on the user's system in that font if it is available to the user; in the next font in the string if the first is not available and so on.  If none of the strings are exactly what you want there is a facility to create a string of your own from all the available fonts.

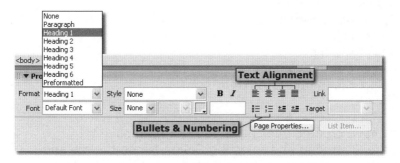

To change the size of text open the Size drop down menu and select a font size from the pre-set sizes available.

To change the colour of the text click on the colour box to access the Colour picker and select a new text colour.

To apply bold or italic styles use the **B** and *I* buttons.

Whenever you press the Enter key a paragraph break will be inserted around the text.  To align blocks of text (or paragraphs) highlight a block of text or place your cursor within a paragraph and select one of the alignment options, left, centre or right.  To indent a paragraph, select the Indent button.

If you don't want a paragraph break inserted between blocks of text insert a line break by holding down the Shift key while pressing the Enter key.

Numbered lists and bullet point lists are created by typing in the list separated by returns, highlighting the list and selecting 'Ordered List' for numbered lists or 'Unordered List' for bullet point lists.  To add new items to an existing list, place the cursor at the end of the line before the place where you want the new item to appear.  Click Enter and type in the new item. To delete an item from the list highlight the item and press Delete/Backspace twice.

Text can be imported from Microsoft Word into Dreamweaver but important formatting elements can be lost. To avoid this:

- Open the File menu in Microsoft Word
- Select Save As
- From the Save as type drop down menu select a file type showing .html
- Open the File menu in Dreamweaver
- Select Open
- Select the file
- Select Commands
- Select Clean up Word HTML
- Click 'OK'

Once you have created your page you can then save it by opening the File menu and selecting Save. Name the file and save it in the appropriate website folder.

To see how the page will appear on the Web and to check that links work you will need to preview the page in a browser. To do this open the File menu, select Preview in Browser and select the browser you wish to use (F12). If you wish to print a copy of your new page, you will need to preview the page in a browser first and print from there as you are unable to print directly from Dreamweaver.

The next step is to import images. Images inserted on a page in Dreamweaver are not embedded but remain as separate files. These should be stored in your 'images' folder in your site files. To insert an image:

- Place the cursor in the appropriate place on the page
- Open the Objects panel
- Select Image
- The Select Image dialog box will open
- Browse to and select your image

Alternatively, drag and drop the image from your images folder in the 'Site Panel'. The image will appear on the page and the following image options will be displayed in the **Properties inspector**:

- **Name** - It is important to name your image
- **Width and height** - This displays the dimensions of the image in pixels
- **Refresh** - This is used to reset the original width and height of the image if you change them
- **Src** - This indicates where the image is located in the website files
- **Link** - This displays the URL of a linked image
- **Align** - This relates to the alignment of an image to text or other objects in the same line
- **Alt** - The text alternative to the image for users with images turned off
- **V Space and H Space** - This inserts transparent space around your image vertically or horizontally
- **Target** - If your image is a link the target will specify which window or frame the linked page should open in
- **Low Src** - You can specify a low resolution version of your image to open while your actual image is downloading
- **Border** - A linked image can be displayed in the browser in a border
- **Map** - This is where you name and create an image map
- **Edit** - This is used to open a graphics programme in order to edit an image

An image inserted in Dreamweaver will appear selected with resize handles (black boxes on the bottom right corner and edges).  The image can be resized using these handles.  To align an image with text, select an image then:

- Click on the expander arrow in Properties inspector
- Choose an alignment (left, right or centre)
- Select the image again
- Choose an option from the align drop down list:
  - Baseline - This aligns the image to the text baseline
  - Top - This aligns the text with the top of the image
  - Middle - This aligns the middle of the image with the text baseline
  - Bottom - This aligns the bottom of the image and the selected object
  - Text top - This aligns the top of the image with the tallest text character
  - Absolute middle - This aligns the middle of the image with the middle of the text
  - Absolute bottom - This aligns the image to the bottom of the text including the descanters
  - Left - This aligns the image with the left of the page and places text or other objects to the right of the image
  - Right - This aligns the image with the right of the page and places text or other objects to the left of the image

You can also import sound, animation or live video using the 'Objects panel' or by drag and drop from the site panel.  Be wary of file size.  Especially in the case of videos.  Large file sizes can mean long download times.

Either text or images can be made into hyperlinks.  With Dreamweaver you can link between pages, jump between items on the same page, link to other websites or set up e-mail links.  If you move files or folders within the Site window any links to or from those files will be automatically updated.

To create a link from one page to another:

- Highlight the text or image that you want to link
- In the properties inspector click on the folder icon

- The Select File box will open
- Select the page to which you want to link
- Alternatively pick up the 'Target' symbol next to the file icon and drag and drop to the relevany page in the 'Site Window'

To create a link between items in the same page you have to set up Named Anchors:

- Place the cursor where you want the user to go to
- Open the Insert menu
- Select Named Anchor
- A dialog box will open
- Type in a name

To link to a named anchor in the same page click on the Point to File icon in the Properties inspector and drag the pointer to the named anchor.

To create a link to another website highlight the text or image that you want to make into a link and type the URL of the website you want to link to in the Link box in the Properties inspector. Be sure to include http:// at the beginning of the URL.

To create a link to an e-mail address:

- Go to the Objects panel
- Click on Insert E-mail link
- A dialog box will open
- In the Text box type the text you want to appear underlined on the page
- In the E-mail box type in the e-mail address

Links will not actually work in Dreamweaver. To check that your links have been successful you will need to preview in the browser by pressing F12.

 **What you need to know**

The purpose of the Toolbar, Status Bar and Objects panel

How do you access the Properties inspector?

How to insert a line break

What is the function of the History panel?

How to import, resize and align images

How do you create a bullet point list?

The different links available and how to create them

Why is it necessary to clean up text imported from Microsoft Word?

## Publishing and updating a website

Having successfully created your website you will now want to get it online. There are still a few things to do first. Many website producers overlook a very important step; proof reading the website. The easiest way to proof read your pages is to first run a spell check by opening the Text menu and selecting Check Spelling, remembering to check that the language is set at UK English, then print the pages from the website and ask someone unfamiliar with the content to proof read them.

You will now need to consider whether you want to add a form to the website in order to gather data. Whatever data you set your form to collect it is useful to include an option for the user to feedback on how easy they found your website to navigate. There are two stages to manage; form production and form processing.

Forms are made up of 'Objects' such as text boxes which the user types into and 'Action' which sends the information to be processed. To enable processing you need a Common Gateway Interface (CGI) script. Check that your Server supports CGI. If not it is probably as well to change Server. If they do, ask if they have scripts that you can use. If they haven't there are scripts available free on the Web.

To create a form:

- Go to the Objects panel
- Select Forms
- Select Insert Form
- A rectangular box will appear in the document window

Go to the Properties inspector and fill in the form properties:

- **Name** - Give the form a name
- **Action** - Enter a link to the script that will process the form
- **Method** - This chooses how the form is to be handled. The default is GET but as this is not a secure method you should use POST for anything confidential

You will then need to create the necessary form objects depending on the kind of information you are collecting.

To create a single-line text field, which requests one line of information, such as a name:

- Go to the Objects panel
- Click on Insert Text Field

Go to the Properties inspector and type:

- A field name in the textfield box
- The number of characters (or width) of the field display
- The maximum number of characters to be inserted

To create a multi-line text field, which allows users to enter several lines of text, such as comments:

- Go to the Objects panel
- Click on Insert Text Field

Go to the Properties inspector and:

- Select the Type option Multi-line
- Set the character width
- Set the number of lines
- Set the word wrap options

To create a password field, which obscures what is typed into it by displaying bullet points or asterisks, go to the Objects panel. Go to the Properties inspector and:

- Select Password
- The number of characters (or width) of the field display
- The maximum number of characters to be inserted

To create a checkbox, which enables users to make selections by clicking in a box:

- Go to the Objects panel
- Select Insert Checkbox

Go to the Properties inspector and enter a name and a value for each checkbox. Choose the Initial State of each checkbox as either 'checked' or 'unchecked'.

To create a radio button, which enables the user to select one option from a group:

- Go to the Objects panel

- Select Insert Radio Button

Go to the Properties inspector and give each button a name and a value. All radio buttons in a group must have the same name and different values.

To create a menu, which also offers one selection from a group:

- Go to the Objects panel
- Select Insert List/Menu

Go to the Properties inspector and enter a name in the List/Menu box. Click on the List Values button and enter the item name that you wish to appear in the menu and the value of that item.

To create a list, which enables users to make more than one selection from a group:

- Go to the Objects panel
- Select Insert List/Menu

Go to the Properties inspector and select List. Enter the name of the list in the List/Menu box. Click on the List Values button and enter the item names that you wish to appear in the list and the value of each item. You can choose the height of the list and whether to allow the user to make multiple selections as well as which list item is initially visible.

To create a file field, which inserts a Browse button and text field to allow the user to attach files:

- Go to the Objects panel

- Select Insert File Field

Go to the Properties inspector and name the field, enter the width of the field and set the maximum characters.

To create a hidden field, which is not visible to the user:

- Go to the Objects panel
- Select Insert Hidden Field

Go to the Properties inspector and enter a unique field name and fill in the value box with the information you want to send with the form.

To create a form button, which allows the user to submit or reset the form:

- Go to the Objects panel
- Select Insert

Go to the Properties inspector and the Submit button will appear as the default. Change the label to the wording you wish to appear on the form.

To create an image field, which replaces the buttons with images:

- Go to the Objects panel
- Select Insert Image

Go to the Properties inspector and enter a name and value for the image field. The image must be a GIF in a graphics programme and must be in the website files.

Remember when designing forms to bear in mind their purpose. If you make the form too difficult or complicated to fill in you will get less response from users than from a simple form.

Before going fully live with your website it is an idea to carry out usability tests. Preview the website in as many different browser versions as possible to see how it looks to different users. Check that the links are not broken by opening the File menu and selecting Check Links and then opening the Site menu and selecting Check Links Sitewide. To clean up the website open the Commands menu and select Clean Up HTML, leave the options on default and click 'OK'.

You will want your website to appear on as many search engines as possible. Search engines operate using keywords which you place on your page as 'Meta tags'. Most search engines index a maximum of 20 keywords and the fewer keywords you use the more relevance each is given. You will also need to write a website description of about 15-20 words which will be used by the search engine to describe your website.

To insert keywords:

- Go to the Objects panel
- Select Head from the arrow drop down menu
- Select Insert Keywords
- Type in your keywords separated by commas

To insert a description:

- Go to the Objects panel
- Select Head from the arrow drop down menu
- Select Insert Description
- Type in your description

Keep a copy of your keywords and description as you will be asked for them when you submit your website to search engines.

To get your website onto the Internet you have to send your files to a remote site which is the server making it accessible on the Internet. To set up a remote site:

- Open the Site menu
- Select Define Sites
- Highlight the site you want to define
- Click on Edit
- Select Remote info
- Select FTP from the server Access drop down menu
- Complete the information provided by your web host
- Click 'OK'
- Click 'Done' in the dialog box

This will make available the Connect, Get and Put buttons along the top of the Site window.

To connect to the remote server:

- Open the website in the Site window
- Click 'Connect'
- The remote website files will appear in the Remote Site area of the Site window
- Highlight the file name in the local website
- Click 'Put'

You now need to set your File Transfer Protocols (FTP). These will have been provided to you by your host. To set your FTP preferences:

- Open the Edit menu
- Select Preferences
- Make your changes in the FTP Preferences dialog box

The FTP options are:

- **Always Show** - This concerns the remote and local website display in the Site window
- **Dependent Files** - This prompts you to upload or download dependent files on checking in or out
- **FTP Connection** - The length of time Dreamweaver will maintain your connection after being idle
- **FTP Time Out** - The amount of time that Dreamweaver will try to make a connection with the server
- **Firewall Host** - If you have a firewall, type in the address of the proxy server
- **Firewall Port** - The default is 21, change if your connection port is different
- **Put Options** - Save files before uploading

Now you have got your website up and running, you will want to make changes to it from time-to-time. Information may change, new products or services become available, special offers or promotions take place or you may just want to update and refresh your images. In Dreamweaver this is managed through Check In/Out. To enable the Check In/Out facility:

- Open the Site menu
- Select Define Sites

- Highlight the website you want to set
- Click 'Edit'
- Select Remote Info
- Select FTP or Local/Network from the server Access drop down menu
- Select Enable File Check In/Check Out
- This will bring up the set up options
- Type in a User Name and e-mail address

To Check In files, connect to the website, highlight the file name and select Check In. Choose whether you want to upload dependent files.

To Check Out files, connect to the website, highlight the file name and select Check Out. Choose whether you want to download dependent files.

There is a useful tool available in Dreamweaver which enables you to make notes on the file to remind yourself of changes made or to advise others who may be working on the file with you known as 'Design Notes'. To set up Design Notes for a page:

- Open the File menu
- Select Design Notes
- A dialog box will open
- Select the Status of the file
- Add any comments
- Insert the date through the calendar icon
- Check Show When File Is Opened
- Click 'All Info'
- Type the required information into the Name field
- Type the required information into the Value field
- The information will be displayed in the Info box

To add Design Notes to an object:

- Highlight the object
- Right+Ctrl click to open the Context menu
- Select Design Notes
- Add your notes

Your website will now be available on the Internet. Submit the details to one or more search engines in order that your audience can find the page. Collect the feedback that you get from your users and look for indications that there is difficulty in accessing or navigating the website. Consider the fact that some of your audience may have special needs. Review your website to look for colour combinations which visually impaired users or those with dyslexia may find difficult. If your website depends on sound to get its point across, hearing impaired users may be disadvantaged.

Remember that different browsers and modems or the availability of broadband will affect the download speed of your website. If you have too many images, some users may give up on your website because it takes too long to download.

 **What you need to know**

The benefits of attaching forms to your web pages

Why is it important to proof read your web pages?

How forms are created and structured

How do you insert keywords and a description?

Why it is necessary to submit your website to search engines

Why should you conduct usability tests before uploading your website?

How to check that links are not broken

What can affect download speeds?

The process of Checking In and Checking Out files

Why is it necessary to consider users with different needs?

Organisations benefit from the use of websites in different ways. Commercial organisations can raise their profile, advertise to an almost limitless audience at a relatively low cost, reduce costs in premises and distribution by selling on-line and attract recruits through advertising employment opportunities. Non-commercial organisations can spread their message worldwide without censorship. The possibilities are endless.

## Information radiates from your website worldwide across the web

# Are you ready for assessment?

To achieve this unit of a Level 3 Business & Administration qualification you will need to demonstrate that you are competent in the following:

- Use file handling techniques appropriate to the software
- Plan and produce websites
- Combine information of different types
- Edit, format and layout content
- Check accuracy, consistency, layout and functioning
- Upload and maintain content to web pages

(Remember that you will need the skills listed at the beginning of this chapter.  These are covered in chapter 1.)

You will need to produce evidence from a variety of sources. Carrying out the following activities will help you acquire competence at work.

**Activity 1**
Design a website home page for your organisation or department.

**Activity 2**
Add additional pages to the website and provide links between the pages.

**Activity 3**
Design and create a form to collect data and attach it to your website.

**Activity 4**
Add sound, animation or video to your website.

**Activity 5**
Get feedback from colleagues on your website and make amendments based on the feedback you received.

Remember:  While gathering evidence for this unit, evidence **may** be generated for units 110, 212, 213, 218, 301, 302, 320 and 321.

# CHAPTER 26
# UNIT 317 – Artwork and imaging software

Improvements in Artwork and Imaging software over the last few years have revolutionised the production of images for display in print or on screen. Modern packages can be used to create and manipulate images for use in Web pages, presentations or in brochures, promotional material and catalogues to a much higher standard than was previously possible.

Using available software, a wide range of effects can be created. Images can be imported or painted and drawn and then manipulated by the use of filters, deformations and special effects.

Artwork and Imaging software allows you to import an ordinary image and turn it into an extraordinary one to enliven your material, or you can start from a poorly defined picture and improve its quality until it is suitable for use. Old, creased and damaged photographs can be restored to a better condition than they were in originally.

As with producing any other document there is a need to check a number of issues prior to completing the task:

- As you will probably be using images imported from other files and the Internet, make sure you check that they are suitable for your intended use

- Check the text to ensure that it is accurate. This means not only grammatically correct but also that the content is correct too. Check that it is consistent throughout in terms of tense as well as substance and that the layout is as intended
- Confirm with the person who the information has been created for that you have understood where it is to be used, when it is required and that it is suitable for the purpose

You will also need to check that the work does not infringe any legislation. The Acts most likely to be involved are:

- **The Copyright, Designs and Patents Act 1988** - This protects the authors of any literary work, including computer programmes, from having their work copied for 70 years from the end of the calendar year in which the last remaining author of the work dies
- **The Data Protection Act 1998** - This prevents you from using any personal information you may hold on any individual for any purpose other than that for which it was obtained
- **The Computer Misuse Act 1990** - This act was passed to deal with the problem of computer 'hacking'. It is illegal to gain unauthorised access to computer material and to modify that material without authorisation

Finally ask a colleague to review your work and give you feedback on how clearly and accurately it will communicate the information to the intended audience.

 When using artwork and imaging software you will use the following skills:

- Planning
- Designing
- Organising
- Communicating
- Using technology
- Checking

These skills are covered in chapter 1.

# Using Microsoft Paint

There are a number of Artwork and Imaging packages available. One of the most commonly used is Microsoft Paint so the examples used in this section relate to Microsoft Paint. Whether you use this system, or another, the principles are the same.

Open the programme and you will see the following.

On the left hand side of the screen there is an assortment of painting Tools. These are explained on the following page.

At the bottom of the screen there is a Palette of colours. This is used to select colours for shape fills, line colours, text and re-colours.

On the left hand side of the Colour Palette is a box showing the active colours. This shows two overlapping rectangles.

The top rectangle is the foreground colour. This is the colour used by the:

- Text tool
- Pencil tool
- Paintbrush tool
- Airbrush tool
- Fill tool
- Rectangle, Polygon, Oval and Rounded Rectangle tools
- Line tool
- Curve tool

The foreground colour is changed by selecting a colour from the Colour Palette and left clicking on it.

The lower rectangle is the background colour. This is the default colour of any new image. The background colour is changed by selecting a colour from the Colour Palette and right clicking on it.

Additional colours are available from the Colour Picker which can be accessed via the Colours Menu.

**Tools**

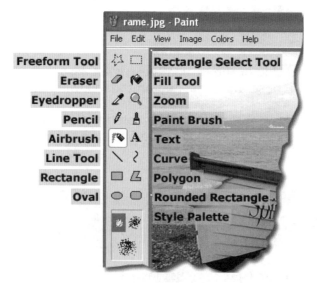

The **Freeform Select Tool** is used to select sections of the image so that you can move, copy or edit those sections without changing the rest of the image. To use the Freeform Select Tool:

- Click on the Freeform Select Tool Icon
- Click on the image where you want to begin the selection
- Drag the mouse around to create the outline of the shape

The freeform shape you have drawn turns into a rectangle on the screen. Your freeform shape is bounded by the rectangle. If you move the selected section of the image it will retain the freeform shape that you drew.

The **Rectangle Select Tool** is used for exactly the same purpose as The Freeform Select Tool except that it selects a rectangular shaped section. To use the Rectangle Select Tool:

- Click on the Rectangle Select Tool Icon
- Click on the image where you want to begin the selection. This will be one of the corners of the rectangular selection area
- Drag the mouse to where you want the opposite corner

The selected section will be bounded by a rectangle.

Having selected an area of the image you can:

- Copy the selected area by pressing Ctrl+C
- Cut the selected area by pressing Ctrl+X
- Paste the selected area by pressing Ctrl+V. You can create a mosaic or collage by pasting the same selected area several times
- Move the selected area by left clicking inside the guide box, holding down the button and dragging the selection to the desired position then letting go. You can create a blurred effect by holding down the Shift key at the same time as you drag the selection
- Stretch the selection by clicking on the square-shaped tabs at the corners and in the middle of the guide box, holding the button down and dragging the selection to change its size
- Apply any of the effects available on the Image Menu to the selection

The **Eraser Tool** changes selected parts of the image back to the background colour. Click on the Eraser Tool Icon. This reveals four options in the 'Style Palette' below the toolbox, of different sizes of eraser. Use the relevant size of eraser for the purpose. Click and drag the eraser over the section of image you wish to erase.

The **Fill Tool** applies colour to a large area of the image. Click on the Fill Tool Icon point to the area of the image that you want to apply colour to and click. Left clicks will apply the foreground colour from the Colour Palette and right clicks will apply the background colour. The colour will be applied to a bounded area so you need to check before using the Fill Tool that the area you want to change the colour of is contained. If not, close the area using the Pencil or Line Tool. If you apply colour and then find it has covered a greater area than you intended press Ctrl+Z. This will undo the fill.

The **Eyedropper Tool** picks up colours that have already been used in an image to enable you to reuse the exact shade elsewhere. To use the Eyedropper Tool:

- Click on the Eyedropper Tool
- Click on the section of the image containing the colour you want to use

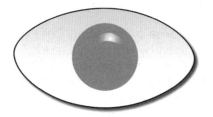

The active foreground colour will automatically change to the colour selected with the eyedropper. Using right click will change the active background colour. This is particularly useful for removing 'redeye' from photographs of people. The Eyedropper will automatically change to the previously selected tool.

The **Magnifier Tool** gives you a closer view of any selected section of the image. Click on the Magnifier Tool Icon and click on the image. You will have options to select from 1x, 2x, 6x and 8x magnification. The Magnifier will automatically change to the previously selected tool.

The **Pencil Tool** is the basic drawing tool. You can draw strokes a single pixel wide in any selected colour. If you hold down the Shift key as you draw you can draw horizontal, vertical or diagonal lines. Click on the Pencil Tool Icon and draw either freehand or using the Shift key for straight lines.

The **Paint Brush Tool** is similar to the Pencil Tool but the shape and size can be changed by selecting from the options in the style palette. If you hold down the Shift key as you paint you can paint horizontal or vertical lines. Click on the Paint Brush Tool Icon and paint either freehand or using the Shift key for straight lines.

The **Airbrush Tool** is similar to the Paint Brush Tool but instead of applying colour evenly, it applies it gradually in a semi-random distribution of pixels. If you hold the Airbrush over the same area it will gradually fill the whole area with colour. The Airbrush Tool has three size options. Click on the Airbrush Tool Icon and paint freehand. With practice a number of effects can be achieved.

The **Text Tool** positions and enters text onto an image. The text can be any colour and font that is available on your computer. To use the Text Tool:

- Click on the Text Tool
- Drag a rectangle onto the image
- A floating window will appear
- Select the Font, size and formatting
- Type in your text which will appear in the foreground colour

The rectangle can be moved by clicking and dragging on its border, or resized by clicking on the tab buttons at the corners and mid points. The Text Tool has two options; the rectangle can be filled with the background colour or the text can appear directly on the image. However, if you click outside of the boundary the text box will deselect and the text will be set in place. If you make a mistake, press Ctrl+Z to undo. Once the text is set in place it can't be edited as text, only dealt with as part of the image.

The **Line Tool** works like the Pencil Tool except that it only draws straight lines and the colour and width of the lines can be changed by using the available options. Click on the Line Tool Icon and select the width required. Click on the image where you want the line to start and drag it to where you want it to finish.  If you hold down the Shift key, the Line Tool will draw only horizontal, vertical or 45° diagonal lines.

The **Curve Tool** is used in a similar way to the Line Tool except that after creating a straight line you can click and drag to bend the line to make one or a maximum of two bends in it.  Be careful as the Undo command will only undo the last change you made.

The **Rectangle Drawing Tool** is used to draw three types of rectangles:

- Outline rectangles
- Filled with outline rectangles
- Filled without outline rectangles

Select from the options then draw a rectangle by clicking on the Rectangle Drawing Tool, selecting a point on the image where you want one corner to be and dragging diagonally to where you want the opposite corner to be.  To draw a square, simply hold down the Shift key.

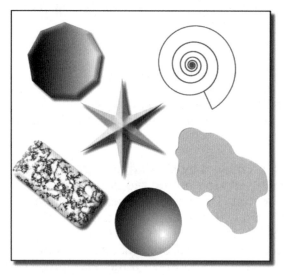

The **Polygon Drawing Tool** draws any other solid shape. Click on the Polygon Drawing Tool, select a point on the image where you want one corner to be and then click on the point where you want the next corner to be and so on until you get back to the beginning.  Polygons have the same options as rectangles.  If you hold down the Shift key the angles of the polygon can only be 45° or 90°.

The **Oval Drawing Tool** works in a similar way to the Rectangle Drawing Tool except that it has no corners. To draw an oval click on the Oval Drawing Tool, select a point on the image where you want the top left of the oval to appear, click and drag down to where you want the bottom right of the oval to appear. The same options are available as before. You will probably find that it takes a great deal of practice before you can draw your oval exactly where you want it. If you hold down the Shift key you will draw a circle.

The **Rounded Rectangle Drawing Tool** works exactly the same way as all the other shape tools to draw rectangles with rounded corners. To create rounded squares, hold down the Shift key.

### Menus

The **File Menu** is where the basic commands that affect the file you are working on can be found. The options on the File Menu and their functions are:

| Function | Shortcut | Description |
|---|---|---|
| **Function** | Ctrl+N | Creates a new, blank (white) image file |
| **New** | Ctrl+N | Creates a new, blank (white) image file |
| **Open** | Ctrl+O | Opens a dialog box to allow you to select an existing image file to open. Only one image file can be open at one time |
| **Save** | Ctrl+S | Saves the file you are working on |
| **Save As** | | Saves the file you are working on with a new file name |
| **Print Preview** | | Displays the image on screen as it will appear when it is printed out on paper |
| **Page Setup** | | Displays options for setting up how Paint will print the file |
| **Print** | Ctrl+P | Displays the Print dialog box, where you can print out the current image file |
| **Send** | | Enables you to send the current image file by e-mail |
| **1,2,3...** | | Opens your recently used files in Paint |
| **Exit** | Alt+F4 | Shuts down the programme |

Paint handles a variety of image formats including bmp, jpeg, png, tiff and gif. Bitmap files (bmp) are used for presentations, documents, Windows backgrounds, or Web pages being viewed through Internet Explorer. Jpegs are used for high colour images on the Internet. A jpeg picture is compressed, degrading the image's clarity and sharpness but reducing the size. For comparison a 400x400 blank pixel image stored as a bitmap has a size of 468kb, but a jpeg is 156 times smaller at only 3kb.

It is advisable to save your file after you successfully complete each major change as Undo will only undo the last change. Alternatively if you Save As after each major change and rename the file you can always go back to the last time you were happy with it if it all goes wrong.

Use the Print Preview mode to check that the image completely fits on the page before wasting time, ink and paper printing it out to find that it doesn't.

The **Edit Menu** is where the commands for making changes in the file that you are working in can be found. The options on the Edit Menu and their functions are:

| Function | Shortcut | Description |
|----------|----------|-------------|
| **Undo** | Ctrl+Z | Undo will remove the last change you made but only the last change. As soon as you click the mouse Undo will be unable to remove any prior change. It works only on the Tool Commands |
| **Repeat** | Ctrl+Y | Repeat is the reverse of Undo. It will reapply the last change that you made |
| **Cut** | Ctrl+X | Used in conjunction with the Selection Tools, Cut will remove the section from the image and place it in the 'copy buffer' |
| **Copy** | Ctrl+C | Used in conjunction with the Selection Tools, Copy will place the section in the 'copy buffer' without removing it from the image |
| **Paste** | Ctrl+V | Paste returns the last cut or copied section to the image, from where you can move it to the desired |

| | | position |
|---|---|---|
| **Clear Selection** | Del | Used in conjunction with the Selection Tools, whatever is in the section will be deleted |
| **Select All** | Ctrl+A | This selects the whole image. You can then use Cut, Copy, Paste or Clear Selection |
| **Copy To** | | This enables you to copy a section or the whole image to another file rather than the 'copy buffer' |
| **Paste From** | | This enables you to paste from the file to which you copied rather than the 'copy buffer' |

The Cut, Copy and Paste functions can be used to repair large areas of damage in photographs. Cut out the damaged area, copy an area containing a similar image and paste this area over the damage.

The **View Menu** has few useful features. You can switch on and off the Tool Box, Colour Box and Status Bar or you can set the Zoom, but this is done more quickly using the Magnifier Tool. You can also use View Bitmap to see the image full size without the window objects in the way.

The **Image Menu** can be used to alter either the whole image or a selected section in a number of useful and interesting ways:

| Function | Shortcut | Description |
|---|---|---|
| **Flip/Rotate** | Ctrl+R | Flip allows you to turn the image or section over. If you choose Flip horizontal the image will appear back to front, if you choose Flip vertical the image will appear upside down but still the original way round. Rotate will turn the image or section through 90°, 180° or 270° |
| **Stretch/Skew** | Ctrl+W | Stretch allows you to change the ratio of the section's height to its width. Skew is similar to |

| | | stretch but affects opposing edges oppositely. This results in an effect that can give an illusion of 3D |
|---|---|---|
| **Invert Colours** | Ctrl+I | Gives an effect similar to a photographic negative |
| **Attributes** | Ctrl+E | Allows you to change the basic image attributes such as height and width, colours and transparency |
| **Clear Image** | Ctrl+Shft+N | This cuts the entire image |
| **Draw Opaque** | | Works with the selection. If Draw Opaque is unchecked, any background colour in your section will be treated as transparent. This can be seen if you move the section. If Draw Opaque is checked, the background colour will remain opaque |

The **Colours Menu** has only one choice 'Edit Colours'. Selecting this will open the Edit Colours window on top of the regular Paint window. Edit Colours allows you to customise your Colour Palette. The Colour Palette is the part of the Paint window from which you select which colour you want to paint or draw with. The basic Colour Palette has only 48 colours to choose from. If you need more colours click on 'Define Custom Colours'. This causes the Edit Colours window to expand allowing you to select colours from the Colour Picker.

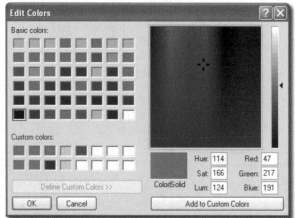

To pick a colour click on the region where your chosen colour appears.  Adjust the lightness or darkness by clicking on the shading bar on the right.  Colours can be selected by entering the appropriate numbers into the Hue, Saturation and Luminosity (HSL) or Red, Green and Blue (RGB) boxes if you understand colour theory.  If not, work with the gamut box.  This is the large box showing all the colours from red to blue (the whole gamut).  Simply move the cursor around in the gamut box until you find a colour you like showing in the Colour Solid box.  Click on 'Add to Custom Colours' and the colour will appear in the boxes on the left hand side of the window.  Click on 'OK' and the colours will be transferred to your palette of colours in the Paint window.

The **Help Menu** does exactly what it says.  There are two options, one of which, 'About Paint', tells you about copyright and licensing information.  The 'Help Topics' option, launches the Help Window for Paint.  The Help Window is divided into two frames.  The frame on the left is the Help Topics index and the frame on the right is where the information appears.  There are three ways to search the Help Topics list, by selecting:

- **Contents** - This enables you to find the topic on which you need help by selecting from expandable directories until the topic appears
- **Index** - This lists all topics in alphabetical order
- **Search** - Enter the topic in which you are interested and Paint will find it

Whichever method you use, when you have found the required topic, step-by-step instructions will appear in the right hand frame.  You can choose to print out pages from the Help Menu by clicking on the Options button at the top of the Help window and selecting the Print command.

## What you need to know

The use of the various Tools available in Paint

What is the function of 'Print Preview'?

How to switch between foreground colour and background colour

What is the difference between 'Flip' and 'Rotate'?

The formats which can be handled by Paint

How do you add colours to the Colour Palette?

The shortcuts for Undo, Repeat, Cut, Copy, Paste and Select All

What is the function of 'Send'?

The artwork and imaging software in use in your organisation

Why is it important to check the content for suitability for purpose?

## More advanced functions

While Microsoft Paint is capable of performing most of the functions that you will use on a day-to-day basis, there are other functions that you will need to have knowledge of. These are available in a number of other software applications including Paint Shop Pro, Photoshop, Fireworks and Corel Draw.

Probably the most useful advanced function is using effects. Available effects include:

- **Black Pencil** - This mimics the result of drawing with a black pencil around an outline within an image to make it more prominent
- **Blinds** - This mimics the result of applying horizontal or vertical blinds

- **Brush Strokes** - This makes a photographic image resemble a water colour
- **Charcoal** - This mimics the result of drawing with charcoal
- **Chrome** - This applies a metallic patina to the image
- **Coloured Chalk** - This mimics the result of drawing with chalk
- **Contours** - This changes images into topographical maps
- **Cutout** - By selecting an area and converting it into a cutout you give the impression of looking through the image to a recessed area
- **Drop Shadow** - This places a shadow behind selected areas
- **Enamel** - This applies a shiny coating to the image
- **Feedback** - This makes an image appear to be reflected inwards in a series of concentric mirrors
- **Fur effect** - This makes images appear bristly
- **Glowing Edges** - This colours the edges of images in neon while blackening other parts of the image
- **Kaleidoscope** - This mimics looking at an image through a kaleidoscope
- **Lights** - This spotlights images with up to five spotlights
- **Mosaic-Antique** - This mimics applying antique tiles to an image
- **Neon Glow** - This applies neon colours to an image
- **Page Curl** - This rolls up one corner of the image
- **Pattern** - This creates patterns from any image
- **Pencil** - This turns images into pencil drawings
- **Polished Stone** - This makes images appear to have been carved out of shiny stone
- **Sculpture** - This embosses the image and applies a coloured pattern
- **Texture** - This mimics an image painted on a textured background
- **Tiles** - This makes an image look as if it was created from tiles
- **Weave** - This applies a basketwork effect to images

A more advanced function is to add layers to images. These are separate, transparent levels and, subject to computer memory size, you can use as many as 100 layers. There are three kinds of layers:

- **Raster** - These host pixel-related data and can only be created in greyscale images or images with at least 16 million colours
- **Vector** - These hold vector objects, e.g. shapes and text and can be added to any image
- **Adjustment** - These contain colour correction data and can only be created in greyscale images or images with at least 16 million colours

Another useful function is to use filters.  There are a variety of filters available:

- **Edge Enhance** - This amplifies edge contrast to increase the clarity of the image
- **Find Edges** - This darkens the image and emphasises its edges to increase the clarity of the image
- **Horizontal Edges** - This darkens the image and emphasises its horizontal edges
- **Vertical Edges** - This darkens the image and emphasises its vertical edges
- **Trace Contour** - This outlines the image by defining a border around it
- **Edge Preserving** - This removes 'noise' from the image without loss of edge detail
- **Blur** - This lightens pixels adjoining the hard edges of the image making for a hazy effect
- **Soften** - This reduces graininess in the image
- **Sharpen** - This improves the focus and clarity of the image
- **Dilate** - This enhances the light areas in the image
- **Median** - This reduces the image 'noise'
- **Texture Preserving** - This removes image 'noise' without loss of texture detail
- **Average** - This removes 'noise' spread over the whole of the image
- **Salt and Pepper** - This removes 'noise' and specks from photographs

Alignment devices can be added to images to ensure that selections, vector objects and brush strokes are automatically positioned.  Grids, which are a network of horizontal and vertical lines, can be applied to images to align objects more accurately.  Guides can be created by use of the horizontal and vertical rulers.

There are a wide variety of graphic formats used in different artwork and imaging software. These are divided into three groups:

- **Bitmaps** - Consist of coloured dots
- **Vectors** - Are defined by equations
- **Metas** - Are blanket formats which explicitly allow the inclusion of bitmap and vector data as well as text annotations

Examples of bitmap formats include:

- **JPEG** - Joint Photographic Experts Group. Used for photographic storage especially on the Internet
- **PNG** - Portable Network Graphics. Used occasionally on the Web
- **TIFF** - Tagged Image File Format. Widely used across a range of applications
- **BMP** - Used to produce large files
- **GIF** - Graphics Interchange Format. Widely used on the Internet as almost any Windows programme can read it, but it can handle only 256 colours
- **PSD** - A Photo Shop format which supports layering

The most widely used vector format is EPS which combines vector and bitmap data with a low resolution informational bitmap header.

The most widely used meta format is WMF or Windows Metafile which is used for data exchange between almost all Windows programmes.

Other formats that you will encounter include:

- **RTF** - Rich Text Format. Understood by many word processing programmes and often used when a document is created in one programme and needs to be edited in another
- **HTML** - HyperText Markup Language. Used in the creation of Web pages
- **PCT** - Macintosh PICT Graphics format. This can be used on Apple Macs or imported into Windows using a Macintosh PICT graphics filter

As with most computer software applications only practice will enable you to uncover the full range of capabilities.

# What you need to know

Other artwork and imaging software
packages available in the market place

What effects are available and what are
their uses?

The legislation relevant to artwork and
imaging

What filters are available and what are
their uses?

How to check the content and layout for
accuracy

What are the differences between
bitmaps, vectors and metas?

The different types of layers that are
available

What is JPEG commonly used for?

In this chapter we have given detailed information on the use
of Microsoft Paint, one of the more common software
applications in use in business and administration.  There is a
vast range of alternative programmes available and, in a
book of this nature, clearly we can't give detailed information
on all of them.  You will need to find out which programmes
are in use in your organisation and obtain the user manuals
to learn their features.

## It used to be said
## 'the camera never lies .........'

# Are you ready for assessment?

To achieve this unit of a Level 3 Business & Administration qualification you will need to demonstrate that you are competent in the following:

- Use file handling techniques appropriate to the software
- Create drawings, artwork and images
- Insert, manipulate and edit artwork and images
- Combine information of different types
- Check images to ensure they are fit for purpose
- Check text for accuracy, consistency and layout

(Remember that you will need the skills listed at the beginning of this chapter.  These are covered in chapter 1.)

You will need to produce evidence from a variety of sources. Carrying out the following activities will help you acquire competence at work.

**Activity 1**
Research the artwork and imaging software in use in your organisation. Read the user manuals and question colleagues competent in their use. Make notes of the information you collect on the features and functions of the software and how to use it

**Activity 2**
Using the artwork and imaging software available to you, create a series of images that you can use to illustrate your organisation's emergency procedures.  Make sure the images are compatible with current Health and Safety regulations.

**Activity 3**
Obtain a photograph of the premises in which you work.  Use the photo to create a design for your organisation's next Christmas card.  Add appropriate text to the card.

**Activity 4**
Design a multi-coloured A4 poster for display on the office notice board to advertise a forthcoming training and development programme OR a Social Club event.  Use at least two effects in your design.

**Activity 5**
Design promotional material for your department or organisation's products or services.  Use at least two effects, four colours and layers when creating your promotional material.

Remember:  While gathering evidence for this unit, evidence **may** be generated for units 110, 212, 213, 218, 301, 302, 320 and 321.

# CHAPTER 27
# UNIT 318 – Design and produce documents

The layout and accuracy of documents produced in any organisation is very important. The key to this is the amount of preparation that you put into it. Most organisations have an agreed policy about the way their documents look to ensure consistency and quality, often referred to as the 'house-style'. The type of document you are asked to design will determine the style you should use. Before actually starting to design any document make sure you have all the resources you will need and that you have considered the most appropriate layout to use.

It has been said that first impressions are made within thirty seconds. The first impression a potential customer gets of your organisation could have a vital effect on their decision whether to do business with your company. A well-designed, correctly spelt, grammatical and accurately punctuated document will create a positive impression which will last.

There is a wide range of software available that will help you to produce the highest quality documents possible. Remember that there are a number of different features that can be added such as images, graphs, tables or diagrams. These should be used with care however, and in agreement with the author of the document. You will also need to follow your organisation's agreed procedures.

After designing a new document you will need to get it approved by the person responsible in your organisation for ensuring that all company documentation is legal, comprehensive and adheres to the organisational house style.

After producing your document it should be checked carefully, errors in spelling or grammar could have a potentially disastrous effect. During production regularly save the document and give it a file name in accordance with your organisation's policy.

Both during the design and production of documents it is important to bear in mind the question of confidentiality and the security of the information contained. Any personal information may be subject to the Data Protection Act 1998, and there may also be commercially sensitive information which would be valuable to a competitor.

Before being printed off the document will need to be stored electronically. After production it will need to be stored in hard copy. In both formats the important thing is that it can be found easily.

 When designing and producing documents you will use the following skills:

- Listening
- Questioning
- Negotiating
- Reading
- Researching
- Organising
- Designing
- Writing
- Using technology
- Checking
- Managing time

These skills are covered in chapter 1.

# Designing documents

There are three types of documents you may be asked to design; stationery, promotional material and forms. Information on structuring reports can be found in Chapter 19.

Most documents are printed on A4 paper (210mm x 297mm) but you may want to consider A5 (half of A4) for memos and leaflets or A6 (half of A5) for brochures.

Stationery design will include letter heads, compliment slips, business cards, memos and fax cover sheets.

**Letterheads**:

- The first thing to decide is the size of the paper
- Letterheads are almost certain to be A4 as they will have to feed through a printer and fit into standard sized envelopes.  If you are going to use window envelopes there is a British Standard which gives guidelines on the areas to be left blank in order that the address appears in the window
- The next things to consider are colour and font.  Do you want black on white or coloured ink on white paper or coloured ink on coloured paper?  Does your organisation have a logo which will need to be incorporated?  Would you prefer a classic, modern or artistic style of font?
- The next things to consider are what information you want to show.  Obviously you will need your organisation's name and address, but do they have a Registered Office?  If so this must be shown as well.  You will also want to show an e-mail address, telephone number, fax number and, if applicable, VAT Registration Number and Company Registration Number
- Where on the page do you want the information to appear?  You might want to put the name and address on the top of the page and all other information on the bottom; you may want all information on the top and only the Company Registration Number and VAT Numbers on the bottom
- Finally, do you want to position things like date, your ref., my ref., on the page at the design stage?  If the letterhead is designed to be used as a template on a

word processor these can be included. If the letterhead is designed to be printed and then used as headed paper, it may be best to leave these to be added at the time the letter is being typed as it is often difficult to line up entries with fixed points on the page

**Matthew and Son Builders**
**Allington Place**
**West Billington**
**WB1 1AD**
**Tel:0224 566854**
**info@matthews.co.uk**

Our ref:   GM/RA/124
Your ref:   VH/AK

17 March 2005

Mr V Harmison
Oval Walk
West Billington
WB2 1AX

Dear Mr Harmison

Thank you for your letter dated 14 March 2005 accepting our quotation to extend your office building.

The work will commence on Monday next and will be completed within 6 working weeks.

If you have any queries please do not hesitate to contact me.

Yours sincerely
Matthew and Son Builders

*G Matthew*

Graham Matthew
Director

Registered office 12 The Street, West Billington, WB3 5JH
VAT Registration Number 123 4560 78
Registration Number 123456

## Compliment slips and business cards

As these are usually not designed to be typed on, it is not as critical that they are of a standard size to fit in a printer. However the optimum size for a compliment slip is the size of a DL envelope, as this means it can be posted without folding. Business cards need to be of a size that will fit conveniently into a wallet or card holder.

The colour and font used on compliment slips and business cards will usually reflect those chosen for letterheads. Compliment slips will contain the words 'with compliments' as well as all of the information on letterheads except Company Registration Number and VAT Registration Number. Business cards will also have the name and direct telephone number of the individual carrying them as well as their job title.

**Memos** should ideally be A5 size, as this will be sufficient for the vast majority of occasions where a memo will be used. You may want to design an A4 version for those occasions where a longer memo is required. They are usually printed black on white unless the organisation's logo requires colour printing. They should be headed 'memorandum' or 'memo' so that the reader can easily identify them as such. Memos from senior members of the organisation may be identified by headings such as 'memo from the Chairman' or 'from the office of the Chief Executive'. If designed as a computer template 'To', 'From', 'Date' and 'Subject' can be positioned.

```
┌────────────────────────────────────────────────────────┐
│                    MEMORANDUM                          │
│                                                        │
│  To:       All selling staff                           │
│                                                        │
│  From:     Sales Manager                               │
│                                                        │
│  Date:     27th August 2005                            │
│                                                        │
│  Subject:  Sales targets                               │
│                                                        │
│  Last week saw total sales of £127,436, an increase    │
│  of 3.1% on last year.                                 │
│  This week we have a challenging target of £148,000,   │
│  or 3.7% on last year.                                 │
│  This will require 100% effort from all of us, but I   │
│  am confident we can do it.                            │
│                                                        │
│  REMEMBER THE PROMOTION ON DISPOSABLE BARBECUES.       │
└────────────────────────────────────────────────────────┘
```

**Fax cover sheets** will probably be A4 size as this is the most convenient for feeding through a fax machine. They are printed black on white as colour is not transmitted and should be headed 'Facsimile'. The only information needed is 'To', 'Fax No.', 'From', 'Fax No.' and 'Number of pages'. You should also leave plenty of space for the message to be added. Following the number of pages, a note reading 'if not all pages are received please telephone................' is useful.

```
┌────────────────────────────────────────────────────────┐
│                     FACSIMILE                          │
│  To:           Peter Robinson                          │
│                Motor Vehicle Repairs                   │
│                                                        │
│  Fax No:       02274 55369                             │
│                                                        │
│  From:         Ronald R. Barker                        │
│                Paving Co. Ltd.                         │
│                                                        │
│  Fax No:       02564 33465                             │
│                                                        │
│  No of Pages:  1 plus this cover sheet                 │
└────────────────────────────────────────────────────────┘
```

The design of promotional material and forms is more complex than the design of stationery. There are a number of rules involved in typographic design which need to be understood and used:

- Bigger or bolder type is seen as more important than smaller or lighter type

- Things that look alike are seen as belonging to the same group
- Things that are close together are seen as belonging to the same group
- Things enclosed in a space are seen as belonging to the same group
- Things that line up with each other are seen as belonging to the same group
- About one in eight men has red-green colour deficiency, so avoid the use of colour coding
- Yellow text on a white background is illegible

Promotional materials include catalogues, brochures and leaflets.

**Catalogues:**

- The size and number of pages in a catalogue is determined by two factors; how much needs to go into it and how much it is going to cost to produce and distribute
- You will certainly want to introduce colour into the design but it is advisable to seek advice from your printer as you will need to specify exact shades of colour and whether the colour is to be applied as a solid or a tint
- You will want to use illustrations, whether they be photographs or line drawings.  Be careful to make the illustrations big enough to enable the reader to easily see what is being illustrated
- Sort the content into categories that the reader will be able to understand so that they can find the item they are looking for easily.  Include a content list and an index to help; if people can't find what they are looking for easily, they will look elsewhere

**Brochures and leaflets:**

- These need to be of a size that will easily fit into a pocket or bag.  This will usually mean A5 at most and probably A6 at best, although some may be printed on A4 paper folded into thirds
- Content must be plain and convincing in its meaning but interesting and memorable to read.  It is not essential to fill all the space available, people will

often be dissuaded from reading brochures or leaflets that look too wordy

- Text should be hard-hitting, with short paragraphs and bullet points used to make it easy to read. Colour can be used to highlight particularly important points
- Use illustrations to reinforce the point you are making; photographs, drawings, charts and graphs are all powerful images as long as they are relevant
- If you are designing a brochure you will effectively have at least four pages on which to present your information. Decide what is going on which page first. Use the front page for impact and the back page for detailed information
- Decide how big the illustrations are going to be in relation to the text and where they are to be placed. Remember to leave a 'bleed margin' of a tenth of an inch (2mm) all around the page to allow for cutting of the paper to size

**Forms** usually contain pre-printed information fields to be filled in later. Good form design encourages people to fill correct information into the correct field. It is important to have the correct fields to ensure you get the information you need. There are a number of things to take into account when designing a new form:

- Notes explaining how to fill in the form should appear at the beginning of the form
- The number of pre-printed words should be kept to a minimum, for instance 'address' rather than 'write your address here'
- Tick boxes are a space-saving device. If you try to draw a square for use as a tick box you may encounter problems if you later try to amend the text. Use a tick box character from the Wingdings font (□) instead
- Signature boxes should be 2½ inches x ¾ inch (60mm x 20mm) to allow space for a normal signature
- Address boxes should contain five lines
- Written answer boxes should allow a ¼ inch (6mm) space between each line

**Jane & Ian Books Ltd.**
Rosedale Avenue, London, SE19 3NW
Tel:020 7075 6541

# Order Form

(PLEASE COMPLETE ALL FIELDS IN BLOCK CAPITALS)

Name
Organisation
Address

Town
Postcode
Email
Telephone

| Title | Price | Qty | Totals |
|-------|-------|-----|--------|
| Better Digital Photography | £21.99 | | £   . |
| Digital Photography for Beginners | £16.99 | | £   . |
| Postage & Packing | £2.95/order | ---- | £   . |
| | | Total | £   . |

**Payment Details**
Please invoice me, using the address above ☐
I have enclosed a Cheque made payable to 'Jane & Ian Books Ltd' ☐
Please debit my credit/debit card ☐
Visa ☐          Master card ☐          Switch ☐

Card Number

Expires End          _/__   Valid from (if applicable)          _/__

Issue No (if applicable)   ___   Last 3 digits of the security No   _____

Poorly designed documents can affect the efficiency of the organisation, so it is well worth taking time to design them as well as possible. Good design will result in an improved company image, increased sales and reduced costs.

# What you need to know

The benefits of well designed stationery

How do well designed catalogues improve sales?

The information that must be included on company letterheads

What documents **must** show the VAT Registration Number if the organisation is VAT registered?

The standard paper sizes

Why should colour coding be avoided?

# Producing documents

Preparation made at an early stage will save you time later. If your organisation has a 'house style' (the layout of a document) make sure that you use it, if not you may be able to set up templates for standard documents on your computer, this will save you time when you are producing that type of document again.  Whatever type of document

you produce you must confirm the purpose, content, style, quality standards and deadline.  You will need to know by when the document is required in order to prioritise your work.

To produce any document you clearly need a computer, a printer and stationery resources.  These may include:

- **Printer** – Media (which gives you a choice of paper), quality settings (best, normal or draft) and colour or black and white
- **Paper** – Headed, letter quality or copy quality
- **Envelopes** - Letters to external addresses will need good quality envelopes while internal memos may be sent using internal envelopes which can be used a number of times.  Consideration should be given to the size of envelope needed.  A document shouldn't be folded more than twice to fit into an envelope. Documents with several pages should be placed flat in an envelope

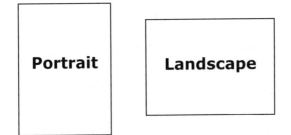

Research the information you need to include in the document. This may come from any number of sources, including the letter you are replying to, previous reports, databases, the Internet and other files. Having decided the content you want to use, you will need to organise it so that you can find it when you need it. It may be useful to produce a first draft so you can see where the content fits into the whole. For a long or complex document you may want to draft the topics or headings to organise the content before writing the detail. You will then want to consider:

- The size of paper to use
- Whether to present your document in portrait or landscape form (orientation). Most standard documents are presented in portrait form. Landscape is used for tables and spreadsheets where it is helpful to be able to see the full row of information at a glance
- Any diagrams or tables you may want to insert into your document. Diagrams will usually be imported from elsewhere, tables are produced from the 'table' menu

Probably the greatest advantage that the word processor has over the typewriter is the opportunity to edit. Functions of the word processor in common use include:

- **Delete** - This allows you to delete a single letter at a time. To delete a whole word at a time use 'ctrl+delete'
- **Paste** (Ctrl+v) - This is used in combination with either the 'cut' or 'copy' instruction. Paste will add the last data selected to the document
- **Cut** (Ctrl+x) - You can highlight a piece of text and remove it from the document. This command then allows you to paste the text elsewhere in the document
- **Copy** (Ctrl+c) - This is used in combination with the 'paste' instruction to duplicate previously entered data
- **Find and replace** (Ctrl+f) - This function is used to change all the examples of a particular word to another word. For instance if you are asked to write a report and you use the word 'company' several times and are then asked to substitute the word 'organisation' there is no need to retype it, use 'find and replace' to change all the examples
- **Inserting special characters and symbols** - This enables you to use a wide range of non-Arabic letters and other signs e.g. ©, é, 'Ω, %
- **Mail merge -** This function is useful if the same letter is going to several recipients, it allows you to change the name and address without having to re-type the whole letter
- **Track changes** - Any changes that are made to text will be highlighted

At any stage during the production of a document you can amend the format of the text. There are various options available in the format menu. It is possible to format characters, pages or whole sections. If you use a format for part of the document and want to use it again later, you can select 'styles and formatting' and the software will show you what you have used previously in the document.

Whatever you are producing you will need to produce it in the accepted style. The style will differ between:

- **Memos** - These will usually simply state the name of the recipient, the name of the sender and the content. They may have the recipient and sender's job titles and departments. They may have the recipient and sender's job titles and departments.
- **Letters** - There is a convention that business letters are produced fully blocked and with open punctuation. Fully blocked means all parts of the document start at the left hand margin. Open punctuation omits all punctuation except that in the body of the letter which is essential for grammatical accuracy and ease of understanding. Business letters are also laid out in a fixed sequence:
  - Salutation (e.g. Dear Sir or Madam for formal letters and Dear Mrs Smith or Dear Jane for less formal letters)
  - Heading, this is not essential but is common business practice
  - Opening paragraph, to introduce the communication
  - Main message, action or results
  - Closing paragraph
  - Complimentary closure (e.g. Yours faithfully in a very formal letter and Yours sincerely in standard business communications)
  - Space for a signature
  - The name and job title or department of the person who is sending the letter
- **Promotional material** - You may need to give each page a header and footer, or page number. It is also possible to number paragraphs and include an index or table of contents to help the reader find their way around the document. Any picture, diagram or table already held on your hard drive or on a disk can be imported. You can also import objects from other

software on your computer, or through a connected scanner or digital camera, or from the Internet. Care will need to be taken when importing non-text objects. Their positioning and size must be carefully considered. Beware the use of images for their own sake.

Remember in a letter 'less is more' where pictures and diagrams are concerned. In brochures and leaflets pictures and diagrams can certainly add to the impact, but you must take care that they are used only when they are relevant and can add to the content.

 **What you need to know**

How to use your word processing package

> Does your organisation have its own house style?

How to make appropriate use of images

> Where would you find appropriate images for a brochure advertising the Cricket World Cup?

The differences in layout between memos, letters, brochures and leaflets

> Would you be able to manipulate images to fit the purpose?

The reasons for changing the orientation of documents

> If you were asked to change every example of 'and' in a catalogue to '&' which function would you use?

## Checking and storing documents

When you have completed the document it is essential that you check for accuracy, edit and correct as necessary. Most word processing packages contain spell checking and grammar checking facilities. Use these first to correct the more glaring errors, but don't rely on them entirely. Check that they are set to English (UK) as many default to English

(US). This can be altered by clicking on the Tools menu and selecting 'Spelling and Grammar'. Select English (UK) from the drop down menu. When the automatic checking is complete, **_read_** the document carefully to look for missed errors, and also for correct use of paragraphs, headings and sub-headings, style and formatting. You may find it useful to remember the 'Five Cs' when checking your documents:

- **Conciseness** - Have you used as few words as possible? Remember, short sentences are best. Avoid the use of conjunctions. Aim to write sentences of 12 – 15 words. Don't use jargon. Try to avoid the use of words with more than three syllables unless this is unavoidable. That way you will learn to write clear and unambiguous business documents
- **Completeness** - Is everything the reader needs there?
- **Courtesy** - Have you been open, welcoming and polite to the reader?
- **Clarity** - Will the reader understand your point?
- **Correctness** - Are all statements absolutely accurate and true?

Be particularly careful to proof-read numbers, dates, times and amounts. Check for errors between similar words such as 'affect' and 'effect' or 'less' and 'fewer'.

You will need to present the document by the agreed deadline and in the style required. If unforeseen circumstances mean that you need to change the style or content, or that you will be unable to meet the agreed deadline, it is important that you report the fact as soon as the situation arises. It is too late to know that a deadline will not be met when the deadline arrives. It is not acceptable to lower the agreed quality standards in order to meet the deadline.

Documents may be stored in hard copy or electronically. Your organisation will have a system for filing hard copies. Electronically the document can be stored by using the 'save as' function on the word processor and naming the document appropriately. There may be a system for naming files such as the originator's initials followed by the date, for example. You may group files into folders for ease of retrieval. Confidential or sensitive documents may be password protected.

With paper records it will be necessary to store the document safely and securely. There are a number of different methods that can be used:

- **Alphabetical** - Filed in order from A – Z. Files starting with the same letter are filed in order of the second letter (Aa, Ab, Ac) and so on. People's names are filed by their surnames and if more than one person has the same surname, then by their first names too, e.g. D Smith, J Smith, T Smith. Names starting with 'The' are filed by ignoring the 'The' e.g. The Federation of Small Businesses and The Mortgage Corporation would be filed under F and M
- **Numerical** - Files are given numbers and filed from 1 to infinity. This is useful for information which naturally lends itself to being filed this way (purchase orders, sales invoices, for instance). There is a difficulty where, for instance, all customers are given numbers and their records filed numerically. If you don't know the customer's number you can't find their file. This can lead to the necessity of keeping an alphabetical list to cross-refer to the customer's number
- **Alpha-numerical** - Files have a combination of letters and numbers. Examples include Postal Codes, National Insurance Numbers, Car Registration Numbers, etc. These are usually large databases as they hold more information than numerical systems and are more flexible than alphabetical systems. The order of filing depends on the sequence of the file name. If file names start with letters followed by

numbers, they are filed in alphabetical order first, and numerical order within each letter

- **Chronological** - This is often used within one of the other methods.  For instance, each customer record is filed alphabetically but the information within the file is stored chronologically, usually with the latest at the front.  This enables a picture of the activity to be gained

Whichever method is adopted if the information is not stored accurately it will be extremely difficult to find.

 **What you need to know**

The use of spell check and grammar check

What are the 'Five Cs'?

How to spell, punctuate and use correct grammar

If you were responsible for the filing of vehicle records by registration number which filing method would you recommend?

Your organisation's convention for naming electronic files

What are the advantages and disadvantages of using alphabetical and numerical filing systems?

The benefits of placing electronic files in folders

Do you know the difference between 'there', 'they're' and 'their'?

When you are producing any document, ask yourself 'for whom am I writing?' Knowing your reader shapes the tone and content of documents. Remember to write to the reader but not down to the reader. Don't allow yourself to believe that correct spelling, punctuation and grammar are old-fashioned conventions. They enable you to communicate your ideas accurately and articulately to your reader. Without them it is easy for your meaning to be misunderstood.

**Well designed and produced documents will be a source of personal satisfaction as well as improved organisational performance**

# Are you ready for assessment?

To achieve this unit of a Level 3 Business & Administration qualification you will need to demonstrate that you are competent in the following:

- Agree the purpose, content, style, quality standards and deadlines for the document
- Identify and prepare the resources you need
- Research and organise the content you need
- Make efficient use of the technology available
- Design and produce the document in the agreed style
- Integrate non-text objects in the agreed layout
- Check for accuracy, editing and correcting as necessary
- Store the document safely and securely in an approved location
- Present the document in the required format within agreed deadlines and quality standards

(Remember that you will need the skills listed at the beginning of this chapter. These are covered in chapter 1.)

You will need to produce evidence from a variety of sources. Carrying out the following activities will help you acquire competence at work.

**Activity 1**
Correct those of the following which are incorrect:

Would we have less problems if we had fewer departments?
Neither Edinburgh or Glasgow is in England.
The customers are always right.
The customer's always right.
The ship's crew was up to its full complement.
The customer's are always right.
The Special Affects Department said that the cuts in their compliment would effect their ability to meet there deadlines.
The Cheif Executive Officer said it was a lie to say that the blame for the accident laid with his deportment.

How many administrators does it take to change a light bulb
The Chair said I will not be able to chair the next meeting I will be on holiday
The computers screens were reflecting the sun and nobody could see it.
The staff canteen had included carrot's and pea's on the new menu.
Wanted, person to operate new computer system that doesn't smoke and drink
She left the document on the desk that she had not completed typing.
To boldly go where no man has never gone before.
'I just hung that phone up'.

**Activity 2**
Design a memo for use in your department.

**Activity 3**
Write a report suggesting ways in which the design of your organisation's current brochures, catalogues and stationery can be improved.  Consider the best way to order the contents of the report. Include charts, graphics, illustrations and photographs where necessary.

**Activity 4**
Design three alternative styles of letterhead to use in your organisation each containing the same information in different layouts.

**Activity 5**
Design a brochure to be used in your organisation using the following:
- Illustrations
- Photographs
- Drawings
- Charts and graphs

**Activity 6**
Design promotional material to be used in your organisation using the following:
- Headers and footers
- Page numbering
- Table of Contents
- Index
- Pictures
- Tables
- Objects imported from a scanner

**Activity 7**
Design a catalogue to be used in your organisation using the following:
- Colour
- Illustrations
- Photographs
- Line drawings
- Table of Contents
- Index

Remember:  While gathering evidence for this unit, evidence **may** be generated for units 110, 212, 213, 301, 302, 314, 320, 321, 322, 323 and 324.

# CHAPTER 28
# UNIT 319 – Plan and implement innovation and change

The most important factor in building a successful organisation is the management of change. It is the only way for organisations to grow and, for those in the commercial sector, to remain competitive. Attempting to resist change is futile. By resisting change you will find yourself left behind by the changes which will occur regardless of your opinion. That results in playing a constant game of catch up with those who embraced the change. You may see those who are constantly seeking to make changes as risk takers but in reality there is more risk in seeking to preserve the status quo.

Almost all change brings both positive and negative results and some people often find it easier to see the negative points initially. Positive results will often take longer to materialise. It may even be difficult to see the positive effects of changes such as the development of a new software package. Your initial reaction may be one of irritation as you have to learn the new software. Perseverance will prove that the new software has many advantages and you will soon wonder what you ever saw in its predecessor.

The catalyst for change can come from one of three areas:

- **Social reasons** - Organisations are affected by the society in which they operate. Demographics, geographical spread and levels of education all inform the range of goods and services made available
- **Economic reasons** - Increase or decrease in the basic standard of living, levels of unemployment, exchange rates and inflation can all impact on the demand for different goods and services
- **Technological reasons** - Methods of production and systems of work are changing rapidly with the continuous development of new technology. Organisations must adapt the way that they do things or become uncompetitive

The engine for innovation to keep an organisation ahead of social, economic and technological change must be the people who work in that organisation. Some organisations are very open about change and train their staff to welcome it with open arms. But others can treat change in different ways. Often the hierarchy of an organisation will encourage lower levels of staff to suggest minor changes and only let senior staff to suggest major or radical changes. The role of middle management is seen as communicating the major changes to subordinates stressing the advantages, while allowing the minor changes to take place. The risk in this strategy is that the subordinates may have ideas for radical changes which they have no opportunity to suggest and, therefore, these ideas are lost. Middle management must ensure that ideas flow in both directions with equal facility.

It is important to react to changes caused by external influences. Potential changes must be analysed to ensure opportunities are maximised and any negative aspects minimised. Anticipating the external change before it happens allows you to be proactive in your response. If you are unable to anticipate the change your response can only be reactive. Changes can be gradual or dramatic. Dramatic changes are often brought about by careful planning and implementation, or in reaction to a crisis which demands an immediate and reactive response. There is no time for debate, action must be taken rapidly and decisively. Once the immediate crisis is averted it is important to look ahead and plan ways in which future crises can be anticipated and their effect minimised.

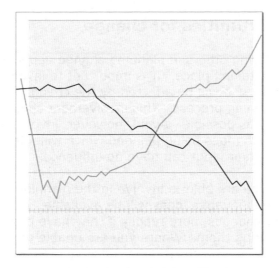

Organisations inevitably change over time. They will follow a life cycle of creation, expansion, contraction and decline. Even apparently indestructible 'organisations' such as empires finally decline and fall. The goal of any organisation is to extend the period of expansion for as long as possible. The acceptance of the need to continuously innovate helps to delay the eventual contraction and decline. Many innovations are fuelled by the need to stay ahead of your competitors. There is a risk in following a policy of change for change's sake. Change should bring recognisable and measurable benefits to both staff and customers.

When planning and implementing innovation and change you will use the following skills:

- Evaluating
- Planning
- Organising
- Communicating
- Negotiating
- Managing resources
- Analysing
- Motivating
- Problem solving
- Decision making

These skills are covered in chapter 1.

# Planning opportunities for change

The timing of involving others in planning change depends on the type of change taking place. It is important to involve as many of the people who will be affected by the change as possible in the planning process. This involvement should take place as early as possible. Avoid, however, involving others too soon in changes being planned which will affect them but in which their input can have no influence.

The more people you are able to involve in the planning process, the more innovative ideas will be available. Also people will accept changes more readily if they have been involved in structuring them. Where you are unable to involve people because the situation is sensitive or change is being imposed externally and there is no room for manoeuvre, inform them as soon as possible of the change and explain why you were unable to tell them previously.

You should set an example to your team by being positive about change and contributing to any debate about the need for change within your area. Give your team goals to achieve in bringing about the change and give them as much autonomy in reaching these as possible. Make the goals SMART:

- **Specific** - 'Increase sales' is an objective, but it is not specific, whereas 'increase sales by 10%' is
- **Measurable** - There must be a system in place to record the achievement of the specific objective. For instance, to measure whether sales have been increased by 10% there must be a record of sales prior to the objective being set and after the objective has been set
- **Achievable** - The objective must be capable of being reached, without being too easy. If there is no possibility of improving sales by 10% then setting it as an objective will achieve absolutely nothing as nobody will make any attempt to achieve it. Much better to set an achievable objective of 5%
- **Relevant** - The objective has to be meaningful to the organisation but also relevant to what the person being set the objective is able to control. There is no point in telling the accounts department that they need to improve sales by 10% as there is nothing they can do about it

- **Time based** - There has to be a date by which the objective is to be achieved. If you set an objective of improving sales by 10% without saying by when, how will you know if it has been achieved

Empower people to initiate change. Teams who are entrusted with planning change will accept the change more readily and indeed will be keen to look for further changes that they can initiate. Conduct surveys with your staff to identify where there is a desire for change. Use the information gathered and involve those who are looking for improvements at work in the change process. Integrate the feedback you have received from customers to identify where changes can benefit them.

Pareto's Law states 80% of problems are generated by 20% of an organisation's activities. Concentrate your innovation on that 20% and you will avoid overloading your staff with too many changes in a short period of time. Organise a rolling programme of change which gives everybody involved time to absorb the effects of one change before they are required to start on another. Avoid abandoning one initiative in favour of another before the first has had time to be fully evaluated as the staff will see this as evidence of a lack of decisiveness and will resist change on the grounds that it will only be transitory.

Change projects require detailed planning. Make an outline plan then fill in the details. For each step decide:

- The required outcome
- How the outcome can be achieved
- How long it will take
- Who will be responsible
- Whether any training is required

When you have completed your detailed plan, check that it meets the following requirements:

- The reason for change is explained
- The desired outcomes are identified
- The route to those outcomes is mapped
- Necessary resources are available
- Communication has been considered
- The need to modify behaviour has been identified
- The individuals responsible have been selected
- The timetable has been set
- Tracking systems have been put in place
- Contingency plans have been included

Before communicating the detailed plan to those involved and the decision-makers, check that it is practical and workable by discussing it with colleagues who may have some experience of implementing similar proposals.  Be prepared to change the details if discussion highlights a problem that you hadn't previously considered.  When you are satisfied that the plan is viable present it as concisely as possible.

 **What you need to know**

The reasons why change is inevitable

How are people an engine for innovation?

The catalysts for change

What is the difference between a proactive and a reactive response to change?

How to react to external changes positively

What should be the next step following
the averting of a crisis?

The benefits of involving others in the
planning process

Why must goals be SMART?

The benefits of empowering people to
initiate change

What is Pareto's Law?

## Implementing change

The critical issue in implementing a change is
communication.  Tell everybody who hasn't been involved in
planning the change as soon as possible to avoid
resentments and confusion.  Don't believe in the adage 'need
to know', telling people only what they need to know
prevents them being aware of any wider implications and will
reduce their commitment to the plan.  If you don't tell them
everything, they will inevitably hear it 'on the grapevine' and
will be suspicious of your reasons for keeping them in the
dark.

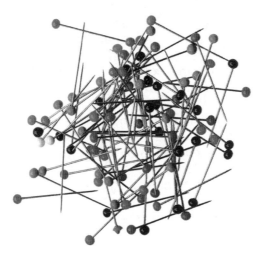

Wherever possible communicate changes verbally as well as
in writing as this will give people the opportunity to discuss
and query the details.  Be prepared to answer queries in as
much depth as possible.  This will increase your colleagues'
understanding and hence their acceptance of the need for
change.  Where changes will adversely affect some

individuals more than others, speak to them individually before announcing the change generally.

Where the change is adverse, it is important that you are realistic when telling people. Attempting to 'sugar the pill' by holding out false hopes will only exacerbate the situation when you have to admit that the worst has happened. Give the reasons for the news honestly and the recipients, while they wont like what they hear, should not blame you for having to be the bearer of bad news. Be sympathetic and if necessary apologetic but be clear that the change is inevitable.

You will need to demonstrate to your team that you are committed to the change. You must set an example by being positive and actively implementing the change. Hold regular meetings with your team to discuss the implications and progress of the change. Encourage members of your team to give feedback and be prepared to make modifications if genuine opportunities or difficulties are identified.

Look out for signs of resistance and try to identify the reasons. If you face active resistance remember that there are often valid reasons for it. Try to find out what they are and deal with them openly. If the resistance is entirely unfounded seek out the ringleaders and attempt to persuade them of the benefits of the change. If they can't be persuaded find a way of minimising their influence. Don't react to aggression with aggression.

You may be faced with passive resistance. This is a situation where people don't argue about the change, they simply ignore it or block its implementation by failing to contribute. You may find it difficult to get hold of these people when you need them, or they may fail to attend agreed meetings. Encourage them to be open about their reasons for resisting the change by asking them individually to explain their position.

Resistance is generally based on one of three emotions:

- **Misunderstanding** - The reasons for and benefits of the change have not been communicated clearly
- **Fear** - The change has been understood but the potential consequences to the individual cause alarm

- **Distrust** - The individual is not totally convinced that all of the consequences have been fully explained, possibly because of a previous bad experience

Misunderstanding is overcome by explanation. Ask the individual to explain what it is in the planned change that is causing them a problem and explain where their misconception lies.

Fear is overcome by reassurance. It is either misplaced, in which case it can be relatively easily allayed or justified. The solution is to be honest and supportive.

Distrust is overcome by time. Most resistance disappears when the evidence tells the person that they were told the truth at the beginning of the process.

Change should be an ongoing process. Where they don't already exist you will need to put in place ways to measure and evaluate the effects of the change. It isn't sufficient to simply look at numerical indicators at regular intervals to measure the success or otherwise of the innovation. It is also necessary to take into account less obvious variables such as the effect on morale, staff turnover or absenteeism. If you have instigated, for instance, a change in the process for dealing with orders and the direct result is a 40% decrease in the time taken to process them, this will seem at first glance to have been a notable success. If, however, two of the three members of staff responsible for dealing with orders have handed in their notice and the third is regularly taking days off, the success is probably unsustainable.

Change can't be seen in isolation. The true measure of success is not whether the change met its immediate target but whether it solved the underlying problem that initiated the need for change. To take the above example, it may well be possible to overcome the immediate difficulty of staff resistance by recruiting new staff who have no experience of the situation prior to the change, and, therefore, producing a sustainable decrease in processing time. The question to be addressed then is 'what was the purpose of decreasing order processing time?'. If it was to solve a problem further along the system, has that problem been solved? The overriding purpose of change in any organisation must be either to increase income or reduce costs.

Evaluation of change may well indicate that the expected benefits have not materialised. This may be because the assumptions that supported the original plan were incorrect or because circumstances have changed since the planning stage. This doesn't necessarily mean that the change must be abandoned entirely. The results should be looked at in detail and a revised plan instigated which will achieve the original goals or, at least, as much of the original objective as possible. The revisions may even strengthen the change process as the weaknesses in the original plan are revealed and the opportunity arises to improve it.

Those responsible for implementing change will lose their enthusiasm over the course of time as they focus on other priorities. If several changes have been implemented simultaneously they may compete with each other for attention. Regularly measure attitudes towards each change and reinforce those which need further support. Don't assume that people are actively supporting change even if the predicted results are being achieved. Negative attitudes may be creeping in unnoticed and need to be recognised before they have a detrimental effect.

Possibly the biggest mistake that is made by agents of change is to stop planning when a change produces the intended result. You should always be looking ahead and planning for the next change. The success of the current change process will have altered the answer to the question 'where are we now?' and this should lead you to re-think the questions 'where do we want to be?' and 'how do we get there?'.

## What you need to know

When to communicate information on
changes

> What methods of communication
> should be used?

How to demonstrate your personal
commitment to change

> Why is it necessary to be realistic when
> communicating changes which may
> have adverse effects?

Ways to recognise resistance to change

> What are the different types of
> resistance that you may encounter?

How to overcome resistance to change

> Why is it important to encourage
> feedback on the effects of change?

The way to consolidate change and move
forward

> How do you measure the results of
> change?

There is no such thing as the perfect organisation or the
perfect process.  Everything can be improved.  Look at
everything in your organisation, including yourself, with a
critical eye.  Move forwards constantly and review
continuously but remember to celebrate your successes and
build on the results of change.

# Anyone who is not moving forwards is moving backwards

# Are you ready for assessment?

To achieve this unit of a Level 3 Business & Administration qualification you will need to demonstrate that you are competent in the following:

- Encourage individuals and teams to challenge existing ways of working
- Identify options for innovation and change
- Plan change, identifying your vision, goals, objectives, timescales and resources
- Agree plans for change with decision makers
- Communicate your plans for change
- Encourage colleagues to contribute to your plans
- Negotiate changes to your plans whilst still focusing on your vision and goals
- Implement change, providing information, support and motivation to those affected
- Identify and solve problems
- Monitor and evaluate change

(Remember that you will need the skills listed at the beginning of this chapter. These are covered in chapter 1.)

You will need to produce evidence from a variety of sources. Carrying out the following activities will help you acquire competence at work.

**Activity 1**
Call your team together to review all of the processes that you are responsible for and identify one which you feel would benefit from change. Create a plan for implementing the change, involving all the people who will be affected by the change and anyone whose permission is required.

**Activity 2**
Implement the change identified in Activity 1, communicating with all the parties involved. Keep a log of all the stages that you go through.

**Activity 3**
Monitor the effects of the change implemented in Activity 2. Keep a record of your monitoring activities.

**Activity 4**
Evaluate activities 1, 2 and 3.  Remember to evaluate the side effects as well as the achievement of the objective/s.  Review whether the underlying problem has been addressed.  Identify what, if anything, needs to be included in the next planning stage.

Remember:  While gathering evidence for this unit, evidence **may** be generated for units 110, 212, 213, 217, 301, 302, 303, 312, 314, 315, 320 and 321.

# CHAPTER 29
# UNIT 320 – Develop productive working relationships with colleagues

A dictionary definition of a colleague is 'a person somebody works with, especially in a professional or skilled job'. This is probably how you think of colleagues, those you share an office with or, at most, those who work for the same organisation that you do. Effectively, however, everybody you come across in your working life is your colleague. This includes all those who work in your organisation whether senior to yourself, junior to you or at a similar level and everybody you interact with outside of your organisation:

- Customers or clients
- Suppliers
- Contractors
- Government bodies such as Tax Offices, VAT
- Local Government officials such as Environmental Health officers, Planning department officers
- Professional advisors such as solicitors, accountants

Once you begin to think of all of these as your colleagues you can start to divide them into groups in a different way than you have in the past. Instead of categorising them as people inside your organisation or outside, you can classify them by their relative importance to your job role. They will each fall within one of three groups:

- Your **primary** contacts. These are the people you work with or come into contact with regularly, probably daily.  Your team, your line manager, your regular customers, your regular suppliers, external contacts that you rely on to enable you to carry out your responsibilities.  These contacts have a direct effect on your ability to do your job

- Your **secondary** contacts.  These are the people you work with or come into contact with less frequently, but you rely on their co-operation in order to carry out your responsibilities.  They will tend to include other departments in your organisation, external contacts such as the local planning department, the VAT office or the company solicitor

- Your **tertiary** contacts.  These are the people you work with or come into contact with only rarely but still need to have a relationship with in order that when you do need their co-operation it is likely to be available.  They may include Environmental Health officers, the Tax Office, senior management within your organisation

Remember, of course, that you will also fall into one of these categories as a contact of each of them.  Once you have identified where each person fits into the three groups you can concentrate your efforts on establishing effective working relationships.  Make sure you know in detail the job roles and responsibilities of all your primary contacts and find out as much detail as you can those of your secondary contacts.  That way you will know exactly who you need to deal with in every situation that arises.  This will give you direct access to the right person to give you information or to obtain the best terms for your organisation in any negotiations.

While concentrating on your primary and secondary contacts don't completely ignore your tertiary contacts.  You may not need them often, but when you do your dealings with them will be much more satisfactory if you have had contact with them since you last needed them.  There is also the possibility that if your, or their, role changes they may become primary or secondary contacts and the positive relationship with them that is already established will be a benefit to both of you.

The way you relate to all of these people will have an effect not only on your performance but also on theirs.  It will also affect their behaviour towards you.  While you may be able to instruct some of them to carry out certain tasks because of your relative positions in the hierarchy of the organisation, you will get much more effective co-operation from them if you have previously treated them with the respect that they are entitled to.

Productive working relationships enable you to recognise the needs of others, work constructively with them to give and receive support when problems arise.

 When developing productive working relationships with colleagues you will use the following skills:

- Communicating
- Managing conflict
- Empathising
- Networking
- Information management
- Leading by example
- Valuing and supporting others
- Involving others
- Providing feedback
- Obtaining feedback
- Stress management
- Prioritising

These skills are covered in chapter 1.

## Establishing relationships

Often you will have a pre-conceived view of someone before you meet them. Either you know them by reputation or you know someone who knows them and has told you their opinion. Similarly, after meeting someone you may well pass on your perceptions of them to others who have not yet met them and therefore affect their views.

Your relationship with others is formed by your behaviour towards them and theirs towards you. If you have a pre-conceived idea of how your relationship will work with an individual, based on either your own experiences or information from other people, the reality will often match your predictions as you will behave towards them according to your expectations of them. But this is not productive. Try to enter each relationship with a completely open mind. Even if somebody else has found the person difficult, it doesn't mean that you will.

If you are in a position where others report to you, you will need to exercise your people skills to establish the right sort of relationship with them. The difficulty you will encounter is in avoiding the two extremes of being aloof from them in order to make it clear that you are in charge, or being too close to them in order to make it clear that you are still one of the team.

Your team will want you to show leadership without imposing your views to the extent where they have no autonomy. You will need to identify what your team expects from you and match it to the way you are prepared to work with them. You can then come up with 'working parameters' within which you will work with your team. These may include:

- Being sensitive to their needs
- Always keeping your promises
- Setting measurable, achievable objectives
- Showing respect and loyalty
- Encouraging initiative
- Supporting self confidence
- Being prepared to listen

However well you match up to these ideals you will still never satisfy everybody all the time. Don't compromise your own standards in an effort to please everybody, it cannot be done.

You will also have contact with various other people within the organisation who do not form part of your team and it is important that you establish productive working relationships with them too. While each of them will have a formal role which you will be aware of, they will also have informal roles which you will need to take into account. Everybody in an organisation forms links with others within the organisation. The formal links are those imposed by the organisation structure or hierarchy. The accounts clerk reports to the accounts manager who reports to the finance director who reports to the Board. At the same time there will be informal links such as:

- **Shared experiences** - Two or more staff may have been to school together or attended the same youth club
- **Social ties** - They may be members of the same football or tennis club
- **Family ties** - They may be related to each other
- **Previous work ties** - They may have worked together in another organisation or department

You may need to bear these informal links in mind when forming relationships. The person you consider to be unimportant and not worth making an effort to influence may have informal ties to somebody that you consider it is very important to create a good working relationship with. Remember that the person you are desperate to impress will be forming pre-conceived ideas about your character based on information being passed to them by others.

One of the best ways to establish a good working relationship is to take other people's priorities into account when making decisions or taking action. Maintaining effective communication with all those who will be affected by your actions will ensure that you don't inadvertently frustrate their intentions. By the same token, of course, they should be communicating with you about their priorities.

An excellent way of destroying a good working relationship is to make promises and then fail to keep them. This applies equally to promises made to people who report to you and to other contacts. If you have committed your team to complete a task by a given deadline you must do all within your power to ensure that they meet that commitment. This means that you will have to:

- Communicate the deadline to your staff so that they know what is required
- Ensure all necessary resources are available so that they have a fair chance of meeting the deadline
- Encourage them to let you know immediately if a problem arises which might threaten the deadline
- Take immediate and effective action to overcome such a problem

You must give the same amount of concern to promises that you make to your team. If you offer an incentive for completing a task by a given deadline you must make absolutely sure that the incentive is delivered or you will lose the trust of your team and the next deadline will be much more difficult to meet. If a member of your team asks you for a favour such as being allowed to leave early on a particular occasion and you agree, you must make every effort to ensure that nothing prevents this at the last moment. If you identify a training need and offer an opportunity to meet it you must follow through and not allow it to be forgotten in the daily routine.

Another aspect to keeping promises is to respect confidences. You may be given access to confidential information in your job role concerning sensitive issues about the organisation or about individuals. You may be told confidential information by a member of your team concerning their private life or someone else's. How ever you come across the information you wont retain the respect of others if you don't keep it to yourself. If it gets out on just one occasion that you have passed on confidential information nobody will ever trust you with their secrets again. The kind of official confidential information you have access to may include:

- Details of salaries
- Staff appraisals
- Medical records
- Disciplinary records
- Sales information
- Purchasing information
- Outstanding debts
- Accounts records
- Past employment records
- Personnel records

You may also have been entrusted with personal information about people's criminal records, driving convictions, drinking habits, drug addiction, family problems or affairs. Where these have no impact on their ability to carry out their duties you must keep the information strictly to yourself. You will have a dilemma where someone gives you information in confidence which you know will affect their job.

If, for instance, the company's delivery driver tells you that they have been convicted of a driving offence and you are aware that this would make the company's motor insurance invalid, you are obliged to inform the company. Advise the driver that their best course of action will be to bring this to their line manager's attention themselves, as they are more likely to receive a sympathetic response. Failing this, the driver will need to know that you will be informing the organisation yourself.

 **What you need to know**

The three groups into which your contacts fall

Who are your colleagues?

How to set 'working parameters'

Why is it important to keep in regular

touch with tertiary contacts?

The difference between formal and
informal links

Why do we have pre-conceived ideas
about people we have not met?

The importance of keeping promises

Why can you not please all the people
all the time?

The importance of respecting confidences

Why may you have to break a
confidence?

The types of confidential information you
will have access to

Why is it important to take into account
other people's priorities?

## Developing relationships

Once you have established relationships with your contacts it
is important that you continue to develop them.  There will
be a number of situations arise that will put pressure on your
relationships:

- You may have to be the bearer of bad tidings.  There
  is a tendency to blame the messenger for the
  message
- You may have to mediate between two of your
  contacts in a disagreement.  Unless you are able to
  suggest a solution which satisfies both you will
  jeopardise your relationship with at least one
- You may find your loyalties are split between a
  contact and the organisation.  If you become aware of
  information which you are obliged to pass on despite
  the adverse effect it will have on an individual you will
  strain your relationship
- You may have to take disciplinary action against a
  member of your team.  Unless this is sensitively
  handled it could affect your relationship not only with
  that individual but with others in the team
- You may have to require greater effort from your
  team.  If your relationship with them is not based on
  trust and honesty, 'wielding the big stick' will affect
  your relationship

Unless you are making a sustained effort to strengthen your relationships, any one of the above points could cause them to break down completely and it is much harder to repair a broken relationship than it is to maintain one.

An important aspect of developing relationships is good communication. Nobody can operate in a vacuum. Everybody needs information and exchanging it is an excellent relationship builder. As with every other skill there are rules to learn in exchanging information.

Always:

- State the facts as accurately and honestly as possible
- Plan how you are going to communicate
- Consider the reaction you're likely to get
- Consider how you will respond to the reaction
- Give the opportunity for questions to be asked
- Choose an appropriate time and place to give important information

Never:

- Give the impression that you are holding back information
- Distance yourself from the information, claiming that you are obliged to pass on something you don't agree with
- Conjecture on gossip as people will interpret what you say as fact
- Be hypocritical, claiming to support something with which you strongly disagree
- Embellish problems in order to increase reaction

Of course, exchanging information is more than telling somebody something. It also involves seeking their views. It is, therefore, a two way process which involves listening as well as speaking. If you are exchanging information with a group of people such as your team you will need to bear in mind that some people will be more forthcoming than others.

Avoid giving more weight to the arguments of those who are more prepared to state them.

You will also exchange information with both customers and suppliers. Customers may be looking for information about prices, products or delivery times for instance or enquiring about their account. You will need to exchange information with them in order to be able to satisfy their needs. If you have a good relationship with them, asking them for information which may be sensitive will be much easier.

Never give a customer any information unless you are sure of your facts. If in doubt, find out before committing yourself as it is much easier to ask the customer to wait while you find out the correct information than it is to explain why the information you gave was incorrect. If the customer is complaining about the service they have received:

- Remain calm and attempt to calm the customer
- Be polite even if the customer isn't
- Remember that you are representing the organisation not yourself. If you have to apologise it is the organisation that is apologising not you personally
- Escalate the problem if it is beyond your authority to resolve
- Never admit liability or apportion blame

Depending on the nature of the organisation in which you work, you may have to deal with customer information of a confidential nature, such as:

- If you work for a financial institution you may have details of customers' debts, mortgages, investments or insurance
- If you work for a doctor or a hospital you may have details of customers' medical records
- If you work for a solicitor or Citizens' Advice Bureau you may have details of customers' criminal records, family matters or wills

If you have access to such information make sure that you don't discuss it in a public place, leave notes on your desk or your computer screen where they can be seen by other people or give the information to anybody who doesn't need it. Avoid giving advice on any of these issues unless you have been trained to do so as your advice will be seen as the professional advice of the organisation you work for.

Suppliers may wish to exchange information with you on a whole variety of subjects. Their prices, their special offers, the reason they can't supply the goods they promised to you for another fortnight. They will be looking for a response from you. They would obviously like another order or your agreement to wait the extra two weeks. Again don't commit yourself unless you have the authority. If you sign an agreement on behalf of your organisation the supplier will expect your organisation to honour it, even if you didn't have your organisation's permission to sign.

Another issue that may arise with suppliers is that they may wish to complain about a member of your team. The natural immediate reaction is to either jump to the defence of your colleague or apologise immediately to placate the supplier. Neither of these is a helpful reaction until you have gathered all of the facts. If it transpires that the supplier has a justified complaint you will have to decide how to deal with the person involved. If the complaint is relatively minor and you believe it to be a one-off situation where your colleague has fallen below their normal standards, you should have an informal word with them so that they are aware of the supplier's concern and can take steps to make sure there is no repetition. If the complaint is more serious or if there is a second or subsequent transgression you will need to speak to them formally and probably record the matter on their disciplinary record.

Another area that may test the strength of your working relationships is where people have differing views of what their, or someone else's, role is. This may present itself as:

- **Uncertainty** - You don't know what you are required to do because it hasn't been made clear
- **Incongruity** - You are either given conflicting instructions because you have more than one line manager or you are given instructions which conflict with your relationship with your staff
- **Overload** - Too much is expected of you, possibly because you have been too efficient at coping with problems in the past
- **Underload** - Too little is expected of you, possibly because your line manager is poor at delegation or because you haven't made enough effort to demonstrate your capabilities

To reduce the effects:

- Don't set people up to fail, allocate tasks according to the abilities and experience of the individual
- Issue accurate job descriptions and ensure everybody understands their implications
- Consult with individuals before altering their job description
- Make yourself available to give any assistance required
- Delegate effectively
- Deal positively with any examples of under-performance
- Organise training to meet any recognised training needs
- Motivate effectively
- Deal immediately with any interference from outside your team

The critical measure of your effective working relationships is what your staff and line manager think about you. Your line manager will probably give you formal feedback during your regular appraisal or they may be particularly good at giving feedback on an ongoing basis. Unless you have a 360° appraisal system in operation in your organisation you will probably have to ask your staff if you are to get feedback. Negative feedback, provided it is constructive, will enable you to spot areas where your skills can be improved. Positive feedback will reassure you that your skills in some areas don't need any attention at the moment. But try to avoid falling into the trap of complacency. You will need to seek continuous feedback if you are to be sure that your performance levels are not slipping.

In the same way that you should be encouraging feedback on your performance in order to improve, you should be offering feedback on the performance of others. When giving feedback remember that it should be based on fact rather than opinion and you must always be prepared to back up your feedback with examples. Positive feedback should reinforce what the receiver has done well and identify opportunities to continue to perform. Corrective action may be necessary where performance has not been satisfactory but the individual should be encouraged to recognise this for themselves. The appraisal should look at performance over the whole period under review, recognise the individual's achievement and produce a development plan which the individual is able to agree with.

The receiving and giving of feedback is covered in greater depth in chapter 1.

 **What you need to know**

The importance of developing relationships

What can put pressure on established relationships?

How to communicate effectively

Why is effective communication vital to

the development of relationships

How to exchange information with customers

Why is it important to receive constructive feedback?

How to deal with complaints

How do you exchange information with suppliers?

How to give constructive feedback

How would you deal with people's differing views of your role?

## Dealing with diversity

The dictionary definition of diversity is 'the state of being different'. You should deal with diversity by remembering that everybody should be shown the same respect, treating everyone as you would wish to be treated. People with disabilities may require help with access to the building. Hearing impaired colleagues may need more visual aids. Visually impaired colleagues may need documents in large print or audio format. Also be aware that English may not be someone's first language.

These are some examples of dealing with diversity. Don't make up your mind about somebody based on appearance, accent, etc. People can have a range of different requirements that means they need help with access, reading or understanding. The important thing to remember is they are all colleagues and should be shown the same respect.

Many workplaces today are far more diverse than in the past. You may well find yourself working with colleagues from a wide range of cultures and diverse abilities. It's in the best interests of everybody that you understand what is meant by Equal Opportunities. For employers Equal Opportunities is about good business practice and can:

- Reduce costs
- Improve efficiency
- Lower staff turnover

For employees it means they are judged on merit, ability and past performance and covers:

- Recruitment
- Promotion
- Training
- Benefits
- Dismissal

Your organisation will probably have an Equal Opportunities programme which will be designed to:

- Improve team success through respect and dignity for all
- Reduce stress levels and therefore absenteeism
- Improve safety performance
- Reduce recruitment costs
- Increase sales through staff commitment

Employers can make these programmes more successful by:

- Outlawing discrimination and harassment
- Treating everybody equally
- Providing advice and training
- Offering flexible working time
- Handling complaints promptly

Discrimination may be direct or indirect. Direct discrimination means treating people less favourably because of their gender, ethnicity or sexual orientation. For instance selecting a male for the supervisor's position ahead of a better qualified female because the majority of the staff are male and traditionally the role has been male.

Indirect discrimination occurs when a rule or practice discriminates against a particular group unintentionally, for instance stating that everyone applying for a job must have been to public school when there is no good reason for this.

Harassment is an unwelcome or offensive remark, request or other act that discriminates against a person by harming his or her job performance or satisfaction. Sexual harassment is a criminal offence. Other types of harassment may be criminal, for instance:

- Offensive jokes, remarks or insults based on ethnicity, nationality or other characteristics
- Bullying
- Threats, verbal or physical abuse

- Threatening or discriminating against someone for reporting a breach of the law

**Disability Discrimination Act 1995 (c. 50)**
© Crown Copyright 1995

**Race Relations Act 1976**
© Crown Copyright 1976

**Sex Discrimination Act 1975**
© Crown Copyright 1975

The following legislation addresses Equal Opportunities at work:

## The Sex Discrimination Acts 1975 & 1986

These Acts prohibit discrimination against people based on their gender or marital status.  It covers two main areas:

- **Recruitment** - This includes the job description, the person specification, the application form, the short-listing process, interviewing and final selection
- **Terms and conditions** - This includes pay, holidays and working conditions

Direct sex discrimination involves refusing to consider somebody for a job because of their gender, for example refusing to consider a male for a job that is traditionally perceived as a female role.  Indirect sex discrimination involves making it more difficult for one gender or for married people to be considered for a job.  For instance if a condition of employment was willingness to regularly move home, this would discriminate against married applicants as they would find this more difficult.

## Race Relations Act 1976

This Act prohibits discrimination against people based on their race, colour, nationality or ethnic origin.  It covers:

- Recruitment
- Training
- Selection
- Promotion
- Dismissal

Racial discrimination may be direct or indirect.

### Disability Discrimination Act 1995

This Act prohibits discrimination against people based on their disability. It describes a person with a disability as 'anyone with a physical or mental impairment which has a substantial and long-term adverse effect upon their ability to carry out normal day-to-day activities'.

### Employment Rights Act 1996

This Act could apply to sex discrimination as it covers the right to return to work after maternity leave.

### Health and Safety at Work Act 1974

This Act could apply to a case of bullying that affects a person's health or safety.

Other forms of discrimination may be unlawful even though no specific law prohibits them, for instance discrimination based on age or HIV infection. However, even these will be subject to new legislation by the end of 2006.

Equal Opportunities at work come down to changing the attitude of people about colleagues who are different from themselves and making the best use of the organisation's human resources. Equal Opportunities policies have the potential to bring out the best in people.

# What you need to know

The definition of diversity

> What is the difference between direct and indirect discrimination?

The benefits of Equal Opportunities policies to employers

> What are the purposes of Equal Opportunities programmes?

The benefits of Equal Opportunities policies to employees

> How does harassment differ from discrimination?

The main provisions of the Sex Discrimination Acts 1975 & 1986

> How can Equal Opportunities programmes be made more successful?

The main provisions of the Race Discrimination Act 1976

> Can you think of some examples of discrimination?

The main provisions of the Disability Discrimination Act 1995

> Who should you tell if you feel a member of your team is being harassed?

Productive working relationships are not formed without a conscious effort. They require a good understanding of others' needs and a determination to work in a professional atmosphere. They are not formed overnight, nor do they necessarily remain stable once created. You have to work on developing them if you are to get the best out of your colleagues, contacts and, ultimately, yourself.

## You are born with relations, relationships have to be earned

# Are you ready for assessment?

To achieve this unit of a Level 3 Business & Administration qualification you will need to demonstrate that you are competent in the following:

- Establish working relationships with all colleagues who are relevant to the work being carried out
- Recognise, agree and respect the roles and responsibilities of colleagues
- Understand and take account of the priorities, expectations, and authority of colleagues in decisions and actions
- Fulfil agreements made with colleagues and let them know
- Advise colleagues promptly of any difficulties or where it will be impossible to fulfil agreements
- Identify and sort out conflicts of interest and disagreements with colleagues in ways that minimise damage to the work being carried out
- Exchange information and resources with colleagues to make sure that all parties can work effectively
- Provide feedback to colleagues on their performance and seek feedback from colleagues on your own performance in order to identify areas for improvement
- Present information clearly, concisely, accurately and in ways that promote understanding
- Seek to understand people's needs and motivations
- Make time available to support others
- Clearly agree what is expected of others and hold them to account
- Work to develop an atmosphere of professionalism and mutual support
- Model behaviour that shows respect, helpfulness and co-operation
- Keep promises and honour commitments
- Consider the impact of your own actions on others
- Say no to unreasonable requests
- Show respect for the views and actions of others

(Remember that you will need the skills listed at the beginning of this chapter.  These are covered in chapter 1.)

You will need to produce evidence from a variety of sources. Carrying out the following activities will help you acquire competence at work.

## Activity 1
Keep a work diary over the period of a month in which you record occasions when you have made time available to work with others.

## Activity 2
Draw a diagram illustrating your internal network showing yourself in the centre and all those you have contact with within the organisation.

Draw a diagram illustrating your external network showing yourself in the centre and all those you have contact with outside of the organisation.

Look at your diagrams and draw connections between people on your internal network and the people on your external network that they have connections with.

Identify what steps need to be taken to improve your working relationships.

## Activity 3
Write a report on the regulations, codes of practice, standards of behaviour and working culture that apply in your industry or sector.

## Activity 4
Make a list of all the members of your team.  Write a short description of the qualities each member has.  Now try to remember what your early views of each were, either before they became a member of your team (pre-conceptions) or very soon after.  Analyse your findings and identify what development needs you or they may have.

## Activity 5
Review your ability to develop productive working relationships with your line manager.  Agree an action plan to improve your own or your team's performance.

Remember:  While gathering evidence for this unit, evidence **may** be generated for units 110, 301 and 302.

# CHAPTER 30
# UNIT 321 – Provide leadership for your team

Leadership is different from authority. Authority derives from your role and your position in the hierarchy of your organisation. You have authority because it was given to you when you were appointed to a position where you have the last word in making decisions. Leadership is the ability to guide, direct or influence people. If you practise authority without leadership your instructions will probably be carried out but you will not get the best out of the team. On the other hand it is possible to practise leadership without authority. People will follow a leader who doesn't have a position of authority if they demonstrate leadership qualities.

Potential leaders can be identified from the following characteristics:

- Experience of leadership whether business related or not
- The ability to see beyond the present
- The courage to welcome challenges
- The need to continually challenge the status quo
- The common sense to differentiate between the practical and the fanciful
- The eagerness to accept responsibility
- The determination to see the task through
- The willingness to accept criticism

- The potential to earn respect
- The tendency to be listened to

Different leaders demonstrate different styles. The effectiveness of each depends on the situation and the style of leadership that the team is used to. Styles that you may recognise are:

- **Dictatorial** - This is not usually the best way to get optimum performance from a team but there are occasions when it may be necessary. When urgent action is required there may be no time to debate. Some teams will prefer to simply be told what to do
- **Laid back** - This style may get the best performance from a team of capable and experienced experts in their field. Interfering with their routines without good reason can have an adverse effect. The laid back leader can empower the team by delegating authority to them
- **Egalitarian** - When this style is used wisely the group is encouraged to participate and discuss while the control remains with the leader. Used unwisely the group refuses to carry out any task without endless discussion and control is handed over to the group

Whichever style a leader is demonstrating they will need certain qualities. Leadership qualities include willingness to:

- Shoulder responsibility
- Set a personal example
- Make decisions based on reason
- Show a concern for people's feelings
- Actively listen
- Communicate effectively
- Use varying motivational techniques
- Give credit where credit is due
- Give positive feedback where improvement is needed
- Be sensitive to the problems of others

It is possible for you to demonstrate these qualities when you are not officially in a position of authority. You will need to recognise the situation in which your leadership of a team is required and will be accepted. Don't attempt to assume leadership of a team that would not accept you or where another member of the team is better placed.

When you have decided the time is right to assume leadership there are a number of steps to follow:

- Identify those who will be willing to follow
- Check you have access to the necessary resources
- Find out what other people in the team are thinking
- Discuss your ideas with all the other members of the team
- Encourage the team to identify with each other and with your leadership
- Set realistic goals for the team
- Recognise and reward achievement of those goals

The art of leadership is to use all the styles adapting to the situation and the people involved. You need to recognise how to motivate your team through empowerment while retaining the option to dictate an imperative when the need arises.

 When providing leadership for your team you will use the following skills:

- Communicating
- Planning
- Team building
- Leading by example
- Providing feedback
- Setting objectives
- Motivating
- Consulting
- Problem solving
- Valuing and supporting others
- Monitoring
- Managing conflict
- Decision making
- Following

These skills are covered in chapter 1.

Leadership can be said to begin with communication. This is the giving and receiving of information and in terms of leadership the most important form of communication is verbal. When speaking to your team there is a set of techniques which will improve the understanding and acceptance of the information by the listener:

- **Launching** - Introduce your main point in your opening sentence so that people don't have to wonder what you are talking about. If you have a number of points of equal importance to introduce deal with them one at a time and then introduce the next
- **Tempo** - Match your tempo to the response of the audience. After the introduction of your main point, give your audience time to absorb the information and ask questions before moving on to the next point
- **Recap** - Make sure your audience has understood and accepted each point by reiterating it and obtaining confirmation. At the end of the whole conversation sum up what has been agreed and what steps are to be taken as a result

When listening to your team watch for:

- **Prejudice** - Everybody will have some pre-formed view about almost any subject. This will inevitably influence the way you hear what is being said to you so make a conscious effort to recognise this fact
- **Body language** - You will interpret the body language of the speaker according to your own experience. In a multi-cultural society this can lead to misunderstanding as body language varies between people of different cultural groups. Be aware of the body language you are demonstrating when you are listening as this can affect the message that the speaker is giving
- **Tone of voice** - You may understand more from the speaker's tone of voice than you do from the actual words being used. People betray their true feelings through the way they say things more than by what they say

Successful team leaders communicate regularly with their team to encourage active participation in decision making. You will probably find that within the team there will be individuals of differing levels of confidence, commitment and ability.  You may have to adapt your leadership style to suit the individual:

- **Supervising** - Individuals who are totally committed but not yet fully competent because of insufficient experience or training in the particular task, will need supervision more than encouragement
- **Mentoring** - Individuals who have been a part of the team for some time but are still not fully competent will need mentoring.  This will involve continuing the close supervision of their work while encouraging and praising them as much as possible
- **Encouragement** - When individuals reach a satisfactory level of competence they will need less supervision but will still welcome encouragement to improve their self-confidence.  At this point you should start to involve them in decision making
- **Responsibility** - When individuals are competent and their confidence has grown sufficiently to work entirely on their own, you can give them tasks to complete without too much supervision

You will need to identify the team's priorities so that the most important issues are dealt with first.  Often urgent issues are mistakenly identified as important when they have little or no long-term bearing on the performance of the organisation.  True priorities depend on having both urgency and importance.  Juggling the urgent but unimportant tasks alongside the important but non-urgent is the real skill.

When you have identified your priorities you will be able to concentrate on setting clear objectives for yourself and your team.  Clarification of the objectives allows all involved to be sure that they are seeking a common outcome.  This makes it easier for them to plan a course of action to reach the objective.  When setting the objective make sure it is achievable as the team will quickly become demoralised if they are set up to fail.  It may be necessary to divide the task into several smaller sub-tasks in order that the team can recognise progress is being made.

The sub-tasks can be delegated to individual members of the team or smaller groups within the team. Effective leaders are invariably good at delegation. Good delegation produces:

- Improved efficiency
- Increased motivation
- More highly skilled team members
- A fairer division of labour through the team

Poor delegation produces:

- Reduced efficiency
- Lower staff morale
- Confusion amongst the team
- Overloading of trusted team members

Avoid thinking that as you can do all of the tasks better than anyone in the team, it will be most efficient for you to do them all yourself. Although the first may be true the second certainly won't be. To effectively delegate tasks:

- Select a member of the team
- Prepare them by explaining the task clearly
- Make sure they understand the required outcome but leave the detail of how it is achieved to their ingenuity
- Make sure they have the necessary resources
- Monitor their progress without interfering. Offer support without imposing your own views on the best way to carry out the task
- Acknowledge their achievement of the task

Remember that delegation is not the same as abdication. If you delegate a task you are still responsible for its completion on time and to a satisfactory standard. If the objective is not achieved you can't blame the person you delegated it to. If you delegated it to the wrong person it is your fault, not theirs. You must also delegate sufficient authority to allow the person to complete the task. If you delegate somebody the task of allocating work amongst their colleagues, for instance, you will need to advise their colleagues that you have given them the authority to allocate the tasks.

There are some areas where it is not acceptable to delegate your authority. These may include recruiting staff, disciplining staff, setting pay scales and dealing with confidential matters relating to other members of staff.

Teams are given cohesion through motivation. Motivation can be defined as 'the amount of effort an individual willingly supplies to a task'. If any one member of a team lacks motivation the whole team effort suffers. The difficulty for the team leader is that different people are motivated in different ways. You will need to recognise what motivates different individuals within your team in order to tailor the rewards that you offer to their individual values. Individuals form patterns of behaviour early in life, which remain with them throughout adulthood. In the same way that cats learn different ways of obtaining food from their owners – some loudly demand feeding, some coax food from their owners by rubbing against their legs, others just wait patiently knowing that they will be fed sooner or later – people fall into one of three patterns of behaviour:

- **Determined and forceful** - These people are driven to achieve and are challenging to lead. The best way to motivate them is to organise team objectives so that these individuals' achievements stand out while contributing to the overall goals
- **Considerate and loyal** - These people are motivated by the success of others rather than any personal glory. They are motivated by the team's achievement and are usually involved heavily in tidying up the details for the go-getters who are racing ahead dealing with the big picture
- **Logical and systematic** - These people are best working alone within the framework of the team. They are motivated by the completion of the task whether or not they are given any recognition for it. They can be allocated the more complex tasks in the knowledge that they will simply get on with the job until it is completed. Avoid the temptation to push them into group activities against their will

Recognition of which of the above groups individual members of your team belong to will enable you to allocate tasks appropriately to make full use of their creativity and innovation and allow each to fulfil their true potential. Team motivation can be improved by:

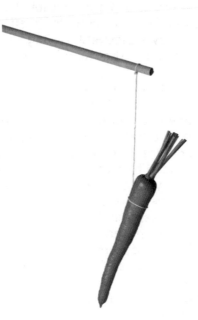

- Encouraging social interaction between the members of the team
- Emphasising the importance of the team as a whole
- Emphasising the importance of every individual
- Providing clear objectives
- Informing the team of the progress they are making
- Acknowledging the achievements of the team and individuals

It is also part of your responsibility as a leader to encourage understanding between members of the team. Understanding enhances the sense of purpose and unity among the team. Open discussion between all those involved is the key to fostering understanding. The challenge is to allow the discussion to air differences of opinion and to manage any conflict caused. This is best done by setting a personal example, not taking offence when your views are contradicted or falling back on your position to settle any dispute.

The benefits of creating a forum where opinions can be freely stated without the loudest voice dominating are that you will get to hear everybody's ideas and encourage loyalty and commitment to the team. To prevent the discussion degenerating into chaos you will need to set and agree ground rules. As leader you will be the moderator between other members so that everyone gets a fair hearing. You will need to be able to:

- **Chair the discussion** - This involves you in making sure that the discussion is not dominated by one person or a few people. Inform all members of the team that only one person is allowed to speak at a time and that nobody should speak until you invite them to. You must then try to ensure that everybody who wishes to, gets a fair opportunity to air their views. Look out for those members who give signs that they have something to say but don't want to put themselves forward and invite them to contribute. It is better to frustrate those who have a lot to say and have to wait their turn to say it than to miss the contribution of those who are not forceful enough to take their turn
- **Restate people's comments** - If the discussion goes off track you will need to restate the position reached by relating the side issue to the point that is under discussion. If those who brought up the side issue wish to have it discussed fully they should be allowed to raise it after discussion of the main topic is complete. There will also be occasions when it is necessary to paraphrase what one member has said so that the other members can fully understand it, particularly in the case of jargon or expertise
- **Mediate between participants** - From time-to-time people become heated in their views and it will be necessary to encourage them to withdraw from the discussion while they regain their composure. Ask other people to give their views on the matter under discussion so that the 'heat' is taken out of the situation. There is a risk that someone will attempt to change the subject in order to divert attention from the confrontation but as mediator you mustn't allow this to happen or the dispute will simply re-surface later. You need to re-focus the discussion to the issue under debate and away from the personalities in dispute. The whole team must then find a solution which is acceptable to all

Where conflict arises between team members outside of the discussion situation there are three ways to deal with it:

- **Use your authority** - Simply tell one of the team members they are wrong and they will have to accept that the other is right
- **Find a compromise** - Identify a situation that will fully satisfy neither but which both will accept rather than acknowledging the other's position
- **Find common ground** - Identify a situation that will enable both to achieve at least part of their goal

The first method very rarely works as the 'loser' will resent your interference while the 'winner' will get little satisfaction out of such an easy victory. They will have made no progress towards persuading their protagonist of the rightness of their view. A compromise will often seem the easy solution but is unlikely to be satisfactory over the long term as both will feel they have not achieved their goal and will raise the issue again at a later date. The ability to find common ground often produces the best long term solution.

Leaders who offer vision inspire their team as much as if they were able to offer improved pay, position or authority. Vision inspires commitment and a feeling of common purpose. If you claim to have a vision you may be dismissed as an eccentric but vision transforms a manager into a leader. It is vision that suggests that things can only get better and this inspires ordinary people.  Leaders present their vision in such a way that others want to achieve it.  Managers present ideas and proposals and may achieve their goals but they are not demonstrating leadership.

 **What you need to know**

How to use speaking and listening techniques to communicate

Why is it important that objectives are achievable?

Methods of involving individuals in achieving team objectives

How do individual objectives relate to the achievement of team objectives?

The benefits of encouraging creativity and innovation

How can you assume leadership of a team when you haven't been given the authority to do so?

The level of achievement expected of your team

What is the purpose of your team?

Methods of dealing with conflict within the team and their advantages and disadvantages

What are the individual objectives of your team?

The legal, regulatory and ethical requirements in your organisation

How can you provide relevant advice and support to your team members?

The various styles of leadership and how they differ

How can you recognise the different motivational methods applicable to individuals within your team?

Leaders take risks and invite their colleagues to join them in exploring those risks. This requires a great deal of commitment and willingness to accept the possibility that their vision will be rejected by those unable to share it. The leader's relationship with their team relies heavily on gaining the trust and support of all the members who may have to accept ideas that they would not previously have considered. If a team has been treated well in the past they will have faith that they are being led in the right direction.

## A good leader believes that their vision is a true image of the future

# Are you ready for assessment?

To achieve this unit of a Level 3 Business & Administration qualification you will need to demonstrate that you are competent in the following:

- Set out and positively communicate the purpose and objectives of the team to all members
- Involve members in planning how the team will achieve its objectives
- Ensure that each member of the team has personal work objectives and understands how achieving these will contribute to achievement of the team's objectives
- Encourage and support team members to achieve their personal work objectives and those of the team and provide recognition when objectives have been achieved
- Win, through your performance, the trust and support of the team for your leadership
- Steer the team successfully through difficulties and challenges, including conflict within the team
- Encourage and recognise creativity and innovation within the team
- Give team members support and advice when they need it, especially during periods of setback and change
- Motivate team members to present their own ideas and listen to what they say
- Encourage team members to take the lead when they have the knowledge and expertise and show willingness to follow this lead
- Monitor activities and progress across the team without interfering
- Create a sense of common purpose
- Take personal responsibility for making things happen
- Encourage and support others to take decisions autonomously
- Act within the limits of your authority
- Make time available to support others
- Show integrity, fairness and consistency in decision making

- Seek to understand people's needs and motivations
- Model behaviour that shows respect, helpfulness and co-operation

(Remember that you will need the skills listed at the beginning of this chapter. These are covered in chapter 1.)

You will need to produce evidence from a variety of sources. Carrying out the following activities will help you acquire competence at work.

### Activity 1

| | | | |
|---|---|---|---|
| Directing | Doormat | Methodical | Naive |
| Nit-picking | Understanding | Friendly | Gambling |
| Risk-taking | Resourceful | Isolated | Plodding |
| Thorough | Sensitive | Impulsive | Arrogant |
| Entrepreneurial | Spontaneous | Dynamic | Practical |
| Self-serving | Highly-strung | Unco-operative | Patient |
| Narrow-minded | Reserved | Idealistic | Tolerant |
| Devoted | Dictatorial | Fair | Impersonal |
| Pushy | Submissive | Rigid | Independent |
| Passive | Calculating | Confident | Principled |

The above words are features of people who demonstrate one of the following patterns of behaviour:
- Determined and forceful
- Considerate and loyal
- Logical and systematic

Identify which features are associated with each pattern and whether in your view they are positive or negative features.

### Activity 2
Think about members of your own team or members of your family or social group. Which leadership style would be most effective with each of them? Write an explanation of your reasons in each case.

### Activity 3
Choose someone who has inspired you. This could be someone you know personally or a celebrity or a historical figure. Write about the leadership qualities that person displays.

### Activity 4
Research the career of a leader who ultimately failed. This could be from history or fiction. Write a report on the qualities he or she lacked which lead to their failure.

**Activity 5**
Next time you have the opportunity to lead team discussions ask somebody to observe how you chair the discussion, restate people's comments and mediate between the participants.  Get them to give you constructive feedback and discuss how you can improve this aspect of your leadership skills.

Activity 6
Review your leadership of team activities over the period of one month, with your line manager.  Record the outcome of the review identifying targets that have been met and areas for improvement or development.

**Activity 6**
Review your leadership of team activities over the period of one month, with your line manager.  Record the outcome of the review identifying targets that have been met and areas for improvement or development.

Remember:  While gathering evidence for this unit, evidence **may** be generated for units 110, 301, 302, 303, 305, 306, 309 and 320.

# CHAPTER 31
## UNIT 322/323/324 Prepare text

Every organisation, whether it be a doctor's surgery, solicitor's office, bank, factory, shop, leisure centre or garage, will have one thing in common - the need to produce text-based documents. These will include memos, letters, reports and minutes of meetings and will be produced from a variety of sources including shorthand notes, audio recordings and handwritten drafts.

Whether you are producing written documents from any of these sources, it is important that you are able to spell, use grammar and punctuation correctly so that the finished product gives a good impression of your organisation and more importantly, conveys the intended message.

If you have trouble with your spelling, there are only two ways to improve – read more books, and practise. The following are 30 of the words most commonly misspelled. If you learn how to spell these, you will be able to spell most everyday words.

| | | |
|---|---|---|
| accommodate | description | privilege |
| achievement | embarrass | proceed |
| acknowledgement | extension | recommend |
| analysis | gauge | separate |
| benefited | guarantee | slight |
| calendar | height | supersede |
| commitment | judgement | through |
| convenient | occurrence | unconscious |
| criticism | possession | weight |
| delicious | precede | yacht |

Of course, if you are using a word processor with the spell check facility operating, it will tell you if you have misspelled most of these words. The spell check can't however, differentiate between words that are spelt correctly but used incorrectly; for instance, if you spelt 'through' as 'threw' the spell checker would not notice. Some of the most commonly confused words are:

- We are pleased to <u>accept</u> your donation.
  Everyone made a donation <u>except</u> Mr. Jones.
- Never listen to <u>advice</u> from your parents.
  I would <u>advise</u> you always to listen to your parents.
- The increase in interest rates will <u>affect</u> everyone.
  The <u>effect</u> of the increase was felt by everyone.
- She thought she was <u>eligible</u> for a grant.
  The letter she received was <u>illegible</u>.
- You must <u>ensure</u> that your car is <u>insured</u>.
- Lowestoft is <u>farther</u> east than Birmingham.
  I need <u>further</u> information on the transport system of Hull.
- There are <u>fewer</u> days in February than in June.
  It is <u>less</u> likely to rain today than it was yesterday.
- My <u>personal</u> opinion is that it will rain today.
  The HR Department deals with <u>personnel</u>.
- I visited the local doctor's <u>practice</u> this morning.
  I need to <u>practise</u> my spelling.
- The <u>principal</u> cause of heart disease is overeating.
  The Minister resigned over a matter of <u>principle</u>.
- The traffic on the M6 was <u>stationary</u> for two hours.
  We need to order some more <u>stationery</u> this week.
- This week's sales were better <u>than</u> last week's.
  We will look at this week's plan, <u>then</u> next week's.
- The girls picked up <u>their</u> handbags.
  The boys will be over <u>there</u> tomorrow.
  <u>They're</u> planning to visit next week.

People often think that grammar is either extremely complicated or that it no longer matters.  In fact, it is relatively simple. and incorrect grammar can lead to serious misunderstandings.   For example, 'Use both lanes when turning right' actually requires drivers to straddle the two lanes – a highly dangerous manoeuvre.  The correct instruction should be 'Use either lane when turning right'.

There are five parts of speech which you need to know:

- **Nouns** - These are the names of things, for instance 'book', 'television', 'Sunday', 'Norfolk'
- **Pronouns** - These are used instead of nouns, for instance 'he', 'she', 'they', 'it'
- **Verbs** - These are doing words, for instance 'run', 'eat', 'listen', 'speak'
- **Adverbs** - These give more information about the verb, for instance 'run quickly', 'eat slowly', listen carefully', 'speak clearly'
- **Adjectives** - These describe nouns, for instance 'interesting book', 'reality television', 'lazy Sunday', 'flat Norfolk'

Sentences are formed by linking parts of speech together. Simple sentences contain a subject and a verb; for instance: 'I am.' 'The new vicar thought he spoke clearly.'  This sentence contains all of the five parts of speech listed above. Can you identify the five parts of speech?  Sentences must start with a capital letter and end with a full stop, question mark or exclamation mark.  Capital letters are also used to indicate proper names (Ahmed, Francesca, Belgrade, Africa), titles (Mr., Mrs., Lord, Sir, Dr.), days of the week and months of the year and acronyms (CIA, FBI, MI5, RAC, BOGOF).

A paragraph is formed by linking two or more sentences about the same subject.  When the subject changes, you need to start a new paragraph.  For instance, this paragraph is about paragraphs, the previous paragraph was about sentences.

Correct punctuation is important if people are to understand what you are trying to tell them.  For instance, if you say 'Fred, the dog is ill' you are telling someone called Fred that the dog is unwell.  If you say 'Fred the dog is ill' you are telling someone that the dog called Fred is unwell.  There are three punctuation marks where the correct use is absolutely vital:

- **Full stops (.)** - These are used to mark the end of a sentence or after abbreviations
- **Commas (,)** - These are used to separate words in a list or phrases in a sentence, or to make sentences easier to read
- **Apostrophes (')** - There are three uses of the apostrophe: to replace a missing letter as in 'I'm, he's' and 'don't'; to indicate something belongs to a single person as in 'Jim's book, Pauline's shoes' and 'baby's bottle'; to indicate something associated with people in the plural as in 'students' fees, administrators' pay' and 'customers' complaints'

Whatever sort of document is produced from whatever source it is important that they are checked for accuracy before being distributed.  Copies of both the finished document and the source must be stored safely and securely.

In this chapter we will look at preparing text from notes, shorthand and audio instruction.  We will look first at those areas that are common to all three and then at the unique features of each in turn.

 When preparing text you will use the following skills:

- Questioning
- Listening
- Reading
- Writing
- Using technology
- Checking
- Managing time

These skills are covered in chapter 1.

# Preparing and producing text

Whatever source material you are planning to use, you will be producing documents in one of the following formats.

**Memos** are used internally within the organisation, but this doesn't mean they are informal. They:

- May be addressed to more than one recipient
- Will usually not include addresses or signatures
- Will simply state the date, name of the recipient, the name of the sender and the content
- May have the recipient and sender's job titles and departments
- Will usually be produced on a template which reflects the organisation's house style

The use of memos is declining in the UK as e-mail communications become more popular. However, most organisations still use memos for important internal messages.

---

**MEMORANDUM**

**To:**      All Department Managers

**From:**    Human Resources

**Date:**    15th August 2005

**Subject:** Bank Holiday Pay


Staff required to work on the Bank Holiday Monday August 29th will receive double-time plus a day off in lieu providing Monday is one of their normal working days.

Staff working on the Bank Holiday Monday when Monday is not one of their normal working days will also receive an extra day off in lieu.

---

**Business letters** are usually printed on paper headed with the organisation's own address and business details. While there is a recognised format to letter writing, each organisation will adopt its own house style. There is a convention that business letters are produced fully blocked and with open punctuation. This means:

- All parts of the document start at the left hand margin
- All punctuation except that in the body of the letter which is essential for grammatical accuracy and ease of understanding is omitted

Business letters are also laid out in a fixed sequence:

- References (this is optional)
- Date
- Name and address of recipient
- Salutation
- Heading (this is optional)
- Opening remarks
- Main message
- Action or results
- Closing remarks
- Compliments

A letter addressed to:

Mrs Jayne Wilcox
12 Manver's Street
London SW19 7ER

can be sent using the following salutations and complimentary closure:

| | | |
|---|---|---|
| Dear Jayne | Dear Mrs Wilcox | Dear Madam |
| Kind regards | Yours sincerely | Yours faithfully |

Someone who knows Jayne Wilcox may well choose to address her as Jayne. If a sender doesn't know Jayne very well they may feel more comfortable addressing her as Mrs Wilcox. The most formal way to address Jayne is to use the term Madam. This might be done by people who don't know Jayne at all. You will notice that as the salutation becomes more formal so does the complimentary closure.

In business, letters are used as a formal means of communication between individuals in different organisations. Over the last few years many organisations have found the volume of letters produced and received each day has dropped because of the increased use of e-mail communications. However, many important external communications are still made by letter.

Mrs Jayne Wilcox
12 Manver's Street
London
SW19 7ER

20/05/2005

Dear Mrs Wilcox

Re: Complaint Letter 17/05/2005

Thank you for your letter dated 17<sup>th</sup> May regarding your complaint about the service you received on the 5<sup>th</sup> May 2005.

I am sorry to hear that you have been disappointed by the level of service you have received from our staff. We pride ourselves on putting customer satisfaction first and I can assure you that I will investigate your complaint fully.

I will be in touch soon by writing. In the meantime if I can be of any further assistance or you require any further information then please do not hesitate to contact me on 020 7091 9620.

Yours sincerely

*AHawkins*

A Hawkins
Customer Services Manager

**Reports** are usually produced in response to a request for information. They may be formal or informal depending on the audience. A report to the Board will generally be more formal than a report to the members of a club. The common thread is that they are written to inform the reader of facts about a subject. The depth of information contained in a report will depend on the purpose of the report and its intended audience.

The type of report that you are most likely to be asked to produce from scratch is a research report. This will involve analysing and interpreting the findings, drawing appropriate conclusions and making suitable recommendations.

All reports will follow a similar structure, however detailed they may be:

- **Front page** - this contains the title of the report, the name of the author and the date
- **Contents** - a list of the subjects covered
- **Executive summary** - a brief outline of the report which can stand alone
- **Background information** - this gives the reasons that the report was produced
- **Methodology** - this tells you how the report was produced (surveys, questionnaires or research)
- **Findings** - there are a number of ways of presenting the findings of a report. These include:

  - by importance (beginning with the central idea)
  - by chronology (in order of events starting either with the latest or the first)
  - by sequence (where one idea follows from another)
  - by comparison (where two ideas are compared in alternate paragraphs)

- **Conclusion** - this section states what the research has led to, and how. Conclusions should be drawn from the information included in the report
- **Recommendations** - actions to be taken as a result of the conclusion
- **Acknowledgements** - in this section the contribution of others to the report is recorded
- **Bibliography** - source material should be referred to, listed alphabetically by author giving the date of publication
- **Appendices** - there may be information referred to in the report which is too detailed to be given in full without distracting from the purpose of the report. The full information is given in an appendix

**Minutes** of meetings are a written record of what took place at a meeting. They can be recorded in a number of different forms:

- **Verbatim** - Everything is recorded word for word

- **Narrative** - A summary of the meeting including discussions and conclusions. Formal resolutions are recorded verbatim
- **Resolution** - A resolution is a motion which has been voted on and passed. Details of the proposer and seconder are recorded with a verbatim recording of the resolution
- **Action** - The agenda item, the outcome or action required and the name of the person or persons responsible for carrying out the action are recorded. The discussions are not recorded

Whichever form of minutes is used they must contain everything of importance.

---

Minutes of Social Club Meeting held on 19th May 2004
West Hotel, Pendleton. 2.30pm.

Those present

Bill Banstow    Chair
Mike Willis     Secretary
Pete Axty      Treasurer
Carol Carter
Brian Williams
Kevin Bissle
Janet Hewitt

Apologies for absence were received from:  Michael Ford

Minutes of the last meeting were approved.

There were no matters arising.

The Chair reported that discussion with management had commenced with regard to the possibility of using the staff canteen for future events.

The Treasurer reported that there were seven subscriptions still outstanding. It was agreed that letters be written to the appropriate members advising them that if payment was not received by 6th June their membership would be terminated.

A.O.B.

Carol Carter suggested that a staff outing to the seaside in August could be arranged.

It was agreed that she would look into the costings of such an event.

The next meeting will be on 16th June 2004 at 2.30pm at the West Hotel, Pendleton.

Whichever form of minutes is used they must contain everything of importance.

It is important to agree the standard of finished product required and the deadline for producing it.  If, having agreed a deadline, you experience difficulties, remember to report the problem immediately.  It is too late to be told that a deadline will not be met when the deadline has already passed.

At any stage during the production of a document, formatting text may be necessary.  There are various options available in the format menu.

It is possible to format

- **Characters** - By selecting 'font' you can change the **STYLE**, colour and size of letters, **embolden** them, *italicise* them, underline them, change the s p a c i n g ,  or add various text effects
- **Paragraphs** - You can align text using the centre or justify options, or by selecting 'bullets and numbering' add bullet points or numbers. You can make other amendments by selecting borders and shading, or by altering the line spacing, tabs and indents
- **Pages** - You can change the size, orientation and margins of pages, or add page numbers, headers and footers or the date and time.  You can insert page breaks to indicate where a new page should begin, or columns to divide the page vertically

- **Sections** - As you will see from the examples above it is not necessary for the whole of a document to be in the same format. By highlighting individual sections of a document you can apply different formats

If you use a format for part of the document and want to use it again later, you can select 'styles and formatting' and the software will show you what you have used previously in the document.

# What you need to know

The different uses of memos, reports, minutes and letters

What is meant by fully blocked?

The importance of meeting deadlines

What type of document will always have a signature?

How to spell, punctuate and use grammar accurately

What forms can minutes take?

The sequence in which reports are presented

What do you understand by an 'executive summary'?

The sequence in which business letters are laid out

What punctuation is used in a letter using open punctuation?

How to use the format menu

If you were asked to emphasise a sentence in a report how would you do it?

# Checking and editing text

There will be occasions while inputting text when the writer's intention will not be entirely clear. You may be listening to an audio tape or transcribing shorthand notes when you come to a word or phrase that you could interpret in more than one way. Always check with the writer as soon as possible. It is much better to ask and get it right at this point than to guess and have to change it later.

In many circumstances you will need to produce a 'draft' copy so that the originator can check that what you have produced matches what they intended. Before even producing the draft, though, you should check your work and correct any errors that you can find.

Most word processing packages contain spell checking and grammar checking facilities. Use these first to correct the more glaring errors, but don't rely on them entirely. They tend to use American spelling and grammar, so will accept 'color' and reject 'colour', for instance.

When the automatic checking is complete, read the document carefully to look for missed errors, and also for correct use of paragraphs, headings and sub-headings, style and formatting. Be particularly careful to proof read numbers, dates, times and amounts. Check for errors between similar words such as 'affect' and 'effect' or 'less' and 'fewer'.

When you are satisfied that there are no further errors that you can correct, print a draft copy of the document and pass it to the originator for them to proof read. This means not only looking for any typing errors but also for errors of context and content. They will mark up the draft indicating any required changes. These may come about as a result of:

- **Input errors** - If you have carried out your checks thoroughly these should be very few and far between
- **Errors in the source material** - If you have produced the text from audio instruction or from someone else's notes, you may have faithfully produced what the source contained, only for the originator to find that there were already errors in the source material

- **Amendments to the content** - Particularly if the originator has dictated the content verbally, it is possible that on seeing the finished product they have second thoughts about the best way to convey the information

---

Mminutes of Social Club Meeting held on 19th May 2004, West Hotel, Pendleton. 2.30.PM

Those present

| Bill Banstow | Chair |
| Mike Willis | Secretery |
| Pete Axty | Treasurer |
| Carol Carter | |
| Brian Williams | |
| Kevin Bissle | |
| Janet Hewitt | |

Apologies for absense were recieved from: Michael Ford

Mminutes of the last meeting were approved.

There were no matters arising.

The Chairman reported that discussion with management had commenced with regard to the possibility of using the staff canteen for future events.

The treasurer reported that there were seven subscriptions still outstanding. It was agreed that letters be written to the appropriate members advising them that if payment was not received by 6th June their membership would be terminated.

A.O.B.

Carol Carter suggested that a staff outing to the seaside in Aug could be arranged.

It was agreed that she would look into the costings of such an event.

The next meeting will be on 16th June 2004 at 2.30pm at the West Hotel, Pendleton

---

So, if your draft comes back covered in red ink, don't feel that you have necessarily produced a poor document. The chances are that the changes have been made by the originator to improve the overall effect.

Probably the greatest advantage that the word processor has over the typewriter is the opportunity to edit. In the bad old days when you got your draft back you had to recreate it from scratch. This meant the chances were that you would

**Unit 322/323/324 –Prepare text 661**

make different errors the second time. Nowadays at least the parts of the text that you wish to keep are still there.

You should therefore make the most efficient use of the technology available to make the alterations that have been requested. Functions in common use in most word processing packages include:

- **Delete** - This allows you to delete a letteror a whole word, use 'ctrl+delete'
- **Cut** (Ctrl+x) - You can highlight a piece of text and cut it from the document
- **Copy and paste** – This allows you to highlight a piece of text and add it to another location
- **Find and replace** (Ctrl+f) - This function is used to change all the examples of a particular word to another word (for instance if you are asked to change the word 'company' to 'organisation' there is no need to retype, just use 'find and replace' to change all the examples)
- **Insert** - This enables you to use a wide range of non-Arabic letters and other characters and symbols e.g. ©, é, 'Ω, %

Having made all of the requested alterations, produce a final draft and pass that to the originator. Hopefully their proof reading this time will result in no further amendments. You will then be able to print off the requested number of copies to the quality standard requested, not forgetting an extra copy for the file.

 **What you need to know**

How to proof read your own work

What is meant by proof reading?

Printers' correction symbols

What two parts of speech are used in every sentence?

Uses of full stops, commas and apostrophes

What function does an adverb serve?

The functions available to edit text

Why should you produce a final draft?

The importance of raising any queries
with the originator before producing the
draft

What types of amendments might be
made to a draft?

## Storing the text

Every document that you produce will need to be stored in
some way.  Your computer will have its own in-built sorting
and storing mechanisms.  You will need to be able to store
information accurately in approved locations and find it again
quickly.  Most systems will include a facility to store the
information in folders within the main directory.  These
should be used to group files together to speed up retrieval.

Paper copies will have to be stored manually.  There are a
number of different methods that can be used:

- **Alphabetical** - Filed in order from A – Z.  Files
  starting with the same letter are filed in order of the
  second letter (Aa, Ab, Ac) and so on.  People's names
  are filed by their surnames, and if more than one has
  the same surname by their first names.  Names
  starting with 'The' are filed by ignoring the word 'The'.
  For example 'The CfA' will be stored under 'C'
- **Numerical** - Files are given numbers and filed from 1
  to infinity.  This is useful for information which
  naturally lends itself to being filed this way (purchase
  orders, sales invoices, for instance)
- **Alpha-numerical** - Files have a combination of
  letters and numbers.  Examples include postal codes,
  National Insurance numbers, car registration
  numbers, etc.  These are usually large databases as
  they hold more information than numerical systems
  and are more flexible than alphabetical systems.  The
  order of filing depends on the sequence of the file
  name.  If file names start with letters followed by
  numbers, they are filed in alphabetical order first, and
  numerical order within each letter

- **Chronological** - This is most often used within one of the other methods. For instance, each customer's records are filed alphabetically, but the information within the file is stored chronologically, usually with the latest at the front. This enables a picture of the activity to be gained. However, it can be used based on dates of birth or start dates

Some information may be marked 'confidential'. Make sure you know exactly what is meant by 'confidential' in your organisation. It may mean senior staff are allowed access, it may mean only the person who created the document is permitted to read it. Access to information about individuals is covered by the Data Protection Act and you must be very careful to comply with its requirements.

As well as the completed document you will need to file the original source material in case it needs to be referred to at a later date. Your organisation may have its own system of referencing documents or you may need to create your own. If you put the same reference that you have given the completed document onto the source material, you will be able to track the source should any query arise later. The source material therefore needs to be stored in a logical manner:

- Hand written notes can be attached to the file copy of the completed document
- Shorthand note books should be stored chronologically with the start and end date written on the front
- Audio tapes should be stored chronologically and labelled with the date

You will then be able to find the source material by locating the completed document in the filing system and using the combination of reference and date.

**What you need to know**

Your organisation's referencing system

> Why is the source material filed as well as the completed document?

Why it is important to be able to locate the source material if requested

> How would you store customer letters?

How to store electronic files in folders

> What does 'confidential' mean in terms of text storage?

### Unit 322 – Prepare text from notes

The great advantage of longhand notes is that they can be prepared anywhere, by anybody without any special training. It's quite usual to see people writing notes on the way to work or back from a meeting. The important thing is to make sufficient notes. If you are preparing text from them yourself you will remember all of the details that you want to include or if someone else is to prepare the text they will understand exactly what you want to say.

# ASAP

When preparing text from notes that you have made yourself, you should have no problem reading them back. On the other hand if you are preparing text from someone else's notes this may be more difficult. Read through the notes to make sure that you understand what is intended. You won't just be typing the notes verbatim, you will be required to sort them into sentences and paragraphs.   Sort the notes into the order that you are going to type them. This may mean making your own notes on them to remind you which part comes next. The more often you prepare text from notes given by a particular person, the easier it will become to read the writing and understand the meaning of their notes.

**Unit 323 – Prepare text from shorthand**

The advantages of being able to take shorthand notes are that you can either take dictation verbatim or make much more detailed notes for your own use than you could in longhand.

Because shorthand is a skill it takes some time to learn, but once you become proficient it will save you a lot of time.

When taking shorthand notes you will be sitting in one place for some time so it is important that you are comfortable. Hold your shorthand notebook in a position that you find most convenient. This may be on your lap or on the desk. Make sure you have a sharp pencil (and a spare in case of accidents). Listen very carefully to what is being said to you. If you miss a word or don't fully understand, ask immediately. It is much easier for the person giving dictation to clarify as they go along than to wait until the end. If you build up a rapport with the person giving dictation you will find it easier to understand what they mean and efficiently record it.

## Unit 324 – Prepare text from recorded audio instruction

The advantages of using audio equipment are that a verbatim transcript will be produced and that there will be no problem in deciphering the hand writing of the person who produces it.  Although it may take a little while to get used to the equipment, once you have mastered the necessary co-ordination you will find it relatively simple.

When preparing text from recorded audio instruction it is advisable to sit with a straight back.  Make sure that your foot is comfortable on the foot pedal and that the headset fits properly.  Listen carefully to what is being said, using the foot pedal stop the machine and type in what you have heard.  Some people will give instruction onto the tape such as 'comma', 'full stop', 'paragraph' or 'new page'.  Follow these instructions even if they seem to contradict the layout that you would expect for the document you are producing.  The more often you use audio equipment the less often you will have to use the foot pedal.

## Whatever source you are producing text from, the more often you do it the easier it becomes

# Are you ready for assessment?

To achieve this unit of a Level 3 Business & Administration qualification you will need to demonstrate that you are competent in the following:

## Prepare text from notes

- Agree the purpose, format, quality standards and deadlines for the text
- Input the text at a minimum speed of 60 words per minute
- Format the text, making efficient use of the technology available
- Check for accuracy, editing and correcting as necessary
- Seek clarification when necessary
- Store the text and the original notes safely and securely in approved locations
- Present the text in the required format within agreed deadlines and quality standards

(Remember that you will need the skills listed at the beginning of this chapter. These are covered in chapter 1.)

You will need to produce evidence from a variety of sources. Carrying out the following activities will help you acquire competence at work.

### Activity 1
Choose a piece of text that contains at least 1,000 words. Switch off the spell check function on your computer. Type the text for ten minutes. After ten minutes stop and calculate your typing speed using the following method:

Count the total number of characters typed including spaces.
Divide the answer by 5 (average length of word).
This gives the gross number of words typed.

Divide the answer by ten (time spent typing).
This gives the gross words per minute (wpm).
Count the number of mis-typed words.
Deduct the number of mis-typed words from the gross wpm.
This gives the net wpm.

If your computer has a word count facility make sure that you use the characters (with spaces) figure.

## Activity 2
Attend a meeting (this could be a team meeting at work, a social club meeting, a meeting at college) and take longhand notes of what is said. Produce a short typed report from your notes. Time yourself inputting the text and count the number of words. Proof read the document and calculate the net words per minute.

## Activity 3
Ask your line manager to provide you with a set of notes which require transcription. Type up the notes and ask your line manager to proof read them and give you feedback. If possible, repeat this activity daily over a one week period.

## Activity 3
You work in an Estate Agent's office in Burnley. When you arrive at work you find the following note:

A new house has just come onto the market can you type the details? 112 Bestonic Street semi situated in a pop. and est. res. location convenient for local schools and shops and town centre, vestibule, entrance hall, lounge, dining room, three bedrooms CH gas garage, upvc DG throughout fully fitted kitchen cloakroom on ground family bath on 1st gardens front and rear

Lounge 8.1x3.48
Dining room 4.72x4.22
Kitchen 2.39x4.5
Bed 1 3.12x4.62
Bed 2 3.61x2.95
Bed 3 3.42x4.56

Make sure you point out that the house has a large well looked after garden, council tax band B photo to follow

## Activity 4
Proof read and correct the following and produce a corrected version. Switch off the spell check function on your computer.

Our ref: DT/GY/1256

Mr G Willims
Apart 21
The shore
Manchster
M6 7yu

23.06.023

Dear nr Williams

Account number 45678956 –Flat 24 tge maltings, Manchester

Thankyou for you're recent enqiry regarding your mortgage, and the interst rates available to you.  I am enclosing a quotition showing what yur new payments would be at a new rate of interst.  Yhjis has been calculated on and Interest only Basis.

At the moment you're monthly payments is ^189.23 vased ib a rate if 6.75%.  Should you decide to except our offer (details )attached, your new repayments would be approx $206.93.  The admin fee of £120.00 gas veeb added ti tyour balance for quotation's pyrposes only.

This offer is valid for 14 day's from the date of the enclosed quotation. you should of receved further details yesterday.

Transferring yourmortgage onto the new rate couldnt be easier,  Simply return the Deed of Variation enclosed, signed by all partied to the mortgage.

We will charge you the aministration fee of £120.00.  This sum can be added to the loan or may be paid by check if you wish.

If you have any questions, plesse contact me on 02356 56998 Monday to Friday between 9.00pm and 5.00pm.

Yours faithfyully


W Gaines
Consultant Mortgage Provider

# Are you ready for assessment?

To achieve this unit of a Level 3 Business & Administration qualification you will need to demonstrate that you are competent in the following:

## Prepare text from shorthand

- Agree the purpose, format, quality standards and deadlines for the text
- Take dictation using shorthand at a minimum speed of 80 words per minute
- Clarify points you are unsure about
- Input and format the text from your shorthand notes
- Make efficient use of the technology available
- Check for accuracy, editing and correcting as necessary
- Store the text and the original shorthand notes safely and securely in approved locations
- Present the text in the required format within agreed deadlines and quality standards

You will need to produce evidence from a variety of sources. Carrying out the following activities will help you acquire competence at work.

**Activity 1**
Choose a piece of text that contains at least 1,000 words. Switch off the spell check function on your computer. Type the text for ten minutes. After ten minutes stop and calculate your typing speed using the following method.

Count the total number of characters typed including spaces.
Divide the answer by 5 (average length of word).
This gives the gross number of words typed.
Divide the answer by 10 (time spent typing).
This gives the gross words per minute (wpm).
Count the number of mis-typed words.
Deduct the number of mis-typed words from the gross wpm.
This gives the net wpm.

If your computer has a word count facility make sure that you use the characters (with spaces) figure.

## Activity 2

Ask your line manager to dictate a document or documents which require transcription. Type up the notes and ask your line manager to proof read them and give you feedback. If possible, repeat this activity daily over a one week period.

## Activity 3

Ask a colleague to read a document containing at least 800 words to you at dictation speed. (This should take no more than 10 minutes.) Take notes in shorthand. Type the document from your notes. Proof read your version against the original.

## Activity 4

Proof read and correct the following and produce a corrected version. Switch off the spell check function on your computer.

Our ref: DT/GY/1256

Mr G Willims
Apart 21
The shore
Manchster
M6 7yu

23.06.023

Dear nr Williams

Account number 45678956 –Flat 24 tge maltings, Manchester

Thankyou for you're recent enqiry regarding your mortgage, and the interst rates available to you. I am enclosing a quotition showing what yur new payments would be at a new rate of interst. Yhjis has been calculated on and Interest only Basis.

At the moment you're monthly payments is ^189.23 vased ib a rate if 6.75%. Should you decide to except our offer (details )attached, your new repayments would be approx $206.93. The admin fee of £120.00 gas veeb added ti tyour balance for quotation's pyrposes only.

This offer is valid for 14 day's from the date of the enclosed quotation. you should of receved further details yesterday.

Transferring yourmortgage onto the new rate couldnt be easier, Simply return the Deed of Variation enclosed, signed by all partied to the mortgage.

We will charge you the aministration fee of £120.00. This sum can be added to the loan or may be paid by check if you wish.

If you have any questions, plesse contact me on 02356 56998 Monday to Friday between 9.00pm and 5.00pm.

Yours faithfyully

W Gaines
Consultant Mortgage Provider

---

**Activity 5**
You work in an Estate Agent's office in Burnley.  When you arrive at work you find the following note:

A new house has just come onto the market can you type the details? 112 Bestonic Street semi situated in a pop. and est. res. location convenient for local schools and shops and town centre, vestibule, entrance hall, lounge, dining room, three bedrooms CH gas garage, upvc DG throughout fully fitted kitchen cloakroom on ground family bath on $1^{st}$ gardens front and rear.

Lounge 8.1x3.48
Dining room 4.72x4.22
Kitchen 2.39x4.5
Bed 1 3.12x4.62
Bed 2 3.61x2.95
Bed 3 3.42x4.56

Make sure you point out that the house has a large well looked after garden, council tax band B photo to follow

Transcribe this into shorthand and then type up the note in full.  Ask your supervisor, team leader or manager to check your work.

(Remember that you will need the skills listed at the beginning of this chapter.  These are covered in chapter 1.)

# Are you ready for assessment?

To achieve this unit of a Level 3 Business & Administration qualification you will need to demonstrate that you are competent in the following:

## Prepare text from recorded audio instruction

- Agree the purpose, format quality standards and deadlines for the transcription
- Input the text from the audio recording at a minimum speed of 70 words per minute
- Format the text making efficient use of the technology available
- Check content for accuracy, editing and correcting as necessary
- Seek clarification when necessary
- Store the text and the original recording safely and securely in approved locations
- Present the text in the required format within agreed deadlines and quality standards

(Remember that you will need the skills listed at the beginning of this chapter. These are covered in chapter 1.)

You will need to produce evidence from a variety of sources. Carrying out the following activities will help you acquire competence at work.

### Activity 1
Choose a piece of text that contains at least 1,000 words. Switch off the spell check function on your computer. Type the text for ten minutes. After ten minutes stop and calculate your typing speed using the following method.

Count the total number of characters typed including spaces
Divide the answer by 5 (average length of word)
This gives the gross number of words typed
Divide the answer by 10 (time spent typing)
This gives the gross words per minute (wpm)
Count the number of mis-typed words
Deduct the number of mis-typed words from the gross wpm
This gives the net wpm

If your computer has a word count facility make sure that you use the characters (with spaces) figure.

## Activity 2
Ask your line manager to dictate a document or documents which require transcription onto audio tape. Type up the documents and ask your line manager to proof read them and give you feedback. If possible, repeat this activity daily over a one week period.

## Activity 3
Proof read and correct the following and produce a corrected version. Switch off the spell check function on your computer.

Our ref: DT/GY/1256

Mr G Willims
Apart 21
The shore
Manchster
M6 7yu

23.06.023

Dear nr Williams

Account number 45678956 –Flat 24 tge maltings, Manchester

Thankyou for you're recent enqiry regarding your mortgage, and the interst rates available to you. I am enclosing a quotition showing what yur new payments would be at a new rate of interst. Yhjis has been calculated on and Interest only Basis.

At the moment you're monthly payments is ^189.23 vased ib a rate if 6.75%. Should you decide to except our offer (details )attached, your new repayments would be approx $206.93. The admin fee of £120.00 gas veeb added ti tyour balance for quotation's pyrposes only.

This offer is valid for 14 day's from the date of the enclosed quotation. you should of received further details yesterday.

Transferring yourmortgage onto the new rate couldnt be easier, Simply return the Deed of Variation enclosed, signed by all partied to the mortgage.

We will charge you the aministration fee of £120.00. This sum can be added to the loan or may be paid by check if you wish.

If you have any questions, plesse contact me on 02356 56998 Monday to Friday between 9.00pm and 5.00pm.

Yours faithfyully

W Gaines
Consultant Mortgage Provider

**Activity 4**
Using any pre-recorded text (a talking book, for instance) type for 10
minutes.  Ask a colleague to proof read your version against the
recording.  Count the number of words you have typed and calculate the
net words per minute.

Remember:  While gathering evidence for this unit, evidence
**may** be generated for units 110, 212, 301, 302, 314, 320
and 321.

# Index

## A

## C